PHYSICAL ILLNESS AND HANDICAP IN CHILDHOOD

Managing Editors: Ruth S. Eissler, Anna Freud, Marianne Kris, Albert J. Solnit

Associate Editor: Lottie M. Newman

AN ANTHOLOGY OF

The Psychoanalytic Study of the Child

PHYSICAL ILLNESS AND
HANDICAP IN CHILDHOOD

Foreword by Albert J. Solnit

NEW HAVEN AND LONDON
YALE UNIVERSITY PRESS
1977

Set in Baskerville type.
Printed in the United States of America by
The Colonial Press Inc., Clinton, Mass.

Published in Great Britain, Europe, Africa, and
Asia (except Japan) by Yale University Press,
Ltd., London. Distributed in Latin America by
Kaiman & Polon, Inc., New York City; in
Australia and New Zealand by Book & Film
Services, Artarmon, N.S.W., Australia; and in
Japan by Harper & Row, Publishers, Tokyo Office.

All the papers included in this anthology were first
published in this *Psychoanalytic Study of the Child*,
vols. 7, 11, 15-18, copyright © 1952, 1956, 1960, 1961,
1962, 1963 by International Universities Press, Inc.
Chapters 1 and 2 are from vol. 7, pp. 69-81, 126-69;
chapters 3 and 10 are from vol. 11, pp. 410-33, 352-80;
chapters 4, 8, and 12 are from vol. 16, pp. 405-22, 523-37,
423-50; chapters 5, 9, and 11 are from vol. 15,
pp. 395-429, 430-53, and 454-81; chapter 6 is from
vol. 18, pp. 636-62; chapter 7 is from vol. 17, pp. 344-62.

Library of Congress Cataloging in Publication Data

Main entry under title:

Physical illness and handicap in childhood.

    CONTENTS: Freud, A. The role of bodily illness in the
mental life of children.—Hospitalization: Jessner, L.,
Blom, G. E., and Waldfogel, S. Emotional implications of
tonsillectomy and adenoidectomy on children. Robertson,
J. A mother's observations on the tonsillectomy of her
four-year-old daughter. Plank, E. N. and Horwood, C. Leg
amputation in a four-year-old. [etc.]
    1. Sick children—Psychology—Addresses, essays,
lectures. 2. Physically handicapped children—Psychology
—Addresses, essays, lectures. 3. Child analysis—Addresses,
essays, lectures, I. The Psychoanalytic study of the child.
[DNLM: 1. Stress, Psychological—In infancy and
childhood—Collected works. 2. Anxiety—In infancy and
childhood—Collected works. 3. Disease—Collected works.
4. Handicapped—Collected works. 5. Psychoanalytic
therapy—In infancy and childhood—Collected works.
WS350 P578] RJ47.5.P45   618.9'2'00019   75-34811
ISBN 0-300-02005-8
ISBN 0-300-02006-6 pbk.

CONTENTS

III. Physical Defectiveness

FOREWORD

ALBERT J. SOLNIT, M.D.

The treatment and observations of children by child psychoanalysts have made signal and trenchant additions to our understanding of how children react to physical deficit and injury as well as to the therapeutic procedures applied for these conditions (A. Freud, Burlingham, James and Joyce Robertson, Senn, Spitz, et al.). In addition, psychoanalysts have made pioneer and continuing contributions to evolving educational and therapeutic measures to protect children from threatening psychological trauma associated with physical illness as well as with the appropriate rehabilitative physical treatments.

This anthology provides persuasive evidence that one cannot understand children's physical health and illness without taking into account their psychological and emotional reactions. Conversely, concern with a person's health and disease must take into account his body's development and reactions.

Accepting the indivisibility of body and mind, we also refer to one group of illnesses as psychosomatic disorders. In this group, the intimacy and intertwining of physiological and psychological reactions are frequently dramatic. Yet, too often the relationship between psyche and body has been taken to be a linear one, whereas in psychosomatic illness it should be understood as a simultaneous interaction to the detriment of both systems. As Anna Freud (1975), upon receiving the 1974 C. Anderson Aldrich Award of the American Academy of Pediatrics, said, "It is an error to believe that an individual's body, his emotions, and his intellect are separate entities which are closed off from each other, instead of realizing that they are interconnected in innumerable ways and that they provide for as well as interfere with each other's functioning." For example, in allergic conditions the immunological and psychological are different facets of the same disorder. The particular expression of the disorder

vii

will be determined by the maturational and experiential mosaic that is uppermost at a particular time or epoch of the individual's life cycle.

We are strongly inclined artificially to split our concern for and our understanding of the child's physiological and psychological selves to the detriment of his recuperative forces and of his future development. Emotional reactions can interfere with or facilitate the individual's self-healing capacities. As children mature and develop, they acquire increasingly complex and independent capacities and tolerances. For the adult observer, the younger the child, the more difficult it is to separate the physiological and psychological reactions. However, as the child is able to verbalize, remember, and observe, and as his object relationships mature, the adults are able to perceive him as a more distinct personality. He becomes increasingly capable of understanding, complaining, and asserting his needs for attention, care, regression, and relief. The older child then is more capable of utilizing explanations and taking an active role in finding relief from pain, deprivation, and overstimulation. In a sense, the older child can protest more effectively when only one part of himself is attended to.

In the case reports included in this anthology, the physical disorder preceded the psychological reactions. That means that the reactions of the mind—the emotional, intellectual, and socializing responses—can be in the service of defense and healing, or they can be reactions that interfere with the child's physiological recuperative capacities or his subsequent psychological development.

As this anthology clearly attests, psychoanalytic contributions to understanding and helping children with physical illness, deficits, and injuries are multiple and have been progressive. As different studies led to new insights, our ways of helping children and their parents became refined and in some instances older approaches were rendered obsolete.

One example would be the insight that children need to be told about a pending surgery, rather than be tricked into going into the hospital or be thrown into utter confusion by the bewildering experiences there. We know from several of the papers in this anthology that the fantasies about physical handicaps or about the treatments of physical illness flourish in the absence of realistic information. Some of the papers also demonstrated that children can cope with frightening events if they are emotionally prepared for them. As the most common specific anxieties were identified, for example, those attached to the experience of anesthesia, the methods of preparing the child and his family for what lay ahead became refined. We know how to provide psychological support during the diagnostic, treatment, and rehabilitation periods, and make attempts to counteract unavoidable deficits in the preparation that may have occurred, e.g., due to lack of time in an emergency hospitalization. We also have learned that fears often do not surface until the "danger" of the hospitalization or treatment is sufficiently defined or abated to allow the child to get beyond the panic or generalized anxiety associated with the anticipation of these experiences. But after the immediate danger is over, the anxiety may surface again or find focused expression in neurotic symptom formation or developmental disturbances as the child attempts to cope with and master the stressful experiences. Therefore, preparation and psychological help are viewed as continuous repetitive processes that should be available as long as they are needed.

The papers selected for this anthology are presented in three parts, though some overlap of focus is unavoidable and even may be desirable. We do not organize the presentation by developmental epochs, by body systems, or by category of illness or injury. Rather, we start with Anna Freud's classical paper on "The Role of Bodily Illness in the Mental Life of Children" and proceed to what is still the most traumatic aspect of these experiences for younger children —hospitalization. This is followed by studies of the child's emotional reactions to temporary and remediable physical illness. Part III deals with the psychological reactions and therapeutic services to children and their parents when the child has a continuing physical handicap or a primary irremediable deficit.

The papers included here have greatly contributed to our understanding of what a child experiences when he is ill. They are major contributions in our efforts to provide children with comprehensive medical care, in which physical and psychological understanding are united and coordinated in the services provided by physicians, nurses, educators, psychoanalysts, psychologists, psychiatrists, and social workers. These anthology papers also have refined our knowledge of how parents and others (physicians and nurses especially) can enable the child to achieve psychological mastery as well as physical recovery

and rehabilitation. The latter depends on whether all the adults involved are successful in putting their best knowledge to work col-
laboratively and harmoniously.

For the young child, well-prepared parents who can stay with
him through the diagnostic and therapeutic excursions at home, in
the doctor's office, or at the hospital are irreplaceable. We aim to
create a climate in which preparatory knowledge can be translated
for the child according to his developmental capacities and psycho-
cultural expectations. When the process is working well, the child
will raise questions in play and words and express fears and expectations which can be accepted and to which there can be factual, matter-
of-fact responses in the home, office, and hospital or rehabilitation
center. Thus, the fears of abandonment and of being overwhelmed
by the pain of the body, by loneliness or loss are central to the anxiety of the young child. It is at a later age that there will be a sense
of hopelessness and helplessness that must be mitigated and coped
with if the child has a chronic illness, a permanent handicap, or an
uncertain future.

As the child develops and as more effective and integrated cognitive powers and emotional responses characterize the older child's
personality and physical resources, he achieves the capacity to feel
the presence of his parents during their physical absence. Thus
school-aged children have different worries and fears about physical
handicap, illness or injury. They are prepared to have the assistance
suggested by psychoanalysts, especially from the new profession, hospital child care workers[1] (Plank, 1971). This profession, a model in
applying psychoanalytic theory to the care of physically ill children,
provides educational as well as emotional assistance, enabling children to cope with variations of separation and castration anxieties
and with the fear of a permanent loss of physical capabilities. For
example, typically the older child is anxious about his body's integrity. He can cope with separation from the parents if he is able to
work through his irrational fears and expectations about his body's
intactness and functioning. Then he can gradually relate to his depressed and anxious feelings and come to grips with the realization
that he may not be able to be the fully equipped and hopeful adult
he wants to be. Rehabilitation then can proceed with the child ac-

[1] Association for the Care of Children in Hospitals.

tively uncovering and releasing his compensatory skills and resources.

In younger children much of how they react to illness and injury is reflected in their behavior rather than by their verbalizations. In older children much of how they react can be heard in their verbal aggressiveness and in their verbal playfulness. It can also be observed in their games, their artistic productions, their humor, and in the range of their emotional reactions. The papers in this anthology are rich in the empirical data. They describe, analyze, and interpret.

Psychoanalysts have pointed to how the ego is buffeted by physical illness, defect, and injury. Their studies, as amply demonstrated in this anthology, have indicated how to strengthen the ego under conditions in which there is, as a result of bodily difficulties, a precarious balance between ego, instinctual forces, and in older children the demands of the superego. In order for the ego's domination to remain viable, the parents must be helped to be the primary agents of support, the auxiliary ego for their sick or handicapped younger child. For the older child, the emphasis must be on helping the child to use mental activity, the trial action of thought, to prepare for and cope with treatment, rehabilitation, handicap, and at times uncertainty. According to the child's developmental resources, mastery will be available through play, through verbalization, and through the calming presence of adults who can accept, understand, and explain in the context of sustained affection, nurturance, guidance, and protection.

As these papers also demonstrate, the role of therapeutic work by psychoanalysts is a crucial one in enabling the child to heal psychologically what he has not been able to mend from the damaging impact of physical illness and its treatment. Throughout, the role of the psychoanalyst has been to serve as a clinical investigator who can bring to bear the full weight of his science and art in understanding, humanizing, and healing the child who suffers from bodily ailments.

This anthology documents the critical insights that have been gained in a period extending over a decade. It is timely because our understanding of psychological reactions and needs associated with physical illness and injury and with the extraordinary technical advances in diagnosis and treatment of physical illness have proliferated at such a rate as to require a survey and inventory of where we have been in the 1950s and 1960s. This is necessary if we are to know how best to guide ourselves through the 70s and into the 80s. Integrating our physical and psychological knowledge in the study and care of children is a crucial and unavoidable challenge if medicine is to retain its association with humanitarian values.

1

THE ROLE OF BODILY ILLNESS IN THE MENTAL LIFE OF CHILDREN

ANNA FREUD, LL.D., D.Sc., M.D.
(1952)

I. INTRODUCTION

When trying to evaluate the role of bodily illness in the mental life of children, we find ourselves hampered by the lack of integration in the material at our disposal. With the present-day division between professional teaching, nursing, child guidance work, child analysis and pediatrics, there is little or no opportunity for the trained worker in one of these fields to function, even in the role of observer, in one of the other services for children. [1]Nursery workers, school teachers and child analysts see nothing of the children under their care when they are ill; while pediatricians and sick-nurses lose contact with their young patients when they are healthy. It is only the mothers who have the opportunity to see their children in health, illness, convalescence, deviating from the norm bodily and mentally and returning to it. On the other hand, during severe bodily illness the mother's own emotional upset and her inevitable concentration on bodily matters act as distorting factors and leave little room for objective observation of the child's psychological reactions.

In recent years a number of analytic authors have made attempts to deal with the effects of hospitalization on young children, a series of studies which culminated in a documentary film.[2] But in the case of these studies the interest of the investigators was directed toward the misery and anxiety which arise invariably when young children are removed from their parents, placed in unfamiliar surroundings and handled and cared for by strangers; hospitalization merely serving as the prototype of a first, short-term separation from home. Instructive as these investigations are as a demonstration of separation anxiety and its consequences, they did not produce—nor were meant to do so—additional knowledge concerning reactions to illness and pain in infantile life.

Data are less scarce where the aftereffects of illness are concerned.

---

[1] A notable pioneer exception from this practice has been established by Dr. Milton J. E. Senn, Departments of Pediatrics and Psychiatry, Yale University School of Medicine, New Haven, Conn.

[2] See Bowlby et al. (1952) [and Anna Freud (1953)].

When describing the neurotic disorders of their children, parents date back the onset of the trouble frequently to some bodily illness, after which the child appeared to be "different." Mood swings, changes in the relationship to parents and siblings, loss of self-confidence, temper tantrums often appear for the first time during convalescence after a severe illness. Symptoms, such as bed wetting, soiling, feeding and sleeping troubles, school phobias, which had existed and been overcome earlier in life, may reappear. Some children who had been considered brilliant in their intellectual performance before illness, reappear afterward in school comparatively dull and apathetic; others surprise their parents and teachers by emerging from the same experience curiously ripened and matured. It is true that changes of this kind may happen after a period of hospitalization. But it is equally true that they happen as well where hospitalization does not take place, i.e., in children who have remained under the care of their mothers during illness and been nursed at home. When considering the effects of bodily illness on the life of the child, it is important to note that hospitalization is no more than one factor among several other potentially harmful and upsetting influences.

II. The Effects of Nursing, Medical and Surgical Procedures

Before we can arrive at a correct assessment of this potentially traumatic experience of illness we have to work our way through the action of a large number of factors which, though they are mere by-products of the situation, are for the child's mind inextricably intermixed with it. The child is unable to distinguish between feelings of suffering caused by the disease inside the body and suffering imposed on him from outside for the sake of curing the disease. He has to submit uncomprehendingly, helplessly and passively to both sets of experiences. In certain instances factors of the latter kind, with their high emotional significance, may even be the decisive ones in causing a child's psychological breakdown during illness, or in determining the aftereffects.

(i) Change of emotional climate during illness.—There are few parents who do not, imperceptibly or grossly, change their own attitude to the ill child. There are some parents, with ascetic leanings, who are afraid of over-indulging and thereby "spoiling" the child at such times, and consequently leave him severely alone, to "sleep out" his indisposition with the minimum of fussing. The majority of parents adopt an opposite attitude. The ill child may find himself more loved and fondled than at any other time of his life; for a child of a large family an infectious disease, with consequent isolation from siblings, may be the one

occasion when he is in sole possession of his mother's time and care. The mother, owing to her anxiety for the child's health, may suspend all considerations of discipline and good behavior and indulge the child's wishes to the extreme. Or, on the contrary, in her preoccupation with the child's body, she may forget the most elementary principles of psychological handling which she had applied in times of health: Shocks, forcible feeding or evacuation of the bowels, sudden separations (for hospitalization), deceptions (before operations) count for nothing with her so long as they ensure that her child recovers. The child, on the other hand, reacts to such unexpected handling as to traumatic experiences, feels bewildered by the upsetting of formerly immovable emotional and moral standards or finds himself unable to renounce the incidental emotional gains after recovery.

(ii) The experience of being nursed.—The child's reaction to the experience of being nursed is understood best in terms of comparison with the better known and frequently described reactions of adults to the corresponding situation.[3] A normal adult who is nursed through a severe illness cannot help feeling at the same time that he is exposed to a series of indignities. He has to renounce ownership of his own body and permit it to be handled passively. He is dressed and undressed, fed, cleaned, washed, helped with urination and defecation, turned from one side to the other, his nakedness exposed to nurse and doctor, regardless of sex, of decencies and conventional restrictions. He is, as it were, under orders, subjected to a hygienic routine which implies a major disregard for his personal attitudes and preferences. Characteristically enough many adults sum up this experience as being "treated as a baby," or as a "complete return to the conditions of their childhood."

On the other hand it would be a mistake to conclude from such statements that the situation of being nursed, by virtue of its similarity to infantile experiences, is less upsetting to the child than to the adult. Observation, as well as theoretical considerations show that the opposite may well be the case. The gradual mastering of various bodily functions, such as independent eating, independent bowel and bladder evacuation, the ability to wash, dress, undress, etc., mark for the child highly significant stages in ego development as well as advances in detaching his own body from that of the mother and possessing it at least in part. A loss of these abilities, when occasioned by the nursing procedures (or by the weakened bodily condition itself), means an equivalent loss in ego control, a pull back toward the earlier and more passive levels of infan-

---

[3] Compare in this connection "The Middle of the Journey" by Lionel Trilling with its striking description of an adult intellectual returning to responsibility for his own health after having been looked after and nursed during a severe illness.

tile development. Some children who have built up strong defenses against passive leanings oppose this enforced regression to the utmost, thereby becoming difficult, intractable patients; others lapse back without much opposition into the state of helpless infancy from which they had so recently emerged. Newly acquired and, for that reason, precariously anchored ego achievements are lost most frequently under these conditions. Many mothers report that after a period of illness their young infants have to be retrained so far as their toilet habits are concerned, weaned once more from spoon feeding, from clinging to the constant company of the mother, etc.

(iii) Restrictions of movement, diet, etc.—In contrast to the comparative ease with which ego skills and abilities are renounced under the impact of being "nursed," children defend their freedom of movement in the same situation to the utmost wherever they are not defeated by the type or intensity of the illness itself. It is well known that, at least under the conditions of home nursing, children with minor indispositions cannot be kept in bed consistently, or at least not lying down in bed. Young toddlers, who have only recently learned to walk, are known to stand up stubbornly in their beds for the whole course even of severe illnesses (for instance measles) until exhaustion forces them to adopt the lying position.[4] Recently some enlightened pediatricians have accepted this state of affairs and treat their child patients, whenever possible, without enforcing bed rest.[5]

The psychological significance of the children's negative attitude in this respect becomes apparent in those extreme instances when child patients have to be immobilized after surgery or in the course of orthopedic treatment. Several analytic authors have observed and discussed the consequences of such extreme restraint of movement of limbs and have pointed out the possible connection with the emergence of stereotyped, tic-like movements elsewhere in the body (David Levy, 1928, 1944), the difference of this mechanically enforced from psychologically enforced restraint (Mahler, Luke, Daltroff, 1945), their bearing on the blocking of aggression discharge as well as on the discharge of stimulation in general with consequent overerotization of the whole body (Greenacre, 1944). Thesi Bergmann (1945), in an observational study car-

---

[4] See in contrast to this the remarks in IV (i) of this paper.

[5] In England, Dr. Elsie Wright, formerly physician at the Babies Hospital, Newcastle on Tyne, impressed on the members of the Cassel Hospital Summer School for Ward Sisters (1949) that in children's wards there should be "no rigidity about the child being kept in bed"; Dr. Josefine Stross, pediatrician, when teaching students of the Hampstead Nurseries (1940-1945) and the Hampstead Child-Therapy Course, emphasized repeatedly that even where children have to be kept off the floor, movement inside the crib should not be restricted.

ried out during three years' work in an orthopedic ward, gives a vivid description of the defense mechanisms which enable the immobilized children to bear the restraint and even to increase their docility when the restraining measures have to be increased. On the other hand she describes the rages and temper tantrums which appear when the restraint is partially, not wholly, lifted or when chance deprivations, outside the expected medical procedure, are added to it unexpectedly. She emphasizes, further, a twofold relationship between the immobilized limbs and other parts of the body. According to her experience, on the one hand the restraint of one limb may spread in the form of inhibitions to other, nonaffected parts; on the other hand certain ego skills, speech, etc., may undergo an accelerated development to compensate for motor restriction of one limb. The same processes as they occur in children with pulmonary tuberculosis are presented in a highly interesting study by Sara Dubo (1950).

These authors' observations are confirmed by much nonrecorded experience of parents and teachers. The heightening of aggression during and after motor restraint (in plaster casts, etc.) is especially well known to the general public. The most usual ways in which this dammed-up aggression appears are restlessness, heightened irritability, the use of bad language, etc.[6]

In comparison with this massive blocking of a whole system of discharge, the food restrictions imposed on children during illness are of minor importance. Normally, in acute illnesses, the physiological lessening of the child's appetite prepares the way for the acceptance of a reduced diet; it is only the children with strong oral fixations, for whom food and deprivation of food have heightened libidinal significance, who react to the situation with fantasies of being badly treated, unloved, rejected. In chronic illnesses (such as diabetes, kidney trouble, colitis, allergies) where dietary restrictions have to be maintained for long periods of time, children are known to feel "different," singled out, discriminated against, or, in defense against being passively deprived, to develop ascetic self-denying tendencies.

On the whole, considerably less harm is done by the necessity of withholding desired foods than by an anxious mother, urging or even forcing unwelcome food on an ill child. It is these latter situations which turn even minor, short illnesses into starting points for serious and prolonged

---

[6] The present author has analytic knowledge of a girl who was immobilized during her latency period for orthopedic reasons. She used to pay her friends out of her pocket money for every new swear word which they brought home from school. The use of "bad language" was the only outlet left for her otherwise paralyzed aggression.

eating difficulties, usually by reviving feeding battles which have raged between mother and child in the nursing period.

For some children the taking of medicines presents a major difficulty. Though the bad taste or smell of the drug is in the foreground so far as the child's conscious reasons are concerned, analytic investigation discloses invariably behind these rationalizations the existence of repressed ideas of being attacked by the mother through the symbol of the drug (Melanie Klein), of being poisoned, impregnated, by her. Laxatives which force the bowels to move, though the child intends otherwise, may form the connecting link between reality and these unconscious fantasies.

In this connection it is interesting to remember that the punitive character of these restrictive measures has always been known to parents and has been exploited by them. To send a child to bed, confine him to his room, deprive him of favorite dishes have been used as punishments over the ages. In certain societies even the forcible administration of laxatives is used for the same purpose.

(iv) Operations.—Ever since the discovery of the castration complex analysts have had ample opportunity in their therapeutic work to study the impact of surgical operations on normal and abnormal development. By now it is common knowledge among analysts that any surgical interference with the child's body may serve as a focal point for the activation, reactivation, grouping and rationalization of ideas of being attacked, overwhelmed and (or) castrated. The surgeon's action, from minor surgery to major operations, is interpreted by the child in terms of his level of instinct development, or in regressive terms. What the experience means in his life, therefore, does not depend on the type or seriousness of the operation which has actually been performed, but on the type and depth of the fantasies aroused by it. If, for example, the child's fantasies are concerned with his aggression against the mother projected onto her person, the operation is experienced as a retaliatory attack made by the mother on the inside of the child's body (Melanie Klein); or the operation may be used to represent the child's sadistic conception of what takes place between the parents in intercourse, with the child in the role of the passive sexual partner; or the operation is experienced as mutilation, i.e., as punishment for exhibitionistic desires, for aggressive penis envy, above all for masturbatory practices and oedipal jealousies. If the operation is actually performed on the penis (circumcision, if not carried out shortly after birth), castration fears are aroused whatever the level of libidinal development. In the phallic phase, on the other hand, whatever part of the body is operated on will take over by displacement

the role of an injured genital part.[7] The actual experience of the operation lends a feeling of reality to the repressed fantasies, thereby multiplying the anxieties connected with them. Apart from the threatening situation in the outer world, this increase of anxiety presents an internal danger which the child's ego has to face. Where the defense mechanisms available at the time are strong enough to master these anxieties, all is well; where they have to be overstrained to integrate the experience, the child reacts to the operation with neurotic outbreaks; where the ego is unable to cope with the anxiety released, the operation becomes a trauma for the child.

In a recent symposium on the Emotional Reactions of Children to Tonsillectomy and Adenoidectomy, a representative group of analysts, psychiatrists, pediatricians and psychologists discussed the subject in the light of these ideas with a view to lessening the traumatic potentialities of the three main factors involved in the situation: reaction to anesthesia, to hospitalization, and to the operative procedure itself. Finding the optimal time for carrying out an operation (Hendrick, Escalona, Sylvester); careful preparation before the event (Fries, 1946); avoidance of separation anxiety (Jackson, 1942), Putnam, Butler); psychiatric support (Rank), facilities for expression of feeling (Spock) were brought forward as the most important precautionary measures (Levy, 1945; Pearson, 1941).

When studying the aftereffects of childhood operations in the analysis of adult patients we find that it is not the castration fear but the feminine castration wish in a male child which is most frequently responsible for serious postoperative breakdowns or permanent postoperative character changes. In these instances the surgical attack on the patient's body acts like a seduction to passivity to which the child either submits with disastrous results for his masculinity, or against which he has to build up permanent pathologically strong defenses.

III. Pain and Anxiety

(i) The mental interpretation of pain.—The manner in which the child invests bodily events with libidinal and aggressive cathexis and significance creates a phenomenon which has baffled many observers. Parents and others who deal with young children comment frequently on

[7] By deciding on the length of preparation time before an operation, two factors have to be taken into account. A preparation period which is too lengthy leaves too much room for the spreading-out of id fantasies; where the interval between knowledge and performance of operation is too short, the ego has insufficient time for preparing its defenses.

the remarkable individual differences in children's sensitiveness to bodily pain; what is agonizing to one child may be negligible to another. The analytic study of such behavior reveals as different not the actual bodily experience of pain but the degree to which the pain is charged with psychic meaning. Children are apt to ascribe to outside or internalized agencies whatever painful process occurs inside the body or whatever hurt happens to the body (accidental hurts, falls, knocks, cuts, abrasions, surgical interference as discussed above, etc.). Thus, so far as his own interpretation is concerned, the child in pain is a child maltreated, harmed, punished, persecuted, threatened by annihilation. The "tough" child "does not mind pain," not because he feels less or is more courageous in the real sense of the word, but because in his case latent unconscious fantasies are less dominant and therefore less apt to be connected with the pain. Where anxiety derived from fantasy plays a minor or no part, even severe pain is borne well and forgotten quickly. Pain augmented by anxiety on the other hand, even if slight in itself, represents a major event in the child's life and is remembered a long time afterward, the memory being frequently accompanied by phobic defenses against its possible return.

According to the child's interpretation of the event, young children react to pain not only with anxiety but with other affects appropriate to the content of the unconscious fantasies, i.e., on the one hand with anger, rage and revenge feelings, on the other hand with masochistic submission, guilt or depression.

The correctness of these assumptions is borne out by the fact that after analytic therapy formerly oversensitive children become more impervious to the effect of pain.

(ii) Pain and anxiety in infants.—Where the direct observation of infants in the first year of life is concerned, the relative proportion of physiological and psychological elements in the experience of pain is an open question. At this stage, any tension, need or frustration is probably felt as "pain," no real distinction being made yet between the diffuse experience of discomfort and the sharper and more circumscribed one of real pain arising from specific sources. In the first months of life the threshold of resistance against stimulation is low and painful sensations assume quickly the dignity of traumatic events. The actual response of the infant, whether it occurs instantaneously, or after a time lag of varying length, or remains invisible altogether, is no reliable guide to an assessment of the shock caused by the pain.

From what age onward the bodily event is supposed to carry psychic meaning for the infant will depend altogether on the analytic observer's theoretical assumptions concerning the date when unconscious fantasies begin to exist.

For the observer of children under the conditions of medical treatment it is interesting to note that older infants (two to three years) may react with almost identical distress to the experience of injections or inoculations and to the experience of sunlight treatment, although the former involves pain (plus anxiety) whereas the latter is merely anxiety-raising without any pain involved.

(iii) Passive devotion to the doctor.—It is the psychological meaning of pain which explains why doctors, and other inflictors of pain, are not merely feared but in many cases highly regarded and loved by the child. The infliction of pain calls forth passive masochistic responses which hold an important place in the child's love life. Frequently the devotion of the child to doctor or nurse becomes very marked on the days after the distress caused by a painful medical procedure has been experienced.

(iv) Reaction to pain as a diagnostic factor.—With young boys in the oedipal stage, their reaction to bodily pain provides a useful key to the differential diagnosis between genuine phallic masculinity and the misleading manifestations of reactive overstressed phallic behavior designed to ward off passive feminine castration ideas. The masculine boy is contemptuous of bodily pain which means little to him. The boy who has to defend himself against passive leanings cannot tolerate even slight amounts of pain without major distress.

IV. The Effects of Illness

(i) Changes in libido distribution.—The casual observer, while following with his attention the loud, manifest reactions to anxiety and pain, nursing procedures and restrictions, is in danger of disregarding another process which, silent and under the surface, is responsible for most important alterations during illness: i.e., the heightened demand of the ill body for libidinal cathexis. Some observant mothers know the mental signs heralding this state and are able to diagnose from them the onset of a disease even before any significant bodily symptoms have appeared.

There are two ways for the patient to react to this demand from the side of the body. Many children who, when healthy, are in good contact with their surroundings, full of interest in their toys and occupations, and in the happenings of everyday life, begin their sicknesses by withdrawing from the environment, lying down on the floor or curling up in a corner, listless and bored.[8] At the height of the illness they lie in bed

---

[8] This refers to cases where such listlessness cannot be accounted for on physiological grounds.

without moving, their faces turned to the wall, refusing toys, food as well as any affectionate advances made to them. Though these reactions occur in certain children regularly, even with harmless sore throats, stomach upsets, raised temperatures, and the most common infectious children's diseases, the impression given by such a child in a state of withdrawal is that of a seriously ill person. Anxious mothers are terrified by this complete reversal in their child's behavior and feel him to be in grave danger. In reality the manifestation is not a physiological but a psychological one and not commensurate with the severity of the illness. It is a change in libido distribution during which cathexis is withdrawn from the object world and concentrated on the body and its needs. Despite its frightening suggestion of malignancy this process is a beneficial one, serving the purpose of recovery.

There are other children who, for some unknown reason rooted in their individual libido economy, use a different manner to achieve the same result. Unable to give their own ill body the additional narcissistic cathexis which it demands from them, they claim this surplus of love and attention from the mothers who nurse them through the illness, i.e., they become demanding, exacting, clinging far beyond their years. In doing so they make use of a natural process dating back to the first year of life, when the mother's libidinal cathexis of the infant's body is the main influence in protecting it from harm, destruction and self-injury (Hoffer, 1950). For the surface observer children of this type are extremely "fussy" when ill, those of the former type are undemanding.

In both cases the gradual return to health is accompanied by a gradual regularization of these movements of libido, though not without difficulties and reversals during which the child appears "cranky." Occasionally the abnormal distribution of libido proves irreversible for a certain length of time and produces some of the puzzling personality changes after illness which have been pointed out above.

(ii) The child's body as the mother's property. Hypochondria.—Some mothers find it difficult to resign themselves to the fact that their children, even after the toddler stage, cannot really be trusted to take care of their own bodies and to observe the rules serving health and hygiene. Whenever a mother reports with pride that her child washes hands before eating without being told to do so, analytic exploration will reveal that the child in question is a severe obsessional and his apparently sensible cleanliness a compulsive and magical defense against imaginary, dangerous contact. Children who protect themselves against colds and drafts ward off fears of death; those who choose their foods carefully do so on the basis of fears of being poisoned; those who refrain from eating too much or too many nourishing foods are obsessed by anxieties concerning

pregnancy. The average, normal child will observe none of these precautionary measures; he will eat with dirty hands, stuff himself, brave wet and cold weather, eat green apples and other unripe fruits unless forced, urged or prevented by his mother. In illness he will at best co-operate with her; at worst he will fight the care taken of him and proceed to use his own body as he pleases. So far as health, hygiene and the nursing care are concerned, the mother's ownership of the child's body extends from earliest infancy, when the mother-child unity is an important factor in the libido economy of both, through all the phases of childhood into adolescence. At this last stage, before independence is finally reached, recklessness in matters of health provides one of the familiar battle grounds for bitter struggles between the adolescent and his mother.

It is interesting to observe that this state of affairs is reversed more or less completely where motherless, orphaned and institutional children are concerned, even in those cases where competent professional nursing care is provided. Far from enjoying the freedom from anxious motherly supervision (as the observer might expect from the mothered child's revolt against her care) motherless children proceed to care for their own bodies in an unexpected manner. In an institution known to the author it was difficult sometimes to prevail upon a child to shed his sweater or overcoat in hot weather; his answer was that he "might catch cold." Rubber boots and galoshes were asked for and conscientiously worn by others so as "not to get their feet wet." Some children watched the length of their sleep anxiously, others the adequacy of their food. The impression gained was that all the bogeys concerning the child's health which had troubled their mothers' minds in the past had been taken over by the young children themselves after separation or bereavement, and activated their behavior. In identification with the temporarily or permanently lost mother, they substituted themselves for her by perpetuating the bodily care received from her.[9]

When watching the behavior of such children toward their bodies we are struck with the similarity of their attitudes to that of the adult hypochondriac, to which perhaps it provides a clue. The child actually deprived of a mother's care, adopts the mother's role in health matters, thus playing "mother and child" with his own body. The adult hypochondriac who withdraws cathexis from the object world and places it on his body is in a similar position. It is the overcharging of certain body areas with libido (loving care) which makes the ego of the individual

[9] A most instructive example of this behavior is the instance of a motherless boy of six years who in a long drawn out nightly attack of vomiting and diarrhea was heard to say to himself: "I, my darling." When asked what he meant, he answered: "That I love myself. It is good to love oneself, isn't it?"

hypersensitive to any changes which occur in them. With children analytic study seems to make it clear that in the staging of the mother-child relationship, they themselves identify with the lost mother, while the body represents the child (more exactly: the infant in the mother's care). It would be worth investigating whether the hypochondriacal phase which precedes many psychotic disorders corresponds similarly to a regression to and re-establishment of this earliest stage of the mother-child relationship.

V. SUMMARY

In carrying further the author's and other writers' studies of separation anxiety (hospitalization) this paper surveys the other factors which play a part in the child's reaction to bodily illness. The effects of the various nursing, medical and surgical procedures which are open to modification are distinguished from those elements which are inherent in the process of illness itself, such as the effects of pain and the inevitable changes of libido distribution. Lastly, a comparison is drawn between the state of deprived children who care for their bodies in identification with their lost mothers and the adult hypochondriac who over-cathects his body with libido after it has been withdrawn from the object world.

In summarizing these factors which play an important role in every normal development the author wishes once more to stress how serious a measure hospitalization is, separating the child from the rightful owner of his body at the very moment when this body is threatened by dangers from inside as well as from the environment.

[For other writings related to the topic of this paper, see Anna Freud (1961) and Thesi Bergmann and Anna Freud (1965).]

PART I

HOSPITALIZATION

2

EMOTIONAL IMPLICATIONS OF TONSILLECTOMY AND ADENOIDECTOMY ON CHILDREN[1]

LUCIE JESSNER, M.D., GASTON E. BLOM, M.D., and SAMUEL WALDFOGEL, Ph.D.
(1952)

AIMS

The psychological significance of surgical procedures in childhood is now generally recognized (Coleman, 1950; Deutsch, 1942; Fries, 1946; Jessner and Kaplan, 1949; Levy, 1945; Lindemann, 1941; Menninger, 1934; Michaels, 1943; Miller, 1951; Pearson, 1941; Pillsbury, 1951). Helene Deutsch (1942) found evidence in the analysis of adult patients that "operations performed in childhood leave indelible traces on the psychic life of the individual." David Levy (1945) and Pearson (1941) found in psychotherapy with children that operations experienced earlier in childhood had a traumatic effect on some patients. In our work with children we were impressed that in some cases the onset of emotional difficulties was attributed to an earlier operation.[1]

Our knowledge of the meaning of operations in childhood comes mainly from retrospective studies. We felt that direct observations of children undergoing surgery would contribute to the understanding of this problem. While we plan to study a number of operations, we began with a most common operation in childhood, tonsillectomy and adenoidectomy (T&A). We were not only interested in the effects of operation, but also wanted to find out how children experienced short-time hospitalization and minor operation.

PROCEDURE

From November, 1947, to February, 1952, 143 children were observed while they were undergoing T&A at the Massachusetts Eye and Ear Infirmary. These children were unselected except for their accessibility for follow-up. This depended upon their living sufficiently close to the hospital and upon their mothers' willingness to co-operate with the study.[2]

[1] [See also the symposium on the emotional reactions of children to T&A (Senn, 1949).]

[2] Studies on which this work is based were supported by a grant from National Institute of Mental Health, U. S. Public Health Service, Bethesda, Maryland.

It is the practice at the Infirmary to admit the child for a period of two days, one preceding and one following operation. The child was first seen by a child psychiatrist at the time of admission.[3] The mother was interviewed by a psychiatric social worker who attempted to get specific information regarding the child's development, previous experiences of stress (illness, operation, hospitalization, life experience), and preparation for the operation.

Each child was observed at intervals during the hospital stay by the child psychiatrist. In addition, nurses who had been informed of the aims of the study made notations of the child's reactions on the ward. Sixty-two children were given psychological tests.[4]

When possible mother and child were seen in follow-up interviews— within a week or two, at the end of a month, and at longer irregular intervals. At present we have three-to-four-year follow-ups on nearly forty children.

LIMITING FEATURES OF THE PRESENT STUDY

Although our study was designed to secure detailed information on each of our patients, we were not always so successful. The greatest gaps in our information appear in the follow-up material. Many of the mothers, who expressed interest in the study when it was discussed prior to the child's admission for T&A, lost much of their enthusiasm once the acute phase had passed and were reluctant to return for additional interviews. When the health of the child improved, mothers were apt to regard a discussion of the postoperative reaction as anticlimactic. With other mothers, where no such improvement occurred, there sometimes was resentment toward the hospital. This seemed particularly true for those mothers whose expectations were colored by magical thinking, as exemplified by the mother who had expected her child's feeble-mindedness to be cured. Several families moved away from the Boston area and were lost for further follow-ups.

Even had we not encountered these difficulties, we would still consider our information as incomplete. Except for the few psychotherapeutic cases our observations are neither extensive nor intensive enough to grasp the full significance of the operation for each child. While in some cases the child's emotional reactions appeared with dramatic vividness, in many we could not properly evaluate the extent to which suppression

[3] Five children were seen two or three times prior to admission, and two had their operation during psychotherapy.

[4] Of these, thirty-three were given a selective battery, including projective tests, for the purpose of predicting the child's reactions. These results are ɪ_ported elsewhere (Rubin, 1951).

and denial may have clouded the picture. We obviously could not deter-mine the extent to which reactivation of the experience in later years might occur.

It should be emphasized that our findings may not be representative of T&A's in general because of the special conditions that prevailed at the Massachusetts Eye and Ear Infirmary. Before we appeared on the scene the Social Service Department, recognizing the importance of prep-aration for the child, had issued a booklet for parents helping them to explain the operation to the child. Nurses, anesthetists, and doctors were all cognizant of the child's emotional predicament and tried to minimize the threat to him as much as possible. It was for this reason that hos-pitalization one day prior to T&A was instituted. It was hoped that this would give the child some time to become acclimated to the hospital and thus reduce his anxiety.[5]

Also, we found that the psychiatrist could not remain a neutral ob-server, but was drawn into a friendly relationship with the child. While this was helpful in obtaining more meaningful material, it modified the hospital atmosphere. The psychiatrist was frequently perceived as a friendly, supportive figure, as was born out by the spontaneous remarks of many children, both at home and in follow-up interviews.

OBSERVATIONS

Preparation

It is generally felt that preparation for a painful and frightening event reduces its traumatic impact. The parents in our study were urged to prepare their children fully and were given a printed booklet by the hospital to assist them. Nevertheless, it was found that in a number of cases preparation was either misleading or grossly inadequate because of the parents' own anxiety about the operation or ambivalence toward the child. In several instances the effect of such preparation was seen di-rectly in the child's reactions.

For instance, *Joseph,* age seven, together with his brother Stephen, age four, was tricked into coming to the hospital by their overprotective mother. She had informed them that they were going to buy a pair of shoes. In the hospital Joseph was restless and when blood was taken he struggled so that it needed four nurses to hold him. He threatened to have them arrested. He would not admit his fears but projected them on his brother Stephen. He mentioned, how-ever, that he expected to be hurt and had fantasies of being tortured. Imme-diately after the operation he appeared warm and relaxed but was "scrapping"

---

[5] Evidence that a friendly, supportive atmosphere reduces the severity of a child's reaction to hospitalization is presented by Huschka and Ogden (1938), Jackson (1942), Pillsbury (1951), and Prugh et al. (1952).

his throat and twisting his neck. His four-year-old brother displayed only general anxiety and cried during hospitalization and at follow-up visits.

It seemed not accidental that Joseph who was completely misled reacted in a panicky and almost paranoid way, with no recognition of the helpful aspects in the hospital, experiencing every manipulation as malicious torture.

Rose,[6] a bright girl of four, had not been told by her highly ambivalent mother either that she would be operated upon or that she would stay overnight in the hospital. Before the operation she was very quiet and restrained, and said that her mother was somewhere in the hospital. The next morning she denied having slept at the hospital and insisted she had been at home. After the operation she seemed depressed, without tears, and maintained that she had slept in her own house. She denied ever having seen the psychiatrist before. One week after the operation she seemed to cling more to her mother than ever before. She would not talk abo : the hospital except for saying that the nurses were mad. She would not recognize the psychiatrist and denied that she had her doll with her in the hospital. Three months after the operation she appeared less tense, and while she still would not talk about the hospital experience she admitted that she had had a T&A, asked if her brother would have his tonsils out, and played out the operation on a hospital set. After seven months she did not play the hospital game any more, but talked about the T&A. After eleven months she liked to see the "play doctor" and play hospital.

Our impression was that the child's denial of reality was to a large extent due to the lack of preparation.

There was quite a range of explanations given to lure the children to the hospital. One boy was told that he was to be fitted with a new pair of tonsils, another that he was going to a new school. A third was told that it would be "like going to a hotel." Two brothers were told they were going to buy some soap. One mother told her four-year-old daughter they would visit the hospital and that she could stay if she liked it.

There were several instances where preparation seemed overdone. This was strikingly illustrated by the mother who started preparation six weeks prior to the operation. She played out each detail of the hospital procedure, going so far as to lay the child on the kitchen table and place an ammonia-soaked rag over her face in order to simulate anesthesia.

Most of the mothers seemed able to prepare their children fairly adequately for the operation. We realize that preparation involves more than simply imparting information to the child. The parents' own feelings can color the presentation of the facts so that the child's apprehensiveness might be heightened rather than diminished. While intellectual preparedness helps maintain a proper reality orientation, it is inner preparedness—i.e., the extent to which the child has been able to master his anxiety and marshall his defenses to cope with the impending danger

6 Mentioned in preliminary report (Jessner and Kaplan, 1949).

—that affects the final outcome. The manner in which this inner preparedness is achieved varies from one child to the next, with some maintaining their own misconceptions and fantasies about the operation, despite their having received accurate information.

The following case is one in which preparation was done with the view of putting the child into a state of preparedness by allowing him to work through his anxieties and mobilize his defenses.

William, age four years, two months

Preoperative preparation by psychiatrist

In the first interview ten days prior to T&A the psychiatrist encourages the patient to play with him with a toy hospital, while talking about a boy who will have his tonsils out. The patient remarks there are no doors. "How do you get out? . . . There ought to be more windows; don't you think so?" The patient asks if the windows were broken and remarks about broken things. "What happened to them?" Psychiatrist gives the reassurance that toys break; other things don't.

Fear of being kept in the hospital

Castration fear

Self-reassurance that one can come out all right and the wish that the operation were over

The patient picks out a boy figure, saying, "He had his tonsils out; he had them out two days ago."

He inquires about exact operative procedures and is given information.

Castration fear—hospital as place to fix up

In the second interview he plays with a farmhouse and animals. He wonders about a horse with a broken leg which he tosses to the hospital to be fixed. He wonders why there are no doors to close in the farmhouse. He says it is too open. There ought to be more room on the edges for the animals to walk around.

Fear of enclosure and too open a space

Considerable anxiety preoperatively

At home, according to mother, he held his penis a lot and wet himself in the daytime three or four times. He ate hardly anything except oranges.

On admission

Armor of familiar things and strengthening himself with his possessions	He brings with him a great number of toys. He speaks of Little Black Sambo who gives his clothes away to the tiger, goes into the jungle, which seems to refer to his anticipation of the operation.
Identifies the hospital with a jungle and himself with a survivor who acquires food	
Fluctuates to the other extreme by identifying hospital with hotel	The patient constructs a house out of domino pieces with a walk around it, saying there are many rooms and how you can have fun in a hotel.
Vaccilates between identification with baby and with father—self-reassurance that shaving (cutting) does no harm, and pain as stimulating pleasure	He frequently uses baby powder, but more often an after-shave lotion, two items he has brought along. Daddy has some, but much stronger. It stings. That feels good.

Evening of the first day

Emphasis on being grown-up	He insists that mother sleeps in crib and that he sleeps in the big bed, but later accepts crib for himself.
Reassurance against castration fear	He speaks about the table being made of wood that won't break; plastic can break. He tests the table and is relieved that it is made of wood. He remarks that sometimes wood breaks but iron bends.

In operating room— waiting

	He is quiet and subdued. He asks questions about doctor's mask, etc., and holds on to lollipops, plays with toy animals. He co-operates with the anesthetist, but under anesthesia struggles—"No, stop it, don't."

Postoperative

He asked whether his tonsils were really out. While in the hospital he was anxious to see whether he could eat a whole meal

Expectation of change which would make him capable of unlimited intake	and whether he could swallow better. He cried when it was denied him. He wanted more ice cream than allowed for. During the night he wanted mother to call the family doctor because he felt awfully sick. The next morning he was playing cheerfully, reluctant to leave the hospital. The parents had the impression he couldn't believe it was all over.
Possessions as fortifying	At home he wanted all his toys and books around him, not to play with, just to be around him.
Identification with aggressor and acting out castration	He pretends to pull off father's nose and fingers. He tries to cut the leg off a flower stand. He plays cutting his own finger and wants a band-aid.
Fluctuates between the devourer and the devoured	On the following day he ate a great deal and wanted to know from what animal meat came. Pointing to his chest, he said: "If it's here, they must cut off his face."
Reassures himself by differentiating between essential and superfluous parts of the body	He plays with a doctor set and a doll as patient, using the headband and stethoscope, like his doctor. He gave penicillin shots in the buttocks. He took a toy dog's eye out and put it in again, remarking that real dogs could get their eyes sore. He asked his mother: "But they stay on, don't they?" Mother confirmed it and the patient said, "Not like tonsils." He told mother when he heard he had to have his tonsils out he was so scared his head almost fell off. He was most frightened after he knew it and before Dr. B. told him about it.
Abreaction by repetition	A week after T&A he dressed up in a doll blanket and quilt, pretending it was a hospital johnny. He declared his window to be the hospital window and that he was going down to play in the hospital nursery. This continued for a few days

and when he had the visit of a friend he played doctor with him, mainly examining his throat and injecting penicillin.

According to his mother, the patient did not wet himself since the operation, except one night after he got a splinter in his finger. He did not hold his penis after operation, ate very well, and seemed relaxed and happy at home and in follow-up visits (two and four weeks postoperatively), without talking about the hospital.

The Hospital Experience

One of the major sources of anxiety for the child in coming to the hospital is separation from those he loves (Edelston, 1943; Huschka and Ogden, 1938; Jackson, 1942; Prugh et al., 1952; Senn, 1945). In our patients we found that separation could have different meanings. For some children separation was experienced mainly as *loneliness*.

After her mother left, *Joanne*, age two and a half, said, "It's dark in the hospital." She cried softly and was quite sorrowful. She climbed up the cribside and put her arms around the psychiatrist, and whenever he returned, she reached out for him.

Not all the children could accept a parent substitute as readily as Joanne. A few spent most of the time lying in a fetal position and gave the appearance of a child in grief. Others were able to obtain some relief by observing that there were other children in distress. For some, separation was so painful that they denied they had been in the hospital overnight, and a few insisted that their mothers had slept in another room.

Some children adjusted rather cheerfully following the mother's departure, but in moments of threat they showed a desperate need for her *protection*.

Frank, age three and one-half, reacted strongly whenever he saw something done to other children; for instance, a child receiving an injection. He repeatedly asked the psychiatrist in panic: "What did they do to her?" The answers did not reassure him and he would persistently ask for his mother at such moments.

Carol, age five, was able to handle the anxiety of not having a protector by assuming the protector role herself. She wanted her mother whenever needles appeared, but was able to decrease her anxiety by adopting a little colored girl who came to the ward. She insisted on mothering this girl although the other child seemed quite self-sufficient.

Several children expressed the fear that their parents would not return. For them separation apparently represented complete *abandonment*. Others indicated in their behavior that they regarded the hospital as a kind of *jail*.

Frequently, being in the hospital presented the child with problems in maintaining his *identity*. The pastel-flowered rompers of the hospital were especially threatening to the masculinity of some of the boys. Being in a crib was upsetting to many of the older children because it meant returning them to the inferior status of the younger child. Some children, who had acquired techniques of mastery for familiar situations, were at a loss as to how to behave in the strange surroundings of the hospital.

Defenses against loss of identity and feelings of unfamiliarity were manifested in a variety of ways. One girl remained at home with her thoughts. She talked almost exclusively about the furniture and what the family was doing at home. Others compensated for their loss of status by bravado and boasting.

The hospital for some children may represent the place where one gets babies.[7]

Roberta, age five, was hospitalized with her brother Robert, age four. One year earlier their mother had given birth to twins. Both children spoke about Robert's bank with six dollars to buy babies. Roberta reported that she had discussed it with her grandmother who said they should get black babies so that she wouldn't have to wash babies so often. After the operation she began to eat enormously and four years later was quite plump. She seemed to use food as comfort, probably to make up for the loss of the tonsils and the frustration of her hope for babies.

Conceptions of Tonsils and Adenoids

For many children tonsils and adenoids had considerable symbolic significance. Such conceptions were frequently fostered by the mother's own tendency to regard the tonsils as the focal point of the child's difficulties. For instance, the mother of a fourteen-year-old schizoid girl hoped the T&A would correct everything that was wrong with her. Two mothers of feebleminded children expected the T&A to make them brighter. The mother of a severely disturbed boy attributed the change in his disposition at age two and one-half to his bad tonsils. Several expected enuresis to disappear. Others hoped for cure of infantile eczema and of asthma.

[7] Beata Rank, in her discussion of Edith Jackson's paper (1942), stressed this point and illustrated it with an example.

For many children the tonsils were the place where the "bad stuff" is. The tonsils were often conceived as demons or dangerous enemies. Thus, one ten-year-old girl thought that if the tonsils "meet in the center you die."

For children with obsessional trends "bad" had a definite moral connotation. T&A was anticipated as an exorcism where the bad will be cut out, torn out with pliers, burned out or melted away with ether. Helene Deutsch (1942) calls attention to the fact that the obsessional neurotic will use organic disease for the purpose of loading and unloading feelings of guilt.

Arthur, age seven, like his father, suffered from psychogenic headaches. He stated that his bad behavior was responsible for his father's headaches. He was sure that his own headaches were caused by his fight with his father, and his headaches made his adenoids grow. Preoperatively he expressed guilt feelings because he had not confessed his sins. Postoperatively his headaches improved.

While most children know that the tonsils were in the throat, for some they were "something deep inside the body." This conception was often maintained side by side with a correct knowledge of their location. Even postoperatively some children located their tonsils in other parts of the body despite having experienced pain in the throat. Most thought it was in the "belly" which for each child had a special meaning.

Donna, age five, stated three months postoperatively that the tonsils had been in her belly. They cut the belly open to take them out. This was connected with her fantasies of getting a baby.

Barbara, age six, pointed to her chest as the site of her tonsils and stated they will squeeze blood out of it. This notion seemed related to her conception of the illness of her father who died of tuberculosis.

For some children the tonsils represented another organ; e.g., testicles, eyes, or teeth.

Lucy, age six, thought her doctor would poke her eyes out. She was offered tonsils in a jar but refused to take them because they were "gushy pushy." She continued to talk about her doctor's eye mirror.

David, age ten, was very interested in the anatomy of the tonsils and described the pictures of tonsils he had seen in *Life* magazine. Nevertheless, two weeks postoperatively he insisted that his tonsils had not been taken out and that he could see them, pointing to his uvula. In the context of this boy's strong fear of mutilation and castration the uvula represented the penis.

Some children regarded the tonsils as analogous to teeth. They expressed a desire to be paid·for the tonsils just as for their teeth and were resentful when no payment was forthcoming. Some expected a second set of tonsils to appear, like teeth.

Removal of the tonsils seemed for some children a threat to the intactness of the body. For some children the tonsils severed from the body and to be seen as objects seemed gruesome. One boy called them "a piece of meat." The operation turned flesh into meat and evoked cannibalistic fantasies. A few children began wondering about animals and where and how the meat was gotten from them. A number of children did not want to eat meat for a while after the operation and we guessed that early devouring fantasies motivated such refusal. Also, other edibles were occasionally renounced. Paul postoperatively would not eat Queen Anne cherries and finally said they looked like his tonsils. Particularly the children with obsessional trends expressed resentment and narcissistic hurt at the thought that the tonsils would be thrown into the garbage pail.

The Meaning of Narcosis

One of the aspects of the operation that loomed large in the expectations of the children—mainly the older ones—was the narcosis. The children invariably called it ether, a word with an aura of mystery.

For a good many children narcosis represented the threat of *death*. Helene Deutsch (1942) has pointed out that ". . . . the fear of death mobilized by the expectation of an operation is connected first of all with narcosis anxiety." While this expectation was common enough, some of the children indicated the fear of death before operation; others expressed postoperatively the feeling of having been suffocated or smothered.

Carol,[8] age six, whose younger sibling died six months earlier, expressed her fear of death openly before operation. She brought a doll dressed as a nun with her. Her play consisted mainly in restoring things to their previous state. Her postoperative reaction was a relief that she didn't die.

For some children the anesthesia had the character of *punishment or execution* and a frequently used defense mechanism against this fear was to be either very good or rebellious. For other children narcosis meant a *murderous or sexual attack*.

Stanley, age eight, whose mother had been very anxious since an older brother died when the patient was two years old, had not slept the night before admission and worried how he would sleep in the hospital. He thought he would get "knock-out drops" and asked at another time if they would "knock me out with

[8] Mentioned in preliminary report (Jessner and Kaplan, 1949).

a hammer." The anxiety was so great that he tore off the mask on the operating table.

Russell, age thirteen, whose father and uncle had died of tuberculosis, described postoperatively how he had seen ether used in the movies: "You count one, two, three." In coming out of the anesthesia he screamed and ran wildly around the ward. The following day he said he had not liked the ether. He said he felt funny coming out of it, but would not talk about it.

At follow-up six weeks later he said the worst thing was the ether—three or four whiffs made him feel funny. He said when half awake coming out of it he felt scared: "I saw two men coming for me with knives and guns. I could see their faces, but they were no one I knew. I was scared. I jumped up and tried to run away. That's when I awoke and the nurse took me back to bed. I was very scared. I thought they were trying to kill me."

In connection with this memory he stated that one of his forms of entertainment was rolling down hill, which made him feel dizzy but good.

He had derived a mixture of fear and pleasure from anesthesia. Such a *masochistic element* was not uncommon among the reactions to anesthesia.

Walter, age five, also was mainly concerned about anesthesia. He had had a previous T&A one year ago, which was followed by enuresis. Seven months after the present T&A he remembered that he didn't like the ether; it smelled awful. He didn't dream under ether but now he dreams there is a whole gang of people coming to kill him, and they tie him up, throw him in the river, and he wakes up screaming, "No, no, no." Then his mother comes in when he does this. He continued by telling that during the T&A he wondered whether his mother left him because she didn't want him.

Death, meaning *separation from mother,* is expressed in the ether dreams of Angela, age eleven. She related a dream she had had during anesthesia. There was a cliff off to the side, and she was on the cliff. A voice was crying, "Mommy, Mommy, Mommy." It was the same dream she had had during narcosis for a mastoid operation seven months ago.

The fear of *loss of control* during anesthesia seemed to be the chief concern of the older children. Sometimes it was the fear of losing control over one's own impulses and at other times the fear of losing control over the environment.

Peter, age twelve, had the experience under anesthesia of things going round and round. Finally he let go when things were black. He thought he would go crazy. He wanted to fight back, but "then they went away."

On the other hand, with some children the thought of getting ether was *reassuring.* They derived comfort from the fact that they would not feel anything. The fear was rather that they might be awake during the operation. For some it seemed that pain was terrifying and they wanted to avoid it by all means. For others the submissive tendencies were *gratified* by having something done to them while they were unconscious.

The Meaning of the Operation

For many of the children the operation had the meaning of *mutilation* or *castration*.

Six months prior to T&A the Children's Medical Service had referred *Michael*, age four and one-half, for psychotherapy when he asked if the pediatrician was the doctor who was going to cut his penis off. For two years his mother had threatened him with castration because of his enuresis.

Michael was prepared in psychotherapy one month prior to operation. After preparation he dreamed he undressed a nurse. In psychiatric interviews he drowned a nurse, exhibited his penis, and the day before admission punched his therapist in the genitals. He expressed his desire to kill his father, and the fear that his father would kill him. He was concerned that a plasticene figure had no penis, demanded that one would be made and placed it.

On admission for T&A Michael was controlled and solemn while his mother was with him. When she left he sent a kiss for his sister but staunchly refused to send one to father. Following mother's departure, Michael cried for several hours, but with frequent visits of his psychiatrist he regained control. He mentioned he won't let himself dream because he dreams bad things. He wet at 6 P.M., but was dry all night. The next morning he was serene, talked freely about the impending T&A, but later on showed more anxiety. While waiting for anesthesia he copied the activities of other children.

The morning after operation he could hardly wait for mother to come and dissolved in tears when she arrived. Two weeks later he seemed subdued and refused to talk about the operation. He "didn't know" what was done to him and reported a nightmare of being killed by a bear. Three weeks later he wanted to get his tonsils back and asked how he might. In play he killed his father in effigy and mentioned his bed wetting. During the next few months he was afraid to leave his mother during the interview, but five weeks after the operation he could verbalize his castration fears and his wish to have as big a penis as his father. He was reassured about castration and in the following interviews appeared happier and more aggressive, poking mother's umbrella at everybody. He played out the T&A, using a sister doll as an object of operation, enemas, and dousing.

His mother described him as being more infantile at home during the first two months, having many nightmares and speaking of castration. Mother wondered why he took her threats so seriously, including such as, "I'll break your legs off if you don't stop running around." He talked about his hospital experience in detail and acted it out with his sister. After eight weeks he seemed more relaxed and mother reported increasingly better adjustment, greater independence and decrease of bed wetting. He was seen in therapy for eight months after the operation.

Two years after T&A he had a herniorraphy at another hospital. The nurses commented on his good co-operation and cheerfulness. His psychiatrist went to visit him. The patient spoke freely about this operation which seemed devoid of the castration fear, which had been so apparent previously while he was at the height of his oedipal conflicts.

Other children expected that the operation might change them from a *boy to a girl or vice versa.*

Rita, age thirteen, called "honey" by her mother, is the oldest of three girls. Her father died of cancer of the throat when she was nine years old and since then the patient has taken care of her mother. On admission the patient had to calm her mother who was extremely anxious about the operation, asking whether children ever died from T&A. Preoperatively, Rita told the psychiatrist that she missed playing baseball with the boys and how much she would like to be a boy and wear blue jeans. But she was glad she was a girl when it came to singing. She finally brought out the fear that tonsillectomy would make her voice sound like a frog and that she did not like the idea of having a deep voice like a boy. The day after the operation she fainted in the bathroom when she looked at her face in the mirror.

This patient had taken over the role of her mother's husband. Her ambivalence about her femininity, we felt, determined her special fear of the consequences of the operation.

Another meaning of the operation was *giving birth.* While this was found predominantly in girls, we found it also in a few of the younger boys.

Donna was a chubby five-year-old girl who had one older sister and a twin brother. She explained to the psychiatrist that her mother wanted one boy. She, therefore, made Donna a girl and her brother a boy. She did this by "cutting his off." When the psychiatrist wondered about that, she stated her mother cut her brother's hair off. If she had cut Donna's hair off, Donna would be a boy, too. But her mother didn't want two boys. The patient was glad she was a girl because when she grows up she will be a nurse. Three months later the patient remembered the T&A and when asked where the tonsils were located, she said: "You know, right here in the belly," pointing to her abdomen. They cut open her belly and took them out. She didn't know why there's no mark or cut. She then referred to her doll as her baby, gave the baby a name, and said her mother bought it in the hospital. During the interview with the psychiatrist she made several drawings. The two which most clearly illustrate her preoccupation with pregnancy are included (see Plates I and II).

Occasionally the child *identified* himself with someone who had undergone a different operation. Here the expectation of the T&A was based on the child's fantasies about the other operation. Thus, a seven-year-old girl indicated she expected her throat to be cut from ear to ear,

PLATE I   PLATE II

which was her idea of the thyroidectomy her mother had during the past
year.[9]

Although T&A is not as common as it formerly was, in some families
it is taken for granted that each child will have it in the course of growing up. In such cases the child often looked forward to T&A as a kind of
initiation rite.

In discussing the children's conceptions of the tonsils, we have already
indicated that the T&A may be regarded as a form of *exorcism* or as
punishment.

There were quite a variety of theories encountered among the children as to how the operation would be performed. There was speculation
as to whether scissors, wires, knives, or pliers would be used to remove
the tonsils. Some thought they might be burned out. One child insisted
that no instrument would be used, but that the ether would melt them
away. One very aggressive, destructive boy gave the following account of
what would happen:

Dickie,[10] age nine, said that the doctors would cut his nose off with a carving
knife, take the adenoids out and then put the nose back on again. He managed

9 *Ibid.*
10 *Ibid.*

to see children in the Eye Ward and stated: "The kids in the other room have no eyes; instead they have bandages on their eyes." He told his theory about the removal of the nose to a girl patient and asked her whether it was true. She indicated her disbelief, but he maintained that it was so. After the operation, he was more quiet than before. He pointed to his nose, saying, "It is okay. They didn't cut it off." He showed his tooth and wiggled it and complained that the doctor bent it. Evidently the castration fear had now been displaced to the tooth.

SURVEY OF THE TOTAL GROUP

Of the 143 children in the study, 80 were boys and 63 were girls. The age distribution of these children is given in Table I. It can be seen that the greatest occurrence of T&A's was during the ages of five and six.

TABLE I
AGE DISTRIBUTION OF PATIENTS WITH T&A

	NUMBER		
Age	Male	Female	Total
Under 3	3	2	5
3	9	3	12
4	9	6	15
5	15	14	29
6	8	9	17
7	8	8	16
8	6	6	12
9	5	5	10
10	6	3	9
11	5	1	6
12	4	1	5
13	1	3	4
14	1	2	3
Totals	80	63	143

Focus of Anxiety

The four main foci were: the separation from the parents and exposure to the strange hospital surroundings, the anticipation of the narcosis, the operation itself, and the fear of needles. Frequently the child had more than one focus of anxiety. We attempted to determine the main foci for each child on the basis of his play, ward behavior, spontaneous questions, and other verbalizations.

We found that the focus of anxiety shifted with age. This is graphically represented in Figure 1, where we have divided our patients into four approximately equal age groups. It can be seen that anxiety about hospitalization and separation is greatest in the younger children. This shifts to the operation and narcosis, the latter with its threat to self-control and consciousness being greatest in the oldest age group.

FOCUS OF ANXIETY FOR DIFFERENT AGE GROUPS

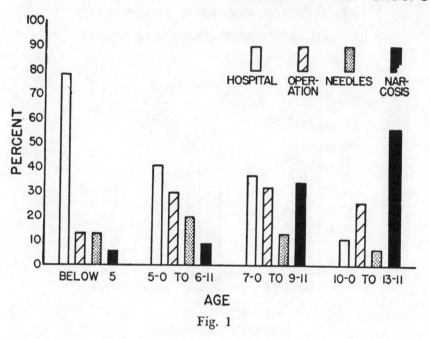

Fig. 1

Effect of Operation

Although the T&A experience seemed to arouse considerable anxiety in practically all the children, the majority seemed to be able to master and integrate the experience without any serious emotional consequences. In some, however, we found that striking changes in behavior occurred, often accompanied by the appearance of symptoms which tended to persist for months and even years after the operation. On the other hand, there were a few cases where definite improvement in emotional adjustment seemed to occur following operation. We grouped our cases according to their postoperative reaction. Those with marked or persisting sequelae were called SEVERE; those with only mild or transitory reactions were called MILD; and those who showed improvement were called IMPROVED. We had sufficient follow-up material on 136 of our 143 cases to classify the postoperative reaction. The relative incidence of each type of reaction for both sexes is shown in Figure 2. It will be seen that the SEVERE reactions constitute about 20 per cent of the group. Little difference between boys and girls was noted.

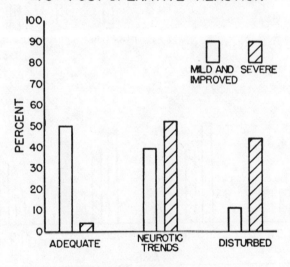

RELATION OF EMOTIONAL ADJUSTMENT TO POST-OPERATIVE REACTION

EMOTIONAL ADJUSTMENT

Fig. 2

A total of 25 postoperative reactions were classified as SEVERE. These included a wide variety of disturbances which are listed in Table II. Of the 25, 13 were boys and 12 were girls. A brief description of their postoperative reactions is given in Table III. Most of the children in this group are discussed in more detail elsewhere in the paper.

TABLE II
TYPES OF SEVERE REACTIONS

A. Eating disturbances
    Overeating
    Undereating
B. Sleep disturbances
    Screaming, nightmares
    Difficulty in going to sleep
C. Speech disturbances
    Voice change
    Refusal to talk
D. Tics and mannerisms
E. Fears: Hospital, white coats, bodily, death, etc.
F. Regressive behavior
    Increased dependency
    Wetting, soiling, etc.

Relation of Postoperative Reaction to Age

Our findings indicate that the incidence of severe reactions was fairly equally distributed among the age groups. David Levy (1945) found among his patients that operations were more frequently traumatic among children under the age of three. There were too few cases in our group to permit us to test this observation. We observed only five children below three years. Of these two had emotional disturbances preoperatively. One was a boy of one year, eleven months, who had temper outbursts with head banging. We were able to obtain only a single follow-up one week after the operation. He was friendly to the psychiatrist, but his mother reported that he had had nightmares the first two nights after the operation. Bowel and bladder control, however, had improved during the week. This "improvement" could have been a sign of his increased anxiety following operation.

The other was a two-and-one-half-year-old boy with whom an early attempt at toilet training had been unsuccessful, and he still soiled at night. He also banged his head when angry and constantly clutched a diaper. We were not able to get any follow-up information on him, but the day immediately after the operation he cringed at the approach of anyone in a white coat. His speech was indistinct and his mother commented that he appeared different and did not seem to recognize her.

The other three included two girls and one boy, all between the ages

TABLE III

DESCRIPTION OF SEVERE REACTIONS

Age	Sex	Postoperative reactions
4	F	Eating difficulties.
4	F	"Not like herself"; dependent; regressive.
5	M	Overeating; persisting nightmares; increase of enuresis.
5	M	Change of voice.
5	F	Persisting fears of hospital; nightmares. Operation complicated by hemorrhage for 4 days, requiring transfusion.
5	M	Adenoid voice for 6 weeks; more anxiety; regression.
5	M	Increase of fears; nightmares.
5	F	Eating difficulties; nasal voice.
6	M	Uncommunicative; night terrors lasting several months.
6	M	Did not eat for 4 days; increased restlessness.
6	F	Nightmares; refused to eat.
7	F	Agitated; depressed; fearful; produced sores on arms and face by picking and scratching. Five days later returned on account of nose bleeding, which we suspected was the result of her picking at her nose. No later follow-up.
7	M	"Scrapping" of throat; twisting of neck.
7	M	Increase in sleep difficulties; grimacing; increase in fear of death.
8	F	Increased dependency on mother and fears.
9	F	Since appendectomy at 5½, fear of doctors and hospitals; would not eat for 3 days; 2½ mos. later, changed from cheerful to withdrawn; eating poorly.
9	F	Severe abdominal pains; night terrors; refused to talk about T&A for 2 wks. No further follow-up.
9	F	Obesity.
9	M	Nightmares; panic of needles and dentist.
10	M	Hysterical aphonia and refusal to eat.
10	M	Nightmares; phobias; throat clearing.
10	M	Refused to eat or talk; increase of hypochondriacal fears.
11	M	Increase of hypochondriacal fears.
13	F	Regressive behavior. Refusal to return to hospital.
14	F	Delusional ideas about tongue and nose.

of two and one half and three years. One of the girls was seen only once, one week after the operation, and nothing unusual was reported. The other girl developed diurnal incontinence which lasted a short time. She also was afraid of a beauty operator in a white coat and two years later cried at the dentist's. Whether the last was associated with the T&A is uncertain. The boy was followed for fifteen months after the operation and no untoward reaction was noted.

Relation of Postoperative Reaction to Preparation

We did not have enough information on our children to determine if preparation was really adequate in the sense of inner preparedness. However, where the parents made a serious attempt to explain to the child what he might expect in the hospital, preparation was classified as ADEQUATE. Where no information was given or was incomplete in essential details, it was classified as INADEQUATE; and when the parents deliberately misinformed the child, it was called MISLEADING.

We have already seen in some of the previous case descriptions that misleading preparation tended to increase the child's feelings of insecurity. Nevertheless, when we considered the group as a whole we did not find that preparation was a decisive factor for the postoperative reaction. In Figure 3, those cases of SEVERE reactions are compared with the remainder of the group in the preparation they received.

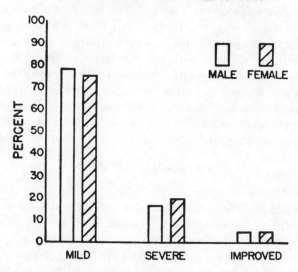

Fig. 3

The slight differences between the two groups are not statistically significant. In evaluating this finding it must be remembered that our children were all seen by a psychiatrist prior to operation. Although his function was chiefly that of an observer, the fact that he encouraged expression of feelings and answered questions may have compensated for the lack of preparation. Although preparation in terms of information did not seem to be a decisive factor in influencing the sequelae to the T&A, intensive study of a few cases demonstrated the importance of inner preparedness [compare with A. Freud in chap. 3, esp. pp. 79–80].

Relation of Postoperative Reaction to Preoperative Personality

Finally we tried to find out if there was any relation between preoperative emotional adjustment and the postoperative reaction. A child was classified as ADEQUATE where emotional adjustment was basically normal with perhaps only a few minor problems. Where clear-cut evidence of neurotic traits or symptoms existed—e.g., enuresis or sleep disturbances— the child was regarded as having NEUROTIC TRENDS. Where the symptoms were severe or crippling with evidence of arrested personality development we classified the child as DISTURBED. These ratings were made on the basis of the anamnesis and the psychiatrists' observations, independent of our knowledge of the postoperative reaction. There was sufficient information available on 130 children to classify them in this manner.

The children with SEVERE postoperative reactions are compared with the others in Figure 4. It can be seen that there is a much greater incidence of DISTURBED children in the SEVERE group. While there was a significant number of children with neurotic trends in this group, there was only one child whose preoperative adjustment was considered ADEQUATE. This was a five-year-old girl who had to remain four extra days in the hospital because of a postnasal hemorrhage and other complications. These findings suggest that the T&A is not likely to be a harmful experience, except in those cases where at least some neurotic traits pre-exist.

SOME ASPECTS OF SEQUELAE

Normal Reactions

The majority of the children we observed had mild reactions for one week or ten days following the operation. They were demanding, irritable, or depressed, had occasional nightmares or other sleep disturbances. These symptoms we, as well as David Levy (1945), regarded as normal manifestations of assimilating the experience. After this initial period, some children tended to suppress the experience, and adapted well on the surface, although many of them betrayed anxiety in their dreams of being chased, cut, tied down, drowned, etc. Other children seemed to integrate

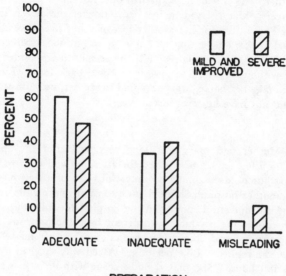

RELATION OF PREPARATION TO
POST-OPERATIVE REACTION

PREPARATION

Fig. 4

the experience by discussing it, especially with contemporaries or younger children, informing them either in a reassuring or in a frightening way, and by repeating it in play.

It is our impression that these children who worked through the experience are less likely to have later reactivation than those who adapted by suppression.

An example of a child who handled her anxiety adequately seemed to be:

Mary, age three and one half, was the youngest of two children in an Italian-American family. Economic stress and problems of the mother (rheumatic heart disease) did not particularly affect her. Mary liked nursery school. She was very close to her mother who, however, did not prepare her for the operation. Two years ago her brother had a tonsillectomy without complication and probably he told her about the experience.

Hospital Observations:

First day—At first Mary asked for Mommy, and wanted to go home, but soon engaged in play with her dolls. She related easily to the psychiatrist and to other children on the ward. She became restless but quieted down when the psychiatrist fed her. She suggested that he eat her and showed him her belly. She then wished he would come home with her. They would eat and go to bed. She mentioned that she was having a tonsillectomy very casually. She spoke about her brother: "He is bad; he is the bad one, not me; I help mother."

Postoperatively—Mary played in her bed, said her throat was sore, but was not crestfallen. She waited for her mother to come, but played readily. She said that she looked forward to eating at home; however, she accepted a lifesaver with pleasure. When the psychiatrist left, she seemed disappointed, and kissed him good-bye without crying. She agreed to come back for a visit. When her mother came to take her home, Mary was glad to see her, but also was concerned that mother did not have her eyeglasses.

Follow-up:

One-year—Mother said Mary got along very well after the operation. She stayed in bed for a few days, and enjoyed the attention and the toys she received upon returning home. Mary compared notes with her brother who had had his tonsils out in another hospital. She had gone to camp meanwhile and had done quite well. She did not mind coming to the hospital for follow-up.

Mary latched onto the psychiatrist (different from the previous one) with no hesitation. She remembered "the thing over my face" (ether mask). Asked what it smelled like, she replied: "Like perfume." Asked why she had them out: "So I could get a doll house." She played out a scene with dolls in which a verbal battle ensued between the girl and the nun with the nun's being ordered around and told off. Asked what had been wrong with her tonsils she replied, "They tickled my tongue but they don't no more." She painted a snake looking at a duck.

This child had resources, facilitating adaptation and integration. The relationship between mother and child was secure and warm. She had reached the developmental stage according to her age without neurotic manifestations. Although unprepared by her mother, she had apparently gained knowledge on her own. The child could express her anxiety quite freely and the defense mechanisms she used were adequate; e.g., she was disconcerted when her mother left, but would transfer her feelings to substitutes easily. She then handled her anxiety in a way comparable to humor which adults use in a frightening situation—by her coquettish and joking manner with the psychiatrist. The jokes seemed to allude to her fear of being eaten up and to her oedipal wishes. This seemed to arouse some guilt feelings which she quickly projected onto her brother and reassured herself that she helped mother. She seemed to take the operation and the consequent throat pain quite realistically whereas some children complained a great deal about the soreness of the throat to a degree which seemed due to an overlay of anxiety. She could take a candy and enjoy it while others were afraid to hurt their throats by eating. Concern of having lost something seemed expressed in her worry about mother's missing eyeglasses. At home she apparently could freely talk about her experiences. Another separation from home three months postoperatively (camp) was tolerated comfortably. In a play interview a year after T&A she indicated some anxiety connected with the operation through a painting of a snake looking at a duck. In all our contacts with Mary she had an appropriate degree of anxiety, sometimes increasing through guilt feelings when instinctual wishes were expressed and immediately being attenuated by successful defense mechanisms.

Except for one passive boy, all children who played the doctor game took over the active role, being either the surgeon or the anesthetist, operating on a doll or a playmate, or giving needles to the patient. In dreams, however, most of the children were the victims of an attack. In respect to dreams there appears a difference between children and adults. Helene Deutsch (1942) pointed out that in a traumatic neurosis the traumatic situation is usually repeated in the dream; whereas in her postoperative patients she has "never seen such a direct repetition of the traumatic experience. If the dream contains direct references to the operation . . ., the dreamer usually appears in the active role. . . ." With our children the dreams usually dramatized the operation in easily recognizable form. References to the operation in fantasies and stories repeated the situation in a romanticized way, similar to the dreams. In play, however, the roles were reversed and the child performed the operation. There is one other difference of children's reactions to those of adults in regard to surgery: The adult, as Helene Deutsch describes it, carries out in postoperative dreams the action usually against a person of authority, a father figure. In so far as the children's doctor games are concerned, the victim is always another child, a contemporary, or more often a younger child.

Symptom Formation

In a number of children, anxiety manifested itself in symptom formation.

In some, *anxiety* was *focused* on and limited, like a phobia, to doctors, white coats, nurses, hospitals, or ether, associated with a reluctance to leave mother or go outside the house.

Sequelae in others consisted of tics or conversion symptoms centering around the area of the operation (mouth, nose and throat).

Richard, age ten, who had undergone a previous T&A at the age five, and was concerned about his dog who had swallowed a fish hook and had his mouth torn, is described in detail by Dr. Samuel Kaplan (1952) as a case of hysterical aphonia following T&A. We found that at a recent follow-up interview, Richard

had no speech difficulties, but an atopic dermatitis and a general apprehensiveness. He still has the notion that doctors will "take up knives and cut" him. He
remembered that for some time after his operation he was scared that he would
not be able to talk.

Edward, an asthmatic boy of five, had a high-pitched voice for several weeks.
His mother kidded him for having a girl's voice. It is our impression that it was
rather a baby's voice. His symptoms seemed largely determined by his identification with a three-month-old brother of whom he was very jealous.

The majority of the children had some *eating difficulties* during the
first postoperative days, with improvement in appetite as they recovered
from the operation. In nine cases we found marked eating difficulties
lasting for weeks or months. Five children began to overeat, and two of
these developed *obesity.*

Camille, age nine, a compliant, overcontrolled girl, knew her mother wanted
the T&A to improve her hearing and to make her eat better. She mainly talked
with the psychiatrist about death. She had a dog, in fact, two. Both of them had
died. The cat also died a year ago after being bitten by another cat in the neck.
She also had a brother who died when he was young (death of infant brother
occurred when patient was four years old). She froze up when the operation was
mentioned and watched with horror another girl spitting blood. Two months
later her strongest recollection of the hospital stay was spitting blood after
waking up. Three and one half years later, Camille was at least 50 pounds overweight, to the chagrin of her likewise obese mother. Whereas Camille was punished preoperatively for not eating enough, she postoperatively could not be
stopped.
    Four years after T&A she appeared shy, scared and mentioned that she had
been frightened at the thought of coming here. She had been at the hospital
a couple of times since her T&A. "I always dream afterward." The only such
dream she remembered was two nights ago: A girl was being attacked by her
father who was a vampire. He was going to suck all the blood out of her. (The
patient's father had left the family five months prior to the T&A to live with
another woman.)
    At the time of operation, this patient was afraid of dying, remembering her
brother's and her dogs' deaths, and identifying herself with the cat who was
bitten in the neck. From the beginning there was an emphasis on losing blood.
At the age of thirteen, the fear of being killed was more definitely in the form of
being attacked by father who sucks out the blood. We assume that her overeating
was related to the fears of death and sexual attack.

Anxiety States

Camille belongs to a group of children who prior to operation were
burdened with apprehensions of mutilation and death. They reacted

to the T&A with persisting heightened anxiety. We will report on four of them in detail to discuss their dynamics.

Francis, age eleven, was described as an overactive boy with temper outbursts, resembling those of his father, a reformed alcoholic who occasionally had epileptiform seizures. Francis had a long medical history, with numerous injuries to his genitals and hands. At two and one half he was scratched by a cat on his penis and appeared terrified. Around that time he was circumcised on medical advice, followed by a period of enuresis. At four he was treated for hematuria, at six for pain in his groin, diagnosed as due to lymphadenopathy, at nine for albuminuria and for a lacerated left hand. His mother noted that the testicles, particularly the left, were frequently missing from the scrotum and that he complained of pain in his penis. At ten his hand was caught in the wringer of a washing machine. The wound was closed under nitrous oxide anesthesia and Francis was discharged after two weeks of hospitalization.

On being admitted for T&A, Francis kept aloof, reading the same comic books over and over. He assured the psychiatrist he didn't mind the operation since his older brother had it when he was three and he, himself, had ether before, pointing to the long scar on his arm. He accepted the anesthesia most obediently. Postoperatively, however, he appeared extremely depressed. He sobbed for hours, covering his head with a blanket, terrified because his throat hurt. Two weeks later he was noncommital, but two months after, he expressed how miserable he felt for five days and how he could not eat or talk. Then he gained 6 pounds. He mumbled that for the time being he was all right, but later on will have to have his tonsils out again. His mother told him, so he says, they will grow back and one has to take them out before he is twenty-one. Taking them out after twenty-one may be dangerous; he may even die. His nineteen-year-old friend said his tonsils will grow back again and if they don't take them out before he is twenty-one, they will grow and grow and choke him. While he said they will grow and grow, he drew a single large elongated object in the air with his fingers. He looked worried and mentioned that a big fat boy in school had kicked him down here, pointing to his genitals. It is a very dangerous thing to be hurt there. One may die. It was bleeding. It was terrible. The same day his mother brought him to the medical clinic, as he was kicked in the groin by another boy. The patient complained to the examining physician about tenderness in both groins, penis, and testicles There were no local signs of injury. [Blos, in chap. 5, further elaborates on the unconscious equation of tonsils and testicles.]

In this case castration wish and fear, accident proneness and conflict about masculinity were strong before T&A. The operation fitted into his fantasy of castration and death—the tonsils representing the testicles which he knew were not at the right place. He expects more to come; he was not satisfied that it was done. The wish for and fear of castration continued with great force postoperatively.

David, age ten, was a forceps baby and had been hospitalized at five months of age for four months because of purulent otitis media; at the age of four and one half for mumps and for pneumonia; at the age of seven he was hospitalized for scarlet fever and for a month following discharge he cried continuously at night. This happened shortly after his mother separated from his father because he was irresponsible, drank, ran around. The patient was very attached to his father although his father was very strict to him. The patient continued to ask for his father. Around the time of separation, he began to wet his bed occasionally and to have nightmares in which someone drowns or is hurt in an accident. Ever since he was afraid of the dark and wouldn't sleep before mother goes to bed. During the past one and one half years David was present when both maternal grandparents fell sick and died.

On admission David at first denied any fear, assuring himself that he won't feel anything, because one gets ether and that he had had gas before at the dentist's. He thought how it would be to get on the table, get ether, get clamps in the mouth to keep it open and long scissors to take them out. Something might happen to him. When he plays he thinks he might die, no reason for it. "I heard one little girl got killed, a truck ran over her." He is afraid something might happen to someone who lives in the house and also to his father. He dreams often of scary things. He became anxious when he had to undress and cried when he had to wear short pants instead of long trousers. Mother remarks that since age six, he has insisted on long pants. On the ward he got more tense, biting and sucking his thumb, mentioning that in case you go into the Army, you can go blind.

David seemed comforted after the priest's visit and passed on to a little girl that the priest had told him: "If the doctors make you die, you have communion in your heart." (Later on he admitted that the priest said no such thing.) In the operating room he asked to see the instruments. He tried to grab the ether cone, cried: "Mama and Lord," then struggled against the anesthesia.

Immediately postoperatively he cried constantly for his mother, lying in the corner of his bed in semiflexion, complaining that the ether had frightened him. "I felt like I was choking." When he woke up, he was scared that he wouldn't be able to talk. He anxiously confessed that he didn't go to church regularly anymore.

Two weeks postoperatively he seemed depressed and timid. His mother reported that he had been weepy since he came home and for the first four days had refused to answer any question about the operation. A month later the mother still complained of his whining and of his not behaving any more like a big boy. He seemed to act out something while asleep: e.g., sitting up in bed, fighting, taking off his pajamas, throwing them into a bureau. His wish to go back to New York, where his father lives, was expressed more frequently. He spoke of visions during ether and how he had felt dizzy after it. He seemed concerned that he was still under the influence of ether because he forgot many things and didn't know what he was doing at night except from his mother's stories. He then mentioned they didn't take his tonsils out: "I still can see them"—pointing to his uvula.

Six weeks postoperatively he was admitted for meningoencephalitis at another hospital, and recovered within two weeks. Six months postoperatively he still seemed anxious and quite preoccupied with the operation. He mentioned that he saw his dog's tonsils, on the side of the neck. "Do dogs have their tonsils out. . . ?" "It might kill them because they can't swallow after the ether."

One year postoperatively he still seemed shy and restless; the content of the interviews revolved around the old theme of mutilation and death. He announced that he wanted to be a pilot later on. "I don't want to be a butcher. I know a butcher in New York who chopped his finger off. I don't know when he did it, but it was off when we used to live there." He likes to paint war pictures. He wanted to know how ether makes you sleep. "How long does it make you sleep?" It seemed just three to four minutes to him. He seemed to allude to the feeling that he was still under the influence of ether. "I wish I didn't wake up at all, because my throat hurt. . . . If you have them out, you don't have to have it again. You don't have to go through it twice." He seemed anxious, hoping for confirmation of his opinion, and inquired why they put a needle in the bottom of another boy to make his temperature go down. One got the impression that an attack on the rear would be even more frightening than another operation. From his mother we learned that the patient continued to have episodes at night, in which he acted wildly agitated. They always came when he was upset during the day. He had none during summer vacation. The mother attributed those nightly episodes to the T&A, because he screamed about knives and people coming to cut him up. He was doing very well at school but was irritable at home and afraid of the dark. He would not go to the bathroom by himself at night. Lately he woke up his mother two or three times a night to take him to the bathroom and when he got there he didn't seem to have to go. In the morning he takes an hour or more to clear his throat. Physical examination revealed no ear, nose, and throat pathology to account for this symptom. Neurological examination was negative.

Before operation David had hypochondriacal fears which we felt were based on his struggle against the wish to submit to the cruel father—to be castrated and annihilated. He covered up his passive, feminine tendencies by insisting on long trousers and athletic activity. The operation seemed to give him a taste of what he unconsciously wanted and intensified the basic conflict. He seemed to expect, wish, and fear a more devastating experience.

Paul, age seven and one-half, had, during his neonatal period, a bilateral otitis media which ruptured spontaneously and he was cranky for the first weeks. He seemed dissatisfied, cried a great deal, and had a feeding disturbance. He suffered from recurrent running ears until he was two and a half years old. When he was seven months of age his father left for military service, and in spite of the father's frequent visits, the patient did not seem well acquainted with him. When his father asked him where his father was, Paul would point to a picture on the mantelpiece. When Paul was six years old the paternal grandfather visited the family and one week after he arrived, he died suddenly of pulmonary infection. The grandfather had gone into coma in the late evening and oxygen equipment was brought to the house. The grandfather died in the early morning. Paul was observed by his sister going into the room and taking the sheet off grandfather's face. The patient seemed not particularly disturbed, but several months later he developed a habit of coming into his parents' room in the evening complaining he was afraid to sleep and wondered what happens when people sleep. The parents had the impression that for Paul sleep was related to his grandfather's death. When guests would comment on the patient's noisy breathing at night, Paul would become upset and his parents felt that he was reminded of his grandfather's labored breathing during the night he died. Prior to his T&A, for which he was well prepared, Paul showed at home a great deal of bravado and was overactive and quarrelsome.

On admission to the hospital, he appeared tense and jittery. He occupied himself by completely covering many sheets of paper with bright-colored crayons. This was done very forcefully so that many crayons broke. He asked all types of questions in regard to the equipment in his room. He reacted with hyperactivity to the sedative the night before the operation, throwing himself about in bed. On the way to the operating room, his chief concern seemed whether they were going to remove a tooth at the same time. When told this would not be done, he appeared rather disappointed. He asked every conceivable question about all of the anesthesia equipment that he saw, tried to delay the narcosis by asking questions, but went under peacefully.

Postoperatively he was proud of his co-operation with surgery and the fact that he held the ether cone over his nose himself. His drawings were full of orange and red skies. After a few weeks he regularly drew pictures of a house with a large red chimney. He made clay models of automobiles, all hot rods, accurate to the last detail, with special interest in large hood ornaments. After the operation he had difficulty falling asleep and would play his bedside radio for hours. The parents noted that Paul made tremendous efforts not to fall asleep. On questioning he described that as soon as he would fall asleep he would begin to hear noises and then he would immediately wake up frightened. It was several months before he related these noises to the noise he heard in his ear during anesthesia. After talking about that for some time he stopped complaining of it. What also grew worse postoperatively was his coming into the parents' bedroom, crying he was afraid to fall asleep because he might die. He would worry about the future, especially the year 2000, or he would think of a date and wonder if he or the other people he knew would be alive at that time. Once or twice he discussed this in relationship to the death of his grandfather. On hearing about someone's death, he immediately wondered how the person had died.

Another symptom, grimacing, appeared much stronger postoperatively. This symptom seemed to be related to two experiences he had at age five and one half. At that time Paul annoyed his dog by shooting at him with a cap pistol and the dog bit Paul's upper lip through, so that it had to be sutured. Around that time his sister got teeth braces and toyed with them by making grimaces with her lips.

Another postoperative difficulty was a provoking negativistic attitude toward his father. He once stated that his father looked at him as though he were going to kill him. When asked whether he was not angry at his father himself, the patient with a burst of laughter said he often felt he would like to smash his father's nose right through his face. After this admission he seemed less provocative and less likely to cry when scolded.

One year postoperatively he read almost one biography a day and became the class expert on American history. He knew the day of birth and the day of death of practically every American of note. At the same time he got passionately interested in riflery and archery. His anxiety and his symptoms gradually subsided, but a striking increase occurred when, one and a half years after the operation his grandmother, who was living in the household, fell in the bathtub and broke one toe. Paul frequently went to her room, was visibly disturbed, would not sleep, and made grimaces. After about two weeks these symptoms subsided.

Steven, age ten, was a shy, pale, undernourished, and subdued boy. His father was a seaman who used to come home only occasionally. He liked his children and favored the patient, but became abusive when drunk. Mother impressed us as being warm, overprotective, anxious, and worried about her marriage, financial difficulties, and her kidney disease. When patient was three years old a younger brother was born. Since then Steven has been enuretic and a poor eater. At the age of six he was struck by a car. Shortly afterward another boy pushed him and he fell. This resulted in a ruptured kidney for which he was hospitalized three months, involving many catheterizations. During the same year the family's house burned down and the parents separated; nothing was heard from the father since. From the age of eight on, Steven had frequent colds and missed school often.

On admission Steven seemed reserved and overcontrolled. He did not sleep much during the first night and remarked the next morning that at 7 A.M. a bell rang like a church bell. In the operating room he lay motionless, staring. He denied fears, assuring himself that he had had ether before. He took the anesthesia quietly and obediently.

Postoperatively he appeared depressed and cried, "I vomited blood." Two weeks later he appeared dejected, moving slowly, talking in a very low voice. He mentioned that they didn't know where his father was and that the father didn't know the family's address, because their house burned down one and a half years ago—while the patient was at the hospital for a check-up. When they came home they found it burned down. Everyone was saved except the patient's dog which was burned to death. He had been vicious and mother wanted to give him away. But the patient liked him very much. Another dog, patient's favorite, was run over by a car. Once father brought patient a guinea pig. A few weeks later it got a fit and died. Patient also had mice which his father had given him. They died one after another.

The mother reported that the patient would not eat for about ten days after the operation, nor would he talk. He said he felt that something was stuck in his throat. Mother thought he kept his feelings about the operation hidden except for praising the nurse because she brought him a radio. While his reaction was a very severe one, the patient seemed to recover three months later, steadily eating better and gaining weight.

These last five patients—one girl and four boys—have certain features in common. They had been sick many times, from early childhood on, had met with accidents or surgery, and had experienced the death of relatives or pets. These events seemed to have left them with the feelings: "It happened before, so it will happen again," and "what occurs to others will occur to me, too." Four had cruel, threatening fathers, to whom they were deeply attached. One (Paul) was in passionate rivalry with his father and projected his own aggression on him. These children seemed to provoke accidents or fights unconsciously. Any threat to the body increased their fears. They repeated the operation in dreams in the manner of a traumatic neurosis. Their play and talk betrayed their preoccupation with the operation only in an indirect way, and hardly referred to it directly in the way the majority of the children assimilated the experience. The dynamics of these children confirm the statement of Helene Deutsch (1942) that when the child is burdened not only with a sense of guilt because of forbidden masturbation but also by death wishes against some person near to him, the expectation that his own death will result from this attitude is a powerful factor in both the early and late fears of operation.

However, other apprehensive children, with a history of traumatic life experiences, felt a relief after T&A; some because the anticipated annihilation did not occur, others because their need for punishment was fulfilled.

Elizabeth, age thirteen, had hysterical character traits, hypochondriacal concerns and a "nervous stomach" preoperatively. Two years prior to T&A, her father had died suddenly and her mother suffered a "nervous breakdown." One year ago her older sister went into a depression. On admission, Elizabeth talked incessantly and referred to her father's death. Immediately after operation she felt relieved and appeared serene. Afterward her appetite improved. Two years later she appeared as an overly made-up coquettish adolescent, mainly interested in her frequent dates with sailors. She remembered that her throat was sore for two weeks, "but it was worth it"; the ether was not bad at all. She did not believe that they really took her tonsils out.

Carol,[11] age six, had a father who drank but had a warm stable relation-

11 *Ibid.*

ship with her mother. When she was three years old her hand got caught in a wringer. Six months before T&A a younger sibling died of whooping cough and pneumonia. Carol on admission talked freely with the psychiatrist about her fear of death. On awakening from anesthesia she expressed relief that she did not die.

Mary,[12] age five and a half, had been an anxious child, clinging to her over-protective mother, very conscious of her mother's severe illness (lymphosarcoma) which had necessitated several emergency admissions. Mary had been hospitalized a few months prior to T&A and at that time raised the roof and vomited when her mother left. When she came for T&A, Mary was frightened, and not communicative, but acted out her fears with her doll, indicating that she believed illness to be the result of naughtiness. She expected her throat would be cut. Postoperatively she described her experience in great detail and wanted to take her tonsils home in a jar. The first night she had bad dreams and did not sleep well, but afterward did not appear anxious and started school without difficulties.

In comparing this group of apprehensive children with those who had severe reactions, we felt that there were both quantitative and qualitative differences in their anxiety. In the severe group there was a special multiplicity of traumatic events. Their anxiety appeared greater and seemed to be related to their highly charged relationship with the father.

Obsessional Children

In a few obsessional children we observed the breakdown of their control and their reaction formation as sequelae.

Eileen, age eight, was described by her mother as a good girl, always concerned about cleanliness. She could not stand dirt and changed her clothes three or four times a day. She had asthma since she started school. Occasionally she had temper tantrums and complained that no one cared if she died. The mother gave us the impression of being an anxious and tense person, preoccupied with the hysterectomy she had had six weeks before. She was ambivalent with Eileen and preferred the younger sibling, a boy. Eileen's toilet training was started when she was six months old and accomplished by the age of nine months. She had five previous hospitalizations and "every disease known to children except diphtheria."

On admission Eileen looked sad and talked a lot. She asked the psychiatrist to put up the side of her crib so nobody could get into it. She spoke of her tonsils as being "rotten," giving her sore throats and belly aches. She asked many questions: Would she feel anything; would the operation be done with a big, big needle and pliers; would she spit blood afterward. . . ? She spat five thousand times when she had her teeth out; was it true that she would not spit blood

12 *Ibid.*

if she could only vomit blood . . . ? From the tone of her voice the psychiatrist got the impression that the patient preferred vomiting, as an event for which she was not responsible, to spitting as an act reflecting aggression. She remarked that she would be braver than the other children and was not going to cry. She continued to ask other girls on the ward what would happen. She recited to the psychiatrist:

> Three little kittens lost their mittens,
> And they began to cry,
> "Oh, Mother dear
> We very much fear
> That we have lost our mittens."
> "Lost your mittens! You naughty kittens!
> Then you shall have no pie."

and the third verse about the soiled mittens. She fussed about being neat and repeatedly wanted to know what time it was. When given the preoperative sedative, she coughed, sputtered and gagged excessively.

On recovery from the narcosis, she screamed, thrashed around in bed, gritted her teeth, and gagged. She became so unmanageable that she was restrained. She vomited all over the place, disregarding the basin and blew her nose without a handkerchief. She had to stay for a third day because she ran a temperature. She seemed completely devastated. Her innumerable questions postoperatively were loaded with concerns about her body; e.g., why did she have a speck of blood on her thigh and a sore spot on the roof of her mouth; why were her eyes sore. . . ? She seemed suspicious of what might have been done to her.

One week later, Eileen did not want to talk with the psychiatrist about the operation. She rearranged the furniture in the doll house, particularly in the bathroom and kitchen. She was careful to keep the doll figures separated from one another. After two months Eileen mentioned at home the ginger ale she got at the hospital and the nice doctor. When coming for one of her follow-up visits she was reluctant to leave her mother. She mentioned that last year when she returned from school she did not find her mother at home. She tried to open the door but could not; then she went downtown with a neighbor. Her mother passed her on the street but did not recognize her. (Mother liked to play sadistic practical jokes on her children; e.g., telling them she would leave for good and enjoying the children's anxiety as a proof that they would miss her.) Eileen added, there was a murderer living in the neighborhood and she was afraid to go to the store because the murderer might go there, too. She also was afraid to walk in the street. She then mentioned dreams about murderers; e.g., one murderer walked in the window all dressed in white and scared her. Three years postoperatively we could obtain information only from the mother. Eileen had been sick a good deal, with asthma, requiring hospitalization. Two months ago she had an appendectomy. On the whole mother thought of her as "kind of nervous."

This obsessional-neurotic child had tried to ward off her anxiety by emphasizing her goodness and neatness preoperatively. When postoperatively she experienced pain, blood, and mucus, she felt overwhelmed. The neat and controlled little girl showed her messiness and hostility.

Other obsessional children had milder reactions.

Douglas, age seven, was described as overly neat and very orderly. Mother complained about his stubbornness.

In the hospital Douglas occupied himself with constructing houses from a tinker toy, mainly heaping the parts into neat piles. He said he didn't know where his tonsils were but put his hand over his throat and asked whether they would "snatch them out." He complained that his two younger brothers ruin his toys so that he locked the toys up. He fingered his genitals and seemed curious about the happenings in the hospital, perhaps wanting to find out where babies come from. The next morning he lay crying in his bed, lonely and upset, missing his mother. He became quite angry at the nurses, threatened to get even with them, ripped his sheet and fingered his genitals. On the way to the operating room he asked a lot of questions.

After the operation he whined, would talk only little in an adenoid voice. He complained that they threw his tonsils in the river and that this is not good. We have only one report on him two weeks postoperatively. He called for the nurse during the first two nights at home but seemed otherwise to get along all right.

Gail, age five and one half, was brought into the hospital by her father, since her mother was too afraid of hospitals and of having to leave the child. Mother gave Gail a tremendous doll to take along to keep her company. Gail clutched her doll most of the time. She busied herself putting the playroom in order, was anxious to wash her hands after the job was done. She was fussy about food, did not want chocolate ice cream. She was anxious to locate the fixtures on the ward-door knob, shade, etc.—and took everything in she could investigate. She complained that she had lost a tooth and maintained her tonsils will not be taken out; she is only going to have them fixed. She did not want to discuss her tonsils any further, as her father had told her not to be scared and "not to think of it." She much preferred to play with the psychiatrist a game of "taking a ride." Shortly before the operation her anxiety mounted.

Postoperatively she cried softly and slept most of the time. During the following ten days at home she complained about having been left in the hospital and she refused to eat; mother forced her to. She talked through her nose and would not mention the operation at home. Father had to urge Gail to go to the psychiatrist at her follow-up interview. She seemed tense, anxious, and less spontaneous than preoperatively. Gail said her tonsils were thrown away and she would not have to worry about having them out again. After four months she still was eating poorly and slowly, although her general health was better. She was able to tell the psychiatrist that she was afraid of needles and remembered coming out of ether. After three and a half years she had trouble with the letter "S" in her speech and had mild food fads, but seemed generally relaxed.

Two other examples show obsessional children with little sequelae:

Florence, age six, was a well-behaved, somewhat rigid girl, described as very good at home, controlled with adults, but aggressive with other children. Pre-operatively she bragged about her being a good girl, made herself a leader of the group and poked fun at the crying of others. Postoperatively she showed marked regression for two hours, acting babyish with her thumb in her mouth. Then she resumed her adult role and boasted how well she behaved. Two weeks later she did not show any particular anxiety. She had told her mother about the operation realistically and discussed it with her sister. Six months later she was reported to be still talking about the hospital.

Tommy[13] was a six-year-old boy whose mother was very attached to him. He seemed to fulfill her wish to be a boy herself. She put him under pressure to achieve, yet he didn't talk until he was four, and insisted on going to bed at seven because he didn't want to get red eyes.

On the preoperative day in the hospital he expressed fears of being punished, was concerned about being good and played that he was the sheriff. His focus of anxiety was the "needles," and he complained afterward that he got eight needles "in the ass." This fear of needles persisted three and a half years later.

Both Florence and Tommy were able to express their fears in words and play more freely than most of the obsessional children we observed.

Aggressive Children

Most of the aggressive children had sequelae for a considerable period of time. However, these sequelae were milder than with children whose aggression was turned against themselves.

Leo, aged five and a half, was described as a hyperactive, aggressive, outgoing boy, imaginative, inventive, making contact easily.

His mother showed great warmth and affection for the patient. She felt "nervous" and overburdened by her two very lively children and by a lack of money, and a duodenal ulcer.

Since age two and a half Leo was a frequent patient at the Children's Medical Service of this hospital; first, because of a limp of the left leg, diagnosed as *pes planus,* and later for tonsillitis and upper respiratory infections. He had four Emergency Ward admissions prior to T&A, and those times was noted to be interested and co-operative. At camp a year ago he enjoyed himself without signs of fear. Three weeks prior to T&A, he had been listless at home, with tonsillitis, and was fretful in the Emergency Ward, knowing he would soon be operated on.

On admission the patient screamed that he didn't want to stay in the hospital. His mother comforted him, telling him he would feel better after the tonsils were out. Leo kept on crying loudly, patting his penis, and looking to

13 *Ibid.*

mother for reassurance. Mother explained that a week ago he had had a leg muscle bothering him so that he could not get out of bed. She believed that he was afraid that something was going to be done to his leg. After he went with his mother to the ward he continued to protest tearfully.

Three hours later he played with other children, was happy and active, talked about prison, and asked the psychiatrist to read him a story. He seemed pleased with the whole situation, was entertaining, joking, and had a push of activity and speech. He ate a good deal.

Some time later he found a pair of glasses in his night table and appropriated them. He put them on and off, proudly exhibiting them, refusing to give them up, saying, "I brought my glasses from home." While he proudly announced, "I'm going to have my tonsils out," he closed and opened doors and put the glasses on and off. He turned to a toy motorcycle, commenting on the missing front wheel. When he sat on it, it cracked. He said, "It's broken," and began to hop on one leg, mentioning that his leg hurt and pointing to his groin. Later he appeared shy and quiet, agreed with the other children that one patient who acted like a tornado should be locked in a closet. "Gonna have my tonsils out tomorrow and the next day I'll go home." He made friends with another patient, who was small and tongue-tied, and assured him the operation would make him better (which had been mother's way of comforting the patient.) He fought angrily when the nurse gave him an injection. Toward evening he lay in his crib on all fours, much subdued, sobbing quietly, and looked blankly at the psychiatrist.

The next day he was happy to see the psychiatrist, throwing his arms about him, showing off with his glasses, jumping up and down and trying to climb out of his crib.

While waiting in the operating room he was boisterous. "I'll eat you; I'll cut off your head! Don't cut my head off!" He yelled at the attendants, "Shut up, you stupid thing!" He jumped about, throwing the emesis basin on the floor, wanting to kill everyone and knock down the whole hospital. He protested, "I don't want my tonsils out; I don't have a sore throat. My mother is stupid to bring me here. I'll kill her." Then becoming playful, he pretended he was an Indian, shooting a medical student and hiding in a tent he made from blankets. He put the ether mask on his face; he's the Lone Ranger. Later the mask was a coffee strainer, baseball mask, hat. He went to the operating room piggy-back, without noise or comment. There, he was apprehensive, looking around the room and at the table, saying, "Light, put the light on." He refused to be covered by a sheet. Anesthesia started with the patient struggling and screaming, "No, don't do that!"

Postoperatively in the hospital he cried during the night for water. In the morning he refused to put on the glasses, saying that they were not his after all. He would not talk, nor look at the psychiatrist. Until four in the afternoon he remained silent and immobile. He then complained about his throat hurting and wanted the psychiatrist to read him a story. "My mother is going to bring me a lot of penicillin. The girl over there is having her tonsils out, too." Because of fever, he couldn't go home that day. The next day he was sad, wanted to go home, but was talkative and interested in a toy his mother had brought him. "I'm going home; I'm glad my tonsils are out. My brother had them out,[14] but he cried and cried. . . . I didn't cry."

At the first follow-up interview, two and a half weeks later, he smiled at the psychiatrist, but was reluctant to leave his mother. He insisted on having his brother go with him for the interview, and all posthospital interviews went on in the presence of his brother. He made a house of clay and told of a lady who lived there all alone; she had no food. He asked the psychiatrist to make a boat and provided a man to run it; this man had only one leg and the patient wouldn't add another one.

Four weeks postoperatively he made fishes out of clay and was worried about the swordfish's having a long thing, saying, "It is his mouth, maybe." He yelled "Stupid! Pumpkin head!" at his brother. In both interviews he was unwilling to talk about the T&A or about the glasses, but said he found the glasses in a drawer.

Six weeks postoperatively, when asked about the T&A he said "They put the thing over your nose and wham!"—running his hands down his body to his feet. He had vomited and they kept him here a long time. He will kill the bad doctors. When asked whether they removed anything else, he answered "No, well, maybe." His brother calls out "his *nose*" which leads to a big laugh from both boys. Both boys are extremely active and destructive during the interview. The patient says he wants to become Abraham Lincoln with a long black beard.

Three months postoperatively his mother complained that the patient's voice had become different since the T&A, "sort of nasal and husky." The patient insisted that nothing was wrong with his voice, that he was making it sound funny. His brother pointed out the Eye and Ear Infirmary and said that was where the patient had his tonsils out. When the psychiatrist remarked that brother had his out there, too, patient cried, "No, he didn't. He's a liar!" The patient banged a table fiercely with a hammer, but was careful not to hit his fingers, using a block to guard them.

Four months postoperatively the patient and his brother played house, locking each other in and out. The patient was generally more co-operative and less aggressive.

During the interviews held five months after the operation, the patient was more constructive and said that the psychiatrist should not give his brother a gun because he goes wild. Grownups never get wild. Father won't let patient have a knife until he is grown up. The patient borrowed a knife from the psychiatrist. He used the knife skillfully and obeyed directions. He again emphasized that only he and not his brother had this T&A at this hospital.

Seven months postoperatively his jealousy of his brother was still great, but he was not as openly aggressive toward him. On the whole he seemed well adjusted.

---

14 Leo's younger brother had a T&A at this hospital one year before.

This boy had considerable fear of mutilation before the operation and afterward a suspicion that something more than tonsils had been taken away from him. This was masked by an increase of his aggressive behavior. For short periods during hospitalization his façade crumbled and anxiety broke through. In the course of integrating the experience, he first used narcissistic pride in his courageous performance as reassurance against castration anxiety. Later he relied on his capacity to control his aggression, which seemed a successful method to decrease his fear of punishment, and a step in maturation.

Constructive Experience

For quite a number of children the operation was a constructive experience, enhancing the development of the ego.

Rosemarie, age eight, was a cheerful girl who made good contact with other patients and felt optimistic about the operation, expecting something will burn out the tonsils.

Postoperatively, she complained of pain for several days and would not speak. Her younger siblings asked if her tongue had been removed. When she recovered she established a new status among her siblings. She continued to be interested in the hospital for three and a half years and had decided to become a nurse on our last follow-up.

This child had suffered a narcissistic hurt by having pain in her throat, which she thought would not happen to her. Having endured it, however, this gave her the feeling of strength in suffering and the experience was in retrospect one of gaining status and identification with a figure (nurse) who was both an aggressor and a protector.

With others it seemed that the mothers' attitude changed because unconscious wishes to punish the child were fulfilled, and the child responded positively—as was one of the relevant factors in the case of Frank.

Frank, age three and a half, had two previous hospital experiences, including a previous T&A ten months before at another hospital. At that time he cried continuously, would eat nothing, and "drove the nurses almost crazy." Mother was certain he would be a problem this time. He did not like hospitals and doctors and was disturbed by barbers' white coats. His mother had not prepared him much as she felt he was too young to understand.

Frank was a premature baby, was neglected somewhat as an infant, was always a feeding problem, had infantile speech, had food fads, was negativistic, and wanted his own way. Mother was overprotective, giving in to his demands sometimes and at other times treating him harshly.

On admission Frank was a small, infantile-appearing boy with infantile speech. His mother constantly admonished him to be a good boy and to eat. He got dressed in his play suit and walked around exploring the hall. He ate just his bread for lunch and that very slowly, watching his mother all the time.

Later in the day he cried bitterly and wanted his mother. He became panicky when he saw another child receiving an injection. He could not be reassured but asked for his mother. He cried whenever a nurse entered the room. Frank played with some of the other children intermittently.

Late in the afternoon and the following two days at the hospital he was subdued. He cried "Want Mommy, want Mommy—when is Mommy coming?" He was unable to use help and reassurance from the psychiatrist.

On follow-ups, the mother reported that he had been a different child since T&A; everyone had noticed this. His appetite and disposition changed for the better. He ate a full meal as soon as he came home, which surprised her. For the first time in his life he slept well. He spoke better, but his mother was upset because he seemed to be taking on an Italian accent, putting a's on the end of everything, like "I wanta my bike." (They lived in an Italian neighborhood and he had an Italian friend.)

It turned out that the mother had treated him quite differently since his operation. She let him play with other children; whereas before she had considered him too sickly to go outside. There were signs of postoperative anxiety; e.g., he would not drink beet juice and was fearful about getting a haircut from the barber but he could be reassured about this by his mother.

After five months his speech continued to improve, still with an Italian accent. He repeated an Italian phrase almost constantly to the family. He grew in height and weight. He frequently dreamed about a dog chasing him. The mother was much less protective of him and allowed him much more freedom.

Two years later he did not remember the tonsil operation. He said he was just a baby. But he recalled vividly a circumcision which he had a year after the T&A. He also had a skull fracture and thereafter was concerned if anyone pulled his hair. Despite these events he was quite mature and masculine.

Severely Disturbed Children

Among the 143 children there were one atypical child and one schizoid adolescent.

Courtney, age six, was an autistic child with arrested development. He spoke hardly at all, was aimless in his activities and unable to make contact with grownups or children. The patient was the only child of an abusive, alcoholic father and an infantile mother who was overdependent on her own mother. She had generalized anxiety and some special fears, for instance, that her house would blow up. She expected T&A to cure the patient's speech. She had prepared him by saying that ether smells like mother's perfume and that he would get ice cream afterward.

Preoperatively he was bewildered, wide-eyed, and restless, repeating over and over, "Mommy gone. Oh, Oh."

Postoperatively he ate nothing for four days, but then showed some interest in a doctor's kit. His mother was disappointed that his speech was not improved. Four weeks later he wandered around, more restless than before and his mother now expressed her fear that he was "crazy" and asked for shock treatment. This behavior continued. Five months postoperatively it was reported that in school he had stopped talking but wrote everything. It would seem that the hospital experience had increased his anxiety and bewilderment. Later he was taken into psychotherapy and is improving slowly.

Sandra, age fourteen, was described as shy, having no friends, staying out of school most of last year, fearful and depressed; she had been a feeding problem in early childhood. She had been placed in foster homes several times for long periods because her mother was frequently in psychiatric hospitals, probably for schizophrenia. The father left the family when Sandra was four years old.

On admission the patient seemed suspicious and hostile. She denied fears and told that she had two bones in her throat which would come out. Immediately after the operation she seemed frightened and complained that her throat hurt more than she thought it would.

Six weeks later she complained that her tongue felt funny and that she missed her period. Nine months after the operation she was fearful and seclusive, preoccupied with her nose, for which she wanted a plastic operation, feeling that everyone was looking at her.

It is not possible to evaluate whether T&A increased the patient's severe disturbance, but it certainly influenced the content of her delusional ideas in regard to her body image. Tongue and nose became the organs of concern, together with upset about menstruation; most likely they were phallic symbols with underlying fantasies about her sex identification.

DISCUSSION

Observations on 143 children undergoing T&A showed that the operation was an important and stressful experience for each child, activating the great childhood fears—of abandonment, of mutilation, and of death; and that it stirred up fantasies of transformation and of getting a baby. Most children were able to integrate the experience as far as we could follow them, but this does not exclude the possibility of a delayed reaction or later reactivation.

Among the children who had undergone an operation prior to T&A were some where the former experience had heightened their apprehension. Others on the contrary seemed able to cope with the later operation better, either because they felt they had mastered it before, or because the reality of such an event was not as terrible as their anticipating fantasies. The impact of a former operation depended also on the type of operation, its specific meaning for the child, and other individual factors.

For a number of children the T&A became a constructive experience, either as atonement for guilt feelings or as challenge to their ego strength and a gain in prestige. For some, the improvement in general health allowed a greater flow of libido toward other people and activities. In some the attitude of the mother changed and a more positive relationship to the child became possible.

For certain children, however, the operation was a disturbing or disruptive experience. Most of these children had neurotic trends or definite disturbances before T&A, or they had experienced but not integrated frightening life situations (e.g., death of a relative). These children were psychologically vulnerable at the time of the operation, and they were unable to assimilate this threat without serious sequelae. For such children, preparation of the conventional kind does little to increase their capacity to withstand such an onslaught. Rather they require working through some of their deeper anxieties. Where there is evidence of a personality disturbance or a history of recent traumatic events in a child's life, careful consideration should be given to his emotional status with the view of postponing the operation or of taking psychotherapeutic measures.

Even with the less disturbed children, preparation involves more than giving accurate information. Where the mother is very anxious about the procedure, as quite a number of our mothers have been, she imparts this anxiety to the small child. In some older ones, it seemed that they could ward off this contamination, or even gain strength by comforting mother. In other cases, where the relationship between parent and child was hostile or highly ambivalent, the mother's attempt at preparation seemed to strengthen the notion that the impending procedure meant being sent away or getting punished.

In regard to the hospitalization it seemed important, as stated in the preliminary report (Jessner and Kaplan, 1949), to allow the child to keep a token—a toy, a penny, a picture, etc.—as a tie to home and as a sign of one's own identity, and if possible to allow the child to wear some of his own clothing. The twenty-four hour hospitalization before operation, devised by the Massachusetts Eye and Ear Infirmary, had a reassuring effect on the majority of the children. In most of them we saw the initial anxiety decrease. For some of the children under four years of age, the effect of a waiting period, particularly over night, was dubious.

In a few private cases, the mother stayed with the child. While her presence certainly was a comforting assurance against the fear of abandonment, we saw on the other hand that if the mother was anxious, the child felt it. The fact that mother could not prevent "the needles" and other dreaded manipulations sometimes aroused the child's hostility against his mother, which in turn frightened the child much more than aggressive acts or words against a stranger like the nurse or the doctor.

On the whole it seemed that a mother substitute—which in our study so frequently became the role of the psychiatrist—was a more adequate solution. A nurse might very well substitute for the mother. The child should feel that one nurse in particular was his protector (A. Freud and Burlingham, 1943) although he could share her with other children.

We also saw that acknowledgment of fear and expression of anxiety in play and talk tended to enhance assimilation. We observed suppression, denial, and overcontrol of fear collapse with a bang, and we can confirm Ives Hendrick's statement (1949) that lack of anxiety is prognostically a bad sign. Encouraging the child to express his feelings should, however, not be misunderstood as inviting the child to give up control completely. The notion of being able to deal with danger and pain has been one of the most reassuring mechanisms for the children. "To cry like a baby," as one of our little girls said, or not to be a "crybaby," summoned ego strength. Another helpful defense mechanism the children showed us spontaneously was the turning of the passive into an active role, by playing the surgeon or the protecting mother for a doll, a Teddy bear, or a young child. The effectiveness with which the child can use his defenses is influenced by the extent to which the adults comprehend that even such a minor surgical procedure has a great emotional impact.

3

A MOTHER'S OBSERVATIONS
ON THE TONSILLECTOMY
OF HER
FOUR-YEAR-OLD DAUGHTER

JOYCE ROBERTSON

With Comments by
ANNA FREUD, LL.D., D.Sc., M.D.
(1956)

At four years and three months, Jean was in hospital for three days, accompanied by her mother, for the removal of tonsils and adenoids. This was a well-managed hospitalization and the outcome was good, but it is clear from the record that the experience was fraught with anxiety for the child.

A PLANNED HOSPITALIZATION

My husband and I believed that hospitalization for tonsillectomy could be traumatic to a child of this age, but that if the mother were present to play a supportive role throughout, the risk of aftereffects could be greatly reduced. The children's physician and the ward sister (charge nurse) were specially sympathetic to our views and interested in the possibilities of nursing by the mother. We discussed the practical implications of my wish to be present during all of Jean's conscious experience.

It was eventually agreed that I should be with her until she became unconscious, and again immediately after the operation. There was initially some reluctance to allow me to be present during the early stages of returning consciousness. They then believed that she would have no awareness in that phase, and that I should therefore be spared the anxiety of witnessing an unfamiliar scene of blood and apparent distress.

Jean and I would share a cubicle in the children's ward. She would be allocated to one nurse in accordance with the practice of this ward, but in fact I would do everything for her except the technical nursing.[1]

1 We wish to thank the staff of the children's ward at Guy's Hospital, London, and in particular Dr. Ronald MacKeith, Children's Physician, and Miss J. Tanner, Ward Sister, for their cooperation in this experiment.

Previous History

From birth Jean suffered from eczema and food allergy, which created problems in feeding and management. The eczema was managed with a minimum of restraint. There was inevitably some frustration and interference during the first two years of her life, but there were no disturbing investigations or treatments and no hospitalization. The eczema then cleared, except for mild spring outbreaks, but left a tendency for common colds to develop into bronchial asthma.

Her social development was slightly retarded by the difficulties of the first two years, but by the age of four this had been largely made up. She had friendly relationships with the children of the neighborhood, and with adults whom she knew well, but was noticeably slow to accept the advances of strange adults. In illness she tended to be more negative and withdrawn than most children.

During the winter preceding her admission to hospital, she had several attacks of otitis media and tonsillitis, and during treatment was found to be allergic to the antibiotics. Since the attacks were becoming more serious and could not be satisfactorily dealt with medically, it was reluctantly accepted that her tonsils and adenoids should be removed.

I intended to say nothing about this to Jean until about a week before the operation, which was arranged for six weeks ahead. But as will be seen from the Diary, I was compelled to begin telling her almost immediately.

Preparation for the Operation

I decided to make no reference to the possibility that she might be subjected to enemas, injections, blood tests, urine tests. I judged that such procedures were best explained immediately before they happened, and that earlier explanation might arouse unnecessary anxiety. I covered procedures in general by saying that in hospital we did not always like what the doctors and nurses did, but that they were always trying to make us better.

When I first told her of the operation I gave no details other than that it was her tonsils which kept making her throat and ears sore, and that in hospital the doctor would make her go to sleep and take them out. I told her she would be three days in hospital, and that I would be with her all the time.

During the next five weeks I gradually expanded this first statement, following the lead given by her questions and behavior. This is the essence of the picture I built up for her:

There would be doctors and nurses looking after her and the other children. On the first day the doctor would look in her throat and ears, and listen to her chest. Next day at breakfast time she would be given a pill. Later she would smell the "funny smell" and would go to sleep for just a little while—it would be a special "tonsils sleep" and not ordinary sleep. She would go on the trolley to have the doctor take out her tonsils, and then he would carry her straight back to her cot in our little room. When she awoke her throat would be very sore, just like a really bad cold. It would be because her tonsils were out. Tonsils were like the loose skin which sometimes hangs painfully around a fingernail—it is sore after it is cut off, but next day it is better. When her tonsils were first out she would not feel well, but I would sit by her cot and read the stories she liked best. Although her throat would be sore, it would be getting better all the time. Her throat would bleed, just like her knee when she fell on it. Some of the blood might go down into her tummy, and then she would spit it up. She would feel better when she had spat it out. We would both want to go home to Daddy and Katherine (her sister), but would have to stop until the doctor told us her throat was better.

Since long before it was known that Jean would go to hospital, there had been in our home two pamphlets showing picture sequences of children in hospital (Robertson, 1953a; Connell, 1953). She became suddenly interested in these and, as will be seen in the Diary, she repeatedly asked to have them explained to her—which I did, in a way I thought applicable to her situation. The first of these Jean refers to as "Laura," and she selected for special attention four pictures showing— Laura sitting in a hospital cot hugging her favorite toys and looking rather sad, being visited by her mother, putting on her shoes to go home, and finally walking out of the hospital gates with her mother. The second pamphlet she calls "Tonsil Boy." This shows a boy going to hospital to have his tonsils out, being undressed, looking at books with his mother and a nurse, being examined by a doctor, smelling the anesthetic, sleeping in a cot with his mother by his side, sitting up to have a meal after the operation, and finally home again.

THE DIARY

I decided to keep a diary of events in the hope of recording a follow-through account of the reactions of a young child to tonsillectomy that would add to understanding of how a child might best be helped to cope with such an experience. In this I shared the interest of my husband who has published on the problem, notably his film "A Two-Year-Old Goes To Hospital."[2]

DIARY[3]

BEFORE ADMISSION TO HOSPITAL

March 1st. Jean was seen by the surgeon today, and he recommended removal of her tonsils and adenoids. This was said in her presence, but as she has been rather deaf because of the ear infection (otitis) she seemed not to have heard. The operation was arranged for six weeks ahead, and I have decided not to say anything to Jean about it until about a week before she goes to hospital.

March 2nd to 5th. During these few days Jean became increasingly difficult about her food. She ate little and appeared angry or unhappy at mealtimes. This puzzled me until I overheard her say to herself, "Don't eat it. Better not eat it or you'll go to sleep." So, although I had planned to give her only about a week to adjust to the idea of an operation and a stay in hospital, I decided to begin telling her at the first opportunity lest her eating disturbance was in fact connected with fantasies about anesthetics.

March 6th. Today I told Jean that she would go to hospital one day to have her tonsils taken out. I chose a moment when she was complaining about having to stay in the house because of a sore throat and cold. Together we looked out of the window and named the children who had been ill and were now well again. I pointed out two children who had had their tonsils out, and Jean added two more names to the list.

She said, "I wouldn't like to go to hospital without you. I would want you all the time. I wouldn't stay there." I told her that I would stay with her in the hospital. She said, "All the mummies don't stay with their children all the time in hospital. Why don't they? Susan's mummy didn't stay with her." I reminded her that Susan's mummy had visited her every day instead: "Susan is a bigger girl than you are. She goes to school and is used to being away from her mummy." Jean said, "Susan didn't like it when she didn't see her mummy in the night, did she?" I agreed that Susan had been a bit unhappy, but because she was seven she could wait until the morning for her mummy; and told her I knew that girls of four wanted their mummies to stay with them, but added that when she was bigger she wouldn't mind sometimes being without her mummy.

I told her very briefly what would happen in hospital—that she would go to sleep, her tonsils would be taken out, and that we would stay in hospital for three days. She did not ask for more information.

---

[2] Robertson, J., "A Two-Year-Old Goes to Hospital." (Film, 16mm., black and white, sound, 45 min.) London: Tavistock Clinic, 1953. Robertson, J., "A Two-Year-Old Goes to Hospital; An Illustrated Guide to the Film." London: Tavistock Publications, 1953.

[3] Events were usually recorded immediately after their occurrence, and never later than the evening of the same day.

March 7th. Jean began eating again almost normally. She searched among her Daddy's papers for the pictures she called "Tonsil Boy" and "Laura." She brought them to me and asked to be told the "hospital story." She searched anxiously for a picture she remembered, showing child and mother going home, and when she failed to find it she appealed to me.

March 8th. At breakfast she examined her fork, and said, "This fork would dig right into my throat, and it would hurt. I've got a big hole in my throat, haven't I?" Later she asked for the stories of Laura and Tonsil Boy. "Why do the doctors wear that thing on their faces? Why must they not cough germs at the ill children? Can I cough at you?"

March 9th. Jean saw me open a tin with a tin opener as she had often done before. She handled the tin opener for a few minutes, and then asked: "What's this for? What do you do with it?" Twice during the day she asked to be told the story of Laura and Tonsil Boy.

When an ambulance stopped outside our flats she said, "Look! The ambulance has stopped because someone is ill." And later, "It's all right, it has gone now." (There is an ambulance station in our road, and she sees many ambulances every day.) Later when she saw an ambulance driver walk by she remarked, "It's all right now. He is going home to tea round the corner."

March 10th. Jean stopped in the middle of her lunch, lay back and sucked her thumb. I asked if she was tired. She sat up and said, "A little girl has died. Michael said she didn't die, but she has." I asked, "Why did she die?" and Jean answered, "Because it was time for her to die." I told her that little girls did not die when they had their tonsils out. She asked, "Why don't they? They might if the Doctor couldn't get their tonsils out properly."

I again explained the hospital procedure, and Jean ran to get the Laura and Tonsil Boy pictures. As I went through them with her, she added some remembered explanations. She counted each picture as a day. For the rest of the day she was active and cheerful, but she slept badly.

March 11th. At breakfast Jean made a fuss about the salt cellar. She refused to let anyone else have use of it, because she wanted to have one of her very own. "Can I buy one for myself on Saturday with my own pocket money?"

March 12th. At teatime she cut her poached egg very carefully, saying, "I want it [the yolk] to run out." She watched her Daddy having tea half an hour later, and said, "Look, when Daddy cuts his egg it all runs out." (A week before this record started Jean had said, "When all the blood runs out of cut and hurt people they die.") She put her thumb and first finger in her mouth and pinched the back of her tongue, remarking "It hurts when I do it."

March 14th. Jean saw a picture of a man, a prisoner being led between two policemen; and for the next twenty minutes she questioned me persistently about "naughty men." "Do children go away when they are very naughty? Were you naughty, Mummy? Did you go away when you were little?" I spoke of the coming hospitalization, and we talked about the reasons for it.

March 15th. At lunch she talked again of knives and forks being sharp. "They could poke our throats," she said, then ate her lunch mostly with her fingers. She pretended to cut my hand and arm with a knife. She asked to be shown the sharp end, then pushed it into her mouth very slowly and carefully until it appeared to touch the back of her throat. She then withdrew it. She said nothing.

March 16th. After breakfast Jean had a temper tantrum and aggressively banged a drum until the top caved in. In the afternoon, while listening to a radio program playing records for children in hospital, she sat handling a little fruit knife. For a quarter of an hour as she listened she made cutting movements on the chair arm, the table, the cushions, my arm, hand and face. When the program had finished, she asked, "Why are those children in hospital? When will they go home again? Read me Tonsil Boy and Laura."

March 17th. Several times today I saw Jean standing quietly putting her thumb and first finger far into her mouth with a pinching movement.

March 19th. Jean bought a gun with her pocket money, and played shooting for the rest of the day. Later she wanted explosive caps to make bigger bangs.

March 20th. She had no interest in games other than shooting—the bigger the bang the more she liked it.

March 21st. This was the first fine day of spring, and our family went strolling in the park. Jean drew attention to herself by shooting everyone she met. When her explosive caps were finished, she wanted to go immediately to buy more and was furious when told it was Sunday and the shops were closed. She could find no pleasure in the park, and asked to be taken home.

March 22nd. There has been no mention of hospital for several days, but Jean has become very aggressive toward me and has scratched and bitten her sister with very little provocation.

March 23rd. Her very aggressive behavior continues.

March 24th. Today Jean overheard an adult talk about a child who had been killed on the road. I spoke with her later about it, but she would not admit that a child could be killed on the road in this way.

March 25th. Her aggressive behavior continues. Temper tantrums in which she throws herself on the floor at the slightest upset have become rather frequent. As she had not mentioned the coming operation for a week, I decided to reintroduce the topic.

After a tantrum I linked her behavior to the operation, and she talked willingly about it. "They will hurt me. Very ill people go to hospital, and they have to go in an ambulance. I don't want to go." At bedtime she said, "Wash my hands when I'm in bed. I'll shut my eyes tightly, then I won't know that you are doing it."

March 26th. Jean awoke in the night screaming. She complained tearfully, "It hurts, it hurts!" and pointed into her mouth as if at an aching tooth. After an aspirin and half an hour in my bed she returned to her own room and slept. This morning I took her to the dentist, but he could find nothing to cause toothache.

This morning Jean did not notice when I undid her nightdress because we were talking. With delight and surprise she explained this to me. "It was just like my tonsils, I did not feel you do it."

March 27th, 28th, and 29th. Many aggressive outbursts.

March 30th. When asked not to scratch her sister, she said, "Well, we didn't talk about the hospital yesterday. That's why!" She found Laura and Tonsil Boy and asked to be told and retold their stories. She dug her fingers into her mouth, and asked, "Which bits of skin will the doctor take away?"

March 31st. At bedtime Jean asked with a whisper for both hospital stories. A few minutes before she had been examining her navel, asking what it was and how it came.

April 1st. We bought some puzzles and other oddments to occupy her while in hospital, and Jean put them in a case under her bed. This evening she took longer than usual to settle down. When I gave her her usual dose of Anthisan (the drug used to control her allergy) she told me to put the bottle into the case with her hospital things. When I said the Anthisan should not go into the case, because it was not yet her turn to go to hospital, her restlessness subsided and she slept.

April 2nd. Today has brought many minor accidents—for instance she caught her thumb in her tricycle and later caught her foot in a chair. Her skin is more sensitive than of late, her eyes and chin become inflamed very easily, and her tummy and thighs show signs of having been scratched a lot.

April 4th. Several of the children were playing hospital in the garden, and Jean was the patient.

April 5th. She talked of other children known to her who had been to hospital. Some time after she had been settled for the night, she called out, "I want to play with the hospital puzzle."

April 6th. Jean had a very active and happy day. When I discussed with her sister the arrangements for her care while Jean and I were away, Jean asked "Why?" as if the whole idea were new to her, and added, "But I don't want to go to hospital."

At teatime Katherine complained of stomach-ache. Jean asked, "Has Katherine got a pain like Susan? Will she have to go to hospital?" Later she asked me to list those of her friends who had been to hospital. She agreed to some names, but denied others. She asked to have a bandage over her eyes.

April 8th. When I told Jean that this was the day for us to go to hospital, she flushed and said, "I don't want to go to hospital—not today. Let's go tomorrow." Half an hour later she said, "Can I take my party dress? Can I take three dresses, and three cardigans? I'll play outside for a few days (!) first." And later still she said, "I might not want to come home again. I might want to stay there."

Saying that she might want them, she asked to take two dollies, dolly blankets, a windmill, and many other toys. To her sister she said, "Mummy will be with *me* and you won't see her."

She played in the garden with her friends for the next hour, dancing and skipping about and behaving as if she were going to a party. She boasted of where she was going. Now and again she came in to me with an anxious face. "I don't want to go to the hospital today," and almost in the same breath, "When is Daddy coming to take us to the hospital? —Daddy must come and bring stamps to me every day.—When my tonsils are out I won't keep getting ill.—When I come home my tonsils will be all gone.—I won't know when the doctor takes out my tonsils."

IN HOSPITAL

On the way to hospital in her Daddy's car she sat quietly, remarking on things seen from the window.. She held my hand tightly and seemed apprehensive as we walked into the office to register, and as we went into the ward. She said several times, "I don't want to have my tonsils out. I don't want to stay in this hospital."

When the doctor and the ward sister (charge nurse) spoke to us she kept very close to me and said nothing. At lunch she ate little, saying it was not the same as we had at home. And again and again she said, "I want to go home. I don't want to have my tonsils out." She showed no interest in the other children. She was cross with me when I picked up a toy for a crying child.

For an hour I sat in our cubicle while Jean went to and from the balcony, reporting back to me every few minutes as one child after another was examined by a doctor in the open ward. She stood watching a toddler who cried loudly when his ears were examined. Her report was: "The doctor tickled him, but he didn't laugh."

We were invited to join some of the "up" children at play on the hospital lawns. Jean soon joined in the games, and all her anxiety seemed forgotten. Her good spirits remained during tea which we had together in the cubicle. After tea she ran on to the balcony and peeped through the window into the ward. When she saw the children were being prepared for the night, she too wanted to have her nightie on; but she agreed that as it was only 4:45 it was too early for her. Instead, she played in her cot and pulled a hospital screen around to make a little house.

At 5 o'clock she was invited into the ward to see television, but unluckily the anesthetist came just then to examine her. She cried when I brought her back to the cubicle, and made examination almost impossible by her struggling and screaming. She took no notice of the friendly advances of the anesthetist.

After the anesthetist had gone I explained the nature of the examinations to Jean, and when the houseman came half an hour later to examine ears, nose, and throat she seemed rather less difficult. But shortly afterwards when she was required to sit on a very small chamberpot to provide a urine specimen she was greatly offended by its size and only used it after much persuasion.

At 6 o'clock she undressed herself and climbed into her cot. She slept immediately. During the night she scratched restlessly in her sleep for two hours, in a way reminiscent of her eczema days two years before.

April 9th. Jean awoke at 6:30 A.M. and wanted to get dressed, saying, "I don't want to have my tonsils out, I want to go home." She played with toys in her bed for a short time, but without interest or concentration.

At 9 A.M. the ward sister came on duty and told Jean she could get up and walk around in slippers and dressing gown. Jean commented, "I like that Big Nurse. She is kind, because she lets me get out of bed." For the next hour she walked about aimlessly, saying again and again, "I want to go home.—I don't like doctors and nurses.—I don't want my tonsils out."

At 10 A.M. she took her premedication (two pills) from me with great difficulty. She could not swallow them, and vomited one. Then she had another in jam. She was very upset by this episode, and I found myself trembling at the knees. She sat quietly on my knee for half an hour, and then had an injection (Atropine) which made her cry bitterly.

She was by now very sleepy and asked to lie in her cot. When I suggested that she should go to sleep on the trolley which was already in the cubicle, she said, "That's only for very ill people, because it has a red blanket." She roused when I carried her to the trolley at 11 A.M., but when I spoke to her she relaxed and slept. In the induction room she roused again at the first whiff of the anesthetic, but seemed to go under quickly. She was wheeled into the operating theater, and my husband and I had an uneasy walk round the hospital block. Twenty minutes later she was brought back to her cot, the operation over.

As she returned to consciousness she became very restless. She kept trying to sit up, with eyes closed; but her movements were so uncontrolled that she had to be protected from hurting herself against the sides of the cot. I talked to her, saying several times, "Lie down, Jean. Put your head on the pillow and I'll tell you a story." But she did not respond, and the ward sister intervened to give a morphia injection which quietened her. It was then mid-day.

She roused every ten minutes and cried a little, but slept again when she heard my voice. At 12:40 she asked for her special "Noddy" story (the story I had promised during the preparation for hospital). At 1:30 she opened her eyes for the first time and looked around the room. She asked quietly, "Are my tonsils out? I didn't feel them come out."

She slept again but awoke every fifteen minutes or so complaining of pain. She calmed down again each time when I spoke or read to her. At 4 P.M. she asked for a drink, took one sip and cried with pain. She continued to awake every fifteen minutes and to say a few words and complain of pain until about 6 P.M.

At 6 P.M. she asked for the potty, but insisted "Not in my bed—on the floor." This was allowed. As she sat she said in a bright voice, and as if both surprised and impressed, "You were quite right, Mummy. My throat *does* hurt a lot—but I didn't feel them come out." She drank a little and cried again. From 6 till 7 she dozed restlessly, whimpering and coughing at intervals.

At 7 P.M. she vomited a fair amount of blood. She had been told that this might happen, and though made miserable she showed no fright. She said, "I dribbled out all the blood, didn't I?" She drank a little water and dozed restlessly again.

Her restless doze continued until 3 A.M. when she became fully awake and apparently properly oriented to her surroundings for the first time since the operation. She asked to use the potty on the floor again. She drank with less discomfort, "I like this drink." She talked a lot: "My tonsils are out now.—I won't keep getting ill.—I didn't feel my tonsils coming out.—When did the doctor take my tonsils out?—Were you there?—My throat does hurt me now.—You said it would hurt.—Can I get dressed when it is morning?—I didn't smell the funny smell to make me go to sleep.—I didn't like the pills, or the prick in my leg.—I didn't feel my tonsils come out; that's funny, I thought I was in my cot all the time.—Can I go home the very next day now that my tonsils are out?—Where is Daddy? Will he come every day to bring me stamps? Why can't Daddy and Katherine stay here too?"

After this barrage of question and comment, which lasted for half an hour, she sang a nursery rhyme, then slept peacefully for two hours. (And so did I.)

April 10th. At 6 A.M. she surprised herself by eating some breakfast. From 7 till 9 she stood in her cot, talking and jumping about and very impatient to get dressed and on to the floor. She said, "My throat doesn't hurt a bit." I was sure it did hurt and told her so. I told her again that her throat would be sore but would get a little better each day. A minute or so later she cried and said, "Yes, it really does hurt."

At 9 A.M. the ward sister came on duty and brought in the mail. She promised that at 10 o'clock Jean could dress and sit on the balcony. Jean was a little shy at first, and would not accept her letter; then with a laugh she snatched it from the sister's pocket. When sister asked, "Do you know where you are going tomorrow?" Jean brightly replied, "Yes— home!" When the sister left Jean said, "That Big Nurse is nice. She gave me postcards. She lets me get up and go home."

A little later she said, "I might want to stay here all the time, and not go home. I might like it here so much I'll just stay."

When I had to leave the cubicle for twenty minutes I gave her pencils and paper to play with. She seemed not to mind my going, but said, "Put up both sides of my cot, and lock them. Then no one can hurt me when you are gone."

She would not let any nurse take her temperature; and each time I acted in their stead she resisted, saying, "I'm not ill. I haven't got a temperature." (Her pulse was always taken when she slept.)

Many times during the day she asked me to tell her how she got her tonsils out. Each time I reminded her of what she already knew: "You had pills and a prick in your leg, and you sat on my knee going to sleep. I was going to put you on to the trolley with the red blanket, but you didn't want that so I put you into your cot. When the doctor was ready to take out your tonsils I carried you to the trolley and I took you to the special room. I was with you when you smelled the funny smell, then you slept the special tonsils sleep. The doctor took out your tonsils and carried you back to your cot. Then I sat next to you and read you a story."

After each telling she was ready with questions: "Where is that doctor now? Where does he live? Will he come again? Where is the special room? My nose hurts. Were my tonsils in my nose too?"

At 10 A.M. we sat on the balcony and played with cards. Although she had been jumping around in her cot, now that she was up she was limp and listless. She objected to my showing interest in another child.

At lunch she tried several times to swallow some semolina, but turned away in pain. I left her alone in the cubicle while I went to the kitchen to find jelly. When I returned five minutes later she was near to tears. Her tumbler of aspirin drink lay broken on the floor. She said, "I couldn't help it. I did drink some of it. I didn't cut myself." She had picked up the pieces of glass and placed them on the side of the sink. When I reassured her that no one would be cross about it, she said, "The nurses are nice. They don't mind."

She went gladly to her cot and slept for three and a half hours. After tea she played on the balcony, then walked with me on the lawns. She was bright and cheerful, saying repeatedly, "I didn't feel my tonsils come out. I didn't know, did I? Which room did I go into to have my tonsils out?" Again I told her how it had happened—the pills, the trolley, the anesthetic, the operation, and return to her cot.

At 6:30 P.M., the time when parents could visit their children in the open ward, we sat and played with a child who had no visitor; and stayed for ward prayers. Ward sister arranged that the hymn should be one known to Jean, and this pleased her very much: "My Big Nurse knows that hymn too."

When she got to bed she seemed very wide awake, and was unwilling to be left alone in the cubicle. She asked me to read a story, then another and another, as if to keep me with her; and she said often, "I want to go home now." She knew that next day she would go home.

April 11th. From 5 A.M. she was impatient to get dressed. She whimpered if my movements in the cubicle took me near the door; she complained that her throat hurt, resisted having her temperature taken, and refused breakfast. I moved her from her cot into my bed, gave her some toys and she cheered up a little. After a while she worried again to get dressed, with such insistence that I dressed her but put her back into her cot. This satisfied her for a while, but soon she became fretful again.

At 9 A.M. the ward sister came on duty and allowed Jean to walk about. She played happily in the open ward, talking to the children there and looking for her favorite hospital toys. She spoke in a friendly way to her Big Nurse, but then shot a flying toy which hit the Big Nurse's leg.

She was glad to see her Daddy when he arrived about 10 A.M. to take us home, but was a little reserved toward him. When the houseman wanted to take a final look at her throat she clenched her teeth and then cried.

AFTER DISCHARGE FROM HOSPITAL

She dozed in the car on the way home, obviously tired, but when we reached home she strongly resisted being put to rest. She silently watched her playmates for a while from the window, then slept for two hours. She awoke in good spirits, and played actively and happily all afternoon.

That evening she would not be left alone in her bedroom. She asked for several readings of Tonsil Boy. I sat on her bed until she was asleep. At 9 P.M. she awoke coughing and crying, "My throat hurts. But I'm crying because I'm by myself." I was unable to settle her, so took her into bed beside me and there she slept restlessly throughout the night.

April 12th. Second Day Home. There were several aggressive outbursts today. Immediately after a drink which hurt her throat, she slapped me hard, saying, "I don't like you, because you took me to the hospital." She saw an ambulance from the window: "There is an ambulance; perhaps someone is in it."

On leaving hospital yesterday we had unexpectedly been presented with Jean's tonsils and adenoids in a small glass jar. This morning Jean held the jar for a long time, peering intently at the contents and tilting them this way and that. I asked her what should be done with them. With great tenderness she said, "I'll keep them. I'll put them on the shelf in my room." I queried this: "Do you *really* want to keep them?" She replied emphatically: "Yes, I do!" She disappeared into her room with the jar in her hand, then returned ten minutes later with a flushed face: "No, Mummy. Let's throw them away."

She herself threw them into the dustbin.

April 13th. Third Day Home. I told Jean that we had been invited back to the hospital to have tea with the Big Nurse. She replied, "Yes. But just to see her, not to stay there." She added, "Why did you take me to that hospital? I wanted to come home the very first minute I was there." She recalled with a laugh how her flying toy had hit the Big Nurse. "I shall get my gun and shoot you all away."

She sat bending her hand to and fro, and pointing to the creases on her wrist, "Look at my hand. There are the lines where it could break off."

She saw three off-duty nurses in the street. She looked casually at them and said, "Yes, they do wear dresses like that." And as we passed the local hospital she remarked, "That's another hospital—not mine."

April 14th. Fourth Day Home. This was a good day. Jean seems to have found her place in the group again. She ate a little at each meal with enjoyment, and asked for her after-meal toffee.

This evening she was asleep by 6 P.M., but awoke at 8 with a heavy nosebleed. She was very uncooperative, would not have a compress applied to her nose nor would she suck ice. This inevitably caused some tension between us, because I knew we might have to return to hospital to have the bleeding checked. But by 10:30 P.M., however, the nosebleeding had subsided and she was asleep in my bed. We both spent a restless night.

Because of the bleeding the hospital doctor ordered 48 hours bed rest.

April 15th. Fifth Day Home. Jean was cheerful and looked well. She wanted to get up, so I let her get dressed and she spent the day on a settee in the living room.

She played a game of not being able to see or hear. She dug a finger into each ear, shut her eyes, then asked me to speak to her, saying, "I can't hear you now, and can't see you."

During the day she displayed and examined her genitals, laughing and looking at me to bring her behavior to my notice.

At bedtime she talked for a long while about her hospital experiences: "When I had my tonsils out I didn't feel it. I didn't hear and I didn't see. Why didn't I? It was funny. First of all I was ordinary asleep, then I smelled the funny smell, but I didn't know because I was asleep. Then I had the tonsils sleep. I would know if I was ordinary asleep."

She was rather lively, and kept bouncing her head on and off the pillow. This seemed to bring a hazy recollection. She said, "Was it yesterday you kept telling me to lay my head on the pillow? I didn't want to— I wanted to sit up." (Her recollection was in fact from the half hour immediately after the operation six days previously, when she had been extremely restless and apparently disoriented and I had tried to get her to keep her head on the pillow. It had been thought unlikely that she would have memory of that phase of recovery.)

She asked again for many bedtime stories, and clung to my hand when I eventually tried to leave the room. She made no complaint when I left the room, however, and was probably helped by the fact that her sister had just come to bed in the same room. She called out several times, but not with anxiety. She fell asleep with a penicillin tablet in her mouth. I opened her mouth to remove it, and was surprised that instead of resisting she seemed to open her mouth still wider and did not wake.

April 16th. Sixth Day Home. When she awoke she sang a song about "wobbly" (her own name for penis). She wanted very much to be active, but had to continue resting on the settee. I said she could get up when her tonsils were better, and she corrected me, "I haven't got tonsils, only a throat. The dustman has taken my tonsils away. I wonder where he puts all the rubbish?" She exhibited her genitals several times during the day.

In the afternoon I allowed her up to play quietly at a table. She resented the restriction on her movements, and was aggressive until the further concession was made that she could walk about. Later she was aggressive again when, after eating a nutcake, her throat pained her.

Looking out of the window at a strange family passing in the street, she said, "That girl was in hospital with me." She went to her room, dressed in her nurse's uniform, and played with her dollies and pram.

At bedtime she insisted on "five" stories. She was quiet for a few minutes after I left her, then cried out for "just one more story." She was obviously tired, held her cuddly, put her thumb to her lips but not into her mouth—she just stopped short of her usual relaxed sleeping position. She asked me to sit on her bed and to sing songs. While I did so she wriggled about, still resisting sleep. She slept well.

April 17th. Seventh Day Home. A good day with only two negative patches. When put to bed she asked for "two stories," then cried when I proposed to leave the room, saying "I don't want to be all alone. Did the hospital doctor talk to you on the telephone today?" I sat on the bed and she fell asleep within a few minutes. She did not suck her thumb. Once during the night she cried in her sleep.

April 18th. Eighth Day Home. Quite a good day, with only occasional aggressive and negative patches. For the first time since the day before the operation she asked to have long plaits in her hair.

At bedtime she refused to be washed or get undressed, and screamed when I insisted. She asked for "four bedtime stories." First of all I retold her own hospital story, and during the telling she made such remarks as, "Yes, I am cross with you for taking me to hospital. I didn't want to go. There was a little child there without his Mummy. I am sure he wanted his Mummy. The big boy won't be cross with his Mummy because he is big. He knows that sometimes children just have to go to hospital.— Yesterday you asked me to shut the door, but I wouldn't. I pretended that I couldn't. I opened it wide and put a chair there, and then I fell down."

Five minutes later while I was reading her stories she sat up, held my hand to her face, and cuddled round my neck: "I *do* like you Mummy. I *do* like you. I liked the Big Nurse—she brought letters to me. I didn't answer when she first asked me, and she walked away—then afterwards I took the letters from her pocket and she didn't know who had taken them." I said, "Shall we go to see the Big Nurse one day?" and she answered, "Yes, just to see her, just to have tea with her."

April 19th. Ninth Day Home. Rather more aggressive and temperamental behavior than during the past few days. She showed more anger against her Daddy. "We could have put a bed in our hospital room for Daddy."

April 20th. Tenth Day Home. A day somewhat like yesterday, with some aggressive and a few tyrannical outbursts. There were many "Why" questions.

She saw a large building which had two open swing doors. A baby lay in a pram outside. She looked intently, and after we had passed she kept looking back. Then she said, "Why is that baby going in there?" I told her that the building was a library. She said, "It looks like a hospital, but it isn't." In the evening she was loudly good-spirited and more affectionate to her Daddy.

April 21st. Eleventh Day Home. A good day. I was out for the whole of the afternoon, and Jean stayed happily with her Daddy. She showed him much affection.

She did not want to be left alone at bedtime. I read many stories, and then sat on her bed until she slept.

April 22nd. Twelfth Day Home. For most of the day she was active and in good spirits, sometimes with a slightly manic tinge. When crossed,

however, she immediately threw temper tantrums. She behaves like the
so-called "spoiled" child. The "Why" questions today were more specifically about marriage and conception.

April 24th. Fourteenth Day Home. The "Why" questions continued
throughout yesterday and today. At bedtime she asked, "Who takes people to prison?" I assured her that children did not go to prison. She said,
"When children are naughty, their Mummy and Daddy make them good
again, don't they?" I suggested that children were sometimes naughty
because they were worried and unhappy about something they could not
understand. She said "Yes," thoughtfully, and twenty minutes later went
on: "I don't know what makes me unhappy. Perhaps I won't be naughty
tomorrow, and won't hit you." She slept easily.

April 25th. Fifteenth Day Home. At breakfast Jean lay back, quietly
licking a grape. With a puzzled frown she said, "It was my Big Nurse who
pricked my leg. I didn't like it. Why did she?" (This apparently referred
to the injection given before the operation by the ward sister—Jean's
"Big Nurse." Until today Jean had insisted that the prick had been given
by a student nurse with whom she had no relationship.)

April 26th. Sixteenth Day Home. She told her sister Katherine with
impish laughter of the time when her flying toy hit the Big Nurse's leg.
She is very keen to have fairness. "She hit me, so I hit her. She hurt me,
so I hurt her" is a recurrent theme. She watched two playmates fighting:
"It's all right, Tommy. You can hit Betty because she hit you. Go on,
Tommy, it's all right."

Later she said, "Hazel nearly died today—she was so sick. She did, she
nearly died. I was sick with all the blood" (recalling her own postoperative blood vomit).

April 27th. Seventeenth Day Home. During last night she had a nightmare, with "doggies" in her bed. At breakfast she grumbled about not
being given a tomato with her bacon; and when given a tomato she complained that it was too firm. She said often, "I don't like you."

She asked to have her toast cut into little pieces, and then divided
them according to size into "mummies, daddies, and children." "I'll eat
the children first. What was the name of the little baby who cried in
hospital? Was it a boy or a girl?—Its Mummy wasn't there and it
cried." I reminded her that the Mummy had in fact visited the child
each day. She said, "But perhaps the baby wouldn't know which was his
very own Mummy. Perhaps they would all wear the very same coats."
I asked: "Do you think perhaps the Mummy wouldn't know it was her
very own baby?" She nodded.

A letter came from the Big Nurse and I read it to her. She took possession of the letter and said she would like to go for tea with the Big
Nurse. She went to her doll's pram and said, "I want a coat for my dolly.
I can't find it, I'll put on her nightie instead. Doesn't she look sweet in
her nightie?"

A few minutes later I heard her singing in her room. "And then her
tonsils popped out, and if I do she'll be sure to die." (In this she was

parodying the end of the nursery rhyme "Little Boy Blue": "Will you wake him? No not I, For if I do he'll be sure to cry.")

Shortly afterwards she came to me and said, "I won't ever have to go to hospital again, will I? I don't want to." When I reminded her that mummies go, for instance to have babies, she said, "When I'm a mummy I won't mind, because then I'll be big."

A little later she came in from the garden to ask: "What is a stomach? Peter [a playmate who had recently had his tonsils and adenoids removed] had something in his nose." I explained about adenoids, and linked it with her nosebleed after the operation. She stood quietly pinching her tongue with finger and thumb, as she had done often before the operation.

Later she was playing doctors with a little boy with dolly for patient. She said, "We must have a doctor, and you be the doctor. You must hurt her leg and then you must make her quite better."

April 28th. Eighteenth Day Home. "I didn't like the Big Nurse pricking my leg. Which leg did she prick? Did she make a hole?" She fell over many times during the afternoon, and each time she came to show me the cuts and bruises on her legs.

April 29th. Nineteenth Day Home. At breakfast she recalled: "When I cut my finger the blood came out. I licked it and the blood went down into my tummy. It doesn't matter, does it? Blood can go down?"

Ten minutes later she called me to the lavatory and said very brightly, "Mummy, I feel sick." I did not take her seriously, and she said again: "I do feel sick—something might dribble out—I did dribble out all the blood, lots of it. Why did I? Why do tonsils make blood in my tummy? I want to go to see the Big Nurse today."

April 30th. Twentieth Day Home (Day of Return Visit to Hospital). She seemed happy to be going to visit the Big Nurse. As we approached the hospital a mother and two children were ahead of us. One of the children carried a case. Jean made a quick inference: "That little girl is going to stay in the hospital. I'm not, am I?"

She showed no anxiety as we went into the hospital. When we reached the ward she skipped ahead of us, almost dancing, and went straight to her former cubicle. She showed it to Katherine, and then took her on a tour of the ward and showed her things with a proprietorial air. She pointed to where the ward sister's hat and cloak hung: "That's my Big Nurse's." She did not talk to the nurses, but smiled and nodded in answer to the ward sister.

Her ball ran into the induction room, and she was hesitant to go after it until encouraged by the ward sister. She tiptoed in, and in picking up her ball she peeped quickly into the operating theater which lay beyond, then hurried out with a flushed face. (She knew the purpose of these two rooms.)

She saw a little girl walk about the ward asking and looking for her mummy. Later she asked: "Where was that little girl's mummy?"

On the way home she said, "I want to visit the Big Nurse again."

At this point it seemed that Jean had worked through her hospital experience. She looked well, ate and slept normally, spoke little of hospital, and showed no special anxieties. She had started nursery school for the first time, and settled quickly and happily. After a few days she insisted that I should not accompany her to school, and went cheerfully with a neighbor and her children. Her increased confidence and independence of me was commented on by our neighbors. Her extreme fear of dogs had almost disappeared, as she herself remarked, "That dog looked at me, and I wasn't even afraid."

For these reasons the Diary was discontinued at this point, three weeks after the operation. But the following narrative, which begins eleven weeks after the operation, shows how external events reactivated her anxieties.

June 23rd to August 28th. Eleventh to Twentieth Week Home. During the first week of this period Jean's behavior suddenly deteriorated. She cried easily, grumbled at everything, threw temper tantrums, refused to go to the lavatory alone "because it comes too quickly," and in general acted much as she had done immediately before going to hospital.

After a few days during which we could not account for the change, we realized that three external events had reactivated her anxieties. These were:

    a. one of her playmates went to hospital to have her tonsils out;
    b. the mother of a neighboring family went away from home for two weeks and left two young children in the care of their father;
    c. the anticipation of our annual seaside holiday.

The Playmate's Tonsillectomy. On June 23rd a five-year-old girl living in the block made it known that she would soon go to hospital, by herself, to have her tonsils out. The other children in the group appeared to take no special notice, but Jean and Hazel became inseparable. Although hitherto they had been only casual playmates, they now held hands, walked about with arms around each other, and whispered together.

A week later, Jean saw Hazel go off by car to hospital; and during the day she spoke of it many times. For the next two days she wore her nurse's uniform most of the time, and came in from play often to ask: "Is Hazel in hospital now? Are her tonsils out? Will her mummy go to see her?"

Hazel in fact suffered a setback. On the second day she had a hemorrhage and a policeman came to tell the mother to go to the hospital. This was known to all the children and there was much talk and reminiscence about blood and operations. Hazel's return was delayed, and Jean became increasingly anxious because Hazel did not come home on the expected day. She asked many times for her, and was irritable, fretful, and easily provoked into tantrums.

Hazel came home after a week, and had to stay in bed for three days. Each morning Jean called up at her window, and became very excited when Hazel appeared and waved down to her. Four days after Hazel had resumed play in the garden, Jean again called up to her window. Hazel was slow to appear and Jean greeted her with, "Hello, Hazel. I thought you were dead. You didn't come when I called you."

Children Left by Their Mother. On July 8th, the day after Hazel's return from hospital, the mother of another family had to leave home for two weeks to care for a sick relative—leaving two children to be looked after by their father. A week later, in response to a remark of mine about mothers looking after children, Jean exploded with: "They don't always. Mary's mummy has gone away for lots of days and left her alone."

Anticipation of the Holiday. From the beginning of July there was much talking over of arrangements for the family holiday which was to begin on August 1st. Toward the end of the month I realized that this was adding to Jean's anxieties, because there were similarities between this waiting period and that which had preceded her going to hospital. I was using similar phrases to deal with her impatience for the holiday as had been used to prepare her for hospital: "Soon we will be going. We will put these things ready in the case. We will have to wait a few more days, because it isn't our turn yet." I talked with her about this similarity, and during the whole of the next day there were no temper tantrums.

Her behavior gradually improved, and by the fourth day of the holiday she seemed to be over this period of difficulty and anxiety. This good state continued when these notes were written up which is three months after our holiday and eight months after the tonsillectomy.

ANNA FREUD

In a recent paper on "The Role of Bodily Illness in the Mental Development of Children" (1952), I stated with regret that professional workers have little opportunity to follow without interruption what happens in a child's mind during the complete course of an illness. I attributed this to our present conditions in child care when doctors and nurses lose touch with their patients when they recover, while teachers, child-therapists or analysts do not meet their charges when they are ill. There remain only the mothers who see their children in both health and illness and in the transitional states between them. But mothers, as I said then, are bad observers at such times, preoccupied as they are with their own anxieties and with the task of nursing.

It is this latter statement which I want to withdraw after reading Joyce Robertson's account of her four-year-old daughter's tonsillectomy. This mother's outlook on her daughter's inner experience remained objective during all the intricacies of the child's disturbed, occasionally negative, at all times highly exacting behavior. She never lost touch with the underlying trend of affect by which the child's reactions were determined and to which her own responses were directed. In following her account we are presented therefore not only with an interesting description of a small girl's behavior under the stresses of operation and hospitalization but also with a convincing and consistent report on the inner struggle between the anxieties which were aroused by the experience and the infantile ego's attempt at dealing with them.

From the first part of the diary which covers the preparatory period we learn that Jean confirmed almost all our theoretical expectations of what operation and hospitalization may mean to children of her age. There was, in the first instance, the threat of the anesthetic, conceived by the child as an oral attack against which she defended herself by a refusal of oral intake. Only the quick understanding and interpretation from the mother's side interfered with more permanent displacement of this phobic attitude onto food, prevented symptom formation and rendered the child amenable to a rational discussion of the danger situation. Separation anxiety arose next with which the mother could deal by reassurance since she had permission to accompany the child to hospital. Next came castration fears, centered around the frightening image of a body hole. Again, Jean had recourse to a phobic defense which made her reject temporarily the use of knife and fork and eat with her hands, an attitude which changed almost immediately to the active use of knives. Jean placed herself in the role of surgeon and operated tentatively on herself. Alternating with this identification with the aggressor, she turned aggression outwards, against members of the family, furniture, etc. Death fears and the fantasy of being robbed of body content (blood) were mobilized next on the id side. To these the superego added an equally frightening moral version of the impending dangers in which the hospital took on the aspect of a prison, the surgeon that of a policeman, and the operation was turned into a major punishment. The anxieties from these sources which flooded the child's mind produced in manifest behavior an increased demandingness, irritability, uncooperativeness and indiscriminate aggressions toward the environment (cutting and shooting). Conversely there appeared also a certain measure of accident proneness and self-injury, the defenses regressing increasingly toward primitive types (psychosomatic symptoms, temper tantrums) as the date of the operation drew near. In the last days of waiting, denials of external reality and internal feelings were most prominent: children are *not* killed, they have *not* gone to hospital, hospitals are nice places where children wear their party dresses, where they want to stay for ever. Jean's final protest against going to hospital may be regarded as belonging to the same defense, i.e., less as a refusal to cooperate than as a vehement denial of her sense of helplessness and impotence to do so.

With the operation accomplished the diary presents a very different picture of Jean's state of mind. We find the diffuse anticipatory anxieties swept away and the child more concerned with the reality aspects of the situation. Even the actual sight of her own blood did not revive her former fantastic anxieties and left her unafraid. What disturbed her most at this time was the interruption in conscious experience caused by the anesthetic. Apparently this connected with some unconscious fantasy of passive surrender to attack. She reacted with a "barrage of questions," i.e., an insatiable demand for reassuring details which might serve to fill the gap. One can well imagine another child answering to the same experience with a phobic attitude toward sleep as the state of unawareness in which "anything might happen." Further, there were the indications of a proprietory and positive attitude toward the hospital and staff which so many children manifest after medical or surgical interventions; in Jean's case this well-known passive-masochistic trend was tempered by an aggressive retaliating wish (hurting the nurse who had hurt her). A heightened impatient irritability on the morning before leaving hospital may well have been due to the child's disbelief in the promise of release.

In the three weeks after their return home, the diary shows how mother and child dealt with the emotional aftermath of the operation. Unlike children who have been to hospital on their own, Jean showed no excessive clinging to the mother. An exception to this was bedtime when —contrary to former habits—she refused to be left alone. We may ascribe this difficulty to the prolonged fear of the passive experience of anesthesia which leaves her suspicious of sleep and increases—at this time only—her infantile dependence on the mother's presence.

There is, further, the interesting incident when Jean decided to discard her cut-out tonsils. Here, the reader is reminded of similar infantile behavior during toilet training when children find it easier to be active themselves in throwing out their own highly cathected body products than to be deprived of them passively. One concludes that Jean's mother had used the device in earlier years of allowing the child to empty her own pot.

Another interesting characteristic of the postoperative period was the marked increase in Jean's ambivalence toward her mother which reminds us of an infant's primitive distinction between the "good" and the "bad" mother.[4] At this time Jean saw her mother actually in a double role, as her protector against danger as well as the person responsible for delivering her to danger. Accordingly, gratitude and anger, love and hate, appeared in quick succession in her conscious feelings, causing difficult and unpredictable behavior. This regression in the relationship to the mother also reawakened the primitive anxieties and, with them, some of the defensive behavior of the preparatory period.

On the other hand, with the operation safely behind her, Jean showed herself less overwhelmed by her anxieties than she had been before and better able to cope reasonably with some of the undigested memories of her hospital experience. She returned gradually to more cooperative and independent attitudes with the need for constant reassurance markedly diminished. The emotional relapse after an interval of two months, although bearing witness to her prolonged vulnerability, also provided an added opportunity for working over and assimilating the experience.

While following the sequence of happenings in Jeans's mind, we cannot help speculating how she would have dealt with the events if— as happens to most children—she had been less well understood, or

---

[4] See Melanie Klein.

among strangers, and deprived of help and support at the critical time. As it was, her battle between id anxieties and ego defenses was played out against the background of her mother's reassuring presence. There was in the child a constant urge to distort and magnify external danger situations and use them as representations of internal threats. This was met by the mother's equally constant, tolerant and understanding behavior which served to undo the distortions, to separate fantasy from reality and, thereby, to reduce the quality and quantity of anxiety to levels with which the child could deal. That she accomplished this without falsifying the unpleasurable aspects of reality is greatly to the mother's credit.

Mrs. Robertson's account of Jean's tonsillectomy seems to me an instructive contribution to our psychoanalytic studies of small children, not diminished in value by the fact that her observations were carried out in the original setting of the child's life and relationships instead of in the analytic setting as we construct it artificially to provoke the repetition of internal events before the analyst's eyes and in the transference relationship.

In her role as mother, Mrs. Robertson kept her account strictly within the limits of her own child's experience and refrained from generalizations. As analytic readers, we may permit ourselves to go a step further and extract from her study some points of general validity. There are, in my opinion, two main respects in which the foregoing description confirms and illustrates our knowledge of the working of a child's mind.

First is the fact that a young child's emotional balance is shown here to be no more than a matter of quantities, i.e., a function of the relation of strength between the id and ego forces. Anxieties are mastered by the ego while they remain below a specific threshold. They become pathogenic, creating neurotic symptoms or behavior problems when they rise above that level, that is, when the defenses are overtaxed or overthrown. If the ego is successful in its mastery of anxiety, the child feels encouraged and relieved. Progress within the province of the ego has been achieved and a potentially traumatic event has been transformed into beneficial and constructive experience, as it has happened in Jean's case.

Second, there is ample confirmation in Mrs. Robertson's account that it is not the external danger, real and serious as it may be, which accounts for the traumatic value of an experience. Injections, loss of blood, surgical interventions, etc., are shown to remain manageable events unless they touch on and merge with id material which transforms them into experiences of being assaulted, emptied out, castrated or condemned.

When looking at the two aspects of Jean's fears, one is tempted to reopen an old theoretical controversy which has been neglected by analysts in recent years; I mean the question whether the phenomenon of "real" anxiety exists at all. Most analytic authors insist that, by the working of our mind, external danger is inevitably and automatically transformed into internal threats, i.e., that all fear is in the last resort anxiety with regard to id events. Personally, I find it difficult to subscribe to this sweeping statement. I believe in a sliding scale between external and internal threats and fears. What we call "courage" in ordinary language is, I believe, no more than the individual's ability to deal with external threats on their own ground and prevent the bulk of them from joining forces with the manifold dangers lurking in the id.

It is this last consideration which may help us also to assess the nature of the mother's achievement in Jean's case. Mrs. Robertson helped her child precisely in this way: to meet the operation on the level of reality, to keep the external danger in consciousness to be dealt with by the reasonable ego instead of allowing it to slip to those depths in which the rational powers of the ego become ineffective and primitive methods of defense are brought into action.

Child analysts and therapists may wonder where, with a mother of such rare insight, her province ends and theirs begins. I suggest the following answer. Mothers—unless specially instructed and guided to do otherwise—should, as Mrs. Robertson has done, limit themselves to assisting the child's ego in its task of mastery, lend it their strength and help to guard it against irruptions from the id. Analysts work in the opposite direction. Under carefully controlled conditions, they induce the child to lower his defenses and to accept the id derivatives in consciousness. The contact with the id impulses which is obtained thereby is used then to effect a gradual transformation of these strivings to which all neurotic anxieties and symptoms owe their origin.

4

LEG AMPUTATION IN A FOUR-YEAR-OLD

Reactions of the Child, Her Family, and the Staff

EMMA N. PLANK, M.A. and CARLA HORWOOD, M.D.
(1961)

Ruth, four years and two months old, made a dramatic entrance into our hospital.[1] She was brought to the emergency room with a high fever in a toxic, but alert condition. While being examined petechiae (small hemorrhages under the skin) broke out all over the child's body, and particularly severely over the lower extremities. She had a stiff neck, pain in the ankles and hips. The illness was diagnosed as meningococcemia (blood poisoning due to bacteria meningococcus). She was immediately started on sulfa drugs by intravenous medication. In spite of therapy, nine hours after her arrival on the Division for Contagious Diseases, the child had a temperature of 42°, blood pressure of 0/0, and seemed moribund. This condition lasted for about four hours, then the blood pressure slowly returned. When it appeared that this child had very little chance for survival a dramatic change for improvement began, which continued.

During the next few days the lesions on her legs and buttocks became larger and darker, and gangrene set in. The need to amputate seemed imminent. On the ninth hospital day it was still difficult to predict the fate of the legs, but it was decided to wait until gangrene or infection would force the issue.

During this whole period the child was fed by nasal tube or intravenously. Sixteen days after the onset of illness, arteriograms were done under general anesthesia to determine the extent of circu-

[1] The Department of Pediatrics and Contagious Diseases, Cleveland Metropolitan General Hospital, and the Department of Pediatrics, School of Medicine, Western Reserve University.

Mrs. Plank was Director of Child Life and Education, Dr. Horwood was Playroom Supervisor in the Child Life and Education Program.

lation in her legs. Her left foot was definitely cold. The arteriograms
fit the clinical observation of the line of demarcation of Ruth's
circulation. It was decided to amputate the left leg just below the
knee and to try to limit amputation on the right leg to the toes. The
little girl was to be moved from the Contagious Division to the general children's ward and to wait there for the right moment for
surgery. We give such detailed account of the medical picture to
show what child, parents, and staff had gone through.

At this point the senior author was approached by the pediatric
staff to enter the case. I was asked to take over the preparation of
the child for the operation and to help the parents accept the tragic
necessity, so that they too could help the child. This was an unusual
request. The doctors usually are eager to do a great deal of the
preparation themselves and to ask a medical social worker to help
the family. In this case, though, it was felt that one central person
should deal with both parents and child. I had been out of town
when the case was discussed in grand rounds; no one wanted the
specific responsibility for the preparation. The anxiety was understandable: most of the young doctors and the psychologist had little
girls of Ruthie's age and attractiveness in their families. Also, the
type of operation must have activated unconscious anxieties in these
men. They found it most difficult to talk with the parents. At that
time consultation with a child psychiatrist was not available to the
staff either.

My first contact with Ruthie was typical of her at that time. She
said: "Leave me alone, I don't want you!" I said that this was all
right, and that I would stop by later; maybe she would like a visitor
or some toys then.

I introduced myself to the mother as a person on the hospital
team who would like to be available to her in talking over what was
ahead. The mother immediately replied: "I don't want Ruthie to
know anything before she goes up to surgery, we couldn't bear it."
I replied how well I understood this wish, but that maybe, if Ruthie
woke up after surgery with one leg and part of the other gone, she
would be very angry with her parents that they had not prevented
the doctors from doing it. Ruthie needed to know that the amputation was necessary to get her well and that the doctors and parents
agreed and would help her before and after surgery. This argument

convinced Mrs. A. She started to tell me a little about the child and herself prior to the illness.

Mrs. A. was an attractive young woman. She was in the second trimester of pregnancy. Ruthie was her only child so far. The mother had had two miscarriages between Ruth and the present pregnancy. She was not feeling too well right now and had suffered from chronic kidney trouble and a peptic ulcer. The father was a strong and tall skilled worker. The family had roots in this community, both sets of grandparents and a great-grandparent living in close proximity.

The mother described Ruthie as a very independent and willful child. She paid little attention to her mother's attempts to in-fluence her eating or to correct her spells of anger. Mrs. A. avoided constant battling and let things go until Mr. A. got home; he set limits and the child obeyed him. Since the illness this had changed; the father was terribly upset, and the mother said he would never agree to have the little girl prepared for the amputation.

Ruthie's development had been quite uneventful. The mother nursed her for three months and weaned her from the bottle shortly after a year. The child walked early and was very skillful and daring in her motor activities. Toilet training was finished at two years with some struggle. The child was a picky eater but well developed.

After my first interview with the mother she suggested herself to bring the father in to see me, too. I met twice with both parents and Mrs. A. helped me to convince Mr. A. that Ruthie should know what was ahead.

Mrs. A. and I went with the little girl to the general children's ward on the day she was transferred. There she settled down without trouble. The staff decided to wait with specific preparations until final medical decisions were made. But both authors would see the child daily in the playroom and would through observing her at play and in relationship to them decide on how best to prepare her.

Once the first resistance was overcome the parents inundated me with questions: where exactly was the amputation going to be, what was the prosthesis going to be like, would Ruthie be able to ride a bicycle, what were the initial costs for the prosthesis and for its re-newal and the like? Several interviews were scheduled for them to get as precise information as possible. They spoke daily about medical plans with the surgeon. The physiatrist explained all questions relating to the prosthesis and to Ruthie's training for ambulation.

Ruthie came from the Contagious Division to the Pediatric Ward three weeks after the onset of illness. The ulcers on her legs and buttocks were very large and painful and had to be treated daily. She could only move her legs from the hip. She saw the horrible black legs when bandages were changed. To reduce the contractions the physical therapist stretched Ruthie's legs daily. Meanwhile the doctors and we—the child care staff—worked on a day-to-day basis with child and family to await the most opportune time for the amputation. This period took about three weeks.

During this time, we got to know Ruthie well. Student nurses told us about the nursing part, we saw her daily for several hours in the playroom, and the family also informed us of changes in the child. We stayed in daily contact with the physical therapist. The observations in the playroom made by the junior author, who became the most important person in helping the child work through her anxieties about her illness, will show how we got our cues for preparing Ruthie and how the working through of Ruthie's feelings proceeded before and after the operation.

Our work with this child should be seen in its general framework. She was one of about fifteen to twenty children for whom we had the responsibility for a day program from 9:30 A.M. to 5 P.M. The playrooms are on the same floor as the treatment room and the children's ward, but definitely divorced from all treatment or nursing functions.

Since the head nurse is often too busy to elaborate on the explanation of procedures, the playroom staff has taken over the function of preparing children in detail mentally and emotionally for procedures and operations. Dr. Horwood reports:

I first met Ruth late in the afternoon of the transfer day. I introduced myself, picked up a doll of hers, and commented on how pretty it was, to which she sharply stated, "It's mine, don't touch it." I put it down and said we also had some things she might enjoy playing with, mentioning a few. She said she liked paints; I brought her some, set them up, and said I would be back to see her the next day.

In looking back, I realize that initially I was quite anxious about seeing Ruthie, because of the severity of her condition. In addition, I had not expected to find such an attractive little girl who at the same time was so very hostile. I feel that because of these factors I unconsciously maintained a certain emotional distance from Ruthie at the start. This gradually lessened as I worked with her, but disappeared completely only when she was no longer on the ward and I visited her in Physical Therapy.

During the first couple of weeks in the playroom, I tried to establish a relationship with Ruthie, help her play with other children, and at the same time to set clear, consistent limits in the playroom that no amount of whining would change. We decided to make no direct preparation for the amputation until medical plans were clearly established and eventually to prepare her only a few days before the day of operation.

There were constant, daily struggles with Ruth in regard to playroom routines; e.g., that she could not continuously go back and forth between divisions; that other children needed me too; that occasionally she had to wait for toys and not grab from others, etc. Through her anxiety she was unable to sustain any activity for more than a few minutes. Furthermore, she was very destructive toward other children and toys, and aroused much negative feeling from both staff and children. Few youngsters ever attempted to play with her. She persistently tried to monopolize a staff member (and often succeeded with new staff). As soon as an activity was started with another child, she immediately wanted to have the same thing.

During daily bandage changes and exposure to the sun lamp, there was constant crying and screaming. Treatments were given on the ward without the presence of playroom staff.

After I had known her for about ten days, I stayed with her while the dressing was being changed. The child could see the whole procedure and was well aware of the grotesque, black lower legs. The doctors, forgetting her presence, frequently alluded to the forthcoming operation, e.g., "We can save the knee"; "It's no good here."

I discussed this observation with Mrs. Plank the next morning. In view of the fact that the child had already heard so much from the doctors, which undoubtedly contributed to any fantasies that she had formed about her legs, we felt it would be wise to start to broach the reality of the plans for her now. Therefore, that day I went to her room before the playroom opened and said, "I know how sick you have been, Ruthie. Everything is almost well now except for one leg. The doctors will have to do something to help you walk again." To elucidate further, I added, "You know that when you touch your leg you don't feel anything?" She immediately changed the subject: "If you touch my TV set, it will break." No further mention was made of this the rest of the day by her or myself.

Two days later there was spontaneous play with the doctor set and dolls. She pointed to one doll, saying, "This one has sore legs. She doesn't want to see them." Several minutes later she referred to another doll: "This one can't stand." She asked for tape and wanted assistance with taping the doll's legs (usually binding the legs together). There was some talk in regard to one of the dolls having had an operation, but she was not interested in discussing it further.

During the next three days, at least once a day she would ask to play with the dolls and adhesive tape and when I would inquire how the dolls were, her answer would also be some version of "They have sore legs, just like I have." Around this time, I began to observe in her play how much interest she showed in being messy. For example, when given paint and paper, she never made a picture on the paper, but instead painted her hands, put her white, fluffy toy dog in the paint (having no desire to have it washed afterwards), got paint on her gown, etc. However, at this time, I had for the first time a glimpse of a rather charming and likable little girl who at times could relate to me without ordering me around.

Here we decided to take a cue from Ruthie's own play and to handle the preparation for surgery largely through the use of a doll. After finding out details about the prosthesis which Ruthie would get following the amputation, we constructed a special doll (later referred to as the prosthesis doll) which would undergo the same procedures as Ruthie. The amputation would be at the correct point, with the diseased part of the leg being blackened. The prosthesis would be of proportionate size, with a realistic leather attachment so that the child could manipulate it herself. It would be of similar color but more rigid and less lifelike than the doll's other leg, so that it would not look as if a leg had grown back.

For raw material I used two dolls of the same size (14"). One had hard limbs and therefore felt quite different. A leg of this doll was to serve as the prosthesis for the other doll, whose lower leg I would amputate. We planned to save the introduction of the doll until the exact amputation point on Ruthie's leg was established.

Some days later Ruthie was extremely upset in the playroom, returning to her original whiney, destructive, demanding behavior. Later we found out that she had been in the Physical Therapy Division and while waiting for a long time to be seen, she had seen three leg amputees.

During the next week she was calmer again. Ruthie was now placed on a low cot where she seemed infinitely happier than in bed. One day on the ward, she was observed to be coloring black the legs of a doll in a picture book.

Surgery now definitely was going to be scheduled in two days. In a conference with the doctors, nurses, and social workers of the floor, it was decided that her doctor would tell her about the amputation in the presence of one or both of her parents. However, that afternoon, he learned from the parents that, contrary to previous plans, they had in their anxiety already told Ruthie about the amputation almost a week before.

The day before the operation, Ruthie was completely unable to concentrate, moving from play with the doll house to the tinker toys, to the playing cards, etc., in less than ten minutes. I therefore decided to start then to prepare her for the details of the surgery. I took her into a side room alone and began by saying, "I know that your parents and the doctors have told you about having an operation tomorrow." She replied, "No, they didn't." I then gave the standard preparation regarding the trip to the operating room and the anesthetic, and explained what would happen while she was asleep. Then we both went to get the prosthesis doll for the first time. I explained and showed her that one leg was black and sick and that the doll was not able to walk. She wanted to hold the doll herself and hold the black leg on. Then I showed her how the doctor would take part of the black leg off, so that later they could help her to walk with the artificial leg. At this point she said, "I don't want to walk." I said, "I can understand that you would feel that way now, but how nice it will be when you don't have to stay in a wheel chair and can walk and play like other girls."

She then asked, "She'll have another leg?" I said, "No, she will not grow one, but she will have a leg she and her mommy can put on just like the artificial leg that was on the doll. It is hard, but it looks like a real leg, and she will be able to learn to walk on it again." Then Ruthie, pointing to the doll's black leg, said, "Throw it away, it's no good." (This was repeated twice.)

Several minutes later, after a doctor had seen her again, and toe amputation on the other leg had also been confirmed, I mentioned that the doll's right toes were sick too, and she immediately said, "Cut them off, maybe you have to cut her foot off, too." I reassured her, "No, it's just the toes, the foot will get well by itself and she will have a special shoe which will match the shoe for the other leg." Later she said, "You be a doctor, I'll be the nurse, and we will tape her," which we did. Ruthie had listened and concentrated during this whole discussion. My anxiety had led me to put the artificial leg on quickly; she was very interested in taking it off, examining the stump, and putting tape on it. She then returned to the playroom and was able to play until lunchtime. When she went to nap later she tucked the doll in with her under the covers. During her physical therapy session in the afternoon she also took the doll with her and was reported to be putting the artificial leg on and off.

The next day Ruthie went to surgery in the early morning. After her return in the afternoon she frequently pulled back the covers, pointed to the leg stump, and said, "See," to various staff members. This was repeated in the next few days. Our first reaction was to try to cover the stump with the blanket, due to our own uneasiness. However, Ruthie tended to keep it purposely exposed, and after several days to take almost no note of it whatsoever.

The next two weeks went relatively smoothly in the playroom. Some of the other children now also came over to her bedside on the ward to talk to her. There was a gradual progression from bed, to cart, to wheel chair, and one day to a small wheel chair which she could happily propel herself. However, because of the need to straighten her legs, the physical therapist wanted her back in the larger wheelchair. This was very upsetting to Ruthie and caused a temporary setback in her ability to play, and again much insistence about being wheeled back to her room in the middle of the morning, etc.

Though less demanding in the playroom, on the ward she continued to order people about and very frequently got her way, particularly with student nurses and with her relatives. She fussed about food, and occasionally wet and soiled herself. Also, she seemed to be quite uncooperative with her physical therapist.

During this time Ruthie made several interesting remarks. To her physical therapist during a therapy session she said, "When will you buy me a new leg?" To one of the other workers in the playroom, "I can do this [touch the floor] with the good leg but not with my other leg." When one day I saw her holding the stump with her hands, I asked whether it hurt a little. She quickly replied, "But it's getting better, isn't it!" Several times she said, seemingly out of clear blue, "I don't want to walk," and I would talk to her about how difficult it was to wait. When other children asked Ruthie about what happened to her leg, without hesitation she would reply, "It was sick and the doctors took it off." Many people, both in the playroom and on the ward, noted that since the amputation there was more open masturbation. However, in the playroom she readily stopped when it was clearly stated that this was something that was not done in public.

Several bandage changes and a postoperative stump revision were necessary during these weeks. The first two changes were done under general anesthesia and caused no noticeable change in her behavior. However, about twelve days after the amputation she again went to surgery, this time without a familiar person, and another procedure was performed, with the child only under heavy sedation. Ruthie was extremely irritable and uncooperative upon her return and almost unmanageable when her mother visited. The child had seen her wound for the first time.

The relationship to me started to get stronger. I was sick and away from work for a couple of days. During my absence there were frequent questions about where I was and when I would be back. When I returned, Ruthie threw her arms around me, asked me where I had been, and said how much she had missed me. This was the first demonstration of any positive emotion for me.

Two days later, another bandage change was done in the morning under heavy sedation, but without anesthesia. She was not allowed to eat before the procedure and remained sleepy during the morning. At lunchtime she asked for her breakfast and was very angry when told that it had not been saved. She refused to eat her lunch and continued to scream for her breakfast. When her mother dropped in after lunch she was completely unable to handle the child. Finally she left with the threat that she would not come back if Ruthie did not behave better. After wetting her pants Ruthie refused to put on dry ones, and the nurses in desperation called Mrs. Plank to the ward. The details of the discussion between Ruthie and Mrs. Plank are interesting because this talk became a turning point in the child's behavior.

Mrs. Plank commiserated with her that she must be very hungry and wondered whether they could not get some food from the kitchen. The student nurse in charge of the child brought toast and milk, but this did not satisfy Ruthie either, and she continued furiously to insist on getting her own breakfast tray, which of course was not available. After a while, Mrs. Plank said that she was not going to stay any longer because Ruthie did not really want her to help, and she had many other things to do. However, if Ruthie would eat her toast now, Mrs. Plank would gladly wait for her and then take her to the playroom. At this point, Ruthie sat up in her bed and screamed: "You are not here to give orders, I am here to give orders," to which Mrs. Plank replied, "No, you don't give orders and I am not here to give orders either. I am here to help you and other children." Ruthie looked surprised and relieved, ate her toast, and was willing to come to the playroom.

There was a marked change in her behavior starting the next day. This pattern continued until the time of her discharge. She spent the next morning in the toddlers' room with me and Jeannie (a girl about her age suffering from a terminal illness) and Roy (a fifteen-month-old-baby). She played some with Roy, sang, and wanted to play school with me being the teacher. Her doll-house play with Jeannie was the first real cooperative play I had observed. Interestingly enough, the main play was dropping the mother down the doll-house stairs on her head. I decorated her wheel chair with her name, which greatly pleased her. In watching her play with dolls I could confirm the observation reported to me by some of the nurses that she always took their clothes off, actually with glee, and had no interest whatsoever in dressing the dolls again. Open masturbation was still present, but appeared to be greatly reduced.

Ruthie's destructiveness of toys and hostility toward other children continued, and their overtures toward her were rare. Nevertheless, one day, Herman (age nine) agreed to help her make play dough upon my suggestion. At one point he told her not to use the rolling pin until the dough was less sticky. Ruthie went ahead and took it regardless. Herman immediately grabbed it back from her, saying, "No, I told you to wait till later." Instead of her usual outburst upon the slightest frustration, Ruthie looked stunned and said nothing, apparently realizing that this sort of behavior would get her nowhere with Herman. This was a great step forward for this little girl.

A few days later, a split-thickness skin graft, taken from the abdomen, was applied in an operation under anesthesia for which it was necessary to apply fully covering casts to both legs. The next day in the playroom we were playing with some shells that a relative had brought her. Pointing to one where the outer part had been chipped off, she commented, "It has no skin." I was then able to discuss her skin graft with her.

Ruthie continued to become more cooperative, less demanding, more able to endure frustration (e.g., waiting while a staff member helped some other child), and more willing to do things by herself. About four weeks after the amputation she was able for the first time to continue an activity even while I was out of the room for a few minutes. After much encouragement, Ruthie was now even willing to wheel herself to and from the playroom.

At this time I introduced some authentic surgery equipment into the playroom: an intravenous setup, surgical drapes, caps and masks, a (dull) knife, and a mask for anesthesia. Here I followed the selection suggested by Florence Erickson (1958). Ruthie was immediately very interested, and she and Yolanda (age eight) performed multiple operations on the dolls, with Yolanda being a sort of head surgeon. Ruthie's operations involved almost exclusively the legs, and she invariably made the incision near or actually right where the vagina would be. This play was terminated only by the playroom's closing and commenced the first thing the next day. One day she mentioned to me that she might have an operation the next morning. I said that I was sorry that I could not tell her more about it because I had not been informed, to which she said, "It's alright, I know you'll tell me all about it afterwards."

The next day under heavy sedation the upper parts of the casts were removed and Ruthie was returned to the floor late that morning. She wanted to go to the playroom immediately. I was firm in stating that I knew she was tired, and she could stay in the playroom only as long as she was cooperative and not whining. Within half an hour she started refusing to put toys away, crying, whining, and we felt it best to return her to her cubicle. This was the last time that I observed such a marked regression to her original behavior.

During the next few weeks Ruthie's legs were healing well, and bandage changes were now done on the floor without sedation and with increasingly less protest. Though it was now possible to reason with her, there were a few last token outbursts in the playroom. We could observe one when the doctor came and proposed a bandage change so that Ruthie would be ready for a visit home at Thanksgiving. She screamed and resisted, but I could explain the necessity of the bandage change to her, adding, "Let's get it over with." At this she stopped crying, said, "Alright," and was willing to go with the doctor. She was home part of Thanksgiving Day with no noticeable change in her behavior upon returning.

Several days later after already having had two dressing changes during one day, when the doctor mentioned that he had to change the abdominal dressing also, she burst into tears. I suggested that we could change the dressing on the doll. She stopped crying, became very absorbed in taping the doll's abdomen, wanted to tape also the doll's legs, and finished by taping the legs together. Still, until the time of her discharge, she occasionally cried and screamed when the nurses took her for a bandage change directly from the ward.

Since the introduction of the surgery equipment she asked to play with it almost daily, being absorbed usually at least an hour and sometimes during the whole day's play periods. In addition to other procedures, all primarily on the legs, she frequently gave injections into the bottom of the doll's feet, taped the doll's legs together, and sometimes first handcuffed the doll's arms before performing an operation. She was also very interested in taking the tape off broken dolls to see what was underneath.

In surgery play I noticed her being most able to sustain cooperative activity with other children and to play in my absence. The first request by another child for her presence was from one of her daily surgical companions, Ernest (age ten). One day when the playroom opened, he said, "You'd better hurry up, Ruthie, if you want to play surgery."

Some of her other play was also noteworthy. She was pretending that a doll was her daughter and was sick in the hospital. I asked her how her daughter was getting along. She said, "She had meningitis, but she is getting better." The same day in the doll house she had the father carrying the little girl and placing her in bed. I asked what the matter was, and she again answered, "She has meningitis." This sort of play and verbalizations were repeated many times in the ensuing weeks. Around this time Ruthie became fond of a two-and-a-half-year-old boy. Once when she was playing with the doll house and he started to move some of the furniture in it, I told him that Ruthie was playing with it now and that he must wait until she was finished (something that I had said numerous times in comparable situations to Ruthie). However, to my surprise, she said, "It's alright, he can play with me." When a movie was shown several days later, she wanted him to be near her and to touch him. (Ruthie had been told before she fell ill that her mother expected a baby.)

Another child, Greg (age six and hospitalized for an infected severe burn on his leg), also interested Ruthie very much. He first came to our attention through his uncontrollable temper tantrums during and following procedures, such as having blood drawn or bandages changed. One morning we noticed that Ruthie stayed to watch these two boys have their blood drawn and tried to comfort them. At other times the relationship of these two children was highly ambivalent. Both had to endure very painful procedures. While Ruthie struggled to get adjusted to her amputation, Greg must have feared that his leg, too, could be cut off if he did not fight every interference. They both received, but also had to share, a great deal of my attention.

One day, when I was holding Greg, and sitting next to Ruthie, I commented to Greg about whether he would get new shoes for Christmas; he said, "Yeah, you get your feet cut off and then you get new shoes for Christmas." Ruthie could take even this in her stride. She made no comment and just went on playing. However, on the whole she and Greg became progressively more disruptive of each other's play, grabbing toys from each other, etc., and it was sometimes necessary to have them play in different rooms.

We still saw evidence of Ruthie's struggle with the loss of her leg. One day, a student nurse was painting a large Santa Claus on a window and the perspective happened to make one leg appear shorter than the other. Ruthie asked the student nurse, "Why is one leg shorter? Did they cut it off, or did you just forget to put it on?"

During this time Ruthie continued to feel progressively closer to me. Once I was getting the puppet stage down for her from a high shelf. It looked as if it could be falling. She stated confidently, "You wouldn't let anything hurt me, would you." Another day when I was late because my car would not start, she expressed concern before I came in. After I arrived she immediately came over to see me and said that she had worried about me, adding, "I could help you start next time." Another day she impulsively grabbed my arm as I was leaving, held it close to her saying, "I love you."

Ruthie made excellent progress medically. The size of the bandages had been decreased almost daily; by now there was none on her left leg stump, and only the right foot was covered. She started standing on her right leg in physical therapy, and tried crutches two days later. She was now spending most of the afternoon learning to ambulate and was eager to go for her exercises, acting very warmly and cooperatively toward her physiotherapist.

It was also remarkable how completely at home she appeared to be with the condition of her legs. For instance, I happened to walk into the treatment room during one of the bandage changes and must have looked slightly stunned, for she reassured me, "It's alright, you can stay with me and watch." Another time in the playroom she told me how soft the new skin felt that was growing back on her leg, and took a worker's finger to touch the skin. Furthermore, there continued to be no hesitation in answering the other children's questions about her legs.

Two incidents in the next few days shortly before her discharge illustrate that she was now able to handle herself in contrast to her initial behavior. When a nurse came in to get Ruthie for a bandage change, Ruthie said pleasantly, "Alright, but can you wait a minute because I have to put the toys away first." The following day, Greg and another boy were playing with marbles. Ruthie went over and took some of the marbles from them. Greg protested and I stepped in and said that Greg was already playing and she could join them if they gave permission. She was silent a minute, then meekly asked and was accepted. The three of them soon made a game of putting the marbles in and out of the can and laughing merrily.

This ends Dr. Horwood's notes.

Parallel with our work with Ruthie, but much less intensive, was our work with the parents. It developed in the following way. There was great 'relief after all details of the illness and the amputation were discussed over and over again. Time was in our favor as the parents had about five weeks to get used to the necessity of surgery. They were most cooperative in helping us with Ruthie's adjustment in the playroom. However, after the date for surgery was finally set, the anxiety of relatives started to confuse both the parents and the physicians. A well-to-do great-uncle wanted to take the child to another hospital to ask for at least one more medical opinion, though

the gangrene was evident and shockingly convincing for both parents
and child. Two specialists on the hospital staff spent hours with the
great-uncle and the father to reiterate their medical plans for the
child. In this critical period—a week end—the senior author did not
talk to the parents. But she was on the ward before the child was
taken to surgery. Both parents were with Ruthie when her bed was
moved to the surgical floor. The mother joined the nurse who had
taken care of Ruthie, but the father turned away and could not face
the moment of parting. Only after the child had left did the mother
break into tears. By that time the father had found himself and
could support her.

The father may have felt shattered and useless at the thought that
a strong man could not protect his little girl and helplessly had to
accept the necessity for the amputation. He reassumed the role of the
disciplinarian in the family after the wound started healing and
appeared to push Ruthie into being a normal child.

Seven weeks after the amputation Ruthie returned home. She
came back to the hospital three times a week for training in ambulation. As her mother's pregnancy progressed, the father brought
Ruthie for her rehabilitation exercises. After her discharge from the
hospital the physical therapist became Ruthie's closest contact. However, she continued to be very positive and warm toward both
authors. Ambulation was interrupted by chicken pox which the
child stood well at home. A month after discharge, Ruthie was a
proficient crutch-walker. Less than five months after the operation,
she was fitted with a left leg prosthesis.

After the operation, the regular contact with the family was
switched to a medical social worker, who among other things helped
the family with getting assistance from the Society for Crippled
Children. Since the prosthesis will have to be changed periodically as
the child grows, this contact is very important.

It is obvious that we were concerned with how Ruthie would
cope with the arrival of the new baby. At the writing of this paper
the little boy is three months old. Ruthie has shown some jealousy,
occasionally demanded to be carried like the baby, but has taken his
arrival in her stride.

On a home visit five months after Ruthie's discharge, the junior
author was met by a confident, active little girl who warmly wel-

comed her, briefly showed her the new baby, and then demanded her full attention. Ruthie moved around the house with a noticeably abnormal gait, but with extreme agility—even climbing stairs. She wore regular oxford shoes. Her mother stated that she was learning to roller skate and to ride a bicycle, and that she played outdoors again.

These skills reflect the parents' ease and lack of need to over-protect her. They make great efforts to create a normal atmosphere for Ruthie to grow up in. Furthermore, Ruthie's mother could ask her if the stump hurt, in the natural tone of voice that would be used to ask if a child was tired. Ruthie has recently been registered in kindergarten for next Fall, and her mother reported that she had especially requested the principal to treat her just as any other girl.

During the visit the mother spontaneously said how much help she thought the special prosthesis doll had been for Ruthie to grow accustomed to the procedures that would have to take place. The mother also mentioned, though, that several times Ruthie had wondered whether a leg would grow out of her stump.

One other point in this case struck us as unusual—the tremendous reaction of the physicians to the amputation itself and to our role in the preparation for it. Some of the doctors had just started their service on the floor shortly before the time of amputation. Others had known the child since the beginning of her illness when death seemed almost unavoidable, and they reacted with renewed anxiety to this new crisis.

The intern, a warm, dedicated doctor, had done a very fine job in helping the parents accept the amputation, and he was the one who told the child. He was rather irritated, though, when we proceeded to give the child the prosthesis doll and discussed the impending operation with her again. Some of the newer nurses and doctors on the floor were actually hostile and angry about our continuing the preparation, and they found the doll "hideous" or "revolting." We needed the active support of the chief resident and the staff doctor in charge of the division to allow us to proceed according to our plan—something that had never been necessary before. Our good relationship was restored immediately when the child was on the way to recovery and when the staff's anxiety was dispelled as they saw the good results.

We will try to analyze what we attempted to do and what we think was achieved. When Ruthie entered the pediatric ward, our clear objective was to lay the ground work and then actually prepare her for the forthcoming leg amputation. We had to take into account her immediately preceding experience in the contagious ward of being critically ill and at one point very close to death, and of having continuously to undergo many frightening and painful procedures. We would be working with a child who had had great difficulty accepting authority even before her illness and who was bright and able to verbalize well. Greatly in our favor was the fact that her intelligent, conscientious parents were, after their early resistance, eager for help with the preparation.

Our general plan before surgery was threefold. First, we felt it essential that Ruthie form a strong, trusting relationship, primarily with one worker from the playroom. Arrangements would be made to bring her to the playroom as much as possible where she would be helped to feel at home. We would strive for consistency and security in the playroom environment and with personnel; we would attempt to be very conscientious in carrying through on plans and promises, but also on limitations which would not be changed by her demands. We would try to help her realize that only when her behavior became more positive would other children choose to play with her.

Second, we decided not to prepare for the amputation too far ahead of the actual operation. This meant that we would not talk about the legs except when she brought up the topic, and even then would introduce no new material.

Third, when time for preparation came, we would try to give as complete information as possible about the amputation. Our general theme in introducing this explanation would be, "Most everything is healing well except your one leg. The doctors will have to help this leg." Gradually we would move toward telling how the doctors would help.

Following the child's lead, we then switched from a direct approach to the use of the prosthesis doll as an adjunct to the preparation, thereby turning her passivity as a patient into activity in play and verbalization.

We do not think that any existing dolls (like the commercially available amputation dolls, where arms or legs can be pulled off) would have filled the needs of this child. Our problem was not to find an outlet for aggression and for atoning for it by restitution through pulling off a limb and sticking it on again, but to help the child to understand and integrate the fact that the useless leg had to be taken off, that nothing would grow back there, but that through the skill of the physiatrist the new artificial leg would take on the functions of the lost one.

Postoperatively, there were several things we had planned to help Ruthie with: verbalize what had happened during the operation, give continual reassurance that the artificial leg would come when the stump was sufficiently well healed; and prepare as completely as possible for any bandage changes, wound revisions, and skin grafts that would occur.

Feelings after the loss of the leg could be expressed in play with the surgery equipment. The word "play" seems inadequate—it was rather an intense, absorbed activity with the equipment, not an outlet for anger, but again an attempt to understand and to integrate. The aggression found its outlet in Ruthie's relation to people —parents, workers, and children—and with some playthings. It decreased proportionately as the leg began to heal and as she knew that she would walk again.

Our methods and goals were different from a treatment situation in a psychiatric setting. We had to work with this child not in individual interviews, but as part of a group program for many children. Though we hoped fervently to be able to help this little girl, we had responsibility for many other children with a great variety of medical and emotional problems, who needed us as well.

Since we function in a department of pediatrics, our work was geared to the needs immediately resulting from the illness and its management, but not to uncovering the child's deeper emotional problems. Eventually we would help her make the transition to returning home and being followed in physical therapy.

Ruthie could modify her original behavior sufficiently to allow herself to use our help. She seemed unusually well able to accept the amputation once it was performed, and afterwards became increasingly better able to cooperate with procedures as time went on. The by-product of this experience was that a warm, likable little girl emerged who could form positive trusting relationships with the unavoidably large number of people who had to care for her.

We found several details the same as Joyce Robertson (1956) described them in her report on her daughter's tonsillectomy: the need to get rid of the diseased organ (by throwing away the doll's black leg), and the open masturbation postoperatively.

We did not start out with a definite and detailed plan how to prepare this child, but were feeling our way. This was such an unusual case that we could not draw on previous experience.

The way we managed to help Ruthie through her illness may be applicable in other children's hospitals. However, one may have to deal quite differently with a child of different background, age, sex, or degree of verbal accessibility. We probably would develop other ways of preparation if the child were a boy or older, though we note that Pearson's Case 1 (1941), the only case of leg amputation on a child we found reported in the psychological literature, concerns a boy of ten whose emotional reaction to the impending operation was markedly similar to Ruthie's.[2] We feel that the manner in which we attempted to work with this girl—with understanding of the meaning of her behavior, though without choosing to work on a deeper level—worked out beneficially.

---

[2] How a nine-year-old boy was "sickened to his heart's core" when he was not prepared for an amputation of the same type is forcefully described in Hawkes's autobiography (1915).

PART II

PHYSICAL ILLNESS

5

COMMENTS ON THE PSYCHOLOGICAL CONSEQUENCES OF CRYPTORCHISM

A Clinical Study

PETER BLOS, Ph.D.
(1960)

I. INTRODUCTORY REMARKS

The psychoanalytic literature contains only scant references to the testicles and their role in the mental life of the male child.[1] This fact alone invites a report on cases with undescended testicles in which these body parts due to their abnormal state assumed a role of specific psychological import. There is no doubt that the male child concentrates almost exclusively on one part of his genitals, namely, the penis, while the other parts (scrotum, testes) are but peripherally and transiently acknowledged. With reference to this fact Freud (1923a) commented: "It is remarkable, by the way, what a small degree of interest the other part of the male genitals, the little sac with its contents, arouses in the child. From all one hears in analyses one could not guess that the male genitals consist of anything more than the penis" (p. 246). However, the male child is not totally unaware of the scrotal region and possesses tactile as well as visual knowledge of it. This is exemplified by the self-observation of a two-and-a-half-year-old boy who had noticed that an undescended testicle had come down into the scrotal sac. He had noticed the change and was perturbed by it. The father, a pediatrician, had paid no special attention to the previous condition and was surprised at the child's self-observation and negative reaction. The little boy wanted it changed back to the way it had been; he "didn't like" two testicles. The change and newness of this body part was initially disturbing to the child but was assimilated within a short time.

---

[1] [Since this paper was written, Anita Bell published a series of studies devoted to this topic (1961, 1964, 1965).]

Analytic experience with male patients, children and adults, bears out the fact that the penis as a pleasure-giving organ is more highly cathected with libido and aggressive energy than the other parts of the male genital. However, under the abnormal condition of an undescended testicle the genitals assume a special role. It is not my contention to infer that in the deviate condition of an undescended testicle, there appears in magnified dimension a primary cathexis of the testicle. Quite to the contrary, I consider the dominant role of the testicle apparent in the following cases to be of a secondary order, namely, determined by environmental influences. I do not consider cryptorchism in itself as pathogenic. Only secondarily, within the matrix of a disturbed parent-child relationship, does this condition acquire a profoundly detrimental influence on the mental development of the child. The anxious (aggressive) preoccupation of the environment with the genital defectiveness of the child eventually designates the testicle as the focal genital part in relation to which the formation of the body image and psychosexual development in general becomes specifically distorted. The genital defect, then, serves in the mental life of the child as the "organizing experience" (Greenacre, 1956) and results in ego deformations of a rather typical pattern. Fantasy life, restitutive acts, ego functions and defensive operations, self- and body image, sexual identification were studied in a number of cases of cryptorchism; three of them are reported here in detail. It must be borne in mind that the usual body-damage anxiety of the male child is in these boys associated with a missing testicle, i.e., with an already accomplished fact over which they have no control. The body-part loss is no longer a threat because it is palpably verifiable. On the other hand, a restitution of the loss is always kept within the realm of possibility as attested by the frequent medical check-ups and interventions. Napoleon's famous dictum, which Freud (1912) paraphrased into saying that "anatomy is destiny," assumes in these cases a special meaning, because here anatomy remains alterable—at least, that is the promise which the environment never ceases to impute. Consequently, anatomical uncertainty is destiny.

It became apparent in the cases presented how the body image is shaped by sensory perception in conjunction with environmental responses to the body and its defect. In this connection it was particularly striking to see that the body change, such as spontaneous descent (case of Larry) or successful operative correction (cases of Steven and Joe) resulted in a rapid shift of behavior, attitudes, interests, and skills. This change cannot be credited to the resolution of endopsychic conflicts alone. The clinical observation of cathectic shifts which were brought about by the restoration of body intactness has theoretical and therapeutic implications which shall be discussed after the case material has been presented.

In all three cases there occurred a mysterious exclusion of the physical condition of unilateral cryptorchism from the rest of the case histories. In two cases the fact of undescended testicles had to be surmised through symptomatic acts of the child. The parents did not mention the child's condition initially, nor did the boy himself ever refer to it. Symbolic representation of the genital defect was abundant in the play material and behavior. In all cases a medical clarification of the genital status was attained. Therapy always came to an impass whenever the medical planning for restorative intervention (injection or operation) was indefinitely postponed. The therapist had hoped against hope that the child after having worked through his fantasies would in due time disclose spontaneously his genital condition. Only under the pressure of medical intervention became such fantasies available in therapy, i.e., could serve as a vehicle to interpret distortions and defenses. Anatomical as well as sexual enlightenment was given in great detail, especially in the cases where the child had to be prepared for an impending operation.

The three boys studied were in the prepubertal age. The orchidopexy on Steven was performed at the age of ten years three months; on Joe at the age of twelve years ten months; spontaneous descent was confirmed in the case of Larry at the age of ten years eleven months. This paper is in no way a report on the therapy of the three boys. Their respective diagnostic categories had little in common; however, their symptom pictures showed significant similarities which were due to the identical genital defect which they shared. The presence of this physical factor indeed blurred the diagnostic and prognostic assessment of the cases to a considerable extent.

Where the maldescent was corrected spontaneously there was far more doubt about and distrust in the permanency of the restoration than in the operative cases. In the latter the action was accepted as final, and more faith was lent to the surgeon's knife than was given to an act of nature. This difference we can attribute to the masochistic and the castrative wishes which contrary to all expectations turned the defective boy into an intact man. He who entered the lion's den had come out alive. Besides the assurance of body intactness, the operation also demonstrated that the body had not been permanently injured by masturbation. Of course, we can detect behind the masculine euphoria which followed the operation an overcompensation of persistent feminine strivings.

The mere condition of an undescended testicle certainly does not lead to similar diagnostic entities, because cryptorchism cannot be considered as pathogenic in itself. However, it lends different conditions some points of similarity since the genital defect assumes in these cases an influence of dominant importance. Whatever the diagnostic category, the "organizing experience," namely, cryptorchism, was the same for all of them. The existence of identical symptoms in our cases became apparent, such as motility disturbances (hyperactivity), learning difficulties, and accident proneness in the form of a compulsive toying with physical danger. To this triad must be added a state of social inadequacy and chronic indecision; furthermore, a tendency to exaggerate, to lie, and to fantasy. Most striking was the disappearance or drastic diminution of these symptoms once the intactness of the genital organ either spontaneously or operatively was established. The clinical material suggests that cryptorchism influences symptom choice, regardless of the nosological designation of the case. It seems that the different disorders represented in the case material found in the genital defect a palpable and visible reality around which the respective pathology of each case was articulated.

II. Clinical Material[2]

The Case of Steven

Steven, a slender, friendly boy of eight, was brought to treatment by his mother upon the recommendation of the school: in the third

---

2 The three boys whose cases are reported here were treated at the Madeleine Borg Child Guidance Institute, Jewish Board of Guardians. The treatment was supervised by the author.

grade, he was still practically a nonreader. He gave the impression of an atypical (borderline) child, with poor motor coordination (clumsy gait, "like a drunkard," inept in games, illegible handwriting); infantile behavior (does not feed, bathe, dress himself; chews on his clothes; messy child: drops ink, flour, food on the floor, spills soil from flowerpots in his room and on his bed); intense preoccupation with death and time; anxious and worried.

Steven was born with the left testis undescended. A tumor on the scrotum was removed at five months. The mother felt that she had caused the tumor "by poking around these parts so much." At seven Steven had a tonsillectomy with subsequent hemorrhages which necessitated his return to the hospital. In the same year he received eight hormone injections which were not followed by a descent of the testis but increased the size of the penis and stimulated the growth of pubic hair. Numerous doctors were consulted. Finally, the source of all of Steven's troubles was thought by the mother to be located in a weak muscle of the left eye, but the ophthalmologist did not confirm this.

The mother was of the opinion that the boy was oblivious of his testicular condition and did not know why so many doctors had examined him. She believed that her show of pseudo confidence and unconcern had protected him from all doubts about his bodily intactness. This defensive attitude on her part was due to her narcissistic involvement with the child: having been disappointed in her own career, in her husband, and in her first son, she had made Steven the center of her emotional life and wanted him to be the genius who would fulfill her wildest ambitions. Steven's father was a passive and withdrawn man who, according to the boy, "did not know what goes on at home." Five years before Steven's birth he had suffered and recovered from a psychotic episode with paranoid delusions. He never showed any interest in Steven's therapy.

During the first interview Steven questioned the therapist as to why he was visiting a doctor again. His guidance teacher had wanted him to go to the eye clinic, but he had been told by the doctor that there was nothing wrong with his eye. In the second interview, he stated that he had kissed a girl and got two sores on his mouth from it; at least, that is what his mother had said, while he himself was not sure: he thought his lips were chapped before.

After this introduction he became involved in dramatic play in which he was the doctor taking care of dolls suffering from a polio condition, having been born with a knife which made them stiff; identifying with the aggressor, he was the surgeon and could be trusted having a sure hand. But at other times his anxiety came through: Steven's grandfather had died after an operation, the nature of which he ignored (actually a prostate operation); but he was sure "it was not in the leg system, it might have been bleeding ulcers." At such times of blatant denial he did not want the dolls to be operated on.

Later in the treatment the boy's play shifted to aggressive themes of shooting and killing; he and his therapist were the two best gunmen in the world. Dynamite (clay) had to be hidden from the outlaws, for it could easily have blown up the world. Over and over he was kneading clay without ever shaping anything; he always wanted the clay he had been kneading to be saved for the next session.

The mother still maintained that the child had no knowledge of his condition. But when the doctor decided to perform an operation, Steven had to be told of it. This the mother did gingerly, only to be interrupted by the boy who told her that he was not stupid and had known all along why people had been poking around there. In his treatment he now openly revealed his anxiety which was so intense that he was unable to comprehend an anatomical sketch his therapist drew for him. His play during these sessions had become very infantile.

Steven made a last effort to dispense with the operation. He wanted to sit in the therapist's chair: "I like to be you and you to be me." Could "hes" be made into "shes"? He was completely ignorant of the origin of babies and the function of the testes: the growing testis "in the stomach" was confused with the foetus. Soon after the boy had admitted that he had always "felt himself" (masturbated) he could listen to the details of the operation. He was then also able to recapitulate his long history of medical interventions. Several months after a successful operation, Steven described the sensation in his testes: he knew what he felt, he no longer was confused.

His play now consisted in building a Stevensville Museum: two marbles of special stone were on exhibit. He soon lost interest in this kind of play and became more oriented toward schoolwork, the boy scouts, friends, chess play, piano lessons, etc. His active interest in the environment reflected the appearance of a belated latency period. Peer relations and organized physical activities began to play an important part in his life. His clumsiness improved noticeably. Near the end of therapy, one year after the operation, he had advanced to his grade level in reading. His critical judgment about himself and others had increased; there was less need to ingratiate himself by being charming and cute; he had made striking gains in the realm of social effectiveness. But in times of stress he reverted to infantile and disorganized reactions. The separation from his mother, which he now aggressively enforced, was laden with guilt and anxiety. The simple comfort found in dependency was no longer available to him. As to the mother, she had been helped to refrain from involving the boy in her own fantasy life; her need to deny his imperfections had significantly lessened. The growing adequacy of the child was recognized by the father who became progressively more interested in his son.

The Case of Larry

When Larry was referred to the clinic at the age of nine years ten months, he presented such a variety of symptoms that it was feared that the neurotic manifestations in conjunction with conduct and habit disorders might mask a more malignant pathology. The major complaints were: soiling, nocturnal enuresis, psychogenic headaches, accident proneness; he fought with other children, refused to do his homework, could not concentrate in school; he had fright reactions to the dentist, to blood, and to monsters which appeared in his fantasies and nightmares; he had difficulty in falling asleep, refused to be covered up or held down. The mother was vague and contradictory in her description of the child: she appeared on the one hand to be indulgent when the child was "nice," but on the other hand she beat him with a strap for misbehaving; she was full of angry contempt for the weak males of her family, her husband and three sons. Larry had two brothers, one two years older and the other four years younger. The father, when he was finally seen, presented himself as a withdrawn man, afraid of his wife's criticism, and carrying out her orders obediently. Actually he had genuine and warm feelings for Larry, and much sympathetic understanding of him.

Larry had been a healthy infant. At two and a half years he was noted to have a hernia and a hydrocele, referred to by the mother as a "skin tumor on the left testicle." The conditions were corrected at a hospital where the child stayed for ten days. During this period he was frightened, depressed, or uncontrollably wild. The hyperactivity accompanied by many accidents had been part of his behavior pattern since that time: the most tragic mishap—it happened while he played in the park soon after he had started treatment at the clinic—resulted in the loss of his left eye. The child expressed to his therapist great rage at his mother who had not told him after the operation that his eyeball had been removed: he had noticed it on the doctor's chart while still wearing his bandage. This irreparable, self-induced injury was subsequently linked to the physical restraint imposed on him during the operation on the genital and to the mother's demand for passivity. A circuitous process had become established: the motoric rage had become turned against the self, bringing about actively what he feared of suffering at the hands of the "monsters."

A ritual accompanying the headaches was soon revealed: they were always due to a "strong light" hitting his eyes. He then had to lie down in the dark with his face covered and he would fall asleep. The headaches always followed an arousal of anger and hostility; they seemed to have started at the time of the operation on the genital. This ritual enabled us to understand the sadomasochistic conflict in Larry.

Ever since the loss of the eye, Larry complained of "bellyaches." A dynamic link seemed probable: the suspicion arose that the boy had an undescended testicle. The mother was questioned, and the assumption proved to be correct. Larry, however, was supposed to ignore this fact. His confusion about operations, needles, hernia contained a tacit accusation against his parents for never having told him the truth about his physical problems. The question arose whether the sacrifice of the eyeball was a substitute body-part relinquishment in order to salvage the more precious ball buried in his belly; or was the self-castrating act a masochistic surrender of his masculinity which brought temporary relief from an intolerable state of panic and terror, namely, to be attacked by a castrating monster-woman? Soiling ceased soon after his fear of going to the toilet was understood as a fear of losing his undescended testicle with his feces.

Finally, the boy's fear of "another operation" came to the fore. He had overheard his father speak of this possibility in case "the testicle does not stay down." This prospect made the child anxious, which in turn aroused in him aggressive feelings toward his parents and resulted in a bicycle accident. He became panicky about an infection of his good eye (which was in perfect condition) and feared going blind; he requested that a night light be kept on in his room so he could see whenever he woke up during the night. This assured him that his eyesight was intact and that his good eye was still there. He dreamed of getting pieces of glass into his good eye and losing it. He dreamed of an "eye bank" where new eyes could be gotten.

Treatment had progressively become the boy's refuge. He used the therapist's name at home to restrain the mother from undue interference. In his sessions he turned tables by playing the role of the teacher, who for so long had been a phobic object, and asking the therapist to be the pupil. At home, he was steadily gaining in independence; he bathed and dressed himself. At school he became more attentive and interested in his work. By the same token he had become more compulsive, and was worrying about his home-work, etc. When the boy urged his therapist to see his father, this facilitated a discussion of the boy's undescended testicle, and the father arranged for a medical examination to determine whether an operation was indicated. The examination ascertained the fact that the left testis had descended, was permanently located in the scrotum but was somewhat smaller than the right one. Larry, of course, knew this.

Constructive self-assertion and compulsive cautiousness gradually replaced the alternating bursts of destructive rages (such as "to blow up the whole family" with his chemistry set) and of the self-damaging activities which once threatened to make an invalid of him. His realistic interest in science had grown steadily; he had set up his own chemical laboratory at home. He no longer threw himself head-long into new experiences but interposed judgment before he embarked on a new course of action. He now played with boys of his own age instead of with younger children. In his daily tasks he took initiative and was no longer a pawn in the hands of terrifying monsters. His aggressive drive had found sublimated expression in his activities: at school he became captain of the safety squad. At home he defended himself against his mother's influence with stubborn determination; nobody else found Larry any longer unreasonably difficult to manage or to get along with.

The Case of Joe

Joe, a tall, heavy, light-skinned Negro with pubescence already manifest, was nine years old when he was referred to the clinic by his school because of his restlessness, excessive boasting, daydreaming, and learning difficulties. He was found to be a lonely and fearful child whose history revealed that his activities had been restricted until the age of six because of a congenital heart murmur and that his urge for activity had then broken through and asserted itself in uncontrollable hypermotility.

The mother, who wanted her boy to be gentle and mild mannered, was doing her utmost to suppress in him all upsurges of male self-assertion. The child's two older sisters had been taught to baby the little "invalid." The father was disappointed in the lack of boyish behavior and interests in Joe, and although a good provider, he was spending little time in the home and did not share in the life of the family.

Joe had been in treatment for three years before his undescended testicles were inadvertently mentioned by the mother. His petty stealing, his tall tales, his constant references to secrets, the compulsive chair balancing which led to his falling, became intelligible when related to the genital defect. It was decided to concentrate on two areas: the ego dysfunction, i.e., his inability to read and the anxiety attached to the genital defectiveness. It was also decided to try and enlist the father's cooperation in spite of Joe's strenuous attempts to leave his father out of his treatment.

The interviews which the therapist had with the father resulted in his taking Joe to the doctor: the course of treatment was explained to the child. The period of injections which followed was one of anxiety for the boy. The fact that "nothing happened" after the injections opened up the frightening possibility of an operation. Joe refused to discuss this, insisting that he had talked to his sisters about it and that there was nothing more to say. His behavior became quite mischievous, almost delinquent, and he was full of complaints about the tutor who, he said, was unable to help him.

The now impending operation was linked by Joe with his tonsillectomy. The doctor might find that the testis was no good, cut it out, and throw it away. His fear of sterility, should he be left with only one good testicle, was talked over with the therapist. Joe could now ask questions about it, and while he felt free to do so, he was at the same time making progress in reading. His tutor also noticed an increased ability to learn and a longer concentration span. Joe at this time introduced a new topic in his treatment, namely, his girl friends. A sudden wave of interest had swept him into the realm of early adolescent emotions. With bravado he told the therapist that he knew everything about sex.

The father's distrust of doctors and the mother's helplessness in planning for the operation ("I only know how to take care of girls") forced the therapist to assume the main responsibility for making all arrangements with surgeon and hospital. Joe was appreciative of this help. Yet for the first time, as soon as the operation was planned, the boy's aggression against his mother came to the fore: she was not helping him, she was trying to make a girl out of him, he was not going to tolerate being treated in this way. He considered it an insult to his masculinity to have a woman doctor examine him at the hospital. At the same time, his fear of castration was being expressed: he often referred to his tonsillectomy when "the knife had slipped and cut a hole in his throat."

As the time for the operation approached, a flood of interest in sexual information burst forth. The rising competition with his father combined with his usual attempt to submit to his mother precipitated an acute struggle in sexual identification which became intensified by the impending operation.

After the operation was performed successfully, it was the healing process in conjunction with the imposed restriction of activity which made the boy anxious and angry. He oscillated between his passive-submissive and his aggressive-masculine trends. The doctor's opinion served during this time as a yardstick for the realistic evaluation of his condition. Joe now desired to learn to swim, to play ball and fight. He expressed the wish to improve himself generally. An itch in the genital area, which he located in his testes, opened up a discussion about masturbation and nocturnal emissions. It was essential now for the therapist, a woman, gradually to transfer the discussion of sexual enlightenment to the father because the excitement relating to such interchange promoted too intense an erotic attraction. The father, in the meantime, had become more accepting of his now "complete" son.

Learning, which had taken a leap since the operation, continued to progress. Joe could do his homework, he went to the library, he asked his father for help and opinion on such topics as elections and strikes. The struggle for his masculinity now dominated his life; therapy entered a drawn-out period of "working through" in which the liberated affects had to be guided into the phase-adequate conflicts of adolescence, preventing the extremes of a surrender to submissiveness or a blind thrust into frantic self-assertion and rebellion.

III. Discussion

Cryptorchism and Family Interaction

The pre-eminence which the genital defect plays in the mental life of the three boys appears to be of a secondary order. The three boys had mothers who promoted feminine tendencies either by rejecting the maleness in the boy who was afflicted with a genital imperfection (Steven, Larry) or by showing a strong preference for a female child and holding out a love premium for passive, submissive behavior (Joe). All three boys were dependent on their mothers in terms of her narcissistic needs. These needs became manifest in the mother's extraordinary ambitions which had to be realized by her male offspring (Steven, Larry), or the mother's contempt of male sexuality which she considered destructive and undesirable; this led to her total acceptance of the genital defect in her son (Joe). In the latter case the genital defect represented for the mother an asset rather than a calamity. Whether the mother concentrated on this imperfection because of her own unrealized ambitions and hopes (overcompensatory expectations), or whether she welcomed the defective state of the son, in either case the attitude of the mother had to be considered as the pathogenic factor of primary order: it had a castrating impact.

This effect became further elaborated by the fathers' remoteness in the lives of all three boys. All concern and initiative had been delegated to their wives. The genital defectiveness of the child engendered in each father a sense of disappointment and dissatisfaction which deepened with the boy's fearful and "unboyish" behavior. The three fathers tried to disengage themselves from the difficulties their sons encountered and it was necessary in each case firmly to request the father's visit to the clinic. The fact that the father was subsequently made a partner and supporter of the son's therapy proved to constitute an essential dynamic configuration for treatment: it represented to the boy the paternal approbation of his male strivings and consequently facilitated masculine identification. As long as the boy was exposed to the mother's belittling attitude of the father, he felt that his own masculinity was acceptable only on his mother's terms.

The fathers responded to an earnest appeal by the therapist with cooperation and active interest. It goes without saying that their own precarious marital position had made them eager sympathizers with their sons' plight, and we gained the impression that the fathers had secretly waited for a cue to speak up and be heard. Forrer (1959) in a report on the mother of a defective child made the same observation, namely, that the belittled and excluded father turned out to be the child's respected and loved parent. The mothers' descriptions of their husbands all sounded alike: "A dull, uncommunicative and unreasonable man" (Forrer, 1959); on closer inspection this man turned out to be an intimidated, shy, but quite capable and loving father.

The emotional distance which the fathers maintained in the marriage extended to their sons who felt deserted by them and left to the controlling (castrating) influence of their mothers. A typical rescue maneuver which two of the boys employed in this dilemma consisted in the idealization of the father, or rather in a summary denial of the negative and depreciatory feelings he extended toward his son. An illusory father image, unshakable by reality, served as an anchor in the masculine position of the oedipus complex and could be upheld only by a scotomatized view of the father's role in family interaction. Joe, emotionally deserted by his father and pressed by his mother into feminine tasks, exclaimed with desperate insistence:

"My mind is my dad." The mother of Larry actually entered into
a conspiracy with her son and allowed him to swim in unsafe waters
in spite of the father's explicit disapproval. Consequently, he and
mother shared a "secret" which aroused oedipal guilt and made itself
felt as resistance in treatment.

While the genital defect occupied all the mothers either actively
("poking around," examining, going from doctor to doctor, etc.) or
negatively (ignoring it, postponing examination, not following or
forgetting medical advice, hoping naïvely for a spontaneous descent
"because the sac is there to receive it," etc.), it was striking to notice
how they either had managed to conceal the genital condition at
intake or had sidetracked it in some fashion to forestall any definitive
clarification. The insignificant role which the mothers tried to attribute to the genital condition was further obscured by their stubborn
emphasis on other issues, such as the child's learning difficulty or his
lack of friends. The referral was usually made by the school because
only under duress could the mother be mobilized to take a step which
would publicly demonstrate her own defectiveness and expose her
inability in modeling the child according to her wishes. The mother's
ambition for the child to be a genius, or to excel academically, or
be perfect and well behaved, reflected her own insufficiency feelings,
forcefully denied in the child by displacement of the genital defectiveness to areas of intellectual achievement and exemplary behavior.
These three boys disappointed their mothers' ambitions; the school
had to impress on the family that their sons had failed. The mothers
maintained an illusory image of their sons in order to ward off a
narcissistic defeat. They maintained the fantasy that their concentration and determination would succeed in changing the child
(Forrer, 1959). They had a tendency toward depressive reactions in
which their aggressive, retaliatory, and castrating wishes toward the
male constituted an essential part.

The mothers' suppressed sadism became apparent in the unreasonable delays concerning medical intervention such as injection
or operation. Their fear of a disaster (e.g., hemorrhaging in Steven's
case) deterred them from an objective appraisal of a medical recommendation. Their impaired judgment appears throughout in relation
to the child, especially in matters of health: this is exemplified by
Steven's mother telling the boy that he got two sores on his mouth

from kissing a girl; or Larry's mother telling him that he gets head-aches from not eating properly. In this connection, of course, the devious and deceptive treatment of the genital condition deserves mentioning; in order not to arouse the child's self-consciousness or suspicion the mother might examine the boy without explanation or by giving an irrelevant reason; the deception appeared also in the falsification of facts as in Larry's case when he was told that he needed injections for a hernia which, the boy knew, had been corrected at the age of two and a half. Such parental opinions are expressed with a single-mindedness of conviction which leaves the boy in uncertainty as to the validity of his own observation, thinking, and experience.

The particular way in which the genital defect is perceived and experienced by the parents, particularly the mother, accounts for the child's preoccupation with the testes. The perpetrator of the body damage is in the child's mind identified with the mother. Her castrating possessiveness and the father's passive aloofness both constitute a matrix of family interaction in which cryptorchism gives rise to a typical symptom picture. The parents' attitude in conjunction with the child's own observation of his anatomical abnormality combine into a body schema, or body image, around which any existing psychological impairment is elaborated. The defective body image itself was found to be responsible for specific aspects of the pathology in each case.

The Prototypical Experience (Trauma)

An operation trauma had occurred in the lives of all three boys. This trauma became subsequently linked to the genital defect and to any medical intervention which might occur sooner or later. Fantasies and drive propensities which had rendered the first operation, such as hernioplasty or tonsillectomy, a traumatic event attached themselves by a process of direct substitution to the genital actuality.

In Steven's case we can recognize in the testicle complex an aggregate of experiences which date from various periods of his life. Their accrued effect appeared in condensed form in his play productions. The first operation (hydrocele) involved the scrotum. The mother's guilt and conviction that she had caused the "tumor" had made her particularly attentive to her son's genital region and to the clumsy gait presumably associated with it. This gait continued to persist up to the time of his orchidopexy. Another body-damage anxiety (castration fear) attached itself to the genital defect and found expression in the doctor play when Steven announced that his doll patients had to have an operation on account of their "stiffness." Steven, the doctor postponed the operation several times; when it was finally performed several of his patients died.

In this connection the consequence of hormone injections at the age of seven should not be overlooked or minimized. The sudden rise of sexual stimulation caused a flooding of the ego by instinctual pressures and became manifest in genital sensations (erections) and erotic feelings (kissing of women). At this very time of increased sexual pressures, a tonsillectomy was performed. This operation made a lasting and terrifying impression on the child due to two hemorrhages which followed the operation and required rehospitalization. Fear of doctors and operations, and fear of death remained with Steven from then on; all three fears found an eloquent expression in his doctor play. Furthermore, he ascribed the death of his grandfather either to the surgeon's clumsiness ("the knife had slipped") or to an uncontrollable bleeding, to a hemorrhage, to "bleeding ulcers." His fear of castration became affirmed by his negation expressed in the statement that his grandfather's operation (prostatectomy) had "certainly not been in the leg system." It is interesting to note that Steven attached the blame for the death of his doll patients to the nurse who was clumsy. He voiced in this accusation what I have already alluded to, namely, that the archaic mother is held responsible for the "genital death" (castration).

In Joe's case the tonsillectomy at four years of age left an indelible impression; the memory of it with the typical infantile distortions offered itself as a model of the impending orchidopexy. The testicle will be excised as the tonsils had been and thrown away if found to be no good. Joe was still convinced that the doctor had "cut a hole in his throat"; this "castration wish" phantom organ he expected to become real by the orchidopexy; i.e., he fantasied that the operation would make him into a girl.

In Larry's case the hernioplasty at the age of two and a half years served as the prototypical experience in which the attack on his eyes (bright light) became linked to body-image anxiety as a retaliation for his uncontrollable rages against the mother. His headache ritual preserved this trauma which he attempted to master by repetition, until it finally yielded to the combined effects of insight into his aggressive urges on the one hand and of the attainment of genital intactness on the other.

A twelve-year-old boy might be mentioned here who had a long history of medical examinations in connection with "one testicle being smaller than the other." Psychotherapy had been at a standstill for an alarmingly long time due to the parents' persistent plea not to have the testicle condition discussed with the boy since this only would make him "self-conscious" and add insult to injury. The boy's symptomatic behavior, such as walking around "blind" (i.e., with his eyes shut) in order to test whether he would hurt himself, pointed clearly to the "testicle syndrome" as described here. This made it mandatory to have the physical condition moved into the focus of awareness through medical evaluation. After the medical examination requested and arranged by the clinic had taken place, it was established that one testicle was atrophied. When the therapist discussed the examination and its findings with the boy he answered that the doctor could not find anything wrong with him. Confronted with the fact he admitted his knowledge of the testicle condition which he had rendered vague and unreal by "not having touched [investigated] himself for quite a number of years." Then he changed the subject, significantly, to a discussion of his tonsillectomy. Soon it became apparent that his knowledge of the male and female genitals was contained in a bisexual, distorted imagery. Only after the body had attained by medical dictum a state of definitive structure—in this case one of permanent genital defectiveness—was it possible to cope in treatment with the psychological implications of the body reality.

The various focal apprehensions as outlined above represented a fusion of the early operation trauma with subsequent drive organizations. Every threat to the body integrity revived the original trauma in a phase-specific modality. By reprojection the child experienced the current danger in terms of the past traumatic event. This might be paraphrased by saying: "What I thought happened to me then will certainly be repeated now." This reasoning is exemplified by Joe's equating tonsils and testicles, and by his belief that the testicle will be thrown away as the tonsils were, and last but not least, by the fact that the early operation was experienced as a castration. These connotations of childhood operations are well known and have been described by Anna Freud (1952), Jessner et al. (1952), and others.

In all three cases it became clear that the genital defect served as the "organizing experience" which subordinated early trauma as well as all subsequent phase-specific anxieties about body damage to the persistent genital defectiveness. How this condition affected the formation of the body image will be discussed later. The facts that the genital incompleteness had existed as far as memory extends and had at the same time remained uncertain as to its ultimate outcome; and furthermore, that operative correction remained for years a whispered prospect, necessarily kept the early operation trauma alive in terms of specific, primitive misconceptions and distortions. Body-damage anxiety became a chronic affect, the mastery of which was attempted by various means. Obviously an early operation trauma is not an obligatory experience in cases of cryptorchism in order to produce disturbances similar to those that are described here. Nevertheless, we shall find that traumatic body-damage anxiety (such as related to body-part loss in, e.g., bowel training or castration fantasies), which under normal circumstances is gradually mastered, remains in an unbound state due to the continuance of the physical defect to which it is attached. The concreteness of the defect in conjunction with the uncertainty of its correction does not allow any definitive settlement of the issue—indeed, not of any issue. It is therefore characteristic of cryptorchism that by its very nature it precludes the definite psychic integration of the defect and instead favors fluid defenses. These were found to yield rather easily under the impact of a definitive physical repair and were then replaced by more stable defenses and adaptive behavior.

Body Image and Ego Impairment

We are well acquainted with the fact that clarity and stability of the body image exert an essential influence on the development and structure of the secondary autonomy of the ego. Any serious distortion of the body image will become manifest in some specific ego impairment. Experience tells us that some component functions of the ego possess greater resistivity to impairment than others.

In cases of body defect the choice of defensive measures as well as restitutive fantasy elaborations are influenced by the nature of the defect and by its physical location. The distinction of inside and outside of the body does not apply clearly to cryptorchism. The defect is palpable and observable but not exposed to the public eye; yet it is not definitive but reparable. These factors determine to a large extent the concept of genital defectiveness which the child evolves. The physical condition, due to its undecided and unpredictable nature, lends itself to the absorption of the specific emotional conflicts and body-damage anxieties which play a more or less transient role in the development of every male child.

The genital defectiveness has played a prominent role in the lives of the three boys from an early age on. Later it became the focus of comparison with and likeness to other boys, affecting the sense of identity and resulting in social incompatibility and maladjustment. Having no friends and not knowing how to make friends was equally evident in all three cases. Steven turned to little girls, Larry to a younger immature boy, and Joe to semidelinquents in order to gratify their social hunger. The emergence of more adequate social relations became evident in all three cases at the end of treatment.

The ego impairments most marked in these three cases appeared as disturbances in learning, memory, thinking, and time-space perception; they could be linked to the mother's inconsistent attitude by which she tacitly forbade the child to recognize his physical defect clearly or to think rationally about it. Furthermore, these impairments were due to a defective body image which had remained undeveloped by having retained primitive qualities of vagueness, of indefiniteness, and incompleteness; in some way, it had never been fully assembled. Peto's remarks (1959) are relevant to this point: "Symbolism in dreams and folk-lore indicates that finding and evaluating external reality is to a great extent determined by refinding one's own body in the environment. Thus the body image is of decisive importance in grasping the world around us. Peculiarities of one's body image may then cause to be conceived as a world which is different from that visualized by the average human being."

The concept of time played a particular role in these cases because only "time will tell" which form the body, namely, the genital, will finally assume. The close connection between spatial perception, spatial conceptualization, and the experience of the body needs no lengthy elaboration. Whenever the body-image formation is impeded a primitive spatial concept analogous to the body form continues to persist despite the fact that other ego functions have progressed normally. Werner (1940) in discussing spatial concept formation comments as follows: "Primitive terms for spatial relations suggest that the body itself with its 'personal dimensions' (Stern) of above-below, before-behind, and right-left is the source of a psychophysical system of coordinates. Therefore it may be inferred that objective space has gradually evolved from this primitive orientation."

The massive influence of body-image diffusion was well summed up in Steven's statement: "They [his doll patients] cannot see, hear or think until the operation is over." We might paraphrase his words by saying that the reliability of the distance perceptors and their usefulness for cognitive processes can be achieved only after the body has attained its complete and definitive form. The consequences of this state of affairs for reality testing and for the sense of reality is self-evident. For the time being then, Steven, as well as the other boys, took refuge in illusory accomplishments, in aggrandizement, in bragging and in fantasies of magic powers. These defenses permitted continuous narcissistic replenishment. I shall later elaborate on how ego impairments were rapidly surmounted after the genital intactness was established once and for all.

Steven, who was easily insulted by criticism, made use of all the aforementioned defenses in order to ward off a narcissistic injury. He considered himself a "magical person" who could make everybody smile at him by smiling at them. Thus he robbed everybody of their aggressive, i.e., dangerous, potential. Consequently, Steven had a poor grasp of social situations and was completely unable to recognize the correct motives in other children for their respective actions. Here we see the influence of the mother who maintained a distorted, idealized concept of her child and easily falsified reality in order to protect him. The mother, in denying Steven's physical defectiveness, devoted all her life's energies to its correction by magic. She gave up work and devoted herself totally to the child's care. The mother's denial became the child's erroneous self-image.

We notice that Steven, despite his "smiling disposition," was preoccupied with time and death. In these fears we recognize the tantalizing waiting time until genital certainty would be attained, as well as a "genital death" fear rooted in the still uncertain state of castratedness. In his earlier figure drawings, Steven gave the girl and the mother figure five fingers on each hand, while he drew a boy with no fingers at all. The boy, he said, is holding on to his parents' hand. Thus, his body deficit was undone by making himself part of a complete and powerful person.

Both Larry and Joe presented learning disturbances which were seriously aggravated in Joe's case by a stubborn reading disability. Again, illusory achievements and lies about school grades appeared as disclaimers of their academic deficiencies. Forgetting, i.e., memory disturbances, presented serious obstacles to a tutorial approach in remedial reading. A decisive turn for the better became noticeable when medical as well as psychotherapeutic attention was focused on the physical condition, its correction, and on body-damage anxiety generally.

The restoration and maturation of ego functions as well as their clinical evidence will be discussed later. Changes in the body image became indirectly observable through psychological tests. Steven's male figure in the second, postoperational test was large, compact, and had five fingers. Larry's "tree," which had first a hole in the center of the trunk, showed later a clear and simple outline without any aberrant features. Examples could be multiplied from the test material. Suffice it to say that the second test gave abundant evidence of a changed body image (self-concept) to allow the conclusion that the distorted, vague, and incomplete body image exerted a pathological influence on ego development. The ego impairments were erroneously treated for some time as if they were the result of endopsychic conflicts only. When the ego impairments were approached via the body image, its correction and completion—that is to say, when the physical (genital) reality was given a definitive structure— then a desirable change in ego functions was finally brought about. The clinical material illustrates the close relationship between body experience, body percept, body image, and ego functions.

Accident Proneness: The Masochistic Surrender

In the three boys hypermotility was conspicuously present. Its relatedness to physical self-damage was constantly demonstrated inside and outside the treatment room. Hypermotility in these cases constituted a complex form of behavior in which the pressure of instinctual drives, anxiety, and defensive operations were tightly organized. Hyperactive, aimless, and erratic moving about had a frantic, searching, anxious quality which at times invited danger and resulted in accidents. The tendency to self-damage, called accident proneness, revealed the child's concept of the genital defect as the result of an act of aggression, of a destructive attack on his body (castration). The identification with the aggressor, namely, the mother, prompted a feminine identification and turned passive submission into active execution. Thus the child made himself the victim of his own aggression.

It is difficult to say to which extent accident proneness or the compulsive toying with physical danger was linked either to passive masochistic castration wishes, or to the avoidance of narcissistic mortification. This avoidance can be paraphrased by saying that it is better not to be a boy at all than to be half a boy. We shall later see how the anatomical condition was unconsciously identified with femaleness. The masochistic yielding to female identity found expression in the many castrative actions of more or less serious consequences. The sense of incompleteness and castratedness was visibly, palpably, and permanently linked to a bodily condition; moreover, the idea of an operation had attached itself intimately to it. Both these factors contributed to the striking concreteness by which body-damage fear and wishes were represented and executed.

The body-damage complex was kept alive by its undecided fate of the testicle, a condition which fostered ambivalent relationships, worked against the establishment of stable identifications, and resulted in a fluid self-representation, particularly relative to aspects of sexual identity, namely phallic versus castrated. The ambivalence of drive propensities in conjunction with defensive maneuvers seemed to move along a circular path with the nodal stations labeled as follows: (conscious) Nothing can happen to me—I am in control of everybody—I know everything; (unconscious) I am not a boy—

I will never be a boy—I shall make myself into a girl—I deserve castration—I shall attack others—Surrendering of a body part is relief, is pleasure—I want castration.

Accident proneness as observed in these cases illustrates the substitution of the genital organ, more particularly, the testicle, by the whole body. This *totum pro parte* principle or the body-phallus equation is well expressed in Steven's play in which the patients have to undergo an operation for their "stiffness." The *totum pro parte* principle receives a massive support from the mother's attitude who customarily used the "total child" as a representation of his defective organ and concentrated her efforts at rectification of the genital defect in terms of substitutive perfections, such as academic excellence. Displacement from below to above is also apparent. In this connection the role of the eyeball as a substitutive organ for the testicle is noteworthy. This substitution is known from mythology and analysis. A blinking tic of an eleven-year-old boy reported by Fraiberg (1960) was traceable to the fear of damage to his testicles. In mythology, King Oedipus gouged out his eyes in symbolic emasculation to atone for his incestuous crime. An eye involvement appeared in all three cases, most prominently in the case of Larry with a self-induced eye loss.

I am inclined to attribute the accident in Larry's case to a compromise formation, consisting in the sacrifice of a body part, the eye, in order to rescue the missing testicle and, furthermore, to bring about the sought-after injury by his active submission rather than by waiting for the expected attack from the "monster woman." The boy's description of the accident clearly reveals the motoric paralysis of a masochistic excitement at the very moment when the stick came flying at his eye. The fear for his "good eye" repeated the original fear for his "good testicle." Both fears subsided with the correction of the genital defect. Larry was the one boy who most vigorously fought against a masochistic surrender, who, it is true, most damagingly victimized himself but nevertheless showed the most striking recovery.

Accident proneness is closely linked to the vicissitudes of the aggressive drive, to the erotization of injury, and to the need for physical punishment as a relief from feelings of guilt. The defective genital became almost automatically associated with sexual guilt since all three boys had progressed to a more or less firm foothold on the oedipal level. The aggressive-drive discharge was restricted to hyperactivity, counterphobic manifestations, and self-damage. In the course of therapy the intensity and primitivity of the aggression became apparent. Quite naturally, the seat of the explosive, destructive, and vengeful energy was to be located in the testicle. This we recognize in the hidden bomb of Steven's play, or in Larry's chemical experiments which were designed to blow up the house. Such expressions of unbridled aggressive fantasies eventually gave way to alloplastic adaptations when neutralized energy became available. Larry, for example, overcame his accident proneness successfully by making it his job to protect others from dangers: he became captain of the safety squad at his school. The other boys showed no signs of compulsive toying with physical dangers after the genital defect was corrected. The repetition compulsion was short-circuited by an anatomical change which facilitated ego alterations of a more complex kind. They became recognizable in characterological modifications and in the development of special, realistic interests and inclinations.

Symptomatic Acts and Organ Symbols

The anatomical defect of an undescended testicle favors expression of the condition through substitutive behavior or through symbolic objects in an effort to master anxiety. The concrete, direct, and symbolic nature of play and behavior are both strikingly demonstrated in the case material. The primitivity of thought implicit in this form of mastery leaves no doubt that the inferred, vaguely conscious temporariness of the defect foreclosed an integration by more complex psychic processes of which the three boys unquestionably were capable.

Werner (1940) remarks that "The structure of primitive thought is concretely determined insofar as it has a tendency to configurate pictorially, and it is emotionally determined insofar as it unites that which is affectively related." The case material indicates that aspects of "quantity" and "size" were definitely equated with power, potency, and masculinity. As another boy expressed it: "If I have two testicles I can have twice as many children." The frequent accidents represented symptomatic acts, explained by each boy circumstantially, but they obviously constituted reassurance actions by reaffirming repeatedly that no fatal damage was done.

The testicle as the seat of aggressive and destructive forces has been mentioned earlier. We can recognize this idea, furthermore, in the defensive belittling of the testicles the bearers of which are fear-provoking men. This attempt to attenuate castration anxiety is well expressed in the marching song of the British soldiers imprisoned during World War II by the Japanese in the Burma jungle: "Hitler has only one big ball—Goering has two but they are small—Himmler has something similar—But little Goebbels has no balls at all."[3]

Joe's insatiable interest in the contents of drawers, his running through the corridors of the clinic in order to see if anybody could stop him; Steven's curiosity about secrets and his use of the number three (male genital) in aggressive play—these incidents illustrate in displaced form the nature of their common concern.

The concrete representation of the testicle by objects is noteworthy inasmuch as it is somewhat out of keeping with the age and intelligence of the three boys. The directness of symbolic representation which we notice in Joe when he stole a ball from the treatment room only to return it after he had undergone a successful operation is almost ludicrous in its simplicity. The same is true for Steven's museum in which he exhibited a special precious marble for everybody to see after a successful operation had brought his testicle into a position where it finally became visible to the world. He also used to roll two small clay balls during the session following the operation; he remarked that he would make two more balls every week and he wanted the therapist to keep them for him. One is reminded of Larry's "eye (ball) bank."

By displacement the testicle is, furthermore, identified with other organs. Consequently, they assume attributes and meanings which render them fitting substitutes for the testicles. In this connection we can speak of organ symbols. The most outstanding substitute organs for the testicles are the following: eye, tonsils, breast, and foetus. (Their relatedness to bisexuality is discussed below.) It is partly the symmetric location, partly the operative history, partly the relatedness to component instincts which are responsible for the fit-

[3] While the melody of this song echoes through the sound track of the movie *The Bridge on the River Kwai*, the words of the song have, of course, been changed.

ness of these body parts to serve as organ symbols for the testicles.

One gains the impression that the genital defectiveness lends itself to direct, concrete, symbolic (substitutive) expression by objects in the outer world and, furthermore, to the use of the whole body or body parts for the mastery of the anxiety which the anatomical defect engenders.

The Bisexual Identity

The defective genital condition is perceived by the three boys as castratedness, i.e., femaleness. In these cases of cryptorchism we did not observe a genuine feminine identification but rather recognized in the self-image the compliance of passive, feminine tendencies to a physical genital reality. The passive tendencies received a powerful recourse from the operation trauma and a ceaseless stimulation from the physical condition of cryptorchism itself. In this connection the following remarks by Anna Freud (1952) are relevant: "When studying the aftereffects of childhood operations in the analysis of adult patients we find that it is not the castration fear but the feminine castration wish in a male child which is most frequently responsible for serious postoperative breakdowns or permanent postoperative character changes." To this we might add the finding that in the case of cryptorchism by the very fact of a defective genital the feminine castration wish did not advance to the state of an integrated self-representation but stayed attached to the genital organ in its physical reality. Feminine tendencies became, therefore, organized around this organ defect and remained in a state of unsettledness due to the implicit reversibility of the condition. The resultant bisexual identity was apparent in play productions, fantasies, transference behavior, and projective tests.

The confusion of sexual identity prevented any clear concept of the male and female genital to develop. An egomorphic image of a hermaphroditic nature became the universal body schema. Joe expressed this confusion in saying: "Does it mean that I have something other boys don't have, or don't I have something other boys have?"

Having one testicle was found to be identical with being half a man and half a woman, with sterility or with femaleness in general. Steven showed his doll patients to the therapist with these words:

"Look at them, they look like nothing." This better than anything else expresses the sense of self Steven had to contend with. In such a dilemma an operation was wanted and feared: in order to retrieve the lost treasure, the testicle, another organ, namely, the penis, might have to be sacrificed. In the overvaluation of the missing body part, we recognize an overflow of cathexis from the penis to the testicle.

Operation anxiety was warded off by identification, by assuming the active role vis-à-vis the therapist. Larry asked his male therapist to be his pupil while he himself was the teacher. The same reversal of roles we noticed in Steven who was the surgeon while the therapist became his nurse. When the operation was imminent, he seated himself in the woman therapist's chair and said: "I like to be you and you to be me." While it is not possible that "hes" can be made into "shes," Steven argued, why not have only "hes"? Then, we might add, castration would be eliminated once and for all. In his logical way, Steven concluded that in that case the "hes" had to get the babies in order to keep the world going. There was, after all, no way out of having two sexes.

This brings us to the equation of the deliverance of the testicle (orchidopexy) and giving birth. The testicle in the abdomen was equated with the foetus. Steven thought that it takes twenty-one days for a baby to grow in the mother, a span of time which represented the exact number of days he had to wait for his operation. Joe's figure drawing of a woman showed two balls in the abdominal region; when this drawing was repeatedly traced as the examiner suggested, the balls moved up in each consecutive figure tracing until they had reached the exact location of the breasts. The association of the absent testicle with the female organ of the breast only serves to emphasize once more the bisexual identity which we have found characteristic for cases of cryptorchism.

It was no surprise then to discover that the orchidopexy evoked a state of dual expectancy, namely, either to achieve masculinity or to meet with final castration. Partly, indeed, a confusion existed as to the simultaneous accomplishment of both. This is apparent, for instance, in Steven's idea that the testicle will be pushed from the "stomach" into the penis; this state of having obtained two external testicles would have canceled out the use of the penis for urination and necessitated another body orifice for this function. Such disturbing admissions were quickly extinguished by aggrandizing fantasies until a recourse to castratedness gained once more the upper hand. These shifts resulted in a chronic state of indecision and of fluctuating sexual identity. Fineman (1959) reported similar observations on a boy, aged five and a half, with a congenital genitourinary defect: "The first attempt to present his actual condition [extrophy of the bladder] to him, although softened by the additional statement that he could do everything else that boys could do, was met by him with considerable anxiety which he spontaneously brought under control by playing at being mother and cooking meals." The acceptance of being a boy took first the form of exaggeration, namely, "fantasies of being a powerful hunter who killed lions and tigers with his father's or grandfather's gun."

The bisexual sense of identity which we observed in the three cases poses some theoretical problems as to identification and instinctual fixation. None of the boys behaved in a, strictly speaking, effeminate or "girlish" way. However, they lacked in boyish assertiveness, in active pursuits, and definitely shrank away from competition within their male peer group. They all responded positively to a changed attitude of the father when he took a more active interest in their lives and acknowledged his own importance and influence in helping his son toward a more masculine orientation. After the father had rescued the son from the castrating mother, after he had shown pride in his son's masculine strivings, a competitive oedipal upsurge became manifest which soon was resolved by an identification with the father. None of the boys offered himself as the passive love object as might have been expected from the prevailing emotional trends. The flight into a feminine position, namely, castratedness, was not anchored in an instinctual fixation nor in a stable feminine identification. No doubt, these tendencies existed as they do in the young male generally, but they never progressed to a passive homosexual orientation. The defense of castratedness is akin to denial in so far as the child denies the genital defect by a radical removal of the last vestiges of maleness which gave rise to anxiety and upset his narcissistic balance. "Being a girl" was never sufficiently supported by a pregenital drive nor ego fixation to prevent a forward movement of the libido; however, the intolerable genital condition in conjunction with the dependency on a castrating mother provided feminine propensities with a ceaseless updrift. The perseverance of the female body image and the defense of castratedness (body-part surrender) was directly related to a body reality rather than to a psychologically integrated drive and ego organization. The bisexual identity reflected a physical reality; consequently, a change of the physical reality brought the provisional state of pseudo bisexuality to an end. The restoration of genital intactness gave masculine sexuality a decisive push. The overbearing quality of this newly acquired and unequivocal masculinity invited, however, doubts as to a completely victorious outcome. We shall return to this question later on.

The Positioning of the Testis in the Scrotum: Its Influence on Integrative Processes

The effects of the newly acquired genital completeness were followed by us with interest and surprise. First of all, it was the rapidity and the scope of ego maturation accompanying the new body reality which called our attention to the fact that the anatomical change itself must account for a specific impetus for ego change. The influence of the new body reality was so massive and immediate that the question arose as to the respective psychological processes initiated by therapy on the one hand and by the anatomical transformation on the other. While it is no doubt true that psychotherapy had, so to say, prepared the mental ground for the genital intactness to take roots or to effect a changed sense of reality, the physical change itself must be credited with an equally important contribution toward the improvement of mental functioning. The most striking changes occurred in the areas of learning, cognitive processes, elaboration of age-adequate interests, social adaptation, and masculine identity formation. The ego impairments affecting all these areas have been described earlier.

Let us first recall that a tacit parental prohibition existed, in all three cases regarding recognition and thinking about the genital condition. In Steven's case the mother's unconcern, her denial, was projected onto the child ("He does not worry, he knows nothing") and impeded his ego development, especially the faculty of reality testing. The child, consequently, lived in a state of confusion, not knowing what was real; he was at a loss to say whether what he perceived was real or what his mother wanted him to know. This global perceptual confusion was counteracted in treatment when the "veil of twilight vision" was lifted and a sense of reality restored. In the psychological test this change appeared as a "differentiated view of the world." Steven had predicted in his play already that after the operation, if successful, his "patients will be their own self again; everything depends on this operation."

It is interesting to note that he as well as the other boys expected a return to a genital state which once must have existed, so to say, in prehistory. They expected to receive what had always been theirs. Steven eagerly investigated his newly acquired testicle and described clearly his physical sensations related to the positioning of the testicle in the scrotum. Before the operation, Steven said he always felt confused. With finality an interim state had come to an end: "Once the operation was over, it was over." After the physical restoration, Steven's emotional and intellectual maturation took a remarkable leap. The infantile self-absorbed child became more and more oriented toward schoolwork, reading, the Boy Scouts, friends, chess playing, piano lessons, etc. Taking into account all the psychotherapeutic endeavors, the rapid consolidation of psychological gains derived a unique recourse from the bodily change itself. Before that change nothing was final or complete.

Larry and Joe were both retarded in reading and consequently seriously handicapped in school. In all cases a reading disability existed (e.g., Steven was almost a nonreader when he started treatment) which was strikingly ameliorated soon after the genital restoration or even shortly before the operation. In Larry an improvement in his spatial perception was also noticeable. The aimless wandering of his mind through horror movies and the destructive use of chemistry gave way to a genuine interest in science. Larry's accident-seeking turned into accident prevention. His second psychological testing showed startling changes: the serious ego impairment which raised the suspicion of borderline functioning was no longer in evidence. His body image had changed radically: the male figure, drawn earlier with fuzzy strokes and vague forms, was now set down with firm outlines and precise shapes. Passive submission had given way to active mastery of the environment. The higher level of integrative processes stands out as the most remarkable finding in his second test series.

Joe showed many of the same features of change described in relation to the other boys. The spurt in ego maturation in his case also was remarkable: learning capacity and handwriting improved, an interest in factual knowledge appeared, concentration span lengthened; moreover, he could for the first time think of the future in terms of a vocation, namely, in terms of being a man when he would be grown up.

All three boys appeared much more alert mentally, and capable of more complex psychic processes after body intactness was established. A higher level of differentiation and integration appeared in their second test series. On the behavioral level this became manifest in the delay of action and the interposition of thought between stimulus and motor discharge. Along with this came a decline in hypermotility, which had been characteristic for the three boys. It is assumed that the anatomical change affected the body image in terms of a definitive masculine identity. The influence of the anatomical reality on the ego via the body image resulted in a firmer sense of reality, consequently in greater clarity of thought and the establishment of more effective, namely, adaptive, defenses.

In spite of these gains we shall not overlook the fact that genital intactness was initially seized upon as the savior who would keep feminine strivings at bay. Efforts at repression or characterological absorption of these still powerful strivings were preceded by an overbearing show of masculinity directly following the physical changes.[4] The thrust into assertiveness following body intactness had two phases. The first was characterized by an upsurge of masculine sexuality and an exaggerated display of forcefulness and cocksureness. An almost euphoric sense of power became noticeable which can be paraphrased by saying: "Now that I am a real boy the sky is the limit to what I can do." Heterosexual excitement (e.g., Joe's pictures of nude women) became—perhaps too soon and too completely—repressed and a tendency to compulsivity and affective constriction took over. No material on the boys' masturbation was forthcoming

---

[4] The positioning of the testicle into the scrotum does not affect—that is to say, does not increase—the hormonal activity of this organ. The suddenness of change in behavior is therefore a purely psychological phenomenon.

which left an unfortunate lacuna in the understanding of their sexual development.[5] There is no doubt that the display of phallic masculinity had a defensive quality. However, its ultimate effect on character synthesis cannot be assessed with certainty before late adolescence.

For the time being, treatment in conjunction with genital restoration had made psychic functioning on a higher level possible. Thus it facilitated adaptive processes and the use of stable defenses less damaging and debilitating than the ones originally employed. One might say that Joe was prevented from entering a delinquent career; Steven was saved from an infantile, autistic state; and Larry was rescued from physical self-destruction. Due to the fact that the defective ego development was firmly attached to a physical condition, the pathological retardations and distortions were, so to say, prevented from inundating the psychic life of the child and from causing irreversible ego alterations. The thought occurred to me that these boys might have been more seriously affected by their environment, especially the mother, if they had not been afflicted by a genital, reparable defect. The concreteness of body-damage fear had not been totally internalized and welded to instinctual and conflictual anxiety. This fact might explain the reversibility of symptoms which in children generally would have indicated a most serious disturbance. Much that seemed at first in diagnostic evaluation as ominous pathology changed radically under the impact of the genital restoration. Psychotherapy alone can hardly be credited with the massive improvements. The idea forced itself on the observer that the physical condition itself represented a reality according to which the ego became modeled and remodeled; furthermore, that which appeared initially as an endopsychic conflict represented in fact a body-reality confusion aggravated by reality fear. As far as the body reality was internalized, psychotherapy was the proper helper; as far as the body reality could be corrected, namely, made definitive, the surgeon was called upon to help. Both specialists have to syncho-

5 I am indebted to Dr. Mary O'Neil Hawkins for the idea that continued examination of the scrotal sac might sensitize, so to say, accidentally, this genital area which thus becomes the seat of erotic feelings. The manual investigation by the child of his bodily defect consequently could turn into a masturbatory activity with the focus of sensation in the scrotal region. Castration anxiety, on the other hand, might lead to a complete desensitization of the genital. Our clinical material is inconclusive as to the particular masturbatory practices in cases of cryptorchism; here further analytic investigation is needed.

nize their contributions in order to discharge their respective functions in a coordinated approach. The cases of Steven and Joe have illustrated this point.

SUMMARY

Three prepubertal cases of cryptorchism were presented. The complementary effects of psychotherapy, physical correction of the genital defect (two operative, one spontaneous), and treatment of the parents, especially the mother, were explored. On the basis of the clinical data the following conclusions were reached:

1. Cryptorchism is not a primary pathogenic factor. The particular way in which the genital defect is experienced by the parents, particularly the mother, accounts for the child's preoccupation with the testes. The perpetrator of the body damage is in the child's mind identified with the mother. Her castrating possessiveness and the passive aloofness of the father both constitute a matrix of family interaction in which cryptorchism gives rise to typical symptoms despite the fact that the three cases belong to heterogeneous nosological categories.

2. In all three cases an early operation trauma had occurred, and served as the prototypical model for body-damage (castration) fear. The genital defect (cryptorchism) served as the "organizing experience" (Greenacre) which subordinated early trauma as well as all subsequent phase-specific anxieties about body damage to the persistent genital incompleteness. An operation trauma per se is not considered an obligatory experience.

3. A distorted, vague, and incomplete body image exerted a pathological influence on ego development. Resultant ego impairments were manifest in defective functioning relative to learning, memory, thinking, time-space orientation, and motility. These impairments could furthermore be linked to the mother's inconsistent attitude by which she tacitly forbade the child to recognize his physical defect clearly, or to think rationally about it.

4. The tendency to self-damage (accident proneness) present in the cases was understood as the child's idea that the genital defect was the result of an act of aggression (castration). Through identification with the aggressor the child turned passive submission into active execution and made himself the victim of his own aggression.

Castrative wishes were clearly in evidence.

5. Cryptorchism favors direct, concrete, symbolic (substitutive) expressions by objects in the outer world, the use of the whole body or body parts for the mastery of the anxiety which the anatomical defect engenders. Substitutive organs (organ symbols) for the testicle were found to be: eye, tonsils, breast, and foetus.

6. A bisexual sense of identity reflected the physical reality of anatomical indecision. The perseverance of the female body image and the defense of castratedness (body-part surrender) was directly related to a body reality rather than to a psychologically integrated drive and ego organization. This became evident through the reversibility of the body-image confusion once genital intactness was established.

7. Coordinated efforts of surgeon and therapist resulted in a striking amelioration of ego impairment. The changed body image exerted an immediate and direct influence on ego functions. What appeared initially as an endopsychic conflict represented in fact a body-reality confusion, aggravated by reality fear. Considering the influence of the anatomical correction on differentiative and integrative psychic processes, the conclusion was reached that the concreteness of body-damage fear prevented total internalization of the body reality and its amalgamation with conflictual anxiety. The delay of internalization was maintained by the reparable genital defect and the undying expectation of a changed body reality. This particular state of affairs in the presence of a bodily defect might explain the reversibility of an emotional condition with severe ego impairments, which in children generally would indicate an ominous pathology.

The findings in this paper are restricted to cryptorchism. It seems that the particular survival value, the interference with perception, with the physical grasp of objects, with phase-specific gratifications, and many more factors related to a defective body part, introduce elements which are absent in cryptorchism per se. The sifting of similarities and differences in cases with other bodily defects lies outside the scope of this presentation. The clinical study of three cases of cryptorchism aimed at an investigation of the mutual influence of body reality, body image, ego development, and internalization within the matrix of a specific pattern of family interaction.

6

THE SEARCH FOR A SEXUAL IDENTITY IN A CASE OF CONSTITUTIONAL SEXUAL PRECOCITY

RUTH THOMAS, in collaboration with LYDIA FOLKART
and ELIZABETH MODEL
(1963)

Sexual precocity is defined as the attainment of sexual maturity some years before the normal time of puberty. Novak (1944) states: "According to most authors, puberty should be considered abnormally early or precocious when it occurs below the age of nine, although some suggest a lower limit of eight." It is always due to hypersecretion of androgenic or estrogenic hormone.

The ovarian hyperactivity (which some authors state may be secondary to some hypothalamic-pituitary stimulus) is manifested by qualitatively normal sexual development, pubic hair, well-formed breasts, and even pregnancy, the last having been recorded as early as six years.

Novak postulates that the condition is dependent on abnormal genetic factors. Paschkis, Rakoff, and Cantarow (1958) on the other hand state: "The possibility that the initiating process affects the ovaries primarily rather than the pituitary, also deserves consideration, especially since gonadotropin excretion in these children is minimal. The ovaries may be unusually responsive to minimal amounts of gonadotropin; other factors not yet understood may have

This case was treated at the Hampstead Child-Therapy Clinic. Miss Lydia Folkart was the child's therapist and Mrs. Elizabeth Model interviewed the mother.

The authors are indebted to Dr. Alfred Model, Dr. H. Nagera, and Dr. H. Rey for information contributory to the assessment of the medical situation.

initiated early maturation of the ovary, which in turn has 'awakened' the pituitary by back action. There seems to be little evidence that the condition is hereditary."

While in some forms of precocious puberty, the patients menstruate but do not ovulate, "in the constitutional group, the patients not only menstruate unusually early, but they also ovulate" (Novak, 1944). In the constitutional type the risk of pregnancy is therefore real.

In both sexes, precocity is associated with early union of the epiphysis (Di George and Warkany, 1959). Although initial growth is well above average, ultimate height is below expectation. However, constitutional sexual precocity may proceed to a normal state.

Sexual precocity of early origin will necessarily generate considerable anxiety in parents and normal siblings. The nature of this anxiety will depend on and interact with the personal sexual orientation of each member of the family. Incest fears will be magnified in all possible heterosexual partnerships within the family constellation, for example, between father and daughter, or brother and sister. The relation between mother and daughter may generate novel competitive anxieties. These in turn will produce defensive measures in the family members in accordance with personal character patterns. The normal protective and educative attitudes of the parents will therefore be complicated in a special way by their own psychopathology.

Sexually precocious children have an abundance of physical energy and strength beyond their actual age, but they frequently appear clumsy. Their vigorous growth unfortunately gives rise to the expectation of behavior far in advance of their mental age and sometimes beyond their physical adaptiveness.

Not infrequently the diagnosis and treatment of this abnormality require some degree of hospitalization and physical examination. Further traumatic factors are thus added to the normal vicissitudes of childhood.

To both child and parent, the age at which precocity makes itself manifest is important. An early precocity, say from birth, means to the parent a long waiting period before it is possible to accept the child as a normal being. Some part of this period is complicated by the recognition that the child is abnormally overgrown, and looks

unusual among other children. To the child, manifest sexual abnormality appearing at or before the time when gender role is
established may have a confusing impact on the body ego and the
ability to establish gender role. Money et al. (1955a) place the age
for the establishment of gender role at around eighteen months. If
doubt about this matter is prolonged beyond this period, they believe it favors psychopathology. In the precociously sexual girl, the
establishment of gender role includes not only the decision to think
of herself as a boy or girl but also the decision as to whether she is
a girl or a woman. Precocious breast development may complicate
the resolution of her penis envy, and her unconscious choice of
sexual role, and at the same time reinforce her fantasies of sexual
identity with her mother.

To accept and understand this abnormal situation and to verbalize the problem it presents to the child at varying stages of growth
constitutes a task which can of course be met, though parental readi-
ness to deal with it is highly variable. We would therefore expect a
qualitative element in child care which varies with the difficulties of
the parents.

While our awareness of these factors has grown in the process of
analytic work, as it will be reported, we had not expected them to
be so outstanding in the analytic picture. Studies of these children
are usually confined to their medical profiles. The single exception
are studies by Hampson and Money, working at the Johns Hopkins
Hospital, who examined sixteen children psychologically, eleven
girls aged from fourteen months to fifteen years, and five boys aged
two and a half to seven years. Information was gathered from detailed histories, test batteries, and interviews with both parents and
children. The evidence on general psychological maturation seems
to be more adequate than that on psychosexual maturation. The
latter, based on interview and interrogation, is difficult to assess and
far from conclusive. Hampson and Money (1955) assert that "Children with idiopathic sexual precocity do not automatically manifest
psychosexual and general sexual precocity along with their somatic
precocity. Psychologically their development resembles in manner
and speed that of their somatically normal siblings and cousins. Like
their dental development, it is not precocious."

It should be recorded that the present study was undertaken in the hope of clarifying the developmental picture of the drives in this one case. Physical maturation and menstrual functioning are not themselves evidence of psychosexual maturity at the level of drive development. Neurological maturation does not necessarily keep pace with endocrine development; and in sexual precocity, the somatic bases for drive development might therefore be at variance with the corresponding psychological development. For this reason it is of considerable interest to compare the libidinal phase development of precocious and normal children of comparable age. If an immaturely structured psyche has to deal with increased sexual drives of an intensity normally found in puberty, one might assume that this situation would highlight the use of primitive defense systems and could easily be compared with normal puberty. This approach proved oversimple and superficial in the face of the complex inner situation which the analysis disclosed.

In our case, the psychobiological effects of the abnormality (constitutional factors) and the effects of the abnormality on family and personal relationships (environmental effects stemming from the abnormality) had to be studied in a familial background dominated by the gross disturbances of both parents. The latter element could scarcely have failed to be pathogenic in the life of a physically normal child. The effects stemming from the abnormality were constantly overlaid by a cycle of environmental factors, originating for the most part from the personality and activities of a traumatogenic mother. Nevertheless, certain elements pertaining to the abnormality could ultimately be isolated in their effect on development.

CASE REPORT

Susan, aged two years and nine months when brought to the Hampstead Clinic, was first noticed to have a white vaginal discharge at the age of six weeks. She was not seen by a consultant endocrinologist until the age of nineteen months. A vaginal smear at that time showed marked estrogenic stimulation. She was admitted for a rectal examination under anesthesia; no abnormal masses were found and cervix and uterus were both normal. At that time the mother stated that the child had a white vaginal discharge for three to four days every three to four weeks and during this time was sleepy, irritable, and emotional. She was seen again at the age of five. At that time her height was four feet (equal to a height age of seven years, eight months) and her weight was four stone, ten pounds (a weight age of about eight years, nine months). Other development was proportional. There was an increase in breast size. The 17-ketosteroids were found to be 5.5 mg. per 24 hours, well above the expected figure for a child of five, but approximately correct for a girl of thirteen or fourteen years. Her pregnanediol output was 0.2 mg. per 24 hours, a normal figure.

Although sexual precocity may be due to a variety of causes, the differential diagnosis in this case clearly established that the child was manifesting constitutional sexual precocity. No abnormality of the brain or endocrine glands was found. In this case no pathology could be postulated other than the abnormally early age at which hypothalamic-pituitary-ovarian activity commenced, and medical treatment was not available or indicated.

Reasons for Referral

At two years, nine months, Susan's main presenting symptom was an inability to allow her mother out of sight. Persistent clinging was said to begin after her hospitalization at twenty months. She became terrified at going into any building, and would drive away whoever attempted to speak to the mother in the street. She screamed when a stranger came to the door of her home, for fear they would take her into the hospital, would clutch her stomach and cry, "Susan's tummy all better now." Following this hospitalization Susan refused to return to the bedroom which up to this time she had shared with her brother John, four years older than herself. At the time of referral there were daily scenes with John. Susan waited for him on his return from school and attacked him with forks and cricket bats. On one occasion when a boy had broken his leg, she attempted to break John's leg and could be restrained only with difficulty.

She was capricious over food, refusing to eat food she had just asked for. There were numerous scenes at mealtimes, where she insisted on putting her feet on the table and upsetting dishes.

Her mother regarded the precocity as a separate problem, in no way related to the behavior difficulties, and did not adduce this as a reason for referral.

History and Family Background

Susan was the youngest of three children, born precipitately when her mother was forty-two years old. At the time of referral the eldest child, Gwen (aged fourteen), appeared the most stable member of the family. John (aged eight) was eventually taken into treatment and later sent to boarding school.

Susan's history was a disturbed one from birth. She weighed eight pounds and was fed by spoon, because for several months, as the mother stated, she continued to discharge quantities of nasal mucus, which interfered with breast or bottle feeding. She was taken into a hospital at six weeks—on the point of choking, the mother said—where she was bottle fed and where it is reported the nasal condition cleared up, though it recurred on return home. She walked at twelve months; her speech development is said to have been normal, and she could whistle at ten months! She was toilet trained at twenty months, though there was a breakdown of this achievement after her hospitalization. She was lifted at night till the age of four.

Mrs. S. first noticed the vaginal discharge on Susan's return from her first hospitalization at the age of six weeks. She also noticed that Susan's breasts were developing at this time. It was not till sixteen months that her persistent attempts to have these facts given consideration were successful. When finally at nineteen months Susan was seen by an endocrinologist, the child reacted with intense screaming to the hospital setting, the presence of a number of students, and the interference with her body for the vaginal smear. Hospitalization was arranged a month later to investigate the differential diagnosis between an undisclosed tumor and a constitutional abnormality, described to the mother as "just a strange development of nature." Susan again proved unmanageable.

Her hospital experiences may be summarized as follows: at six weeks a ten-day stay on account of nasal mucus; at nine weeks a month's stay on account of gastroenteritis; at nineteen months the taking of a vaginal smear; at twenty months a nine-day stay, with a rectal examination. At this time the diagnosis of constitutional sexual precocity was made, the presence of a tumor having been excluded.

It was stated that after the hospitalization at twenty months, a change in her object relations took place. Before this she easily attached herself to people. This event was said to mark the onset of her withdrawn states which lasted in an intense way till she was over seven. Before this and following the hospitalization, it was stated that she scarcely spoke to anyone outside the family and withdrew when any attempt was made to establish contact with her.

At three Susan was a well-made child with dark hair, cut in a sleek bob, and noticeable for beautiful dark eyes. She was attractively dressed and could have passed for a schoolgirl several years older. When first seen, she sat anxiously on her mother's lap with her face buried in her mother's shoulder. From time to time she sucked a piece of rag from which she was never separated. There was a strange contrast between her round babyish face and her mature little body, shapely hips and calves, and the noticeable development of her breasts, though she was dressed in a fashion which did not draw attention to these. Her expression could be eager and lively, though more often she lapsed into vacancy.

Susan showed herself at an early age very competent at household tasks; she could bathe herself and do her own hair at a normal age. She loved most to play with her dolls of which she had a great number. While her mother encouraged her household activities, other members of the family thought them a nuisance and tried to interfere. Susan would then become babyish and demand to be cuddled. She found it difficult to wait for a response to her wishes, and her mother tried to avoid scenes by as far as possible never directly refusing anything. Mrs. S. often pacified Susan by promises for the future.

At the time of referral, and for several years afterward, her general health was poor. She suffered from continual colds and minor ailments, was an excessive thumb sucker, and alternately masturbated compulsively. Her mother regarded the thumb sucking as an acceptable alternative to masturbation.

At three she was already attending nursery school, and was regarded as withdrawn and the kind of child it was easy to overlook. This continued to be the school picture for some years. She appeared not to learn, made no friends, and other children did not seek her company.

Susan was too withdrawn to have a mental test done before

treatment commenced, but a year afterward she achieved an I.Q. of 102 on the Stanford Binet Scale, though it was felt that 117 was a closer real estimate, allowing for her chaotic behavior and the domination of her response by fantasy.

Mrs. S. was a tense, excitable woman, intelligent, hyperactive and erratic. While she had a warm relation to her children and there was considerable latitude in the home, all her arrangements had an air of constant crisis in which she played a central and dramatic role. The unfortunate quality of her maternal care was accentuated by her need to subject Susan to overfrequent medical attention, the absolute necessity for which was often in doubt but proved difficult to gauge because of Susan's abnormality. The timing of the interventions and the mother's emotional approach to them were inevitably traumatogenic. Reference to the records of other clinics confirmed that Mrs. S.'s dramatizations on the theme of illness and the medical mismanagement of her children were as much in evidence in the early years of her marriage as later. When Gwen was six years old, she attended a London clinic because of excessive masturbation. Mrs. S.'s preoccupation at this time, brought as her husband's, was revealing: "My husband wonders if Gwen's genitals are deformed." John was then one and Susan not yet born. John was also taken to this clinic at the age of three, following his violent reaction to hospitalization for alleged constipation. The clinic clearly felt that it was Mrs. S.'s gross anxiety over her children's bodies that drove her to seek help.

It was a measure of Mrs. S.'s distress that with Susan, in whose case there was every justification, she did not present her child's body as the reason for seeking help, but used Susan's difficulties in separating from her. Superficially Susan's precocity may have been less devastating to her than to a more normal mother. Only at a late stage in Susan's analysis was Mrs. S. able to admit how distressed she had been to hear other mothers comment on her child when she towered over other children in a school play. There was no doubt that Susan's abnormality focused her mother's disturbance without being in any way the central feature of it.

A simultaneous analysis of both mother and child was indicated but not available. Instead Mrs. S. was supported in weekly interviews throughout Susan's treatment. It seemed at first that she would use the opportunity entirely as an abreactive therapy for her own pent-up needs. Her verbosity had the quality of the flight of ideas of the hypomanic: her paranoid ideas, especially against doctors, had an intractable and delusional quality, and her distortions on the theme of her own body states were clearly deluded. She constantly provoked crises which reverberated on her family, but equally and unpredictably had long active and constructive periods. In the handling of her children she was often surprisingly open to influence, and kept a humorous and benevolent relation to her therapist for seven years. Basically her personality remained untouched, though her acting out could be directed away from the children. In type, she approximated to the "chaotic mother," producing a state of "organized chaos" which distracted and bewildered her children (Winnicott, 1961).

Mrs. S. saw her husband as an ineffectual, wavering man, afraid of physical contact with her, whose acute anxieties about transport led him to leave home in the early hours, miserly and unpredictable about money, and with "uncanny" ways. Only in the later stages of Susan's analysis did he emerge as an acute obsessional character, who withdrew into a small workshop, relatively unrelated even in his business life to genuine adult interests, yet with surprising understanding of his children's sublimations and often a sensitive protagonist for them against the world outside the family. To his children he seemed often remote on account of his withdrawn states.

The Treatment

Susan's analysis extended from the age of three to the beginning of her tenth year, sessions being gradually reduced in the last two years. The first years of her analysis were marked by two outstanding features. It seemed as if all libidinal activity with considerable areas of ego functioning were forbidden, and that all areas of libidinal development were functioning simultaneously in an agglutinized fashion (Greenacre, 1954). For the first nine months of treatment Susan insisted that her mother remain in the treatment room, expressing fear that otherwise she would become excited and unmanageable. Babies were sent to the hospital for eating sweets, water play might lead to drinking something messy like urine, "and if you drink a lot of water, it has to come out." Susan was lifted at night around this time, but no restrictions were placed on her intake of liquids. Her hands had constantly to be washed after sand play, "'cause Mummy be cross and Susan be cross." She restricted her urination for long periods and was afraid that to cuddle her Teddy would be too exciting. Susan feared that all these activities would find appropriate punishment in the hospital and in separation from her mother. She had above all a great wish to gobble people up and have them to herself, the punishment for this wish being nasty medicine and the extraction of teeth.

Susan's fantasy that she was a baby was fortified by the severe ego restrictions she imposed on herself in an endeavor to reduce excitement of any kind. When inevitably she could not always contain herself, she begged the therapist to join in her activity, to suck her own fingers, and suggested the therapist was disgusting and might have pooh-pooh in her pants. Both were forbidden to look, listen, or talk because they were dirty babies whose tongues could be cut out. But it was also clear that Susan was longing to talk about her problems with her unusual body and had great fears of doing so. Not only was talking itself exciting and liable to produce a situation in which she would feel overwhelmed, but Susan had a store of information about her body, secretly gathered from her mother's conversation and her own observation, which in part defied her ability to integrate and which on the other hand had implications too painful and frightening to allow of integration. Operations on her dolls indicated distorted fantasies of body functioning side by side with other play clearly based on a normal body image. Teddy's badness was extracted from his legs and poured into his eyes; he would scratch himself and infect his eyes, mouth, and hair with the badness of his legs. Covert references to hair, her genital discharge, and unusual height came only very slowly into the analysis. Her inability to control the discharge, conceived as an anal and urethral function, which could then through masturbation infect the whole of her body, accounted for some of the limitations she imposed on her activity. She felt she had infected her hands and, through them, her eyes and her tonsils; even her pubic hair was the result of her messy play. These features of her disability were confused with and ascribed to her lack of a penis. She felt that only a penis would remedy her defects. She was uncertain whether she or her mother was responsible for this great lack. "Once," she said, "I had a penis, but I put my finger through it and it bust." She then began to wash her doll's hair, saying it would look smashing, but added, "I used to cry when my mummy washed my hair and I fell down and it broke and it was a plastic and then I was another Susan."

Her anxiety about her abnormality was woven into all her object relations, dominating and further restricting her ego activities. Her brother John seemed to Susan the most fortunate one in the family. She drew him with a proper body and a gun in his belt, and represented herself beside him by vague lines and circles. He was clean, while she was messy. She often spoke of herself as John's twin, and drew them both with a seed bag in each hand, sowing seeds. She imagined she had a penis hidden in her pubic hair or that her height was a compensation for the lack of it. John was ashamed of Susan's appearance, and he and his friends tended to withdraw from her or tease her. Susan responded by roaming naked around the house and attempting to alleviate her own anxiety by frightening the boys. This behavior proved to be a repetition of exciting and frightening romping games with John when they shared a room in her infancy, the room from which she anxiously withdrew on her return from the hospital. Her later fury against him could be attributed to her feeling that he had remained normal and active in spite of these games, while she had been damaged. She constantly referred to these games in the analysis by means of current fantasies in which she and John were clambering about together on rocks.

While the normal girl's phallic wishes are entrenched in a firmly accepted body and a self, which she would like to exchange or enlarge by her phallic strivings, Susan saw herself at times as a nothingness—vague lines and a circle in her drawings. She seemed unable to differentiate herself from her clothes, and her sense of her body was related to whether she was dressed in a skirt or jeans. Her therapist once said, "You look nice in your skirt," and Susan replied with puzzlement, *"In* my skirt?" Having talked of herself as a boy or a baby, she would immediately ask anxiously, "But I am a little girl?" She often spoke of herself as a "big-little girl," and at other times she said, "I feel more like a lady than a big-little girl." On several occasions she suffered mild states of depersonalization. At these times she could not bear to play pretend games and would counter a make-believe remark with "But I am real." She seemed afraid she would disintegrate, and drew pictures of herself in pieces. Her intense anxiety over her body seemed to lead to a partial decathexis of her self-image, and her anxiety over what other people could or might do to her body led to a parallel inability to grasp their identities. Told that a lady might be coming to take some pictures of her, she asked anxiously if the lady could be telephoned to find out her name as if this would help her to maintain a grip on the situation. This lady was confused with the X-ray specialist who might undress her.

Susan was at times clearly unable to maintain the reality of herself and her objects in the face of intense fantasy, a phenomenon which at the outset of the analysis could have seemed not too unusual for her age. At a later stage, the bizarreness of her mother's outspoken fantasying had to be considered as a factor contributing to Susan's tenuous hold on reality in the area of her sexual life. Finally, the inherent weakness of her ego structure and its inability to handle her internal problems were brought into relief.

Susan spoke rarely about her father. In the first week of treatment she asked for a swing to be drawn with daddy on it, a reference to some pleasurable activity with her father which she resolutely refused to pursue. Instead she said that Dorothy, her teacher, used to swing her.

Susan longed to be able to break through her father's reticence. While he joked about her precocity, calling her Jayne Mansfield, an actress famed for her large breasts, his anxieties led him to be embarrassed about her in public and unresponsive to the point of appearing to shun her. After a wedding party when he had failed to take notice of her or to talk to her, she played that her doll's daddy was cross with her because she was a messy girl, and angrily tried to cut off pieces of her own hair and stuff them into her therapist's mouth. When her therapist tried to reassure Susan that their talking was different from her mother's and could help her to win over her father, Susan began excitedly to prepare a meal for them both, inviting the therapist to take the role of father. She was immediately overwhelmed with anxiety and tried too late to stop the game, saying she must not eat her mother's dinner. Then she lay on the floor twisting her legs and body in acute sexual excitement and asked to be spanked. This outbreak was much later repeated, very unfortunately before Gwen's boy friends.

Susan's states of disrupted identity and the confusion of her body image could now be seen to relate in part to recognition that her precocity made her in reality a sexual threat to her mother. In the case of her brother, Susan aggressively exploited her realization that her pubic hair created anxiety in males, but divested herself symbolically of it to appeal to her father. Reassurance that he could be brought to love her released the fantasy of an avenging mother, and precipitated an anxiety attack with a break-through of aggressive sexuality. Her mother's persistent and anxious interference with her body thus represented to Susan the danger of actual castration in constantly changing forms, an interdiction on assuming a feminine role, and a relegation to a sexual limbo. Susan once said that she thought of herself as a little girl who, having left her mother, was all alone out in space. Susan's precocity thus robbed her of a feminine role and of a normal child's measure of safety to indulge oedipal fantasy. In this respect her situation invited comparison with the sexually seduced child.

The fluctuations of Susan's self-images seemed to be caused by attempts at denying this dangerous uniqueness by establishing a different kind of common identity with each of her objects in turn. Susan drew a picture of her father as a house with a tall chimney extending over all the rooftops. Inside a witch was extracting some glass from his forehead. She represented herself outside as a flower that had grown too tall and was dying. Both father and Susan were thus castrated by the witch mother while simultaneously possessing male attributes.

While Susan's fantasies were not basically different from those of a more normal child, the quality of her anxiety and the extensive ego modifications stemmed from three areas in her personality where her resources were defective: the narcissistic, the object-related, and the more strictly oedipal. All the evidence indicated that Susan lacked the support of a normal relationship with her father and brother. The fact that they possessed a penis was, for her, of exaggerated and central significance, and left little room for normal interchange. The reality involved in her own sense of castration and their anxious rejection predated her oedipal phase and attenuated her resources for dealing with this problem. Instead the normal child's wish for a penis was in her case reinforced by her wish for a normal body conceived as male. Whatever assumptions one might have been tempted to make about the impact of Susan's precocity in producing an abnormal drive development had to be weighed against the poverty of inducement to an aim-inhibited relationship, a poverty which stemmed in part from Susan's defective personality and in part from the anxieties she aroused in her objects. In these circumstances, sexual acting out would have been an economic possibility in a child whose normal drive endowment was not in doubt. Only in the last stages of the analysis did a further important determinant of Susan's sexual exhibitionism emerge, namely, that Mr. S. frequently seduced Susan by undressing before her at bedtime. This could be directly related to the restriction of her visual activities and to the outbreak of anxiety before Gwen's boy friends in which she turned passive into active and repeated the exhibitionistic behavior she had manifested to her therapist earlier in the analysis.

Susan's relation with her mother was intimate, warm, and alternately compliant and controlling. It manifested itself most positively in her play with a vast number of dolls and teddies, whom she tenderly cared for and protected; even more adaptive were her constant visits to a neighbor's twin babies with whom she played mother expertly. The dolls represented Susan herself, and her vigorous and sadistic control of them expressed her resentment that she was often prevented from doing much that she felt capable of.

Susan's compliance with her mother's fiction that she was too young to understand about her precocity was based on her taking over her mother's defenses which then enabled her to deny her satisfaction in listening intently to her mother's hypochondriacal ruminations on her own and her child's body. Susan would sing a little song called "Agony," equating her own medical experiences with her mother's sexual and feminine agonies. In one of her drawings they held hands, having placed a little mouse on each other's heads. Susan felt they were both subjected to frightening and magical experiences which made them uniquely different from other members of the family. When Susan spoke of herself as "a little girl with crates of milk in her bottom," her discharge featured to provide an organ identity with her mother's breasts. Her self-esteem was thus nurtured regressively, and her aggression defended against.

Mrs. S.'s projection of her hypochondriacal anxieties onto the child and her attempt to deal with them in relation to Susan's body (projective identification) were fundamental issues which emerged clearly even in the limited treatment it was possible to offer the mother. This situation made Susan's defense system and the defensive character of her fantasies of identity with her mother, based on their common wish to exhibit castration, the most intractable in the analysis.

Constant transference interpretations of her defenses against aggression had slowly enabled Susan to become more efficient at expressing her anger at her enforced passivity and more effective at equipping herself with useful knowledge about her own and her mother's medical procedures. At this point she developed a chaotic mode of speech and behavior (for the most part confined to the analysis) reminiscent of a borderline child. Her material for many months was expressed through primary-process functioning, over-condensed and symbolic at many levels, replete with cover memories and often unintelligible. Some more intelligible fragments, which focused interpretations at the end of this period, indicated that Susan attempted to explain her abnormality in terms that involved her mother and herself in mutual bodily damage. While the ambivalent nature of her fantasies was now more strikingly evident, they still expressed Susan's wish for an undifferentiated union; a constant pull toward symbiosis marked all her object relationships. The deep ego regression in which her fantasy life at this time involved her arose when the release of aggression through analytic work threatened this narcissistic maneuver.

Susan's birth was allegedly "six weeks overdue" and precipitate. One day she stuffed her doll under her dress and ran excitedly around the room. Her therapist was told to catch the doll because if she fell she would die. She must be X-rayed when she was pulled out, to see if she was still breathing, as now she was ripe. Her blood had to be extracted—it was red, blue, and green—and new blood injected. In this story Susan's mother was responsible for her condition because she let her "fall out." In another version, Susan was responsible for her mother's condition. Susan was in bed with mother and jumped about and kicked her in the tummy. Susan then had a bath and they went away on holiday. Everything happened in a hurry. Susan climbed about on rocks and when John came out, he said, "I am sorry you are so sad. Come inside." So Susan dived in head first. The substitution of "falling in" for "falling out" was the key to this anal birth fantasy which proved crucial in her diminished self-esteem. Susan was relieved to be told that her own intra-uterine kicks had not injured her mother, nor had her mother's delay in arriving at the hospital injured her in any way. While the rocks refer to her anxiety over her early games with John, to which she also attributed her abnormality, the meaning of "falling" was over-determined. It involved her fantasies of sexual experience with her father *in utero* (Leuba, 1950), and more deeply buried references to her experiences of anesthesia conceived as a sexual union. The latter were clarified only at a later stage of the analysis and disclosed her wish to be devoured in an ultimate union with both parents.

Shortly afterward, Susan enumerated the reasons for all the hospitalizations there had ever been in her family. When the subject of her own hospitalization at twenty months was broached, Susan asked for information. She was told that her mother had been worried because her body was growing so fast. The doctor said she was rather a special baby who would always be ahead of other children till they caught up with her at fourteen. Then they would all be the same again. Susan listened with rapt attention and asked for the story to be repeated. Soon thereafter Susan introduced the subject of menstruation, and the way was now open for a fuller discussion with her. The narcissistic distress she had suffered was greatly eased from this time with the reassurance that other girls would share this function with her. Her ability to integrate the information was evident in the direct ego advances she made almost at once (aged five years, ten months). Most importantly, she began to look forward to her future. Referring to the twins in a slightly later session, she said, "When I am grown up, I shall have a husband *instead*." This was the first occasion on which she gave evidence of imagining a normal future for herself.

The Emergence of a True Oedipal Phase

Susan's libidinal development closely approximates the phenomenon of "agglutination of phases" (Greenacre, 1954). Postulating that the overlap of phase development may be considerably greater than has been thought, "that in fact all lines of activity are present in some degree at birth or soon thereafter," Greenacre concludes, "it is the maturational peak and its relative prominence in the total activity of the individual organism that marks the phase; and the succession of maturational peaks which creates the appearance of a succession of phases." Severe prolonged stimulation or multiplicity of simultaneous stimulations may result in a flooding of the organism with excitement; and where all channels of discharge are utilized, there may be a generalized acceleration of all drives and a kind of basic amalgamation with sacrifice of special direction and appropriateness.

In Susan's case, the evidence is conclusive that though she received above-average care, her life from the outset was beset with maternal anxieties of a quite unusual type. At every stage of her development Susan was confused and disturbed by the impact of her mother's chaotic personality. It is likely that her early feeding problem resulted from Mrs. S.'s libidinal incapacity to deal with her nasal blockage. Frustration of her sucking needs from birth contributed to the persistence of gross oral features in her autoerotic activity and in her fantasy life as well as to the incorporative nature of her object relations. The sexualization of her perceptive activities also stemmed from this source.

There is every reason to suppose that Mrs. S. had handled Susan's toilet training not strictly but in an emotional way. Moreover, the hospitalization at twenty months and her mother's preoccupation with her genital discharge were influential factors in the persistence of her anal and urethral preoccupations. Little is known about the earlier hospitalization for gastroenteritis, which also must have played a significant role. Susan's strong reaction formations of disgust toward her own body may have derived initially from the frustration of her sucking and certainly from the handling of her discharge, the continuation of which served as a constant provocation

of her anal impulses. Anal and oral anxieties were closely interwoven in her poisoning fantasies.

While the wish for a penis appeared as an organizing element in
her fantasy and the wish to share in her mother's bodily experiences
was also a constant, undoubtedly oedipal element, a specific phallic
response with true competitive strivings was barely apparent. The
quality of her anxiety, her ego modifications, and the blurring of
self- and object images gave the impression of being defensive
against a loss even more fundamental than is involved in oedipal
frustration. It was less that she was retreating from an oedipal position than that nascent oedipal wishes were threatening an already-
precarious position where she felt unsure of her personal emotional
existence.

In the early stages of analysis Susan's self-representation was
similar in some respects to that of the fetishist. At one level she was
well aware that she was a little girl and would be a woman. Equally
she was aware of the sexual identity of her objects. At the level of
her primitive fantasies, these distinctions were obliterated, and
reality was replaced by a belief in the universality of the penis on
the one hand, and the universality of castration on the other. The
remarkable feats of integration which she attempted at both these
levels were possible because there was no primary defect in her
synthetic function. These endeavors were necessary because the in-
soluble problem of her precocity reactivated basic narcissistic anxieties, which threatened to overwhelm her ego.

Susan's considerable adaptive capacities indicated a primary
development in which ego integration had already taken place in
large measure and was supported and developed by a very great
degree of good mothering. Autoplastic modes of discharge (illness
and prolonged autoerotic activity) were influential in limiting the
degree of vulnerability of the ego (Anna Freud, 1954). But the
failure of the synthetic function in the area of the "equilibrium of
the instinctual drives" (Hartmann, 1939) interfered with processes
of fusion in the drive systems, with consequent heightening of mo-
mentum in each. Her early unrestrained attacks on John and later
outbreaks of exhibitionism reflected this defusion and represented
defensive attempts against a deeper ego regression.

Passive fantasies of incorporation by the idealized and degraded part objects marked the onset of this regression to primary-process functioning, releasing new aspects of both her self- and object images. Jacobson (1954) refers to the temporary weakening of the perceptive functions which accompany such fantasies of refusion of self- and object images. Susan's case is remarkable for the short spans of time in which each endured, often changing several times within the compass of one story. This situation reflected the fluid boundaries between self- and object images, the split in her ego organization, and the extent of her ambivalent conflict.

While the distinction between herself and her objects was so difficult to maintain and the cathexis of whole objects so inadequate, it is doubtful if it is right to speak of a true oedipal complex. With the ego's acceptance of the need for temporary frustration which followed on her enlightenment about her abnormality ("I shall have a husband, instead"), reaction formations in the form of pity, shyness, and consideration for the frustrations of others led Susan to a more real appraisal of her objects. An oedipal *conflict,* in contrast to what might be called her pregenital battle for phallic equivalents, could then develop.

At the age of five years eight months, Susan was hospitalized to undergo an operation for squint. When she returned from the hospital where she had been unusually happy and had participated in the school activities provided on the ward, she absolutely refused to speak or enter the treatment room and for three months had to be interviewed in the waiting room, where she was clearly the object of much curosity. She reproduced in this way the situation of her original hospitalization, silently soliciting interest in her new accomplishments while indicating in her drawings that bad analytic sexual talk was not in order. On occasions, however, she was sexually most provocative, sitting with her legs apart, or crawling round the floor, her face covered with a beret, and noisily and excitedly playing at being a cat licking milk from a saucer. One day she drew a forest with a little girl riding. Instantly she became frantic with anxiety, asked whether anyone had ever seen a tree with so many little twigs on it (pubic hair), and was that what a tree should look like? Was the little girl alright?

The pleasurable attention Susan was receiving as the focus of interest in the waiting room released memories of the original traumatic hospitalization at twenty months. She had been given anesthesia for a rectal examination (the beret on her face) when she became uncontrollable after being separated from her mother. It is not known in what form the anesthestic was administered. Susan also reacted with ego restriction to the excitement engendered by returning to her therapist with many new accomplishments. The splitting of the ego in the defensive process was thus seen to have originated in her attempted denial of the hospital experience with the overwhelming excitement and aggressive stimulation it involved.

At the age of six and a half years, Susan had her first period. Her second followed after an interval of six months, and thereafter she was regular. She was well prepared for the event and though it brought considerable excitement and anxiety, and a profusion of fantasy, this differed from the normal girl at the menarche only in that it was readily accessible and achieved a degree of belief (*Ichzugehörigkeit*) which is unusual. Her disappointment that she had not gained either a penis or a baby led to a pronounced reaction against the physical and verbal exhibitionism in her family and to the revelation that she identified her whole precocious little body with the penis which she and her mother so coveted. She felt that by maintaining her body and its precocity as an object of sexual interest, she fulfilled this need for her mother.

From this point on, Susan gradually developed her awareness of people. New phallic (oedipal) elements appeared in her relation with John and her father. Her envy of John was tinged with admiration, and a wish to catch up with him in school. She became aware of her mother's disturbance and the distress it caused to herself and the family, and was gradually able to be more detached. Her father's weakness and the impingement of his obsessions on the family were also admitted. A true oedipal conflict now emerged and could be analyzed as it manifested itself in the transference, in regard to her family, and via displacement outside the family. Her sexual deprivation was expressed in fantasies of starvation and her aggression in a tantalizing untidiness, directed against her father's obsessional rituals at mealtimes. In the untidiness, Susan was abetted by her mother, and identified with her mother's casual attitudes to her cleanliness training. Mrs. S.'s conflicts in this area of child care led her to project her distress onto her husband, while she maintained an overtolerant

attitude herself. This pattern was carried over into her preoccupation with the discharge, and underlay Susan's complaint of her
mother's part in alienating her from her father.

Susan now found constructive ways of coming to terms with her
father's personality. Memories of early swinging games and of being
carried half asleep in his arms were re-enacted in the transference.
The memory of the swing brought in the first sessions now appeared
as a cover memory for all these events. The idea of swinging away
from the father's body contained both the denial of the penis as a
male organ and a condensation showing the origin of the penis-body
equation in excitements, disappointments, and anxiety, which primarily concerned her father. Fenichel (1936) stresses the importance
of the prevalence of oral wishes in girls' fantasies of possessing and
being a penis. "They identify themselves, i.e., their whole body, with
a penis, via the pathway of oral introjection. The idea of having
bitten off a penis or of having otherwise incorporated it is the continuation of the unconscious equation 'body = penis.' This equation,
the aim of which is in fact that of a *totem* being taken into the body
of the object, may therefore be regarded as a passive complement to
the fantasy of swallowing a penis." Fenichel also stresses the heightened effect which the oral-sadistic tendencies have on the voyeuristic
impulses.

With the emergence of Susan's fantasies of the primal scene
in the final stage of the analysis, her fear of losing control was centered on ideas of becoming "hysterical," being hypnotized, and going
"out into space" in a capsule. Susan linked the latter idea with a
capsule given her against her will in the hospital and with a recent
fainting fit of John's. These fantasies culminated in a panic attack
on an escalator. Susan broke into a sweat and was "safe" only with
her mother's arms around her. It was now clear that Susan equated
the primal scene with her struggle to resist anesthesia at twenty
months. The fear of "falling into space" was identical with her fear
of being overwhelmed by sexual fantasy (Leuba, 1950), against which
her internal resources in terms of maternal identification seemed too
precarious a protection.

Susan's inability to establish a workable identification with her
mother, a shift from "being one with" to "being like" (Jacobson,
1954), could now be seen from a developmental angle. Loewald

(1951) describes how the child's attitudes to reality, and his ability
to build boundaries between his outer and inner world bears the
imprint of the stages of his relation to his object. While the primary
narcissistic identity with the mother constitutes a libidinal motive
force for the ego's striving to progressive differentiation and unifi-
cation of reality, it is also the source of a threat to perpetuate and
re-establish this position and engulf the emerging ego into its original
primary narcissistic unity, "an unstructured nothingness of identity
of 'ego' and 'reality.' " Susan experienced castration in terms of a
fantasied loss of identity both from the anticipated satisfaction of her
phallic (oedipal) wishes and when she retreated from these to an
"engulfing mother." Susan's fantasies of her own birth, where she
was poisoned, overwhelmed, engulfed in the dangerous womb, and
threatened with suffocation and extinction, represented an alternative castration threat. This fantasy seems to bear the imprint of
memory traces of her feeding situation.

Susan's experience of body interference at twenty months and
the reinforcement of her primary narcssistic fantasies by the administration of anesthesia provided a basis in reality for her essentially
neurotic fears of loss of identity. This event occurred at a time when
the boundaries between inner and outer reality were still fluid and
her sexual identity was not yet fully established. Fantasies of oral
impregnation arising in the current oedipal situation reactivated
her wish for the mother's breast. Her fears of disintegration could
now be seen as rooted in an ambivalent wish to be taken into her
mother's arms. Fenichel comments: "The intention of disproving
oral-sadistic tendencies against the penis by the fantasy of harmonious
unity with it—'I am myself the penis'—seems in typical fashion a
continuation of the intention of disproving oral-sadistic tendencies
against the mother's body by means of the fantasy of harmonious
unity with it." Fantasies of unity with the mother's body or the
penis alternated in Susan's sexual identity.

Present Interests and Achievements

Susan at ten years of age is a normally adapted latency child.
Although the tallest in her class, she is in no way conspicuous. Her
mother finds Susan a competent and reliable help in the home. In
her relationships with her parents, she is able to take a tolerant

account of their difficulties and can discuss her problems sensibly. While she is entirely competent in managing her periods, before a recent visit with a school friend to Ireland, she had a serious discussion with her mother about the difficulties that might arise. Toward the end of her analysis Susan summed up the advantages she had gained from it as follows: "When Mummy wants me to change my clothes all the time, or wear something I don't want to, I just say, 'Oh Mummy don't fuss.' I never thought I would do that ever." Susan had no minor illness either neurotic or physical in the last year of her analysis.

In the seven years of treatment, Susan lost more than a third of her treatment sessions, and was simultaneously absent from school, on account of her own or her mother's indispositions. Ultimately, it became clear that the impact of Mrs. S.'s anxiety on her medical advisers provoked at least one long and unnecessary hospitalization (for a nonexistent heart condition). It could be surmised that many of Susan's absences for minor illness had been encouraged by Mrs. S. and had not been strictly necessary. Despite the long absence from school Susan is in the top group of her class, except in arithmetic where she is average. Her imaginative powers are now used for integrated story writing, which is ambitious and well organized. Her stories sometimes run into several chapters. At the end of treatment she expressed her pleasure in her own absorbed functioning as a writer, saying, "I never thought I could do a thing like that. It's like being out in space." Her drawings have received merit awards in newspaper competitions.

Her ability to verbalize discriminative judgments is probably unusually high as a result of her long period in treatment. She applies this ability equally to her inner and outer life. She recently volunteered the thought that she must have liked the smell of her rag dolly, because it smelled like her mother.

Swimming remains one of her favorite pastimes; she has won various badges, including one for lifesaving. On the whole, her activities tend to be solitary; in a group, she likes to take the role of instructor, telling stories or teaching others to swim. She has no particular interest in her appearance, though she dresses neatly and attractively. While her sexual fantasies involve boys in her class, they are tentative and not carried into action. She is contented at home and has no wish to leave her family. Susan looks forward to her future, but for the moment is quite content to be a little girl.

SUMMARY OF CONCLUSIONS

1. Susan's behavioral disturbance was first recognized after her hospitalization and anesthetization at twenty months. These events accentuated the passive-active conflict normally developing at the end of the second year. The fluidity of her instinctual organization and the immaturity of her ego at this age provided fertile soil for fantastic solutions in her assumption of gender role.

2. There was no timely suggestion that help could be made available for both parents and child. The parents' continued anxiety over her precocity added a special quality to Susan's object relations and complicated the problem of her identifications. The structuring of her narcissism was more than usually impeded, and her self-esteem became dependent on defensive fantasies involving her body image.

3. Fixation points induced by the quality of her earliest maternal care also predisposed her to continuous instinctual stimulation at all levels and partial ego regressions against which her primitive defense system could not be effective. Spitz (1954) emphasized that "it is the fixation point in the mother's personality which causes a disorganization in the orderly development of the child."

4. In the context of her later phallic (oedipal) development Susan's precocity and her ambivalent object relationships led her to see herself as a real rival to a mother with omnipotent powers of retaliation.

The fantasy of actual sexual rivalry with her mother, focused on the possession of secondary sex characteristics, accentuated her castration anxiety. The peculiar intensity and macabre quality of her fantasies owe much to the strength of these anxieties. But Susan's castration anxiety was also reinforced by a primitive fear of ego dissolution inherent in very early fixation points.

5. Susan's display of secondary sex characteristics functioned to aggravate the castration complex of the males in her environment, so that the quality of the consequent rebuff of her oedipal wishes intensified her tendency to regression.

In an impressive article,[1] Comfort (1960) suggests that at a time in human evolution prior to the development of the latency period, castration anxiety, which seems inappropriate to childhood in any known society, may have had the effect of restraining males from being competitive before they were mature. Avoidance of the sexually displaying female could serve to keep them out of the competitive struggle while still maternally dependent. The penis envy of the girl coming to normal adolescent expression in decorative symbols and cryptandric behavior would help in reversing the male anxiety response to the female genital and thus facilitate the expression of adult sexual drives.

6. The analysis afforded no evidence that Susan's physical precocity was accompanied by the quantitative increase in sexual drive that we associate with puberty. Her pathology is more readily explicable on other grounds. Identical pathological manifestations, involving phase agglutination, with marked passive features in all drive systems and ego regression, are observed in a group of cases in which early seduction and maternal frustration are common but which lack the feature of precocious puberty.

In analogy with what we know about the formation of neuroses, it might be assumed that the intensity of her pregenital relationship to her mother (accompanied as it was by manifestations of phallic exhibitionism) was in part the outcome of regression from an increased genital drive. The following facts argue against this view:

a. The main manifestation of conflict occurred in the area of Susan's narcissism; it was at this point in the analysis that her main regression, including regression to primary-process thinking, was evident (age four to five and a half years).

b. The onset of menstruation was not accompanied by a similar phenomenon (age six and a half years). Nor did any increase in defensive struggle which might have been a negative indicator of increased drive activity occur in relation to the onset of menstruation. It could scarcely be expected that an increase in genital drive would fail to exacerbate the genital anxieties of such a young child with so inadequate an ego. In the absence of increased inhibition or other evidence of increased defenses against sexuality, there is a

[1] My attention was drawn to the relevance of this article by Dr. Alfred Model, R.T.

very strong *prima facie* case for the hypothesis that Susan's precocious physical development resulted in no increase of psychic sexual drive.

c. Susan's development to the present shows none of the features of adolescence. She has reacted to her oedipal situation (the true oedipal phase) instinctually as a four-year-old, though with the added insight contingent on her long period in analysis. No wish is evident to break her object ties. At the height of her oedipal frustration, fantasies of street wandering similar to the prostitution fantasies of the adolescent were evident, but their outcome was only that Susan asked for more liberty to go about alone.

Analysis has contributed to the containment of her sexuality ·by the reorganization of her personality, and made possible the emergence of a true latency period.

7. The analysis affords overwhelming evidence that constitutional sexual precocity is a major problem for both the child and her family, in which psychological help for a considerable period may be needed. It is doubtful whether a true estimate of the child's internal disabilities can be gauged even by such intensive interviews as were undertaken by Hampson and Money (1955). In Susan's case the degree and nature of the impact of massive family defenses on the child's own defense system would have proved impossible to judge. Family casework over a long period by an analytically trained adviser, capable of eliciting and handling the transference manifestations of anxiety, would alone provide an adequate diagnostic plan.

7

EGO SYNTHESIS OF A LIFE-THREATENING ILLNESS IN CHILDHOOD

JEROME KAVKA, M.D.
(1962)

Despite numerous studies in which psychoanalytic insights have been brought to bear upon the relation between illness and character development, students of child psychopathology, including Anna Freud, have alluded to the absence of exact observations on the psychological effects of illness. In a recent panel on the psychological consequences of physical illness in childhood, Edith Buxbaum offered a partial explanation: people, in general, do not like handicapped children or adults. This attitude is based on a deep-seated horror of and resentment against illness, feelings which are also expressed by parents toward the sick child. In support of this she noted how often curative measures take a restrictive form. Similar attitudes, she suggested, may account for the reluctance of psychoanalysts to observe the effects of bodily illness (see Calef, 1959).

The following report is based on the supposition that by a detailed study of the evolution of the transference neurosis, the analyst can secure reliable information regarding the integration and synthesis of physical events in the life of the child as reflected in the ego's adaptation to these events. Re-enactments and reconstructions of extreme traumas, such as serious physical illness, may provide instructive examples not only of ego synthesis but of the related interpersonal transactions, and thus help to affirm or modify current theories of character development and neurosis.

The psychoanalytic treatment of an adolescent boy revealed the mechanisms used by his ego to integrate a life-threatening illness, which began at the height of the oedipal period of development. The combined traumatic assault of the illness, the required medical treatments, and the alarm reactions of his parents were superimposed on an unconscious castration threat. The obvious danger to his life was in the center of the parents' conscious interest. This emphasis as well as their consequent attitudes and behavior were later used by the patient as the main, though preconscious, focus in the evolution of the transference neurosis. In other words, there was a constant concern about physical health and disease and preoccupations with disaster and death. The data of the treatment ultimately tended to confirm the classical theory that castration anxiety underlies the fear of death.

SUMMARY OF DEVELOPMENTAL HISTORY

A highly intelligent nineteen-year-old university student was referred to me because of decreased interest and poor performance in academic work which seriously threatened his career. According to his parents, he was chronically irritable and doubted his career choice; but their main concern was that he engaged in daring physical activities, such as extremely long walks in bad weather, lifting heavy weights, etc., which could result in the flare-up of a chronic disease. The parents as well as the referring analyst informed me that a diagnosis of reticulum cell sarcoma (Hodgkin's disease) had been made following the biopsy of an enlarged lymph node when the patient was five years old. He had received intensive X-ray radiation and nitrogen-mustard treatments at the time and again at the age of eleven years. At the time of referral, there had been no recurrence for a period of eight years. The patient had never been told the truth about his illness. When one of his vertebrae was involved during puberty, he was told he had osteomyelitis, which euphemism he would use to refer to the events of his illness. Presumably, he was not conscious of the gravity of his past illness.

After an evaluation I agreed to accept the patient for psychotherapy, eventually perhaps for psychoanalysis, under one condition: since I had been informed of the diagnosis, I would be ruled by honesty and discretion in my conduct with him; while I would make no effort to reveal unsolicited information to him, should he directly ask me what I knew, I would feel obliged to tell him what I had been told. The possible consequences of panic, depression, and rage to the parents were discussed with them. They agreed to the condition and the therapy proceeded.

The dormant physical illness with its implications of fatality presented, along with the compact made with the parents, possible countertransference difficulties. For the most part, however, I felt comfortable in my dealings with the patient. While sensitive and empathic at more intense periods, I did not become helplessly involved with sympathy and identifications in matters pertaining to the illness. There were no direct manifestations of the disease process during the four and a half years of the treatment.

I shall summarize the patient's developmental history as it unfolded in the treatment and shall focus mainly on the important memories and the fantasies associated with them.

The patient had distinctive physical features: he was thin, pale, and had a slight hunch in the upper back due to the spinal involvement. He was gawky in his movements, and, in general, gave the impression of an unsturdy physique. Not until later in the treatment did the bespectacled scholar substitute gazing at girls on his way to the office for reading the books constantly in his hand.

Frightened at first, he assumed a cautious, if respectful attitude. He resented his parents for having suggested psychiatric treatment and viewed his referral as another step in his mother's campaign to restrain his independence. Nevertheless, he soon avowed his dissatisfaction with himself, and expressed a desire to become comfortably independent of his parents, to do well in school, establish a career, and to have more satisfying relations with his peers. As he talked, his confidence in me increased to the point where he was soon able to confess perverse fantasies and fetishistic preoccupations, which he preferred to communicate in a written note:

> When I was a rather small boy, certainly before I was ten years old, I became obsessed with the horror of suffocation in general and hanging in particular. It was really a pseudo-erotic stimulation, and has persisted until the present with, I think, less poignancy. As a matter of fact, this realization was the original reason why I came to despise capital punishment. This is my own declaration to myself that my mind can discipline its own impulses.
>
> My strongest memory, which may have something to do with this, is of the time that my mother took to telling me "go hang yourself" when I irritated her. She says this was when I was eleven. I thought it was sooner. She still thinks she was righteous.

Like the other, this preoccupation has not affected my interest in women. However, I have only dreamed of girls twice or so in my life, and neither of these dreams was a true "erotic" dream since they provoked no discharge. My true erotic dreams have all been concerned with this perversion. However, even in dreams, the sadism has been muted. Sometimes it is masochistically expressed.

My other claim on hell is, since childhood, in various forms, depending on age, a fascination with handkerchiefs, especially neckerchiefs, which brings this into some sort of relation to the above. As a boy, I used to watch Westerns. At that time, the neckerchief was a symbol of masculinity. Since puberty, the significance has reversed and preserved itself, depending on the circumstances. When I was in kindergarten or first grade, I refused to carry a handkerchief, to my mother's chagrin which is always ready at hand. One day, when she and my sister escorted me to school, I was forced to carry a woman's handkerchief, which mortified me. That is all I can recall relating to this.

It seemed to me that this form of communication, with its exhibitionistic display of language and forced intellectual style, represented during this early phase of treatment a carry-over from the academic sphere and implicated the treatment in a student-teacher relationship with overtones of supplication for acceptance. The content, nevertheless, revealed his intelligence, his attempt to establish psychological connections, and some capacity for insight. One may note the masculine-feminine struggle and the anticipatory association between male pride, castration anxiety, and, as he called it, mortification. The tone of the communication, while tinged with masochistic self-pity, was assertive and individualistic and contained unveiled antagonism to his mother.

He cooperated during the exploratory phase and revealed that he had been somewhat prepared for help from outside the family, having for years turned to a physician friend of his parents for guidance and inspiration, which he felt he had now outgrown. As he looked back on it, he now regarded this guidance as overmoralistic, pushy, and too reminiscent of his parents' excessive stimulation. This evaluation seemed to express a certain wariness concerning the possible influence of his parents on me; it also reflected some degree of conscience anxiety which was apt to be mobilized in the permissive environment of the office.

He freely criticized his parents, especially his mother, who, he said, "babied" him. In this he was not incorrect, although in his rationalizations he obviously overlooked both his own provocativeness and his submissiveness. During later, critical phases of the treatment, the mother, a compulsive character with hysterical qualities and a whining voice, often sought help from me, especially when the patient was "acting up" with her. Separation from him increased her fears for his health. Yet she was able to leave on her occasional vacations with the feeling that he was in safe hands.

The father was a highly successful professional man of compulsive character make-up, a sensible and kindly person, if formal and stiff. Two recurrent notions were often associated with the father: as a youngster the patient was discouraged from entering his father's study and this had disappointed him; he could not imagine his father "unbending enough" to enjoy sex.

The only sibling, an older sister, left for an out-of-town college when the patient was eight or nine and returned when he was thirteen. She left home permanently shortly thereafter to marry and raise a family. She was remembered mainly as being seductive inasmuch as she and mother often walked about the house half-dressed and without regard for the excitement which this caused in him.

In reviewing the history as it emerged, piecemeal, throughout the analysis, traumatic incidents and screen memories of traumas dominated the dated remembrances. The few preoedipal memories consisted essentially of some excitement around a miscarriage of the mother when he was between one and three years of age. Details remained obscure, but fears and anxiety related to blood were relived and recalled. Reconstructions and some memories revealed an ambivalent attachment to a "nanny" who cared for him between the ages of one and six years and who was responsible for his toilet training. Considerable urinary and anal aggression was expressed, reconstructed, and re-enacted in the course of the analysis. His expletives were urinary or anal (pissed off, shit) until later in the analysis when they assumed a more phallic, aggressive character.

Beginning with age four years, fears of expanding objects such as balloons and umbrellas screened anxiety over erections. There was a recollection of tumescence at age five when he had masturbated in his mother's presence; she had voiced various warnings to stop and told him to "go hang himself." On one occasion she struck him for masturbating, and he was filled with murderous rage. Fears of a magician and his kerchiefs necessitated his fleeing home from school at the onset of latency. Also, an invitation to a father-and-son dinner aroused fears in him that he and his father would be hung when they got there.

A number of memories dating from the ages of five to six years appeared to be screens for the biopsy of a lymph node which had resulted in the diagnosis of his physical illness and fearsome radiation therapy. He recalled his parents' fears for his life when he had what he referred to as "measles" characterized by "lumps." Measles was obviously a euphemism for the enlarged nodes, just as osteomyelitis later became the euphemism for the spinal involvement. His fright of the radiation machines was expressed in oral-cannibalistic anxieties as he recalled being taken to a hospital where he seemed to have seen "a big cruel turtle eating a dead bird." Exposed to separation and danger in the hospital, the idealized mother came to his aid in a fantasy; "I am a goldfish in a bowl of cold water. A beautiful girl comes to the edge of the water and talks to me and I talk back."

Between the ages of six and nine years, and following his hospitalization, loving memories of both parents emerged, including nostalgic reminiscences of summer vacations and the warmth of sleeping beside his mother. These pleasant memories concealed some anxiety since he sought his mother's side because of nightmares. Also, he recalled embarrassment over her return of his affection. The latency memories revealed a fascination with a hanging in a Western movie he attended with his mother at age seven. The theme of a Western-style hanging later became the framework of pubertal and adolescent masturbation fantasies. The fetishistic and obsessional preoccupation with kerchiefs, necks, and hanging was embellished and varied in many ways, but most importantly by the eventual addition of his fantasied rape of the bereaved wife during or after the hanging of her husband. This fantasy thus disclosed the oedipal theme barely disguised.

On the whole, and as would be expected, the latency period was relatively quiescent by comparison with the periods immediately preceding and following it. However, a dramatic and violent end to the latency period was ushered in by a sudden hospitalization at age nine years when the patient developed pneumothorax requiring a two- to three-month stay at a hospital for treatment and observation. At that time, he consciously feared for his life and regressed to urinary incontinence. The seductiveness of the hospital experience was exemplified by a later urinary retention when he was embarrassed over mother pouring water on his genitals to stimulate urination.

At the age of eleven years, the patient developed a more intense fascination with neckerchiefs which to him symbolized masculinity. Further hospital treatment at the age of twelve years, when his ego was stronger, was no longer fraught with terror. At the age of fourteen years, while ambulating with crutches, he developed a direct interest in real women. His later adolescent memories, from ages fifteen and seventeen years, included his grandmother's death of apoplexy and mother's hysterectomy.

The Course of the Analysis

The first seven months of treatment were preparation for analysis. The therapeutic approach was cautious because he had not come of his own accord and resented his parents' suggestion of psychiatric treatment. Furthermore, he was initially somewhat cynical; his "what can this do for me" attitude reflected rebellion against authority and a continuation of a self-destructive pattern evident in his academic work, in his personal relations, and in his attitude toward his body. In his somewhat being "eased" into analysis, he resembled the frequently reluctant adolescent who will characteristically attempt to deny defects, deformity, and mutilation of body or character by evasion, displacement, projection, or other defensive devices. However, with sufficient distress, good intelligence, and increasing trust in me, regular analysis was instituted. He came four times weekly, used the couch and free association, and abided cooperatively with the external rules of analysis to the end.

The diagnosis at the beginning was that of a character disorder with immaturity, emotional inhibitions, and neurotic manifestations, but with the evolution of the analysis an obsessional neurosis became more evident; there was the history of preoedipal precocity and regression to pregenitality when at the height of the oedipal period he was faced with extreme danger to his life—a trauma which was repeated at the prepubertal and pubertal periods.

Soon after treatment was initiated he began to masturbate compulsively and defiantly continued as he moved from autoerotism to object relatedness. Sadistic phallic fantasies with the penis as a hurting organ emerged, and he challenged me to stop his masturbation as his mother had done with her threats. On the other hand, he feared attack by me and implored me not to punish him as his mother had done. Confronted by my noninterference, he made spontaneous efforts to be a "good boy" by controlling masturbation. As a substitute, however, he shed his shoes, wrist watch, and keys, and picked at his clothing while on the couch. His desire to be close to me alternated with withdrawal as he felt he was getting too excited by sadistic and masochistic fantasies. In a fairly rapid regression from the phallic position, his actual shedding of clothes and his attempts to use free association recalled early toilet-training experience. Getting things "off his chest" was similar to going to the toilet, while revealing his thoughts and feelings was a form of nakedness and recalled diapers and dirtiness. Elements of phallic anxiety were mixed with anal anxieties as he recalled his fears of the magician and his disappearing act—now it's here and now it isn't. He attempted to provoke arguments with me, while in reality the number and intensity of his arguments with his mother diminished considerably in the first year.

With the approaching first long vacation from analysis, he feared losing control of his emerging phallic sadistic impulses in the absence of the analyst as controller. I was seen as the abandoning mother whom he wanted to shoot. The second line of diversion was an attempt to convince me not to go away since vacations were "whoring, bad, dirty." As his efforts to change my plans failed, he regressed to the arch weapon—illness; he developed a cold and "needed" a doctor to remain with him.

When the analysis was resumed three weeks later, he reported that during the vacation he had had back pain which recalled the hospitalization during puberty—the whole experience now summarized as punishment, mutilation, and castration. Oedipal fantasies now were associated with masturbation. Murderous, choking impulses toward the father were rationalized as due to the father's sadism; father, being a biologist, tore wings off insects. Though the patient began to assert himself with a girl, his fantasies while "necking" were of an incestuous nature. These fantasies were rationalized as "not too bad" since his mother was able to arouse every kind of excitement in him in the past except desire for sexual intercourse. Under the increasing tension of urinary and phallic impulses with simultaneous remembrances of feelings toward his parents, he made an important anticipatory remark at this point in the analysis: "A wonderful thing has happened to me since I came here. Remembering makes my life seem whole again."

Following a series of alternating pleasurable regressive fantasies—head on mother's lap, nursing, looking up into her face—and frightening suffocation fantasies, he reached a high point of emotional tension after one year of treatment. After masturbating with fantasies of women's scarves, intense castration anxiety was ushered in with the dream of a tornado. Sex was connected with death and hanging with deprivation—loss of love. While there was no evidence of guilt feelings, there was a fear of reactivating the old "infection." I understood this to refer to the reactivation of the infantile neurosis. Strong attraction to older women and a dream about an older woman aroused intense fears for his penis and recalled radiation therapy, which he equated with punishment for his phallic impulses. As he unfavorably compared his penis to that of older men, he concluded that radiation, used as punishment, made him impotent. During fantasies of hanging, choking, and dying, he recalled the anesthesia experience too as punishment for phallic impulses. From the analytic material it appeared that his illness had occurred before the period of phallic primacy and while urination had represented the only permissible cathexis of the penis. Phallic impulses had just been emerging and genital primacy had not yet been inaugurated.

In the transference situation, he recalled his mother's love for him when he was six or seven years old. He had experienced this as exceptional permissiveness and now expressed it with simultaneous disparagement of me. Strong sadistic feelings erupted under great pressure of incestuous fantasies. At this time a dream representing an attempt to deflect sexual feelings away from the incestuous object initiated an effort to find a girl in real life. He began to "neck" more

aggressively with girls. At the same time, the father reported by
telephone that the patient was recklessly exposing himself to cold
weather; this behavior represented a counterphobic denial of his
vulnerability displaced onto the weather. As he enjoyed necking,
his fears of being punished increased in intensity. The oedipal
conflict became obvious as he expressed satisfaction over the death
of a gorilla in the local zoo and simultaneously experienced "puzzling" hostility toward me. Castration anxiety was most intense when
he introduced the gorilla's death; he commented that he was now
learning things about himself he should have known long ago, by
which he referred to the reactivation of death wishes toward his
father now displaced onto the analyst. Following another entreaty
for me to interdict his masculine endeavors, a dream revealed that
he had conceived of the X-ray therapy as a castration threat and
punishment for his sadistic impulses. Until that time he had occasionally used regressive homosexual defenses to ward off intense
castration anxiety, but now a sexual interest in my wife ushered in
a more consistent use of passive, submissive devices. He regularly
began going to toilets in the building, hoping to meet me there
sometimes. He then switched to violent attacks on his mother and
began to see me as his mother who refused to accept his love in the
place of the father's love. In a continuous homosexual flight from
castration anxiety, the father now was all good and the mother all
bad. He envied people's closeness to each other, yet feared being
crushed in sadistically conceived primal scenes. Thus, at the end of
the second year of treatment, he was switching back and forth between heterosexual impulses directed to girls reminding him of his
mother and homosexual impulses induced by regressions. With each
increase in masculine assertiveness outside the office, he showed a
corresponding increase in apparent maturity in the office. He now
felt more adult, and for the first time was able to place his coat in
the closet instead of throwing it down casually. However, assuming
a more adult role again increased his castration fears and revived
fantasies about radiation and how it may have affected his potency.
He began to wonder about his sperm, which he studied under a
microscope. He visited his physician for information, but was quite
hesitant and vague in seeking it. It was apparent that he was not
yet ready to accept the truth of his past experience. The desire to

know something from adults continued, but in the disguised form of seeking advice on the choice of a career. Increased interest in his career and improved studies also represented identification and rivalry with adults—he too could have what adults have.

Upon reaching twenty-one years of age, he made heroic attempts to be a man. He changed his style of clothing to a more mature one and proudly announced that he had registered to vote. At the same time, he realized that his notion of being adult implied cruelty and destructiveness to women as he indulged in sadistic fantasies toward women in the waiting room. His aggressiveness had mobilized hostility instead of affection.

The first murmurings about leaving occurred in the third year of analysis. Independence meant relief from incestuous fantasies which were diminished only after a great struggle and augured another round of oedipal fantasies. Now I was identified with his father; this became clear in a dream. After a brief vacation in which he feared for my safety, he had open fantasies about caring for his mother after his father died. When his father undertook a plane trip, he feared for the father's safety and called his mother ugly in an attempt to deny his attraction to her. This attempt was unsuccessful, because he could not get his mother off his mind while he masturbated compulsively day and night. Again the retaliative fears appeared, this time in the form of fearing a recurrence of the "bone thing"; so he had himself X-rayed.

After a longer vacation, regressive homosexual devices again came to the fore. He wanted to be accepted as a girl. Many pregenital anxieties appeared—rape, murder, and choking fantasies; fetishistic preoccupation with scarves, polymorphous-perverse manifestations—in an attempt to avoid increasing attractions to women in the waiting room. He struggled intensely to give up masturbation. While reviewing pubertal anxieties over his illness, suicidal impulses were overcome by a strong life-preservative tendency. He referred to "a little nodule of feeling coming out" which showed how difficult it was for feelings to emerge, and also that he associated the illness and castration. It was becoming clear that he had experienced the removal of the nodule as a punishment for phallic impulses. He also recalled castration fears in the form of dissolution feelings with the nitrogen-mustard injections.

As the phallic impulses toward women and the phallic rivalry with me in the transference increased, the intensity of castration anxiety also increased and manifested itself in a remarkably strong fear of renewed medical treatments. He feared lung collapse and radiation; he developed spots before his eyes and anticipated the return of all his previous illnesses. In an effort to divert the image of his mother and sister in his masturbation fantasies, he turned to women in the office and the analyst's wife, and even to his father's former secretary. With each diversion, the anxiety mounted and he again anticipated the end of analysis. One year before termination, he developed an attachment to a physically handicapped woman. Overt sexual exploration of the female body gradually replaced the frightening incestuously toned masturbation. His intellect was freed and his course work improved as he looked forward to ten years of productive work.

After several months of regressive shifts related to sadistically conceived primal scenes, he began to make realistic statements: "Life is not going to be a bed of roses. I want to be a man, but I fear getting sick." Following a triumphant dream, "I made it—a great accomplishment," there was intense excitement involving love for the mother and hatred for the father with a subsequent fear of dissolution in orgasm. His parents' solemnity during his first illness was related to his feelings toward his parents at that time. Acting outside the analysis, he began to manipulate the girl's genitals with fantasies that both parents would die. Soon phallic preoccupations assumed a more genital character.

The oedipal neurosis reached a full climax in the fourth year of analysis as he began to have erections on the couch and strongly controlled his impulses to masturbate in the office. In a dream he asked a girl "where to put the fluid." A great deal of hostility was displaced from the genitally refusing mother onto me. He viewed me as refusing his penis and therefore his masculinity. This he associated to his mother treating him as a weakling and as if he were going to die. Dying was related to castration in a dream of his teeth falling out.

After failing to fulfill his oedipal attraction to mother in the transference, the other aspect of the family romance was relived in his affects and re-enacted. He became strongly competitive in and outside the analysis and was very eager to have heterosexual relations. Simultaneously, he pursued his studies diligently and secured an advanced degree. With his academic triumph, he planned slowly to abandon the analysis, insisting upon reducing his hours and arranging a termination date, which was agreed upon.

Several weeks later, he had intercourse for the first time in his life. He was relieved not only because his penis remained intact, but also because he was able to give a woman pleasure in this way. He now felt he could make plans for leaving home, his euphemism for abandoning infantile claims, and he even began seriously to consider marriage. These plans to marry resulted in apprehensions regarding his health. He felt his parents had misinformed him about the dangers of sexual intercourse, and he had now disproven these apprehensions. This led to associations to other forms of misinformation and he spontaneously connected his fears for his life with fears of castration. "I used to believe doctors were taking retribution and now I realize they saved my life." The link between his illness and castration was still preconscious. As he planned marriage more seriously, he told his girl friend of his "osteomyelitis" and arranged a visit to his physician to obtain an opinion concerning his physical status. It dawned on him that I was a doctor and in the course of asking my opinion, he casually asked whether I knew anything about his state of health. In an ensuing discussion, I told him what I had been told: that he had been treated for Hodgkin's disease as a child. The name was unfamiliar to him, and he remained calm as the general nature of the illness was discussed briefly and discreetly. I suggested that he could now talk more freely with his medical consultant. His reaction after this hour was considerable relief, even mild euphoria. "I feel very good, like after I passed my exams. Before, I felt things were done without any reason. Now, I don't have to feel bitter. While I am tempted to use this information as a club, I feel more responsible and less like a child. I feel very grateful to you, but I want to see Dr. X as soon as possible." This exchange took place one month before the previously established date of termination of the analysis and was most likely influenced by the pressure of the anticipated separation from me.

Although he seized upon the diagnosis in an obsessional way, that is, he now had a magical word to grapple with, he was, in a long discussion with his physician, finally able to come to terms with the facts of his life. He was told by his physician that in view of the quiescent course of his illness in recent years, the original diagnosis remained in doubt, although at the time it was made there was no doubt. The patient, in the face of increasing frankness, changed remarkably. He felt more secure and made the poignant remark, "Every day I live is an act of defiance of my folks. I wanted the privilege of worrying about my own life."

Until then independence had meant the death of his parents. Now he wanted to be recognized as a man and not be prevented from leaving the analysis. After some vacillations and renewed fears that a node in his neck similar to that which had precipitated his illness at age five might reappear, he fearfully anticipated leaving the analysis but remained undaunted in his desire to separate. A number of rebirth fantasies emerged toward the end. In his last hour, he expressed phallic defiance: "My penis is better than yours."

The patient still had to accomplish a number of tasks: to be more independent from his parents, to establish and maintain an adequate heterosexual adjustment, to work effectively over a sustained period, and to have meaningful interpersonal relations. At the conclusion of the analysis, signs of movement in these directions were clearly evident. He had by this time become a serious student, secured an advanced degree, and progressed toward a definite career, the latter interestingly in a field involving the study of basic life processes.

While I would have preferred a more extensive period of working through, particularly of the preoedipal aspects of his neurosis, the patient was not tolerant of the need to continue at the time. On the other hand, the analysis had achieved definite structural changes in his personality. He had made his first satisfactory heterosexual adjustment, which ultimately led to marriage, though the fact that he chose a girl with a physical handicap suggests that compromises were being made. He cared for his health in a more realistic fashion, no longer feeling compelled to indulge in extensive counterphobic maneuvers. Also, he improved in his family relations to the point of more realistic, if not more pleasant, adaptations. He developed capacities for insight of which he had previously been afraid or unaware. There was a marked softening of a severely critical superego. He was able to tolerate separations with little or no anxiety, although this was now tempered by the new, marital attachment. He found more direct means of satisfying his instinctual impulses, which were no longer expressed in symptoms or masturbation, and he increased his capacity to sublimate. Finally, his ability to test reality was shown in his ability to deal with the facts of his past illness without the extensive use of denial.

The analysis of his oedipal neurosis as well as of his equation of fears of dying with castration fear enabled the patient to accept his current reality and the unique meaningfulness of his own personal life history. As a consequence of his unresolved obsessional neurosis with traumatic features, he had been afraid to live. In this, he had been encouraged by the well-intentioned protectiveness of his parents. He had complied with his parents, and implicitly with me, not to know the facts of his life.

Discussion

In studying the after effects of childhood operations, Anna Freud (1952) found that in a male child it was not the castration fear but the feminine castration wish which was most frequently responsible for serious postoperative breakdowns or permanent character changes. In these instances, she suggested, the surgical attacks on the body act like a seduction to passivity, to which the child either submits with disastrous results for his masculinity or against which he has to build up permanent pathologically strong defenses. In my patient, struggles against passive submission were strikingly evident in the amplitudes of his swings from submission to assertion, the latter often of a counterphobic nature. Anna Freud was so impressed by the importance of the submission factor that she felt the reactions of boys in the oedipal stage to bodily pain could provide a useful key to the differential diagnosis between genuine phallic masculinity and misleading manifestations of reactive, overstressed phallic behavior designed to ward off the passive feminine castration idea. The masculine boy, she stated, is contemptuous of bodily pain, which means little to him. The boy who has to defend himself against passive leanings cannot tolerate even slight amounts of pain without major distress.

Emmy Sylvester indicated that early insults cripple the development of the ego, while traumas which occur after consolidation of the ego and of object relations affect ego functioning (see Calef, 1959). I would say that in my patient, his physical illness influenced the manner of ego functioning rather than crippled his ego development.

The emphasis on phallic imagery in this patient's associations was determined by the time of onset of his illness, the phallic-pregenital period. At that time the phallus was already cathected, and the anxiety concerning his body was therefore phallic anxiety. The clinical evidence suggests that dissolution anxiety was related to somatic experiences, particularly those caused by radiation. He also reacted to panic states in the parents, the manipulations and restrictions necessitated by the gravity of the illness. Various aspects characteristic of the illness such as nodal enlargement were symbolically incorporated into the infantile anxieties and later emerged in the course of the transference. Something could be said about the relevance of pregnancy fantasies in relation to having a node removed in a passively disposed boy. Considerable preoccupation with a miscarriage of the mother when he was one to three years of age was not elaborated in this account, but fantasies were worked over a number of times in regard to this supposed event.

Unresolved pregenital conflicts strengthened the fixation points to which he regressed in life and in the transference situation. There were many manifestations of polymorphous-perverse sexuality, fetishism, and accented urinary and anal sexuality. The frequent shifts of pregenital cathexes gave evidence of an unstable refuge in pregenitality into which he had been pushed by his mother's overstimulations. Upon entering the phallic and oedipal periods, he was "dropped" by his mother inasmuch as she did not accept his more mature sexuality. This attitude of his mother's as well as his incapability of achieving adequate discharge left him in an unresolved oedipal neurosis. This neurosis was further fixated by his illness which by overwhelming the ego prevented further mastery and which led to increased infantilization by the parents.

Among his regressive manifestations, one is struck most by the intensity and chronicity of his fetishistic fantasies and behavior both in his life and in the treatment. All his fetishistic preoccupations could be traced back to the period following the onset of his illness. The earliest ones, dealing with mother's underpants, women's kerchiefs, and magicians' scarves, reflect anxiety over erections, the anatomic differences between the sexes, and separation from the mother. His latency and pubertal preoccupations disclose conflicts over masculinity and the unsuccessful integration of libidinal and aggressive drives. These resulted in the delayed appearance of orgasm and the related fears of dissolution. The patient recalled infantile masturbation which he resumed during the treatment in late adolescence, but he did not recall pubertal masturbation. The analysis of his fetishistic fantasies accompanying masturbation revealed a high degree of overdetermination, some degree of accidental association, and some degree of anxiety-influenced misperceptions. Two examples will illustrate the latter. "As a child, I thought HAND-KERCHIEF was HANG-KERCHIEF." This misperception, he felt, was influenced by his mother's curse, "go hang yourself." He also confused the words "scarves" and "scars," an obvious reference to surgery. Again, balloons were part of the anesthesia experience as was the feeling of choking.

Greenacre (1953, 1955) and Socarides (1960) in their studies of fetishism suggest that the fetishist has a body-image disorder. According to Greenacre, internal traumas, rage, spasms, fevers, and anesthesia create severe disturbances of the bodily sense of self, with feelings of immanent dissolution. In her cases she also found disturbances in the phallic phase which led to an exaggeration of the oedipus complex. The clinical material reported here seems to be an apt illustration of these conclusions. The traumatic assault of surgical experience, radiation, and chemical suffusion, as well as the fact that these events took place in a climate of understandably frightened parents lent reality emphasis to the unconscious fears of retaliation for unconscious impulses. Synthesis of an adequate body image in this patient was made particularly difficult by two factors: reality events lent support to his worst unconscious expectations, and he reached the phallic and oedipal phases without having consolidated his pregenital development.

While more genuine masculinity provides protection from the insult of pain and illness, immaturity, whether chronologic, fixated, or regressed, results in a state of helplessness which precludes effective mastery of reality or even of unconscious fantasy. Anita I. Bell stated that mastery requires a fusion or neutralization of aggressive and libidinal instinctual energy—processes which free the ego for reality testing and object relations. Excessive defused aggressive energy is used masochistically or sadistically (see Calef, 1959). According to Lucie Jessner, the crucial issue in illness is the struggle to maintain the bond to the loved person: "The effect of illness is that libidinal investment of objects suffers a narcissistic regression altering body and self-images. The image of the parents changes. The parents' helplessness, anxiety, and incapacity to protect the child become painfully clear. The powerful protector turns into an archaic devouring monster in retaliation for the child's impulses. Identification with the parents becomes disturbed" (see Calef, 1959, p. 158).

After the establishment of genital primacy death fears represent castration to the ego and in such a predisposed individual may reflect castration anxiety. Threats to the organism before the establishment of genitality are threats to the whole body as well as to the developing ego which is still relatively helpless. This patient experienced considerable conscious relief after he learned the facts of his medical history. Perhaps because he had not known them, he appeared to be less concerned with the actual threat to his life except in so far as he equated it with castration. Eissler (1955) indicates that the fear of castration is so great, presumably after genital cathexis, that the destruction of one's self appears preferable. "Man's reaction seems to be, with surprising frequency: rather dead than castrated." He implies that man cannot tolerate life without the prospect of pleasure.

This patient's discovery of his illness, in addition to the resolution of his infantile neurosis, constituted a mastery by the ego which could now facilitate a psychological freedom where he had not even that before. His ego's need to maintain an unbroken representation of the future (Eissler, 1955) probably led to his marriage.

PART III

PHYSICAL DEFECTIVENESS

8

MOURNING AND THE BIRTH OF
A DEFECTIVE CHILD[1]

ALBERT J. SOLNIT, M.D. and MARY H. STARK, M.S.S.
(1961)

The study of human crisis permits the extension of our understanding of psychological health and illness and how they overlap.
These opportunities become especially fruitful when the observer
is also the person offering professional assistance to those whose
crisis requires them to seek help.

However, these professional people require a comprehensive
theory of human development to clarify and organize their observations and to make possible formulations that lead to a useful course
of action. Psychoanalysis is such a theory of human psychology. In
recent years the health care professions have had opportunities to
integrate insights from this theory into the care of the child and his
family in many different crisis situations (Bowlby et al., 1952; Burlingham and A. Freud, 1942; A. Freud, 1953; Jackson, 1942; Lindemann, 1944; MacKeith, 1953; James Robertson, 1953, 1958; Joyce
Robertson, 1956; Solnit, 1960; Solnit and Green, 1959; Solnit and
Stark, 1959; Spence, 1946, 1947). When a defective child is born, the
pediatrician and his colleagues can make observations of the family's
reactions to this catastrophic event. These observations may indicate the factors that shape the family's trauma or that lead to the
family's adaptive responses.

The material on which this study is based has been collected

We wish to acknowledge with warm appreciation the helpful suggestions and criti-
cisms of Berta Bornstein, Ira Gabrielson, Sally Provence, and Milton J. E. Senn.

from pediatric, psychiatric, and casework contacts with mothers and their defective children. The theoretical approach to our work is founded on the psychoanalytic explanation of the process of mourning as applied to the mother's reactions to the birth of a defective child (Freud, 1917, 1923; Bibring, 1959, 1961; Janis, 1958a, 1958b). Freud's contributions to the understanding of narcissism and its vicissitudes (1914) are essential for the study of object loss—in our case, the loss of the longed-for healthy child.

The psychological preparation for a new child during pregnancy normally involves the wish for a perfect child and the fear of a damaged child. It is very likely that there is always some discrepancy between the mother's wishes and the actual child; to work out this discrepancy becomes one of the developmental tasks of motherhood that are involved in the establishment of a healthy mother-child relationship. However, when the discrepancy is too great, as in the birth of a defective child, or where the mother's wishes are too unrealistic, a trauma may occur.

The study of pregnancy—what Ernst Kris (1955) termed a normal illness—reveals a loosening up of defenses and the more direct, and at times more threatening, access to unconscious representations, wishes, and scars (fixations). In a normal pregnancy, labor, and delivery, there are psychological rearrangements and achievements necessary for the developmental advances leading to early motherhood (Benedek, 1959; Deutsch, 1945). These changes, often subtle, appear gradually over a period of time, and are best seen in the interacting development of mutuality of mother and child (Erikson, 1950). The mother's anticipation of the baby, especially of the first, is in many ways like adolescent turmoil because the adult psychic structure is gradually prepared for the birth of a new individual and the crystallization of a new unfolding within the self.

The image of the *expected baby* is a composite of representations of the self and of the love objects (mother, husband, father, and siblings). The composite representation includes the image of the expected child which has been conveyed to the expectant mother by her own mother. Each of these kaleidoscopic shifting impressions summon up for recollection and emotional review older issues, conflicts, and fears. This anticipatory process is part of the normal preparation for motherhood. As a preparation it repeats and solves again certain of the basic conflicts and identifications that the expectant mother had with her own mother.

However, this preparatory and adaptive process is abruptly interrupted by the birth of a defective or retarded child. Although the mother's reactions to her defective child are to a significant extent shaped by the type and degree of defect, they also are greatly influenced by her own past experiences with parents and siblings as well as by other significant life events. Conflicts in the woman's relationship to her own mother and in regard to her own femininity are often reawakened during the psychological work of the pregnancy (Bibring, 1959, 1961). The vicissitudes of this psychological preparation (Janis, 1958b) are outside the scope of this presentation, but an awareness of these preparatory developments in the mother will heighten the understanding of the impact of the disappointment, feeling of helplessness, and sense of failure that the individual woman experiences when the child she bears is obviously blighted.

There are many aspects of the diagnosis and treatment of defective children and their families which it will not be possible to encompass in this paper. However, the thesis of this paper will be of little value if one does not at the same time take into account specific factors, such as familial disease, previous trauma to the mother, family constellation, the genesis of the retardation, and the severity and characteristic of the defect. It will be noted that "defective" and "retarded" are used interchangeably in this paper, simply indicating that all of the children referred to are retarded and that the defect is more or less apparent.

In an experiment created by nature, the birth of a defective or deviant child, one can observe more directly the "sudden" loss of the baby that was expected; and the "sudden" birth of a feared, threatening, and anger-evoking child. The course of motherhood, a developmental process, is influenced by the characteristics of the baby, first by his appearance and gradually by his responses. Significant deviations, such as gross retardation or obvious congenital defects, may limit or interrupt the mother's developing capacity to accept the new child who is totally dependent upon her.

In a recent article, "Is Grief a Disease?" George L. Engel (1961) has drawn attention to the importance of the mourning process in human development. Borrowing from Freud's (1917) and Lindemann's (1944) work, Engel describes mourning in terms that are useful for this presentation. "Grief is the characteristic response to the loss of a valued object, be it a loved person, a cherished possession, a job, status, home, country, an ideal, a part of the body, etc. Uncomplicated grief runs a consistent course, modified mainly by the abruptness of the loss, the nature of the preparation for the event, and the significance for the survivor of the lost object."

In the mother's mourning reaction to the loss of the healthy child, her wishes for and expectations of the desired child are crushed by the birth of the defective child. Her anxious fears of having a damaged child are realized. These disappointed, highly charged longings for the normal child may be recalled, intensely felt, and gradually discharged in order to reduce the impact of the loss of the expected loved child. This process, which requires time and repetition, can liberate the mother's feelings and interests for a more realistic adaptation. The mourning process makes it possible to progress from the initial phase of numbness and disbelief; to the dawning awareness of the disappointment and feeling of loss with the accompanying affective and physical symptoms; to the last phase of the grief reaction in which intense re-experiencing of the memories and expectations gradually reduce the hypercathexis of the wish for the idealized child.

In childbearing, the simultaneous loss of one child—the expected and narcissistically invested one—and adaptation to the deviant or defective child makes a demand that is very likely to be overwhelming. There is no time for working through the loss of the desired child before there is the demand to invest the new and handicapped child as a love object.

It is as though the work of preparing for the new child has suddenly become useless. Established libidinal pathways and attachments are abruptly terminated, and at the same time a demand for new libidinal cathexes is made.[1] The unexpected aspect of the birth at a time of physiological and psychological depletion is an essential factor in the traumatizing effect of the experience.

Thus, at the time the mother is prepared to be nurtured by the satisfaction of her creative experience, and to begin nurturing her

[1] To some extent a similar situation occurs when there is the unexpected birth of twins or of a premature child.

child, her adaptive capacities are sapped because she has failed to create what she intended, and feels damaged by the "new" child—the defective organism to whom she has given birth. Just as pregnancy itself is a normal crisis in which there is no turning back, so defect or retardation is a condition which cannot be undone. The irretrievable nature of the retardation adds to the mother's trapped feeling—she has failed to achieve what she has so laboriously prepared herself to create or produce. Fathers, too, will have similar or related reactions. For the purpose of this discussion, and because the mother's vulnerability is much greater, we limit our primary considerations to the mother.

Although each situation has to be individually analyzed for the highly specific considerations essential for planning and treatment, in our experience there are two extreme reaction patterns that delimit the continuum of the pathological reactions to the birth of a defective child. The manifest reaction and the underlying feelings should be differentiated. At the one extreme is the guilt feeling leading to the mother's manifest dedication of herself unremittingly and exclusively to the welfare of the retarded child. At the other extreme is the parents' manifest intolerance of the child and the almost irresistible impulse to deny their relationship to the child. The underlying narcissistic injury is intolerable. The following example illustrates the first extreme.

Jimmy, the first-born child of a young couple, was severely retarded. His mother was unable to care for her second child, Danny, who was normal, because of her "devotion" to Jimmy. Her inability to accept the reality of the retarded child began when she left her pediatrician who had advised institutionalization shortly after Jimmy's birth. It became necessary for the paternal grandmother to live with them in order to organize their household and to care for Danny shortly after he was born. The father's dissatisfaction with this plan finally resulted in a request for consultation in regard to long-term planning for Jimmy.

At the other extreme, Arnold's mother had apparently accepted the interpretation of slow development in her son soon after a difficult birth. During his first year, the parents arranged for Arnold to be placed in a foster home because they felt unable to care for him. From the many medical recommendations sought, the parents favored that one which said institutionalization at a training school would be advisable. Arnold was only slightly retarded and made good strides in his development at the foster home, eliminating the need for a training school. The parents said they could accept Arnold only if it could be guaranteed that he would be "perfectly normal." Otherwise, they feared he would "damage" their family life. Their move to another locale, which made it impractical for them to see Arnold, was to some extent determined by the father's occupation, but it also represented their effort to strengthen the denial of their relationship to their son in order to avoid the intolerable narcissistic injury evoked by their contacts with him.

There are elements of both denial and guilt involved in the reactions of parents to the birth of a retarded or defective child. However, the defenses represent the modes of warding off depression, guilt, and feelings of narcissistic injury. The defenses are selected from the interaction of the individual's characteristic patterns of defense and influenced by the predominance of the painful affect evoked by the birth of a defective child. By taking into account the parents' feelings of loss, defeat, and resentment about their defective child, and their individual ways of coping with their feelings, the interpretation of the child's diagnosis and its implications can be made more effective.

When the mother wards off her feelings of grief by establishing a guilty, depressed attachment to the retarded child she may fail to relate adequately to other members of the family because she feels she must give her life to the care of the damaged child. Conversely, the mother may identify with her defective child. In identifying with her defective offspring, the mother feels narcissistically wounded. This narcissistic injury is often intolerable, because the mother feels painfully defective as she is caring for her retarded child. The mother's withdrawal then becomes a denial of the needs of this child, which the following example illustrates.

Sally, two years of age, the second of two girls, had been examined by two doctors. When she was eight months old, a substitute for her doctor (the family doctor was ill) told the mother that Sally was a Mongol and "there would be trouble later on." This mother, aged twenty-nine, worried about the above statement for nearly a year. Her husband thought she was foolish to worry. Both parents knew Sally's development was delayed, but the father thought she would "catch up" in time. Finally, the mother was able to ask her family doctor about Sally. She had hoped that since he had not mentioned it, perhaps it was not so. He told her that he had been concerned about Sally since birth and agreed with the diagnosis of Mongolism. He said he had not brought it to her attention because nothing could be done about it. He pointed out the fact that her eyes were far apart. He agreed to arrange a consultation for Sally with a specialist in child development.

The mother told the social worker, who worked with the consultant, that she thought Mongolism was a strange disease, and she blamed herself for Sally's condition. As a child, the mother's poor vision required her to attend a sight-saving class in school. She associated the doctor's comment about· Sally's eyes with her own visual defect. She also blamed herself for marrying a man twenty years her senior; she had read that older parents tend to produce retarded children.

Because of her painful feelings of inadequacy the mother had found herself withdrawing from Sally and spending more time with her seven-year-old daughter who provided evidence of her mother's adequacy. Sally was kept in a crib a good part of the day.

As this mother was given a descriptive picture of the extent of Sally's retardation (her motor development and adaptive behavior were about that of an eighteen-month-old child) and some suggestions regarding the everyday care of her child, she began to realize that Sally's future was not so hopeless. When she could talk about her disappointment and fears for Sally's future, her own poor vision, her marriage, etc., she felt less guilty. Her pent-up energies were then released to be used constructively for both of her little girls. She devoted more time to Sally, provided her with suitable toys, and began to explore nursery school opportunities that would be available when she was older.

The lack of opportunity to discuss the child's diagnosis can create a situation in which the parents feel overwhelmed and unable to gauge the reality of their child's retarded development. Denial then serves to ward off the anxiety and depression. The following vignette illustrates such a situation.

Susan, a first child, was born abroad when her father was in Service. The baby was born in the seventh month of the mother's pregnancy, weighing 3 lbs., 4 oz. Three convulsions occurred on the second day of her life. Because of her prematurity, she remained in the hospital for eight weeks. No definite diagnosis was discussed with the parents. This was a difficult time for the parents because Susan was in a critical condition and fed poorly. When Susan was brought home she continued to be a source of anxiety to the parents because she failed to thrive. By eight months, she was not rolling over, and she was returned to the hospital for further studies. The parents said they would never forget the words of the physician at the time of her second hospital discharge: "You might as well put her in an institution and let her die in peace." The harshness of such words added greatly to the suffering already experienced by the parents and interfered with the mother's recognition of the reality and with her mourning reaction. The mother blamed herself for not seeking out her obstetrician a week before delivery when she was having some abdominal pains. She reasoned, if she had gone to him then, her child would not have been retarded. The thought of institutionalization caused her to cringe with anger.

It was not until there was ample opportunity to review their hopes and to discuss their fears for Susan that the parents were able to utilize a thorough evaluation and interpretation of the child's development in a continuing relationship with the pediatrician and social worker. One might say that interpretation began with what was the parents' reality, their state of grief, and then under the guidance of a skillful pediatrician they were prepared to deal with the reality of their child's condition.

In many instances the initial diagnosis has been made accurately and with adequate consultation, and has been presented to the parents in a simple, straight-forward manner, taking into account their fears and questions. However, several months later the physician is surprised to hear from a colleague or neighboring clinic that his patient is "shopping" and has presented a distorted picture of the situation. Upon reviewing this very common complication of interpretation, we have been able to demonstrate in many instances that the parents' distortion was an unwitting one that stemmed from two main sources: (1) the inability to tolerate their painful reaction to the reality of the diagnosis or to accept the first diagnosis; and (2) the lack of what might be termed follow-up. Once the physician has conveyed the initial diagnosis to the parents there is a tendency to think the interpretation of mental retardation is completed when it has only begun. The main reason for this misconception by the physician is that he has not understood the repetitive aspect of the mourning process in the mother's reaction. If the therapist has not sensed or understood the need that parents have to grieve about their tragic "loss," he will feel ineffectual and reproached by the parents when they indicate their need for repeated opportunities to review and to re-examine the past in the current "loss."

Interpretation is a continuing process which utilizes interviews with the professional person to establish a sense of confidence and trust that will promote the parents' gradual understanding of the child's defect. In this atmosphere of trust and confidence the parents are enabled to express their critical and fearful questions to the pediatrician; and the physician can describe what is known and what is not known about the retarded child in a manner that increases the parents' understanding. This understanding refers to objective and subjective components—to the comprehension of the child's condition, and to the realization by the parents of their inner reactions of disappointment, resentment, humiliation, and loneliness. Many of the subjective reactions will be experienced as repetitions of previous losses or disappointments. The pediatrician, nurse, and social worker should not make interpretations of unconscious feelings or thoughts; or attempt to make connections for the patient between past experiences of loss and the current subjective responses to the birth of the retarded child. The psychiatrist who otherwise may interpret unconscious conflicts also may avoid such interpretations because of the narcissistic involvement during the mourning period.

The medical personnel should clarify the reality of the child's condition as the parent is able to bring up each one of his questions and fears. This clarification which strengthens the reality-testing capacity of the parents will indirectly reduce the distortions responsible for unrealistic connections between past and present. In this way the dynamic interpretation of the reality aids the working through of the mourning process as one of the major avenues to the mastery of the traumatic experience.

Ideally, the parents, especially the mother, will experience what Freud (1917) described: "Each single one of the memories and situations of expectancy which demonstrate the libido's attachment to the lost object is met by the verdict of reality." It is the physician or social worker's responsibility to facilitate this process, which is gradual, repetitive, and which requires that the "verdict of reality" be offered in a useful manner. This implies that at every stage of translating the defective child's condition to the parents, the language, sequence of thoughts, and focus of the interpretation will take into account other important factors involved in the parents' reactions. These factors would include the stage of the mother's development, her current situation, and the ways in which her past experiences, cultural and personal, influence her adaptation.

As we have indicated earlier, there are many aspects of working with the parents of retarded children that we are not considering in this presentation. One aspect is the mother's relative neglect of the other children if her attachment to the retarded child is abnormally intense. Another aspect that needs to be emphasized is how often the normal child reacts with fear, depression, and guilt when he has a retarded sibling. There are many measures that can be taken to help the normal sibling of a retarded child which cannot be discussed in this paper.

It becomes clear that the unexpected advent of a retarded child can have a traumatizing effect on the development of the mother and on the interactions and elaborations of family relationships. The ghost of the desired, expected healthy child continues to interfere with the family's adaptation to the defective child if the mourning process becomes fixed as the sustained atmosphere of the family.

DISCUSSION

Interpretation of mental retardation to parents should be synchronized to the mourning reaction. In this presentation, interpretation refers to a dynamic continuing process of successive translations and clarifications, rather than to a single definitive explanation. Such interpretations are communications that facilitate the recognition of reality and promote one's adaptation to the demands of reality. The effectiveness of these communications depends upon a relationship with the interpreter that will enable the parent to express highly charged feelings and to remember the past as it relates to the present. What are referred to as interpretations for the mother with the abnormal child are also the principles upon which are based the explanations and anticipatory guidance of the mother with the normal child.

Coping with the outer reality of a child with a congenital defect and the inner reality of feeling the loss of a desired, normal child requires a great deal of mental work. Such psychic work is slow and emotionally painful, and it proceeds through the gradual and repeated discharge of intense feelings and memories. These mental and emotional reactions enable the parent to recognize and adapt to the reality, the retarded child.

The mother's reaction to a dead child is different from her reaction to the birth of a defective child (Provence, 1961), though certain aspects of these differing mourning reactions are similar. In both situations there are: feelings of loss; intense longings for the desired child; resentment of the cruel blow that life's experience has dealt; and the guilt that the dead or defective child may evoke by representing the consequences of unacceptable feelings or thoughts. The main difference between the two reactions is the persistent effect on the mother of the living defective child who realistically requires care and attention. The daily impact of the retarded child on the mother is unrelenting. Attempts to withdraw libido from the "lost," normal child are disrupted by the demands to cathect the living, blighted child. When the defective baby dies, the libido can initially be withdrawn and then become available for new attachments without the daily corrosive reminder of failure. Probably, the process of mourning cannot be as effective when the retarded child survives.

When a person is mourning, his ability to recognize, evaluate, and adapt to reality is often significantly impaired. It is for this reason that the physician often turns to the father or grandparents in the planning for the newborn defective child. Sometimes immediate planning may require this. However, from the point of view of the mother's development and the child's care, it is essential to gauge the mother's mourning reaction in order to know how and when to help her to take an active role in planning for her child's care. The continuation of mourning into a persistent, depressed, self-reproachful state may be encouraged if the mother's mourning reaction is not understood, and if the care of the child as well as the planning are carried out without her active participation. Obviously the mother needs a great deal of support and time in order to deal with her feelings of failure. The father, too, will require such aid.

The gradual investment of feeling for the child who was born cannot be hurried and will proceed along a realistic line if the mother's capacities to think, feel, and talk about her disappointment, sense of failure, and feelings of helplessness are not impaired by the atmosphere of the hospital and the attitudes of her physicians and nurses. Surely the medical personnel's feelings of helplessness and defeat in regard to the retarded child are among the important reasons that parents may fail to receive understanding support. A common obstacle to the mother's adaptation is the urgency that the physician may feel in developing a plan because of his fear that procrastination may damage the mother. One sees the exaggerated effect of the physician's anxiety in those situations in which there is the conviction that the defective child should not be seen by the mother, but should be rushed away to an institution so the mother will not form a guilt-laden attachment to the child. This attitude reflects a misunderstanding about: the precision of the prognosis; what constitutes the mother's preparation for and reaction to the newborn child; and the physician's own reaction to the situation of his patient being defective. A correct understanding of the crisis will lead to a conservative attitude toward prognosticating; an expectation that the mother will need time and help to deal with her own reactions to having a defective child; and the awareness of the physician's own feeling of helplessness and resentment that his work has failed to produce a normal child.

Often this behavior of the medical personnel to the birth of a defective child mirrors the mother's psychological state. By wishing to send the child to an institution before the mother sees the child, they are reacting partly to their own feelings of helplessness and failure; and partly they are dramatizing the loss of the normal child that the mother feels. Perhaps there is the unconscious notion that if the defective child is sent away before being seen by the mother she will have a better chance to regain the lost, normal or idealized child. It is equally wrong to insist that a mother and father see a malformed child when they wish to avoid it and express their strong opposition to the experience.

The physicians and nurses can invest the deviant child realistically for the mother. This provides her with an opportunity to take an active role in planning for her child; to increase her self-esteem through the evidence that she can feed and care for the child; and to receive the satisfaction of those reactions that the retarded child demonstrates in response to the mothering care.

If the defective baby is a second or third child, and the older children are normal, the impact may be somewhat less though it follows the same pattern of mourning. If the retardation defect is not evident at birth but only gradually becomes apparent to mother and physician in the first year or two, the mourning reaction is less acute, but its structure is very similar. That is, there may be a nagging fear that the child's development is lagging and a gradual awareness of the child's inability to respond. In this more gradually developing situation the difficulty in recognizing, identifying, and adapting to the reality of the child's retarded development may be drawn out over a long period of time. However, the gradualness of the recognition may also strengthen the denial of the reality, leading to the more tortuous and chronic mourning reaction. In a sense the parents may become fixated between the recognition of the deviation of their child and the denial of its implications. For example, the parents may steadfastly deny the child's defect or slow development, but continue to seek special help to enable their child to overcome his difficulties. In a recent discussion, Helen L. Beck (1959) stated: "The parents who come to a mental retardation clinic are as a rule quite aware of the fact that they have a problem. They may, however, deny its nature."

In order to facilitate the work of the mourning process, the mother needs: physical rest; an opportunity to review her thoughts and feelings about the wished-for child; a realistic interpretation and investment of the feared, unwanted child by doctors and nurses; and an active role in planning for and caring for the newborn child as she is able. These are the measures through which the mother can minimize or overcome the trauma of giving birth to a retarded child. The physician, nurse, and social worker will take into account these dynamic psychological reactions of the mother in order that their use of the interpretative process becomes an essential aid to the mother in mastering this crisis in her development.

SUMMARY

Our work in psychoanalysis, child development, pediatrics, and social work has reflected a continuing interest in the mutuality of theory and clinical work. The present paper arose from our observations that the theory of the mourning process was essential in order to understand the depressed reactions of certain mothers to the birth of their children. Although this could be observed most clearly and dramatically when a defective child was born, it was apparent to a lesser degree in the birth of children who were not overtly or significantly abnormal. One mother's depressed mourning reaction occurred when a son was born. In later years she said that it took her three months to resign herself to the loss of a daughter and to accept her son.

Another interest served by this paper is the opportunity for the application of insights from the study of human behavior to the care of the child in a family. The critical application by pediatric colleagues of suggestions and explanations resulting from this study has sharpened the analysts's clinical work and theoretical deductions. Observing and theorizing are reciprocal activities. While the pediatrician can make certain observations that are not available to the analyst, the former needs a general theory of human behavior to help him organize and comprehend his observations. Certain of the theoretical and clinical formulations in psychoanalysis suggest applications in a nonanalytic setting. Often these are guides to be used in child rearing or in the prevention of trauma when a child is physically ill. The pediatrician is in a position to apply many of these insights and to raise questions that stem from his clinical experiences. In a recent symposium on psychosomatic aspects of pediatrics, Anna Freud (1961) said: "I can only say that if I were a pediatrician I would start a fight for the pediatrician's influence from the start."

In our investigation of the grief reaction of mothers who have given birth to defective children, we were able to demonstrate that the physician's awareness of the mourning process enabled him to provide effective therapeutic help to the mother and her child. Additionally, the physician's awareness then extended to the concept that a mother's depressed reaction to the birth of a normal child might reflect her feeling of loss because of a significant discrepancy between her expected or wished-for image of the child and the actual normal child.

9

THE ANALYSIS OF A BOY WITH A CONGENITAL DEFORMITY

ANDRÉ LUSSIER
(1960)

This paper is based on the analysis of Peter, a thirteen-year-old boy born with malformed shoulders and abnormally short arms terminating in hands having only three fingers and no thumbs. When Peter entered analysis,[1] the over-all measurement from his shoulders to fingertips was scarcely eight inches. As far as is known, the psychodynamic implications at the unconscious level of so severe a congenital deformity have not previously been described in psychoanalytic literature. The positive results presented here are to be attributed to the inspiration and close collaboration of the staff of the Hampstead Child-Therapy Clinic under the direction of Anna Freud.

A special objective of the analysis was to compare the castration anxiety associated with such a gross bodily handicap with that of a neurotic youngster having no physical abnormality.

A finding of unusual interest in this analysis was the specific constructive function assumed by the fantasy life in the development of a number of permanent skills—ego abilities.

BACKGROUND INFORMATION

Much of the information about Peter's family background came from the reports of social workers and Hampstead Clinic personnel

[1] This case was treated by the author in the Hampstead Child-Therapy Clinic under the individual supervision of Dr. Ilse Hellman which is gratefully acknowledged.

who had interviewed Peter's mother at various times prior to and during his analysis.[2]

The whole subject of Peter's birth and early childhood was fraught with anxiety for his mother. She said she had never got over the shock of seeing him for the first time . . . it was terrible! Never before had she spoken of this to anyone.

She was certain that Peter's deformity had been caused by her mother-in-law with whom she had not got along at all well. The mother-in-law, she said, used to "row" her during the pregnancy. This quarreling she knew to be bad, and one day to avoid a scene on the street she tried to pass the mother-in-law "without taking any notice of her." The ruse failed and the incensed mother-in-law seized her *by the shoulders* to bring her to a halt. While she was not injured, she was greatly upset by the encounter and her feelings were hurt. She was three months' pregnant at the time and was sure that Peter's deformity was a direct consequence.

Peter's birth was an easy one, his mother reported. She was not told of the child's deformity at the time of the delivery and discovered it only when the baby was first brought to her. The sight was a terrible blow. "His arms were so tiny," she recalled.

The Parents

Peter's mother said she had had a happy childhood and had been devoted to her own mother. She described herself, however, as having always been highstrung, and according to a medical report had suffered from neurasthenia when she was thirteen years old.

Her husband was the first boy ever to take any notice of her. Their marriage followed a five-year courtship. In 1940, when Peter was a year and a half old, the father was called up for army service, and the mother took Peter back to her native town to live with her parents. Except for leaves, the father was away until 1946.

A second child, a daughter, was born in 1941 when Peter was three.

When Peter was five, his maternal grandmother took ill and Peter's mother had then to keep house for four men—her own father and her mother's three brothers.

---

2 Mrs. Bianca Gordon, psychotherapist with the Hampstead Clinic, saw Peter's mother at regular intervals.

The maternal grandmother died three years later. Peter's mother said she thought at the time she would never get over her mother's death. In fact, she said, it had kept coming back into her mind ever since, accompanied by what she described as horrible thoughts.

Peter's mother was a Roman Catholic but did not attend church. Her husband, she reported, did not believe in religion. Actually, the mother had little to say about the father. He was an engineer's mate, and while not regarded as an impressive figure for his son, was nonetheless looked upon as the authority in the family. Following his return from the war, he got along well with Peter, then seven, and often played with him.

After the war, the family lived in a poor district and the parents were far from satisfied with their housing. The mother said she would have liked to have had a house with a garden where Peter could have played without being seen by the passers-by. Moreover, the fact that Peter had to sleep in the same room as his sister disturbed his mother, especially in view of Peter's handicap.

Peter as Baby and Boy

Peter's mother breast fed him until he was two months old when she had to wean him because of cracked and festered nipples, caused, she felt, by her own worrying. She had found it difficult to handle Peter because he could not put his arms around her. In the bath she would support him with one hand under his neck, and was constantly fearful he might slip out of her grasp and drown.

During the first six months Peter cried almost nightly. To comfort him his mother would carry him about and give him "gripe water" but would not feed him because she "kept to a schedule." Apart from this, he was a healthy baby and no trouble. His mother started training him to use a pot when he was two months old and said she had persevered in this training to have him clean and dry by about seven months.

During his first year Peter was twice separated from his mother for periods of about six weeks each while he was in the hospital for surgical interventions to separate the webbed fingers of his right hand and to provide greater mobility in shoulders and arms, one of which, the left, had no elbow.

From early infancy, Peter was clever with his feet and could pick up things with his toes. While learning to walk, he would fall down frequently because he seemed top-heavy.

The mother told the social workers that she had taken Peter to doctor after doctor, always in the hope that he could be "cured" although she had been repeatedly told that his condition was beyond remedy. When the doctors explained that Peter's left arm had no elbow she at first accepted the fact but soon began to believe she could see one and even that Peter was beginning to bend his arm a little.

When he was three, the sister was born. Physically normal, Mary was the second and last child. During this pregnancy the mother had imagined she was going to have another boy whom she was already calling "Stephen." She told Peter about "Stephen" and when Peter was naughty she would threaten him by saying that "Stephen" would not come to life because of his bad behavior. She claimed she had never been afraid that this second child would be deformed.

The mother reported that Peter and Mary got along well together, that Peter was fond of his sister, and that Mary, in turn, would "stick up" for Peter. Sometimes, however, Peter would torment Mary and his mother had to "smack him." During the analysis, very little emerged about the sister. Clearly, Peter compensated for his insecurity by regarding the little girl with her normal arms as no more than a baby, and consequently no threat to him.

When Peter's mother took him out as a baby and young child, she would cover him up to hide his arms. She said she felt very ashamed of him. She was especially embarrassed when people stared, and this uneasiness continued right up to the beginning of the boy's analysis. On his part, Peter would react to stares by turning to his mother for reassurance, but she would "just feel ashamed" and could not comfort her son. She realized she was failing Peter, causing him suffering and making him more insecure. Even so, she did not believe in spoiling him, although, she said, it was hard at times not to do so.

By the time Peter was about ten years old, he had acquired the hard-earned skill of feeding himself, even being able to use a knife and fork, although still needing help to cut meat. He was described as a very clean eater. He could partially dress himself. He could put on his socks and shoes but could not do up his laces and needed help with some garments. He also needed help in the toilet right up to the beginning of his analysis. Shortly thereafter, however, the slight growth of arms and shoulders associated with puberty made it possible for him to take care of himself in the toilet.

Peter started going to school at the age of three. He was enrolled at a regular neighborhood school and did well there. At seven, he was transferred to a special school for the physically handicapped. Here he gradually lost interest in schoolwork, becoming more and more preoccupied with his daydreams. His studies suffered to the degree that he was regarded as a backward pupil. His backwardness was, in fact, one of the motivating factors in the later decision to give him analytic treatment.

When he was about eight and a half, Peter began arriving home from school with his pants soiled. This continued for about four months. His mother blamed the school, explaining that Peter was too shy to ask for help when going to the toilet. The soiling never occurred at home.

Only two months after this problem had been overcome, Peter began wetting the bed. This happened right after another hospitalization for surgical intervention preparatory to the fitting of artificial arms.[3] He continued wetting the bed nightly for about five months until medication prescribed by his physician gradually cleared up the symptom. Enuresis, however, recurred a year later. His mother blamed herself for these troubles as she was still upset by the comparatively recent death of her own mother.

At the age of nine, when Peter was still able to read only a few words, mostly two-letter or three-letter words at that, he was given a Revised Stanford-Binet intelligence test which rated him as a low normal (I.Q. 85-90). Subsequent observations suggest the rating did not do justice to his intelligence.

The Problem

Manifest behavioral difficulties already referred to were instrumental in bringing Peter into analysis at the age of thirteen. The nocturnal enuresis appearing at the age of nine following the surgical intervention, and recurring at ten, was one of these. The backward-

[3] Before his physical growth stopped, surgical work had to be done to the inner articulations of the shoulder as a preparation for the future fitting of better artificial arms.

ness at school was another. But, as soon became clear during the analysis, the fundamental problem was an emotional disturbance expressed in a continuous and inventive evasion of factual truth and in the creating of a fantasy life of remarkable complexity and color. There were, too, some depressive tendencies.

For a boy with Peter's handicap and experiences, such difficulties were to be expected. But unexpected was the way in which Peter failed to exhibit either masochistic satisfaction, passivity, or self-pity —three characteristics only too readily associated in our mind with the psychology of many disabled people.[4]

Peter did not like to be handled, nor did he want to be regarded as an object of pity. He did not seem to derive or want to derive gain or gratification from his disability. Dominant in his behavior was the active striving toward the achievement of his goals.

The Analysis

The analysis proper, consisting of intensive work in daily sessions five days a week, lasted for about twenty months. Contact was maintained for a further sixteen months, but during the last year Peter's visits were irregular, varying from about once a week to once a month toward the end.

Compensatory Mechanisms

The early stages of the analysis produced many illustrations of the psychological mechanisms Peter was using to cope with his deformity. Three were dominant. He sought to push his handicap out of existence by intensive denial of its reality; he built a fantasy world from which he excluded his physical handicap; and he developed certain reaction formations as defenses against insecurity and inferiority. His aim, both consciously and unconsciously, was always to prove to the world that whatever anybody else could do with normal arms he could do as well or better with short arms and without artificial aids.

Early in the treatment, the sessions were filled with talk of his splendid exploits and great hopes. He would see himself excelling in all kinds of competitions and activities in none of which he would make even the slightest allowance for his handicap. In his fantasy

4 Conclusion drawn by Anna Freud following her diagnostic interview with Peter.

he was a remarkable tree climber, for example, and also something of a champion at cutting down trees, both obvious impossibilities. He boasted how skillfully he could ride a bicycle. He liked to imagine himself, too, as the youngest trumpet player in the world. "I want to be the best, alone on top, no one better than me." His greatest wish at this time was to own a trumpet.

The need to show off was continuously apparent in his behavior and his fantasies. He wanted his analyst to know that he was physically the strongest of his gang. He did, in fact, carry a large dagger at his side which he would brandish as a symbol of his prowess. Heroic in its denial of the deficiency of his arms was his boast that he could "slap the other boys in the face so hard!"

Again and again he would tell how he planned to organize special shows in London at which he would be the featured attraction, diving headlong from the Tower Bridge to the astonishment of the skeptical crowd.

Peter especially liked to acquire things that other boys did not have, so he could provoke their envy. "Look, you haven't got what I've got." "See my big dagger, mine is bigger." He expressed this kind of feeling more vehemently and more frequently than would the average boy.

His deep-seated insecurity due to his deformity constantly impelled Peter to essay exceptional feats of daring or skill. The day he started taking swimming lessons he commented: "I am looking forward to swimming with my girl friend; I want to show her that I can swim; perhaps she does not think I can do it well. . . . If I have enough pride, I will get my swimming certificate." Then he recalled an earlier incident at the pool when, feeling unsure of being accepted by the poolside gang of young swimmers, he had climbed to the upper springboard to display how fearless he was. When the other boys saw him up there, he said, they became frightened for him, and when he realized they were frightened, he jumped into the water. The boys were impressed. They applauded him and accepted him. This story shows how desperately hard Peter was working to prove he was in no way inferior to his peers in achievement.

During the first months of the analysis, it could be said that the intensity of Peter's fantasy life was so great as to verge at times on pseudologia phantastica and to carry him close to borderline capacity in reality testing. One day, full of excitement, he reported: "I have just won a bike by answering questions." The fact was he had entered a daily newspaper contest by answering questions and sending in the contest entry. At the time, this action was all the foundation he needed on which to build the belief that he had already won the bicycle. Moreover, he had moved on from this belief in ownership to the planning in minute detail of a 400-mile trip.

At this stage his fantasies were so intense that their realization in actuality seemed to him to be at most no more than a matter of time. This conviction led him into a number of dangerous situations such as that resulting from his bravado on the high-diving board.

Castration Anxiety

Peter's castration anxiety soon assumed a paramount place in the analysis. Paradoxically, his anxiety was in no way different in type from that of any physically normal neurotic boy except in that he had a permanent unconscious need to compensate for the lack of normal arms.

Peter's castration anxiety was related to masturbation fantasies and activities, to oedipal strivings, and to the resulting guilt and fear of punishment. In his case, the arm defect was unconsciously feeding the castration complex. The defective arms were, in a sense, equated with "defective" genitals and thus were unconsciously taken as evidence of actual castration.

Peter had all the classic masturbation fantasies but with unusually strong exhibitionistic components. In these, his symbolic exhibitionistic masturbating was always followed by symbolic castration.

The exhibitionism was shown in the fantasies in which he performed as a trumpet player and was cheered by huge, delirious crowds. Similarly in other fantasies, he performed notable exploits on a bicycle for which his photograph would appear in the daily papers.

The sense of guilt arising out of his strong sexual feelings for his mother and the consequent fear of punishment were shown through such actual dreams as this: He was riding his bicycle at great speed . . . he became more and more excited, then started going down a steep hill . . . his mother was there watching his performance . . . she laughed and was quite "thrilled" . . . a crowd of bystanders was equally thrilled . . . at the peak of his excitement he found he could not control the speed at which he was racing downhill. "I am going so fast it isn't possible to put the brakes on. I can't stop. I have an accident and break my leg."

It is interesting that Peter had a variety of fantasies revealing oedipal strivings in which he had to go to the hospital for a broken leg, not an arm.

In some fantasies so much emotional significance was attached to cycling that Peter's legs symbolically became his genitals. Cycling was sexualized and consequently injury to legs represented punishment by castration. The same process was also apparent in those trumpet fantasies in which the trumpet was broken.

This sexualization was so intense that Peter said he had to avoid thinking about *his* bicycle or trumpet at night. "It makes me feel too hot and too excited, and then it is hard to fall asleep."

Still another instance of phallic displacement was Peter's frightening dream of lying in bed, face down, and finding a big snake under his tummy. Peter used to masturbate at night lying on his "stomach."

During the period in the analysis in which Peter was longing for a bicycle or a trumpet, there were a few episodes of homosexual anxiety. He had indeed to miss some sessions to avoid becoming "too excited" while talking to his analyst.

The Significance of Enuresis

From the material provided by the analysis it became evident that the enuresis associated with Peter's intense oedipal fantasies had two meanings for him, as it does for most enuretics. It meant prohibited sexual activity accompanied by castration as punishment. And simultaneously, it had the reassuring meaning of an undamaged, well-functioning penis. For Peter, castration anxiety was intensified because unconsciously he equated his arm defect with castration. This unconscious equating of a real with a symbolic handicap intensified both his denial of his deformity and his great need to overcompensate for it. The arm defect, in itself a visible handicap, also greatly increased his need for displaced phallic exhibitionism.

Most of Peter's dreams show that this phallic exhibitionism was a basic factor in his bed wetting. For example, he had many dreams involving aeroplanes. In front of an amazed crowd including either his mother or the Queen, he would pilot a plane at a terrific speed. Then he would crash in water and break his leg. The dream sequence was obviously one of masturbation-erection, enuresis, castration-punishment. After Peter had been in analysis for about a year, the enuresis disappeared.

THE CONSTRUCTIVE ROLE OF FANTASY

The extent to which Peter was able to make constructive use of fantasy in the formation of ego abilities was the most unexpected development of the analysis.

As mentioned earlier, the boy entertained, for a time, a number of unrealizable fantasies such as climbing and cutting down trees. These soon dropped out of the analysis completely. But other fantasies and hopes, which my colleagues and I admittedly felt to be equally unattainable, remained for some time as central points of interest until these too were dropped one by one from the analysis but for quite a different reason. They moved out of the realm of fantasy into actual accomplishment. During the analysis, Peter learned to play the trumpet well enough to plan a career as a performer. He learned to swim and dive well enough to earn a lifesaving certificate. In this he measured up to the standards required of all applicants; no special allowances were made for his deformity. And he learned to ride a bicycle in the face of the opposition of his apprehensive parents. These accomplishments showed that Peter had a more generous and, at the same time, more realistic assessment of his capabilities than did his parents, his analyst, or the other professional consultants. Moreover, he seemed to have at his disposal an almost inexhaustible fund of energy.

That Peter should talk about his hopes and fantasies just so long as they remained in the realm of unreality was an unusual and fascinating aspect of the analysis. He presented a succession of foci of intense interest—the trumpet, the swimming, the bicycle, and others. Each of these was talked about with great excitement, elaborated in imaginative detail, then dropped abruptly the moment Peter took action to make it a reality. For example, the entire subject of trumpet and music dropped out of the analysis when Peter was finally given a cornet. The analyst would therefore have been unaware of the details of the boy's real achievements but for the reports of the therapist who interviewed the mother.

It could be said, then, that the analysis dealt at any one time only with the residue of Peter's fantasy world, and the work of the analysis could be described as the continuing transformation of fantasies into ego abilities executed in reality. Peter was using fantasy to conquer reality. And through this process he was seeking a secure ego identity.

It was significant also that Peter's most highly charged fantasies all revealed strivings toward a masculine identity. This was particularly apparent in the way the trumpet and the analyst served alternately as means of achieving masculinity. When Peter felt he was gaining enough satisfaction from his trumpet, he felt he could dispense with the analyst by missing sessions.

Multiple Mechanisms

At this point it might be well to note that any one of Peter's activities must be recognized as having been brought about as the result of the interplay of more than one mechanism. Phallic displacement, overcompensation, and reaction formation were involved in the trumpet playing before large audiences, in the display of badges won in swimming, diving and lifesaving, and in the wearing of a dagger at his side. One striking instance betraying the extent to which Peter's short arm threatened his masculine pride was the determined attempt at fourteen years of age to win membership in a fishing club whose minimum age requirement was sixteen. He set his heart on this goal because he was convinced that, should he succeed on grounds of actual performance as a fisherman, the world would cease to entertain doubts about his potentialities. He would then belong to the category of men. Moreover, membership would entitle him to wear "a big badge" on his coat which he could show to all his friends. Here again, drawing upon his tremendous reserves of energy, Peter did win the coveted membership on merit despite his age.

From Fantasy to Reality

Some considerable time after Peter's fantasies relating to the trumpet had moved out of the field of the analysis, he brought the subject back in again in an unforeseen way. One day he brought his cornet (trumpet) to the analytic session. Secure now in his real achievements and repeated successes as a musician, he somehow felt able to bring this once highly cathected subject again to the attention of his analyst.

"You want me to play?" he asked, his eyes radiant. Hesitation and shyness were brushed aside by the determination to demonstrate his skill. He communicated the feeling that nothing in the world could have prevented him from playing.

On this occasion, Peter was wearing his new artificial left arm. He said this would be his first time to play for anybody while wearing the artificial arm, and that playing would be much more than normally difficult. The wonder was he could play at all. As the artificial left hand could not grasp the cornet properly, he perforce had to use his undersized, thumbless right hand with its three slender fingers to help hold the instrument while simultaneously fingering the valves. For extra support, he put one foot up on a chair so he could rest the cornet against his knee. In this awkward and little-practiced position, he played relatively well.

After playing several selections, one of which he had composed himself, he commented that "the next time" he would play twelve tunes in a much better way without his artificial arm. After a moment's reflection, however, he said it would probably be better for him to try to learn wearing his artificial arm because the arm would give him a better appearance on the stage. The comment indicated how far removed Peter was from seeking a masochistic advantage from his handicap, or, to express it in other terms, to exhibit with his defect.

Comparisons of Peter's fantasy life with that of more physically normal adolescents revealed one fundamental difference in the relationship between sexual (masturbatory) fantasies and symbolic activity. When a physically normal youth abandons a sexual fantasy, he almost invariably jettisons all related symbolic activity and interest. Peter, in contrast, was able to transfer the interest associated with symbolic activity to constructive activity. For him, fantasy was the precursor of, not the substitute for, real striving. His early intense preoccupation with his trumpet fantasy, for example, later became the driving power that carried him over the arduous road to competence as a musician.

Observations made by Anna Freud concerning the fantasy life of the physically normal boy indicate how unusual was Peter in this respect. Anna Freud (1936) writes:

> We must not suppose that an adolescent ponders on the various situations in love or on the choice of a profession in order to think out the right line of behaviour, as an adult might do or as a boy in the latency-period studies a piece of machinery in order to be able to take it to pieces and put it together again. Adolescent intellectuality seems merely to minister to day-dreams. Even the ambitious phantasies of the pre-pubertal period are not intended to be translated into reality. When a young lad phantasies that he is a great conqueror, he does not on that account feel any obligation to give proof of his courage . . . in real life . . . He [the boy] evidently *derives gratification from the mere process of thinking* . . . His behaviour is determined *by other factors* and is not necessarily influenced by the results of these intellectual gymnastics [pp. 175-176, italics added].

How different is the story of Peter, the boy who left little or nothing of his fantasy world behind him with the passing of puberty.

Explanations of Peter's psychological processes must be tentative pending corroborative findings in similar cases. A hypothesis could be: Nothing of Peter's fantasy world could be abandoned or left behind because every part of it had to be put at the service of an unconscious need, the need to find substitutes for the growing of longer arms. This mechanism of transformation would be part of a never-ending denial of inferiority. And the deformity would be a perpetual stimulus for compensatory strivings.

CHARACTERISTICS OF THE DISABLED

The belief that "as long as one is convinced one can do something, one can do it" has helped many people to worthy achievements. But it can also be conveniently used to feed daydreaming while inhibiting activity which would put the conviction to the test.

So far as physically disabled people are concerned, surface observation shows that, according to their reactions, they can be divided into two categories, the active and the passive ones, the doers and the dreamers. Apparently, in the analytic literature, more attention has been paid so far to the passive than to the active type. Veterans hospitals are still caring for many patients described as "passive-dependent personalities." Typically these patients use their noncongenital handicaps, consciously or unconsciously, as justification for passivity and dependence. They stop striving for attainable achievements and make inaction morally acceptable by considerations of self-pity. The handicap becomes the pivot for a multitude of unfruitful fantasies and excuses for resignation.

These passive individuals preserve the conviction that they could accomplish great things by avoiding test by action. Analogous is the frequently encountered case of the student with poor grades who does not dare work hard for fear he might shatter the gratifying belief that he would be at the head of his class if only he would apply himself. Here again reality is a threat and is sacrificed. Passivity and fantasy leave no room for achievement.

Not so with Peter. He dared to put his "dreams" to the test. For him there was nothing mutually exclusive between the appearance of compensatory fantasies on the one hand and compensatory actual improvements in ego performance on the other. Peter's real achievements were so well integrated, so positively ego-syntonic, that it seems we must look beyond pathological mechanisms for a comprehensive explanation.

Turning passivity into activity is there, but it is only part of the picture. It will be shown later that the fear of passivity played a part in spurring the boy to greater endeavors. But a purely defensive reaction cannot be the sole impetus for so many positive undertakings. If it could, it would produce reaction formations of classic, crystallized structure whereas Peter's behavior approximates much more closely that resulting from sublimation. It might be better to say that Peter's functioning could serve as an illustration of the adaptive function of fantasy life, according to Heinz Hartmann's elaborations of Anna Freud's views on the denial of reality by fantasy. Hartmann (1939) wrote:

> . . . what are the positive adaptive elements of fantasy? . . . It is possible, and even probable, that the relationship to reality is learned by ways of *detours*. There are avenues of reality-adaptations which, at first, certainly lead away from the real situation.

The function of play is a good example . . . Another example is the auxiliary function of fantasy in the learning process: though fantasy always implies an initial turning away from a real situation, it can also be a preparation for reality and may lead to a better mastery of it. Fantasy may fulfill a synthetic function by provisionally connecting our needs and goals with possible ways of realizing them . . . there are fantasies which, while they remove man from external reality, open up for him his internal reality [pp. 17-19].

Peter's condition, furthermore, should not be compared too narrowly to that encountered in certain character disorders and in manic-depressives who exhibit much compulsive, compensatory activity. Peter was all this—and something more. He looked forward while the others looked backward. His progress was more than a reactive defense. He actually achieved increasing emotional security as he went along. His actions and integration regularly operated to reduce the tension between "wanting" and "being able" to do something.

Compulsive work, counterphobic reaction, reactive compensatory mechanisms, all have something static about them. Peter's activity, in contrast, was creative. There seems no doubt that Peter is an excellent example of an "active disabled" person. The people who belong to this category do not usually seek psychiatric help, and their reactions are usually dismissed as "normal." Whether or not Peter's drive toward activity is characteristic of all the individuals who belong to this group, or whether we have to regard him as exceptional, will have to be decided in the future when more detailed analytic studies of such persons are made available.

Artificial Arms and Ego Identity

Peter had first been provided with artificial arms several years before his analysis. But for the most part he could not be induced to use them with any regularity. By using his own arms he was putting his inborn physical equipment to the test. After all, Peter had always known his body as it was. For him, his body ego was intact. While others may have been shocked by the sight of his arms, Peter himself was not. His body image had been unchanged all through his life. If there were any element of shock for him, it could only be brought about by the disturbing experience of comparing himself to others, an experience bound to jeopardize his security and self-confidence.

If, then, he so consistently refused to use the artificial arms, the reason must have been to valorize those very body parts that threatened most to feed an inferiority complex. His intense motivation toward action and achievement was a measure of this need to prove his own natural body adequate to every challenge. Yet his competition with other children was of a normal kind. The intensity with which he resorted to the mechanism of compensation in displacement was proportional to the intensity of the threat of inferiority and failure in the experiences of competition. The threat to his inner security first posed by his mother's shame served as a trigger for more compensatory performances.

We hope we correctly use Erikson's concepts and terminology (1956) in stating that the artificial arms were completely excluded from the field of Peter's identity. They were not given even the smallest part to play in his drive toward levels of performance adequate to his ideal ego identity. The sense of *self*, of *his* personality, of *his* potentialities, he felt should be based solely on the physical equipment nature gave him.

Peter's first direct reference to his arms after several months of analysis had nothing to do with his desperate wish to see them grow. On the contrary, it was a protest against having anything further done to his arms as they were. The occasion was the relating of a dream of castration anxiety in which he was walking on railway tracks when a train (the analyst) roared up to him too quickly to be avoided, hit him, and mangled his arms.

Peter himself linked this dream to the previous operations he had undergone preparatory to the fitting of artificial arms. Peter had greatly feared that the hospital doctors might decide to cut off the short arms in order to replace them with artificial ones. The surgeons had, in fact, suggested that this might be necessary in order to fit the newest, most improved type of artificial arms. Peter opposed the possibility with intensity.

Obviously such an ablation was conceived of by the boy as a brutal attack from the adult world, a cruel attempt to deprive him of any chance to reach a meaningful sense of identity. It could destroy any possibility of reaching a reconciliation with his body ego. It could be so traumatic an experience as even to pave the way for depression or devastating passivity.

It should be noted here that there was no evidence that self-pity motivated Peter's exploits. He would go out into the streets with his trumpet at Christmas and other times to play tunes and collect money from the passers-by. In this kind of activity where, if anywhere, self-pity could be expected to reveal itself in passive exploitation, Peter's whole objective was to impress people by his performance, not by his handicap.

SEXUALIZATION

The transformation of fantasies into the ego constitution was not achieved without hazard. For the main fantasy, that of becoming a musician, the process at the instinctual level was for a while a precarious one. During one phase, the musical activity was a highly sexualized, aggressive activity which threatened to interfere with Peter's musical training and performances. He enjoyed, for example, playing with the trumpet pointed as "high up in the air" as his arms would permit. When this playing with trumpet raised was accompanied by real erections in the presence of girls during a concert, Peter had to stop playing because of the sexual excitement. The resulting anxiety tended toward inhibition rather than sublimation. Fortunately, the problem was left behind after the phallic content in the activity was interpreted, thus desexualizing it without destroying it. Toward the end of the analysis Dorothy Burlingham summed up this aspect of Peter's progress: "His ego and id seem to be well lodged in his music, which might enable him really to do something with his gift."[5]

REALITY AND DEPRESSION

Two questions which presented themselves again and again during the analysis were: Why did Peter keep his real achievements out of the analytic sessions for so long? Why did he seem to cease being thrilled by anything as soon as it stopped being a fantasy?

[5] Dorothy Burlingham, Co-director, Hampstead Clinic, during a case conference.

One hypothesis is that a coveted object (trumpet) or function (musician) was unconsciously equated to the growing of longer arms. While such objects or functions remained in fantasy, they held great emotional significance for Peter, but the moment they entered the real world, they lost their symbolic meaning. This process of converting fantasy to fact was one of painful disillusionment in that it meant abandoning a "dream" through which Peter could keep alive his deeply cherished hope for normal arms. His unconscious reaction was to devaluate the real object or function. It could be expected that the process would have a depressive effect, and this did, in fact, occur. At times when he had nothing exciting to talk about in the realm of fantasy and thus felt he had to talk about himself (reality), he would become depressed.

Earlier, when the trumpet was still an object of fantasy, Peter had fully expected to receive one as a birthday present. When it failed to arrive, his disappointment was so great that he became depressed, lost interest in eating, could not sleep, and missed sessions. However, as the analysis proceeded, he developed the ability to accept disappointment and the disillusionments of reality without experiencing such deep feelings of depression.

Important also in Peter's personality was an unconscious feeling of incompleteness expressing itself endlessly in attempts to compensate for his deformity. This feeling developed in spite of the strong body ego which made him resist the use of artificial arms. Toward the end of the analysis, it was apparent that Peter would never be able to feel he had achieved full masculine status. Unlike most physically normal men who reach a relatively satisfactory state of equilibrium in their male role, Peter gave indication that he would always need some mechanism to deal with the psychic effects of his deformity. Achievement and success would be needed again and again to bolster his masculine ego.

This mechanism was seen in operation on a number of occasions. For instance, after six successful months as a trumpeter in a band, Peter began talking about forming his own band where he would be the leader, "the boss." But, he emphasized, he had no intention of showing off. This was in contrast to the exhibitionism he had displayed earlier. In talking about "his" band, he said he would not want to make it too obvious that he was the conductor. He would just like to give a discreet signal to start the band playing. Surely the other members of the band would not like him to show off too much and he would not want to make them envy him.

Further, revealing his need to devaluate arms of normal length, Peter commented that he particularly disapproved of the usual behavior of most trumpet players on the stage. He described them as "being foolish with their trumpets . . . showing off by throwing them up in the air . . . and playing in the sky." Peter, of course, could not flourish his trumpet in this fashion. In a matter-of-fact way, he summed up: "A trumpet is meant to play music, not to make a big show."

In the foregoing, Peter's psychic handling of his physical defect might be compared with the way in which young girls typically deal with a castration complex. They depreciate their own bodies but take pride in their pursuits. It is as if they were to say: "My body is of no consequence, but what I do is marvelous." Similarly, Peter's phallic exhibitionism found expression through achievement.

Oedipus Complex, Regression, and Adolescence

One day Peter came to his session fully determined, for the second time, to play the trumpet for his analyst. On the one hand, this was a sign of increasing security and reconciliation with reality. On the other, it revealed strong oedipal rivalry and forewarned of the danger of regression to a passive-masochistic state.

Unconsciously, this performance meant that he could do in front of his analyst something the latter was incapable of doing. It proved to be too daring a show of his phallic superiority as it was followed by nightmares in which his trumpet was broken into pieces and in which he was run over by horses and gorillas. In the nightmares he was reduced to a castrated, female condition. He had many ensuing fantasies, verging into real beliefs, in which his analyst was jealous of him, was unhappy that he had become a musician, and was displeased that he had got a bigger trumpet. (Peter had recently changed his small cornet for a trumpet.)

Earlier in the analysis, the rivalry in the transference and the anxiety accompanying it did not go too deeply and were expressed quite simply. He would say: "I would like to be the boss here, too, and make you talk to me and not only me talking to you . . ." One day, a necessary visit to his dentist provoked a nightmare that was related to the transference relationship: Two very big men seized him and took him by force to the dentist; they were ugly and wanted to take out all his teeth. After relating this dream, he went on without a pause into his own fantasy: "A boy is in the dentist chair; the dentist takes a hammer, hits the boy, and takes out all his teeth. Then the boy wakes up [recovers consciousness], takes the hammer, knocks down the dentist, and takes out all his teeth." This tooth-for-a-tooth fantasy was related with great gusto.

But the feelings which emerged at this later phase presented greater difficulties. Peter was no longer cooperative and said he wished to see the analysis come to an end. He would reiterate that he did not feel like coming any more. He would insist that he was cured, not having wet the bed for so long. His father told him it would be a waste of time to go on. It was obvious that Peter no longer found the analysis exciting. He felt he had nothing more to expect of it. It was now even disappointing. Above all, Peter did not feel like talking about his trumpet. He wanted to keep it to himself, away from the analysis, away from the analyst he was sure was opposed to his becoming independent and grown up with his big trumpet. He was convinced that the analyst was envious and consequently ill-disposed toward him. His resistance at this stage almost reached phobic proportions. He was very anxious in his silences, in his avoidance of any mention of his prized trumpet. Through dreams and fantasies, it became obvious that he was afraid of being deprived of this most exciting possession. He had to keep all his strong feelings about it from the analyst. Symbolically, he was hiding away his pleasurable, exciting erection, and his unconscious fears of castration were expressed in nightmares in which his trumpet was broken while he was on his way to a session.

A little later the masturbation displacement, the guilt, and the castration anxiety became even more dominant in his dreams. In place of the gorillas of previous nightmares there appeared an even more obvious representative of the superego, the policeman. Peter reported the following nightmare: He was playing jazz with his trumpet as a member of a nightclub dance band when several policemen rushed in; he became so upset and frightened that he dropped his trumpet to the floor where it smashed into pieces. He woke up sweating profusely. Following the sessions dealing with this dream, there was a gradual lessening of the sexualization of Peter's musical activity.

Some earlier indications of the intensity of Peter's oedipal strivings were noted during the first phases of the analysis. Peter used to say that he very much liked to act in school plays, "specially the grown-up parts where I can let myself go with rage, telling off the others . . ." He particularly enjoyed making a noise, especially whistling or sounding off with his trumpet. The significance of this can be more readily appreciated when it is known that whistling was forbidden at home during the day in order not to disturb the sleep of the father who worked night shifts. The making of noise was perhaps his favorite way of expressing his opposition to his father. Another cathected area related to his oedipal rivalry was the great temptation to remain awake as late as possible at night; this meant consciously daring to do what his father did.

In the latter part of the analysis, the mother and mother figures came more and more to the foreground. Some ambivalence had first been observed. On the unconscious, negative side, his mother was a bad, orally depriving mother. He dreamed that he had not enough to eat, that she had given him "much less sandwiches" than she had given his father. His father thus "had better chances to grow."

This negative aspect, however, was much less important in the analysis than his febrile desire to impress the mother and win her admiration and love. His yearning for her love and approval came out in a recurring daydream in which the Queen honored him for his fishing abilities by inviting him to dinner and presenting him with £1,000 for fishing equipment. Another revealing daydream found him planning to work and make money to buy a better house for his mother.

An almost incredible feat throws further light on Peter's oedipal strivings. He set himself the task of building a real bicycle without his parents' knowledge. A friend who was in on the scheme let Peter use a shed at the back of his house. Here Peter gradually assembled the parts as he was able to save his money, bit by bit, to buy them.

As the project progressed, Peter's excitement ran high. The analytic sessions were filled with vivid fantasies of how at last he would be able to perform on his bicycle for his mother. One could feel the boy's determination to let nothing stand in the way of the fulfillment of this dream, not even the disapproval he knew he could expect from his parents who had always opposed the idea of bicycle riding for Peter.

As with the trumpet, Peter surprised everyone by achieving his goal. He became a skillful cyclist.

The Mother's Changing Attitude

About halfway through the analysis, there was a significant change in the mother's attitude. She began to tell her therapist how much happier she was feeling about her son. With each of Peter's successive achievements—fishing, playing the trumpet, swimming, lifesaving, diving, and bicycling—she would express surprise and a growing pride and pleasure. More and more he was becoming an indispensable part of her life. She was finding that she liked having him around the house. One time when he was away at camp for a few days, she said how much she was looking forward to having him back and hearing him practice on his trumpet again. His deformity no longer caused her embarrassment and shame.

This change in his mother's attitude was a source of great satisfaction to Peter. As all his hard-won feats had been undertaken basically to win her love and admiration, her pleasure and pride made him very happy and promoted his growing sense of security. Evidence of the oedipal coloring of his strivings and the assurance that he was becoming "the little man" of a proud mother was the simultaneous wish of mother and son for another baby in the family. Previously both parents had maintained that they did not want another child. Now, only the father was still against the idea.

Hazards of Passivity

During the latter phase of the analysis Peter's fight against regression to a masochistic, passive-feminine relationship in the transference became a major issue. Evidence of this struggle had appeared earlier in the form of an unconscious wish to be beaten by the analyst. There was also an earlier dream of a car accident in which he received an injury that left him with an opening into the middle of his body, a condition he equated to the female sexual constitution.

While his determination to achieve independence led him to "cut" several of his sessions and to argue for a reduction from five to two or three sessions a week, the latent wish to become more dependent betrayed itself in several slips of the tongue in which his plea for fewer sessions came out as one for more sessions, actually "seven" sessions a week.

The analytic interpretation of Peter's conflict around dependence-independence produced some therapeutic results. These were manifest in his increased self-confidence, and in an easier, freer relationship with his analyst. As should be expected in the analysis of an adolescent, this development resulted in an increasing detachment from the analyst and a decreasing interest in continuing the analysis.

At this point I realized that Peter was no longer talking to me as a patient. He had, as never before, a matter-of-fact way of expressing his intentions; he now had the direct, open manner of an adolescent boy determined to see to his own affairs. With a sense of purpose and self-assurance, he explained how he now felt about the analysis. Reasoning logically, he wanted me to understand that after school he would like to follow his friends rather than attend a session. He wanted to do what the other members of his "gang" or club did at that particular time of day; he wanted to participate in their games; he wanted to go out with girls. The more fully his passive wishes were analyzed, the more urgent became his adolescent self-assertion and revolt. Accordingly we let Peter go on his way toward the independence he was seeking—and that meant the end of the analysis.

TECHNICAL PROBLEMS

As Peter made no mention of his arms in the early analytic sessions, the question as to whether or not the analyst should himself introduce the subject was raised at a case conference. Anna Freud recommended against this, suggesting that the analysis should be conducted like any other, with no topic being avoided or introduced. Interference, she felt, could result in bypassing the full analysis of his personality. She pointed out that the material then being presented concerned Peter's fear of castration. Dealing first with this anxiety would have certain advantages. As castration was not a reality, interpretation of his fears in this area would be more reassuring than interpretation of those having a basis in reality—the malformed arms. She also saw in this procedure a safeguard against Peter's depressive tendencies.

Throughout the entire course of the analysis, the requirements of Peter's ego functioning were respected. And nothing seems to have been lost by following this procedure. His real-life activities and achievements came late but safely into the analysis. After the interpretation of much of the castration material, Peter himself introduced the subject of his arms. This occurred in a depressive context, revealing that he had been harboring the illusion that the analysis would make his arms grow. He had dreamed that he was working in a coal mine with adults; a "big accident happened" and completely cut off their air supply; he fainted and woke up in a hospital, saved from death because he had been given *artificial* air; and he completely recovered. In the dream, the hospitalization was followed by normal life (normal arms). But in real life, his hospital experiences for the fitting of artificial arms were not followed by "real arms." Nor did the analysis bring about the growth of longer arms. There was no magic. At long last he was able to speak of the hopelessness of his wish.

Weathering this critical period of disillusionment, Peter went on to new achievements. Gradually, the enrichment of his real abilities and his growing self-esteem made it seem likely that he would continue to make reasonably satisfactory progress toward adulthood without further help from his analyst.

10

THE RELATIONSHIP OF PSYCHOLOGIC STATE AND EPILEPTIC ACTIVITY

Psychoanalytic Observations on an Epileptic Child

LOUIS A. GOTTSCHALK, M.D.

(1956)

In the investigation of epileptic phenomena, there are few detailed clinical reports available that describe the epileptic activity and the sequence of interpersonal and intrapersonal events during which the seizures take place. In certain types of paroxysmal activity, variously called "psychic equivalent seizures," "affective epilepsy" (Wilson, 1940), and so forth, it may become impossible to differentiate between epileptic experiences (and behavior) and nonepileptic experiences (and behavior). This is especially likely to be so when the presumed seizure activity involves complicated and highly integrated patterns of behavior and psychologic processes. On the other hand, just as the clinical phenomenon of the "Jacksonian march" gives a rough representation of neural structure and function, so the detailed description of more complex types of epileptic sequences may reveal relationships of brain structure and function to psychopathologic processes or relationship of psychologic stresses to brain function. Previous reports (Gottschalk, 1953, 1955) have provided evidence that psychologic factors, as well as other factors, can contribute to the form and frequency of seizures and associated clinical manifestations [see also Meers (1966)].[1]

The present paper is about a ten-year-old boy, Ned, who was observed in psychoanalytic psychotherapy for a period of twenty-eight months and who was followed by correspondence and occasional interviews for another period of five years. This boy frequently had one of his three types of seizures during the therapeutic sessions in the playroom; and the type

[1] Part of this study was done while the author was a Research Associate at the Institute for Psychosomatic and Psychiatric Research and Training, Michael Reese Hospital, Chicago, Illinois.

of seizure repeatedly observed during psychoanalytic sessions can most accurately be labeled as an "atypical or psychic equivalent" seizure. The observations made with this patient illustrate not only the therapeutic value of psychoanalytic psychotherapy in the management of certain types of epileptic individuals, but also demonstrate the value of psychoanalytic study of epilepsy as an important avenue of furthering our understanding of the neural basis of emotional disorder.

A brief summary of the kinds of seizures Ned developed in the chronological order of the appearance of the manifestation follows:

1. His atypical seizures were precipitated usually by looking through an ordinary window screen or occasionally by looking at checkered or striped patterns on clothes, tablecloths or drapery. (These seizures will henceforth be designated as "screen spells.") These episodes had had their onset when he was five years of age, soon after the father had to leave home to enter active duty in the army. The fits consisted of spells of staring through a window screen and were accompanied by unco-ordinated, generally symmetrical stereotyped shaking of the upper extremities. According to the parents, the arm movements, with accompanying head and neck motions, suggested to the parents protective or warding-off actions against some threat to the child's head and neck. These seizures lasted from one to forty-five minutes. Ned would generally remain standing, would only rarely fall or bite his tongue, could not be communicated with during the spell, and could not recall what he had been doing during the spell. Neurologists, pediatricians, psychiatrists, and electroencephalographers who studied the boy between the ages of five and ten concurred in the opinion that these episodes were of an epileptic nature.

2. His grand mal seizures were rare. The first one had occurred at the age of nine years, and one such seizure had occurred each year thereafter, accompanied by tonic and clonic phases and biting of the tongue on two occasions. The grand mal seizures all evolved during "screen spells."

3. The psychomotor seizures appeared at the age of ten years. Typical in their pattern, lasting from fifteen to thirty minutes, these were paroxysmal episodes of complicated and rather highly organized motor activity, with a prominent destructive component, e.g., tearing clothes to shreds or breaking furniture. The boy had no notion what led to these seizures and could not be communicated with during them. After the seizures he could not recall what he had done during them. It was these seizures that motivated the parents to bring him for psychiatric evaluation and treatment.

POSSIBLE PATHOGENIC FACTORS IN THE EPILEPTIC SYNDROME

There was no familial history of epilepsy or migraine and no relevant history of trauma or infection. The patient's birth and development during infancy were free from any known symptomatic disorder. All neurological examinations revealed a normal state except for bilateral construction of the peripheral visual fields ("tubular vision"), first appearing at the age of ten years four months and lasting two months. Thorough neurologic and ophthalmologic studies revealed that a disturbance of the form fields and not of the color fields was involved in this visual symptom, but there was no detectable structural or anatomical basis for it. The visual field defect cleared up soon after the advent of psychotherapy and did not recur.

The first electroencephalographic recording, done when he was six years old, showed 3 c.p.s. spike and wave discharges, a little more pronounced from the right hemisphere.

Electroencephalograms done at the ages of seven, ten, and eleven were generally similar to the first electroencephalogram but showed a progressive trend to irregular slow wave activity (3-4 c.p.s.) without regular spiking. An electroencephalogram at thirteen, taken shortly after the termination of psychoanalytic treatment, gave evidence of focal slow activity in the right parietotemporal region.

Ned was described by his parents as a boy who, except for his seizures, was customarily conforming to their standards, though clinging and demanding of indulgence. He was adjudged by psychiatrists who had seen him previously on consultation as "very immature and rather effeminate" and as "a boy with whom it was difficult to establish close rapport." He was an only child.

Psychiatric and social casework studies of the mother revealed that she was a compulsive, perfectionistic person, whose relationships with others were characterized by very little investment on her part. She was mainly interested in people in order to get support and approval from them. She was inclined to be overindulgent and unduly intimate in Ned's rearing. She kept in constant attendance during his baths and frequently undressed in front of him or slept with him up to the time he began psychologic treatment. On the other hand, she showed poor tolerance to the least signs of independence and hostility he manifested toward her. She encouraged him to learn to cook and do housework. She had a tendency to tell him in what respects she considered the father inadequate.

The father was a passive, self-depreciative person who had difficulties in dealing with men in competitive situations or adequately asserting himself when someone's demands were actually excessive, e.g., an employer's. As the oldest son in the family, the father had had to take over the financial support of his own siblings at the age of fifteen because of the economic failures of the paternal grandfather, a temperamental chronic alcoholic. The father worried that the patient wanted to replace him, just as the father had replaced the paternal grandfather. The father dealt with his rivalry with his son by reaction formation, by constantly giving him gifts, exposing him—when not pushing him—to the mother's confusing intimacy, aloofness, and compulsive demands for cleanliness and orderliness. Though the father wanted to do so, he had difficulty in experiencing a warm interest in and real companionship with his son.

Events Occurring at the Onset of Patient's Seizures

The onset of Ned's first seizures ("screen spells") occurred at the age of five years, in 1943, shortly after the father departed for active duty in the army. Interviews with the mother revealed that at this time she turned to the patient for security and that she also directed some of her anger, aroused by her husband's leaving, at the patient. Her inconsistent seductiveness and compulsive restraint were most pronounced toward him at this time.

No life situations of significance are known to have occurred during the time of onset of Ned's grand mal seizures, at the age of nine years, and his psychomotor seizures, at the age of ten years.

Effect of Anticonvulsant Medication on Clinical Manifestations Before the Start of Psychoanalytic Psychotherapy

From the time of onset of his first seizures, the "screen spells," many of the standard anticonvulsant regimens, including use of a ketogenic diet and administration of bromides, phenobarbital, diphenylhydantoin, and trimethadione (tridione), or combinations of these, had been tried. Such medication had effected no essential change in the frequency or form of his seizures. At the time psychotherapy was started, however, the patient had not taken any medication regularly for about one year, being given only a capsule of phenobarbital (30 mg.), usually after a fit.

Because of the distressing effect on his parents of the destructive aspects of his psychomotor seizures at the time psychotherapy was started, another trial of diphenylhydantoin medication was made—diphenylhydantoin, in a dose of 0.09 gm. twice a day. With the disappearance of the psychomotor spells after the first six months of psychologic treatment, the administration of diphenylhydantoin was discontinued. No anticonvulsant drug of any sort was administered during the remainder of the course of psychotherapy.

PSYCHOANALYTIC OBSERVATIONS

At the initial interview, Ned was observed to be a large boy for his age, plump, pink-skinned, with regular facial features. He wore glasses. Throughout this session he kept a knitted cap on his head. He was restless and moved about the playroom continually, sometimes apparently for purposes of exploration and orientation, but oftener without discernible reason. He glanced out of the playroom window through the window screen furtively, without any immediate or noticeable reaction. He then began playing actively with a dart gun and holster, while explaining he had seen several doctors previously at the clinic. It seemed, he explained, that he had "hypnotic powers," could hypnotize himself by looking through a screen, "a habit, very silly." He went on to say that he wanted to get rid of the habit because Dr. H., his pediatrician, told his mother he should. As soon as any questions were asked, he regularly responded with the remark, "I don't know," but often would later elaborate spontaneously with a more detailed and pertinent answer. He volunteered tensely that he liked to come and see doctors, psychiatrists, because he liked "to be amused." When his next responses were awaited without his implicit plea to be entertained being satisfied, he remarked petulantly, "I love to play and amuse myself." He did so for a while with different play materials. Returning to the gun and holster and strapping it onto himself, he tried pulling out the gun rapidly and pulling the trigger, observing that he had to practice because he "might be slow on the draw, the gun could get caught in the holster . . . happens sometimes to cowboys." At the close of the session he said he had to shoot the dart gun four or five more times. He did so and then observed, in a tone of threatening reminder, "I like to be amused so much; do I have to go?"

During the next several treatment periods Ned revealed that he thought his psychomotor spells were like uncontrollable attacks of rage. He indicated these seizures were precipitated by seemingly trivial frustrating incidents, such as the interruption of a radio program he was listening to with an advertisement by the program's sponsor. His demands for dependent gratification (to be amused) increased in the playroom setting and when frustrated in these demands he appeared to express his reaction in his play: for example, he would build high towers of blocks and then invariably knock them over and remark that tall towers always topple over easily. He then began to confide, anxiously, his fear of hurting someone in a display of aggression, citing instances at the age of five and later when he threw snowballs or rocks at passing autos, once broke a window, and feared he injured someone. The following hour he announced he had had a psychomotor spell after his pediatrician had put him on a diet because of being overweight. Then he related how he had once had a fight with a boy who made a slanderous remark about his parents. He said, with flashing anger, that he could kill somebody who said anything against his parents; he could even kill a "grownup" like me if I said any such thing.

He now attempted to express and to check his rage and to communicate the reason for it. These activities became the central issue of treatment. In games, such as checkers, he attempted to control my moves by sounds and gestures, drumming on the table, muttering, whistling. When reality testing exposed the lack of magical effect of these procedures, he became provocatively hostile, shooting at me with a dart gun. At the same time, he sought control of and protection from his destructive fantasies and impulses and I informed him I would check him if he could not do so himself. A rigid self-control over affective displays began to show itself.

During the first three months of treatment the "screen spells," which had occurred one to several times a day, became decreasingly frequent and disappeared for about six months. In the meantime the psychomotor seizures became more frequent, the number ranging from two to eight a month. No grand mal seizures occurred during this period. Then, as the patient began to be able to communicate the various components of his psychomotor seizures, i.e., the thing he was doing and what feeling he had about it at the moment just preceding his psychomotor spell, and what he did, thought, and felt during and after the seizure, his psychomotor seizures disappeared fairly rapidly. No further frank psychomotor episodes occurred after the sixth month of psychotherapy. In view of this, the diphenylhydantoin sodium, which had been administered with the beginning of psychotherapy was then discontinued. In these circumstances, no recurrence of the psychomotor fits was noted. Situations which previously had been followed by psychomotor spells were then followed by typical temper tantrums, which the patient could describe and discuss fully. He could also give a more detailed report of his emotional reactions during the temper tantrums. The incidence of these temper tantrums gradually decreased during therapy and became progressively milder and briefer. During the last eighteen months of treatment they occurred only rarely.

On the other hand, as psychomotor seizures waned and disappeared, the "screen spells," which had practically stopped at home, began to recur first at home and, by about the fifth to the sixth month of treatment, they began to occur during the therapeutic sessions in the playroom.

About this time, he asked several times whether I had been in the army, and told me that his father had. He scrutinized my face carefully and observed that I looked as if I had been in the army, meanwhile pounding a ball of clay with his fist, rolling it into long thin cylinders and naming his creation "snakes that could bite." He made a pouch-like receptacle of the clay and then suddenly smashed it flat as a pancake and made a hole in the middle of it. Then he rolled another thin cylinder of clay, wound it into a flat spiral with a knob protruding from the center, and cut the knob with scissors and then with serious preoccupation, without any show of feeling except slight tension and a startled reaction after completion, he unraveled the thin cylinder of clay and cut it into even one inch sections. On my asking, "Are you frightened?" he retorted, irritably and seemingly obtusely, "I'm not angry!"

Now he became resistant to coming to the sessions, covered his head with his jacket in the waiting room, imputed magical powers to me, and expressed suspicions I would tell people his secrets. I informed him I knew he was anxious about his secrets, I did not know why, and I would not know any of his secrets as long as he did not want to tell me about them. Then he had his first screen spell during a treatment session. It lasted four or five minutes. He stood before a screen, tended to look upwards, made masturbatory movements on a pencil he held in his hands, while he rubbed his genital region against the wall and made jerky ducking movements with his head as if suffering or dodging some dangerous object. During the spell he dropped the pencil out of his hand, bent over to pick it up, and resumed his jerking. The seizure lasted until I told him the session was over and then without a pause he turned away from the window and screen and walked out of the room. The resistance to coming to the treatment sessions continued. He explained, "I don't like coming because I have secrets I don't want to give up." I reiterated that I would never know any of his secrets as long as he did not want to tell them. And I added that the only thing I knew about him was that he was a very angry boy. He seemed somewhat relieved, remarked that he knew he had a bad temper and that was why he was afraid to argue with anybody. Outwardly he became more friendly to the idea of therapy, several times put his arm up across my shoulder as we walked to the playroom, asked for rules of various games, asked for help to solve jig-saw puzzles. Now screen spells occurred in the playroom clearly whenever some dependent demand was frustrated in the transference. He would get up and walk to the screen and soon start shaking. During one of these episodes, while carrying on a conversation with me, he simultaneously reported he was having "a dream." In this waking or hypnagogic "dream," he said he was with many little people, all very much smaller than he; suddenly in the "dream" he wanted to return home with his parents, he did so and felt better.

Though no associations to the dream were provided, I privately speculated that the "dream" represented the ambivalent attitudes he had about his treatment—a wish to be in the clinic where other children ("many little people") were, and to get help for his problems and also a contrary wish to escape from the possible exposure, in the treatment, of his overwhelming hostile emotions and conflicts. I also considered the possibility that the "dream" represented a wish to be the center of attention and care rather than to tolerate the frustrations of sharing affection with rivals.

Subsequent sessions tended to confirm' these speculations. Ned made further abortive efforts to effect control of me by magical wishes and gestures in competitive games; and when these did not suffice, he openly asserted his rivalry with me with the addition of some element of compromise, e.g., he said that though I could defeat him in most games of pick-up-sticks, he was better than I in picking up difficult sticks.

Furthermore, he now began to request, then demand, to be taught how to hypnotize, and to be hypnotized. If I hypnotized him, he said, then I could get secrets out of him. I told him if he wanted to talk about his secrets he had my permission to do so. Hypnosis was not necessary, I said. Persistently and in a whining manner, he elaborated that it was very important for him to learn how to hypnotize. Then he could hypnotize others, his friends, particularly his mother. He could make his mother do things for him, wait on him. He could control her. (With an air of finality I declined, saying that hypnosis was not so powerful as he thought.) With this, in crescendo order, he worked himself up from desultory and increased motor activities to a full-blown temper tantrum, threatening to throw playroom objects at me. When I indicated no alarm at this display and casually but firmly told him he was not to throw things at me, he appeared relieved. Still somewhat restless and excited, he became confidential and teasing; he kept looking out of the window without having a spell and repeatedly invited me to look and peek out of the window with him at events going on outside, mentioning that there were some pretty nurses he could see. I told him to enjoy himself, but at the moment I did not care to look out the window.

Now a period ensued of open cooperation in the treatment. He showed growing interest in the precipitating factors for and the frequency of his various kinds of paroxysmal motor excitement. The nature and function of the "screen spells" continued to remain unknown for a time. But it became clear that what once had all the clinical earmarks of true psychomotor seizures, the spells that had developed relatively recently in his life, became, during the process of treatment, an explosive affective and motor discharge, about which he could report the precipitating situation, the overwhelming impulses he experienced, and the fear, shame or guilt he felt about putting these impulses into action. The realization that it was possible to describe to someone else (in verbal terms) his subjective experiences was associated with a dramatic decrease in the frequency and a change in the quality of the psychomotor seizure. Concomitant with his increasing ability to master the mode of expression of his chaotic affects, the psychomotor type of fit was successively replaced by an exacerbation of the "screen spells" and finally by temper tantrums of shorter and shorter duration.

His parents began to regard Ned as a much more reasonable, understandable boy, who asserted himself angrily when blocked from doing what he wanted to. He was gradually able to win some independent privileges, by his self-assertions. He got a job as a delivery boy. He started coming to the clinic without the company and protection of his mother. But his increased openness and frankness confronted his parents with new problems difficult to cope with. For example, in the presence of his parents, he would caricature them, putting on either his father's or mother's hat, demanding in appropriate intonations that his father, and likewise his mother, do that or this—a kind of play acting in the role of the aggressor that the parents found amusing at times, more understandable certainly than fits of anger. But his role playing became distressing to both of his parents, more so to the mother, when his play became vituperative and caustic, as it frequently did.

Fortunately, the transformation of his "psychomotor seizures" to attenuated temper outbursts and his improved social and school adjustments led his parents to enthusiastic and staunch cooperation with the psychotherapeutic program. Their cooperation in encouraging Ned to continue his psychologic treatment was important at this time, for Ned's screen spells—which had temporarily abated in the beginning of treatment—now recurred as frequently as ever and became a focal point of the therapeutic interviews. It seemed that one means of discharge of instinctual tensions, derivatives, and defenses against these drives had been abandoned for another channel of discharge, older in the patient's life history and more complex.

His investigatory interests in the playroom and his transference reactions began to change and became more specific. He stated: "Not long ago I wanted to be a doctor. You know, now I don't want to be a doctor any more? Not a regular doctor anyway. I'd rather be the kind of doctor they have in a crime laboratory. That would be more exciting! I visited an FBI crime lab. with my father not long ago."

He evidenced increasing interest in and use of certain playroom materials about which he had previously shown only brief curiosity—a magnifying glass and kaleidoscope. During one session while playing with the kaleidoscope, he suddenly became tense, put it down, and asked me whether I would play checkers with him. When I declined, he returned to the kaleidoscope, became aimlessly restless and went up to the window screen in the room, looked through it for a while, without developing a spell. (I observed casually to him that I noticed he did not have one of his usual spells when looking through the screen in the room.) Very seriously he explained that the playroom screen faced the wrong direction—it should face south. Also, he added, he had to look upwards for a while to have a spell. At this point, he did so without having a spell and then explained that yesterday he had been looking through the kitchen screen door, was shaking, and had scraped and hurt his nose against the screen.

At the next session he at first reported that he had got tense and angry when an uncle had clipped a bit of his hair to get gum out of it. On talking more about this experience he indicated that he expected that his uncle was going to cut his scalp or clip his ear, and he was prepared to defend himself aggressively against this fantasied attack. He was relieved to experience no injury.

With anxieties about the matter temporarily allayed, he apparently felt reassured enough to proceed spontaneously with the recital of some "new discoveries" about himself. He recognized, he related, that when he stood at a screen and had a screen spell, he "shook all over like a hula dancer." He continued, "I try not to do it but I can't help it. The screen ought to be on a certain side of the room for me to have a spell." Later, on questioning him about spatial relationships, he drew diagrams of room arrangements of the homes in which he lived from age three to five and from five to the age of ten. In both plans it was obvious that he could see directly into his parents' bedroom from his bedroom. In the apartment where the patient had lived from the age of six to the age of ten, the doorway to his parents' bedroom was noted to be on the same side of the room he indicated a screen should be to produce a screen spell on looking through it. It developed that there was actually no door—but only an open doorway—between his room and his parents' and by lying on his bed he could see his parents' bed. He could not remember that there were any curtains or checkered screens present between his room and that of his parents during the last five years, but there had been checkered bedspreads and tablecloths in the household. He appeared astounded after drawing the diagrams of the living arrangements that the sensation that he must look to the left and upwards through a screen to have a spell was coincidental with the direction he would have to look when lying or sitting on his bed to see through the doorway into his parents' bedroom. He anxiously denied ever seeing any sexual activities going on between his parents—though he did not deny looking. He suddenly disgressed, however, and burst forth with associations about his own sexual activities and conflicts. He denied any masturbatory activities: "I never did anything of that sort—well hardly ever. It can lead to a rupture. I only touch it when I wash or urinate or when it itches. The fellows in the neighborhood talk dirty about sex. I think some of them are going to drive themselves insane." With this beginning, he began to elaborate on his sexual activities, fantasies, and play with other children. Although he could not be explicit why he felt so, his attitude about his own sexual interests and play were that they were dangerous, forbidding, and could only eventuate in his own or someone else's destruction and that it was equally dangerous and forbidding to put any of his erotic thoughts and wishes into words. It is interesting to note that at this time all screen spells stopped for a period of a month. He timidly acknowledged masturbatory activities and sexual interests in girls but did not feel inclined to elaborate on these topics. On the one hand, he stated he knew all about sex and how babies were made because his mother told him. (It turned out later, he was quite confused about these matters.) On the other hand, he displayed an ambivalent urgency to know more. He put two airplanes in front of the playroom window screen and shot at them with a dart gun, while talking about his parents' not understanding the needs of a young boy. He reported dreaming of a dead uncle who looked at him from a coffin with his eyes closed; he worried that his uncle's spirit might throw a curse on him. He said he was having trouble going to sleep at night, suffering headaches "behind my eyes," first behind one eye and then the other eye. At this time he broke his glasses and though he got a new pair, he generally refrained from wearing them. He reported that he looked out of the window only in the daytime when he could see. At night he had tried looking but could not see because of the darkness; so he did not look then.

His anxiety mounted and he volunteered he felt uneasy when he came to see me, he did not know why, but felt scared; but also he felt he needed my help. He briefly again begged to be hypnotized, and he asked, "Why does a hypnotist look in a person's eyes?" Then, still discussing the matter, he volunteered, "I hypnotize myself at the screen, you know? I get in complete control of myself, like in a trance or having a dream." Then he expressed some preferential interest in the women's role. He complained that his father had to go to work and he had to go to school in the morning, while his mother stayed home, and all she had to do was a little housework. He himself liked to cook and clean he said. He would rather be like mother and stay home and rest and loaf.

He related that he was having distressing dreams but could not tell me about them—they were "too personal." Finally, asking for a pencil and paper and saying, "This is safer," he wrote: "I was pretending I was fucking a girl in my dreams." And, "Somehow I like to see girls tortured, I don't know why." Elaborating on these written statements, he confessed he had had sexual dreams nightly since the age of five. And at the age of eight he had tried performing sexual relations with a girl per rectum, had been caught by his mother and father, was scolded and threatened but not whipped. He had fantasies of raping a girl in an alley and having people watching him from their kitchen window; they would call the police and get him jailed. He said that he used to sleep in bed with his mother when his father was away on a trip, as late as one year ago, and he would start jerking and shaking, kicking at his mother, and he would pull the covers away from her. "I got an urge to look up a girl's dress or see through their dress." This burst of confessional material was accompanied by vasomotor reactions, tension, and finally mild crying as he left saying, "I needed to get this load off my mind."

A long period of confessions and relatively free reporting of fantasies, affects, and conflicts followed. Oral incorporative preoccupations were prominent. He said he had the idea that something bad, something alien, was inside of him. With a tone of revulsion in his voice, he reported that he liked to eat phlegm from his throat and "buggers" from his nose. When he was "a very little boy" he urinated in a cup and drank it. And now he loved to eat raw meat, raw hamburger and garlic. He wondered whether these habits had something to do with his trouble, whether there were some impurities in these things. An aunt had told him it was bad to eat raw meat because he might get a tapeworm. His trouble was that he ate too much. His mother and pediatrician had said he was overweight. (He weighed 125 lbs. and was now eleven years old.)

The following hour he talked about how much fun it would be to break all the windows in the apartments on Lake Shore Drive. This reminded him of the time he threw a rock at a passing car and broke a window; it was dangerous and someone might have been killed, he reflected. At this moment, he walked to the playroom window and looked out through the screen and his arms and legs jerked briefly. He stepped away from the screen and reported that he jerked because he thought he might get hurt if he hurt someone. He channelized these conflictual fantasies into hyperactive shooting with the dart gun for a few minutes and then expressed a more elaborate fantasy. He wondered, he said, when a gangster shot a girl why the gangster did not have sexual relations with the dead woman; he would think of doing it. Continuing, he reported that he played with two boy friends at this sort of game. One played the part of the gangster; another, the part of the girl: "He is a good actor." He himself took the part of a detective, most of the time. And they played at having sexual intercourse in various ways. Near the end of this session, he touched on a matter that, presumably, was a stimulus for some of his hostile fantasies. He mentioned that he loved movies. "One movie actress, Oh, boy! her legs when she dances, how sexy she is!" This reminded him that he had often seen his mother with her corset or girdle on (glancing through the window). He could see the door of his parents' room from his bed. He ventured that he would like to see his parents have intercourse; he never had, but he usually imagined they were having intercourse when he looked at the door. He remembered feeling left out, hurt, and angry when his parents went to their bedroom and made him stay alone in his own bedroom.

The next session he reported having had a nightmare. In the dream he was sleeping and someone came in and removed his covers. He awakened, felt anxious, went to his parents' room, and complained to his mother that someone removed his blankets. He did not speak to his father. His mother told him to return to bed. Associative material, verbal and nonverbal, revealed his rage at the parents' interest in one another exclusive of him, and secondarily his rage that his father interfered with his dependent and erotic interests in his mother. A diffuse pervasive fear of retaliation for his destructive rage was present. The jealous rage and fear of retaliation was interpreted.

He accepted the interpretation with a conditional "maybe," looked out of the window through the kaleidoscope, briefly jerked his arms and legs defensively—like a prolonged generalized startle reaction—and said:

"I jerk like I'm afraid of something." Then he reiterated in more detail: "I'd like to see my parents screwing. I've always wondered what they do at night. I was always curious about what went on in their bedroom and wanted to be in there with them too."

There followed several hours during which he elaborated on his erotic fantasies and indicated further information about the function of the screen and his "screen spells" as a substitute means of discharging inhibited conflictual tensions. The recurring conscious conflictual theme presented at this time was a wish to rape a girl, blocked by the fear of incarceration or injury by the police. He revealed some common childhood misconceptions about the processes of procreation, parturition, and childbirth. Sexual intercourse, he figured, occurred via anal copulation. The baby developed in the stomach and was given birth via a process of defecation. The fetus' umbilical cord was attached to the mother's navel from the inside. And a woman with an injured breast could not, he felt, conceive another baby; one of his mother's breasts was injured when he was a baby and she was going to have an operation on it soon. She could not have any more babies. (A breast operation on his mother was actually impending.)

He wondered whether he was nearsighted and had to wear glasses because he had hurt his eyes by looking through screen, especially because he kept trying to look through the tiny holes in the screen. He related that when he went to the screen he would first start looking downwards through the small holes and then his eyes seemed pulled upwards, into the sky area, and to the left. Something attracted him toward the left and upwards. At this point he demonstrated exactly what happened to him at the screen and developed one of his characteristic spells of jerking and shaking his arms and shoulders. But at my encouragement he continued talking, telling of a series of three visual hallucinatory experiences he was having, in the following order:

(1) "I see a farm woman, wheeling a wheelbarrow toward me from my left. A package is in the wheelbarrow. Wrapped. A toy for me. It might be a red light, a railroad crossing bar, a caboose. The woman with the wheelbarrow is sexy. I'd like to f— her" (giggling and jerking).

(2) "A ray of light, powerful, is coming from the upper left, down across the blue sky."

(3) "Two sailors are sitting in a boat, stripped to the waist, one behind the other, talking. The boat is next to a dock."

While he was still standing facing the window screen, I asked him for his associations to certain items in the waking dreams. He responded as follows: "I get that idea about the woman whenever I think of anything bad. I jerk as if something stops me from thinking or doing anything more. A caboose is the rear end of a train. The ray of light is like part of God, letting me know he knows everything and to beware. I don't know what else to say about the two sailors, except that one was behind the other."

I told him I realized he was in a hurry to copy a grown-up man and have sex relations, but he was terribly afraid someone would get hurt and he was trying to figure out what to do about this problem. He responded to this interpretation with the equivocal statement that he liked to cook, stay home, be like his mother, but he would rather be like his father.

For a period of many sessions thereafter he frequently went to the screen and had spells, the form of the seizure and the content of the verbal productions undergoing remarkable transitions:

(1) (#48). He looked through the window screen for a while and reported that he saw a man pulling on a rope. At first he seemed to be pulling it downwards from the roof of a house. Later, the man seemed to be pulling it out of the ground. The patient had occasional jerking and shaking movements of his arms while looking through the screen. He rubbed his eyes after reporting what he saw and sat down and complained that looking strained his eyes. He said he thought a lot about seeing naked women, and that he had a feeling of pleasure going to the screen and looking through it. The rest of the session he indulged in compulsive play by himself with the pick-up-sticks, not asking for my participation.

(2) (#49). He was generally uncommunicative and sulky. At the screen, he put his hands in and out of his front and back pockets, sometimes grabbing through his pockets at his genitals or buttocks. Between these movements he made other motions that looked like he was hitting himself or defending himself. I commented he looked like he was having a fight. He immediately walked away from the screen and asked whether he could go to the toilet and have a bowel movement. Upon returning, he volunteered that his parents tried to stop him from looking through the screens at home and he resented their interference. I reminded him I had not been stopping him.

(3) (#50). At the screen he revealed offensive and defensive, well-coordinated movements with his arms and hands. He touched and grabbed briefly at his buttocks; then jerking his hands away, he grabbed briefly at his genitals—going rapidly from one to the other for about ten minutes. I said I wondered why he never finished doing what he wanted with his hands. He said nothing, but the jerking, defensive and offensive movements with his hands stopped and he began to masturbate genitally

with some coital movements. When told at the end of the session that it
was time to leave, he reported he did not recall what happened while he
was at the screen. I told him what had occurred and he appeared surprised.

(4) (#51-53). Screen spells continued occurring in the playroom.
During one of the spells he remembered that, though there was no door,
there was a checker-painted screen between his room and his parents'
when he was between the ages of three and five.

Masturbatory activity during the spells was accompanied by visual
imagery of having sexual relations with a girl and hurting her. At the
screen he acted out terror, guilt and self-punishment at his own erotic
and hostile impulses. After I described his screen spells to him, he remarked that he did not ordinarily express his feelings well and that he
had a difficult time communicating what he wanted except in his spells.
He now related that he masturbated regularly in his bed or on the screen
porch. He reported feelings of depersonalization and dissociation when
he masturbated; for example, he said, "I'm a brave, dirty guy, I'm somebody else when I masturbate." And then he claimed that he clearly remembered biting his mother's breast when he was a baby, and it was
because of his biting that his mother had to have a breast operation not
long ago. Also, he said his mother told him he used to bite her breast and
she had said it was his fault she had to have an operation. (The mother
denied ever having said such to the patient, but she probably said something like this which the patient unconsciously distorted.)

(5) (#54-58). The screen spells began to occur with decreasing frequency in the playroom. Instead, he spent the time in activities of open
rivalry and aggression in games, play, and talk with me.

He confessed that he went to the screen when something happened
that made him angry. The anger was aroused by the frustration of dependent wishes and the frustration of erotic wishes, especially by his
mother (but also, by other adults, including me, as was repeatedly observed in the playroom sessions). When he was so angered, he became
afraid he would "go crazy," would kill someone, felt anxious and guilty
and punished himself (actually hit himself, as was seen during the therapeutic sessions).

(6) (#90). The destructive, magical potentialities of looking were the
prominent theme of this session. After having a screen spell he reported
he had the impression that while he was pushing and leaning against the
wall, looking out the window, the wall seemed to move out, as if he had
pushed it out with his knees. He reported that it was terrifying for him

to imagine he had such powerful thoughts, looks, or movements, and it was reassuring to learn he did not have them.

(7) (#92). When he first came into the playroom, he reported becoming periodically enraged at his "boy friend," E., for looking or staring at him. For doing so, the patient had wrestled with E., had become so infuriated at him, he had nearly strangled E. Ned's mother warned him not to become so violent in his wrestling with E. because "it might be fatal."

The immediate question that occurred to me was: what provoked the patient's fury in this situation? Some answer was given by the patient himself during this session as he stood at the screen and reported a vivid visual fantasy, accompanied by appropriate motor accompaniments. He saw E. coming at him with a long pole with a big ball at the end; the ball was burning. Ned was terrorized because he had the idea E. was going to ram this pole up his rear end. So, it appeared that Ned's anger was a fear-inspired warding off of a fantasied brutal anal attack by his "boy friend" and the idea of E.'s attacking was a projection of his own sadistic concept of the masculine role.

Because the patient always turned his back to me when he looked out of the playroom window screen, I ventured to ask him whether he had the idea he had to get hurt physically if he depended on me too much. He started to say something, blocked, left my side and went to the screen, had a brief episode of his old stereotyped screen spell, came back and sat down near me, went back to the screen, returned to his chair, all the while speechless. I stopped his returning to the screen after he made several such trips back and forth and asked him what was the matter. Rather tangentially he first told me that he lost contact with me when he went to the screen and he was not sure whether or not he wanted to do so. Then he said he had thought sometimes maybe it would "be nicer" being a woman in sex relations. Then, apparently digressing, he said he had learned to get along well with all his teachers at school; he was using "psychology," which on further explanation by him turned out to be a kind of extremely unctuous courteousness. Now he complained of having had pains recently in his penis, recalled that E. carried a knife and had once accidently stuck him in the belly with it when the blade was closed. He made no connection between these associations, but he became immediately more relaxed and comfortable.[2]

---

[2] Such a sequence of clinical observations might be interpreted in a number of ways. I saw the chain of Ned's reactions and associations as a transference expression of his rebellion against his passive, masochistic concept of the dependent, submissive role, and this type of adaptation was temporarily brought to the fore in connection with conflicts about oedipal wishes. No interpretation was made at this time.

In subsequent sessions, his masochistic concept of the submission or feminine role and his sadistic concept of the dominating or masculine role were acted out less in his play with contemporaries and in his screen spells. Instead he put his ideas and concepts more and more into words and on such occasions he experienced "scared feelings" that were clearly anxiety attacks.

When he became openly competitive with his peers, his father or me, he was less inclined to overshoot the mark and worry that he was supposed to destroy ruthlessly his rivals. When he became openly dependent and submissive, he became less fearful of losing his individuality or being damaged. But a restless attitude of wanting to be done with boyhood and a premature desire to assume the sexual prerogatives of manhood and fatherhood persisted. This attitude seemed almost indelibly implanted in his mind by the experience of having been designated by his mother as the "man of the house" during the period his father was away in the military service for three years starting when Ned was five years old.

Unfortunately, the regular psychotherapeutic work with Ned had to be discontinued at this time before it could be completed, for I was obliged to move to another city for military service. But by correspondence with Ned and his parents and through occasional interviews, a five-year follow-up of Ned's condition was made possible.

At the time when his treatment was interrupted, his "screen spells" occurred rarely in the playroom and infrequently at home. No psychomotor seizures had recurred for two years and none were manifested for a five-year period following termination of his treatment. Two grand mal seizures occurred during the twenty-eight-month period he was being observed intensively. They appeared at a time when he was making efforts toward breaking away from parental supervision. The first grand mal spell happened after eighteen months of observation when he prepared to come, on his own insistence, to the therapeutic sessions without the company of either of his parents. The second one occurred the day after termination of his treatment, although he was superficially gleeful about the ending of treatment because he wanted to regard the termination as a sign he had matured and developed to the point where he could be the master of his own strong chaotic impulses, he was still fearful what he might do without the limit-setting of a good parental figure.

One year after the termination of treatment, at the age of thirteen years and ten months, with his parents' permission, he went away from home to a summer resort to work as a bus boy and waiter. His parents allowed this because he had been free of all seizures during this time and because he had grown rapidly in the ensuing year and was now almost as tall as his father. They reasoned, incorrectly, that he was as mature in his psychologic integration as he looked physically. Within a week after arrival at the summer resort, there was a recurrence of his grand mal seizures, each one occurring during the course of a "screen spell." The compulsion to stare through window screens had recurred soon after his arrival at the place where he was to work for the summer months. The boy's father wrote me on July 24, 1952:

> On the 28th of June, Ned went to a camp in the north woods to work as a waiter and bus boy. We did not tell the owners of the camp about Ned's ills. Ned did not want us to do so. He said he would not go to the screens and therefore would not have any seizures. On July 11th, Ned had a seizure early in the morning while in bed, looking out of the screen. His roommate told us that he did foam at the mouth. After that he went back to work, but did not feel well, complained of pains in his stomach.
> On July 19th my wife and I went out to visit Ned. We saw him and he did not feel well and wanted to go home. On July 21st Ned had another seizure the same way. We can now put his seizures as definitely coming on from the screens.
> I asked Ned why he didn't stay away from the screens. He said that it feels good while he stares through them and he wants more and more.
> Now that they have returned what do you suggest we do? . . .

From our previous work together and additional information Ned was able to tell me later about his experiences that summer of 1952, it was possible to piece together the psychodynamic mechanism leading to the seizures.

The temptation to act out his aggressive sexual fantasies and the fear of retaliation or loss of parental care should he gratify these impulses became overwhelming in the setting of the summer resort.

The outcome of these inner conflicts was a pleasurable compulsion to go to a window screen and look through it. Thereupon, as our previous studies revealed, he re-experienced and acted out on himself in an abortive way, his forbidden impulses and the punishments for them.

After further correspondence with Ned and his parents, Ned was advised to resume taking anticonvulsant medication, namely, sodium diphenylhydantoin .09 gm. twice a day. Though his "screen spells" had never been blocked by this medication, there was sufficient reason to expect that the final consequence of some of these "psychic seizures," the grand mal seizures, could be blocked by dilantin. Furthermore, Ned was now aware of the sources of his anxiety about his dependent and sexual

urges and was not so desperately self-critical and punitive about the
sexual and hostile reactions he had to seductive or controlling women,
such as his mother. Therefore, it was believed he might find a better way
to handle the tensions generated by these conflicts than by compulsively
acting them out while looking through a window screen. His parents
never did understand the full details of his emotional problems and I
did not pass along to them the "secrets" that Ned had entrusted to me in
strict confidence. He told them himself, however, much more about his
inner experiences and conflicts than he realized he could, and he found
them, as might be expected, quite understanding and accepting of him
in comparison to his threatening fantasies of parents or other authority
figures.

After the brief episodic recurrence of the screen spells and grand mal
seizures in 1952, there was no recurrence of any seizures throughout the
next three years. From the viewpoint of his parents, Ned matured well
without any notable signs of emotional instability. Quotations from a
chatty letter about Ned from his mother illustrate his clinical course,
from one point of view.

Dec. 12, 1954

. . . We have lots of good news to report. So here we go.

Ned was very good all summer. He did not stand at the screens,
and he would say to me that the screens do not bother him any more.
He feels that he has the screen spells licked.

Ned has been taking the sodium dilantin twice a day, and he has
not had a grand mal seizure since starting this medicine (in 1952).

He is feeling less nervous than he was, accepts things in a different
light, gets along better at school (with a G average). He has a tough
time though on his tests. Can it be that he gets too nervous and can't
think? Algebra is his tough subject. He was warned against taking it
by his advisor in school, but Ned wanted to take it so that he can go
to college. However, he is getting some outside help and seems to be
catching on.

He was 16 years old Sept. 26th, has learned to drive the car, has
not applied for his driver's license as yet. He is sort of afraid on
account of the passage in this booklet which I am enclosing. [The
booklet cited State regulations disallowing the awarding of a driver's
license to an epileptic person, except with a physician's statement that
the seizures were well controlled.]

Dr. Gottschalk, I want you to know that Ned has been doing
everything a boy his age should do. He plays a fair game of golf and
his social life has been good.

Ned has had a part-time job after school but he quit because he
found it too much for him. He had to travel quite a distance.

Ned is a fine boy, and we are proud of him, the way he has
accepted his sickness and hasn't been ashamed of it.

We are very thankful to you for the help you have given us, for alone we would have been lost. We are always thinking about you and will never forget you. So the best again to you and yours.

A follow-up interview with Ned when he was seventeen showed that he was still seizure-free. He was dating girls and was comfortable in his relationships with them. Compulsively looking through window screens no longer attracted him. He was advised to continue taking sodium dilantin medication, .09 gm., twice a day, because it was felt that this medication, though it had not been found previously to stop his screen spells, did block the grand mal component of his epilepsy.

Whether the emotional trigger mechanism for his seizures is less likely to operate as he continues to mature and find more adequate ways of managing his psychologic conflicts will have to be determined in the future.

DISCUSSION

A résumé of the psychological factors activating Ned's seizures is helpful as a point of departure for discussing the theoretical implications of the empirical observations made during this boy's psychologic treatment.

Screen Spells. A characteristic chain of events was observed to culminate in screen spell in the playroom. (1) Ned would be either engaging the therapist in some play or talking with the therapist. In this interaction, an incident would occur which Ned would presumably experience as a frustration, the frustrating agent being either someone that Ned was telling the therapist about or the therapist himself, e.g., the therapist or someone else did not fulfill some explicit or implicit demand of Ned's. (2) The pattern of Ned's immediate activities would abruptly change, whatever he was doing or saying. He would turn and walk toward the window, on reaching it would glance slightly upward through the screen, and would often reiterate that at times he was unaccountably and irresistably drawn to the screen. (3) Generally, staring less than half a minute through the screen did not lead to a typical screen spell. During this half minute, verbal interchange with Ned was open. When questioned, he never saw any relation between his compelling feeling to go to the screen and the context of the immediately preceding interactions with the therapist. He never volunteered that he experienced any feeling of anger, fear or frustration. In fact, he usually denied any such feeling when he was asked. But an accurate and acceptable interpretation of the preceding situation and Ned's presumably covert aims and feelings could at this point prevent the development of a screen spell. (4) If Ned looked through the screen for longer than about half a minute, a screen spell of varying duration invariably occurred during the first year of psychotherapy. Thereafter, modified screen spells, during which he was communicating his subjective experiences, lasted as long as five to ten minutes and could be terminated voluntarily by himself or on request.

Grand Mal Seizures. Grand mal seizures were never observed in the playroom. In all instances in which they occurred, however, it was observed by his parents, or other observers, that grand mal fits developed some time during prolonged screen spells. Psychiatric investigation added the information that the infrequent grand mal seizures tended to occur during a period when he had been making efforts, often premature, toward independence from parental control and support.

Psychomotor Seizures. No psychomotor seizures were observed during sessions in the playroom. Retrospective verbal comments by Ned about the situations and his personal feelings and aims just preceding the onset of such seizures gave evidence that a sequence of events obtained somewhat similar to those with the screen spells. That is, Ned experienced some feeling of deprivation which was shortly followed by a psychomotor seizure. The deprivation, as reported by Ned, was typically of a trivial variety. For example, on one occasion he reported that he had been listening to a cowboy radio thriller and the program was interrupted by the announcer making a commercial; Ned felt furious, briefly, at the interruption, and a psychomotor seizure occurred. Ned could not report what he did during the seizure. Only his parents could give a description of the behavioral details. Nor could Ned recall any of his thoughts or feelings during the seizure episode. On another occasion, he reported he had been bouncing a tennis ball against a blackboard. He missed several shots, felt furious, and started to break his tennis racket. A psychomotor seizure, with the usual wantonly destructive components, followed.

A perhaps essential differentiating characteristic of the intervening variables in the psychologic precursors associated with the psychomotor seizure as distinguished from the screen spell was the fact that Ned could report feeling angry (out of proportion, of course, to the situation) just before the onset of the psychomotor spell; whereas he was aware of no emotion or frustration just before the onset of a screen spell—only a compulsion to go to and look out of a window screen.

Psychologic State and Epileptiform Activity

An unusual feature of this boy's behavior was the phenomenon of the so-called "screen spells."

From the psychoanalytic point of view, these episodes would, at first sight, appear to be a kind of hysterical conversion phenomenon. Various aspects of the seizure manifestation lend themselves well to the inference that a forbidden impulse and the punishment for it are being expressed. Also, condensed and symbolized in these spells appear the scoptophilic activities of the little boy trying to discover what his parents are doing in their bedroom, the jealous rage concerning the father's prerogatives with the mother, the guilty fear of his sexual impulses to the mother and aggressive impulses to the father, the attempted solution to these forbidden impulses by displacing the one impulse to the other parent or to the self, and by the converting of the elements of the psychologic conflict into somatic manifestations. Finally, there is the regressing to earlier psychophysiologic levels of integration and the forgetting (or lack of awareness) of the psychologic experience and motor behavior while at the screen. Supporting evidence that Ned was capable of dealing with emotional stress through conversion mechanisms was the episode he had of "tubular vision" for which no structural basis could be demonstrated and which cleared up soon after psychotherapy started.

Further evidence of the importance of the role of psychologic conflict in not only the content but also the pathogenesis of the screen spells was the fact that the frequency and form of the usually stereotyped screen spells could be modified by psychotherapy. During psychotherapy these spells were modified to the point where the boy was able to report, just before or during a spell, thoughts and feelings that were highly unacceptable to himself, and concomitant with these communications to the therapist, his motor behavior during the seizures changed and typified the elements of the psychologic reactions he was in the process of putting into words. The boy revealed a terrible fear of punishment and abandonment for his forbidden impulses and primitive tensions. As he learned, from experience with me in the treatment situation, that his aggressive fantasies and fears of retaliation were not appropriate to current realities, he found more effective ways of integrating and discriminating between his perceptions of his past experiences and his expectations accompanying his preparations for action in his current adjustment problems. With these dynamic changes in his personality, a pronounced decrease in the frequency of his seizures occurred.

But the presence of these emotional conflicts and psychologic mechanisms, and the repeated observations that their stirring up could precipitate the screen spells, do not completely explain the mechanism of this epileptiform activity. Other boys have similar conflicts and psychologic mechanisms without having any seizures at all. And there are other features of the patient's clinical manifestations not accounted for very well by a primarily psychological theory. When these spells began, at the age of five, an electroencephalogram revealed 3 c.p.s. spike-wave rhythms that, in terms of our present-day knowledge, are thought to signify the presence of a neurochemical disturbance (secondary to many different possible factors) involving thalamocortical function (Williams, 1953). The screen spells were quite stereotyped for years, which is customary with an epileptogenic seizure; in fact, they did not vary in form until the boy was in psychoanalytic therapy. Though they were not blocked by anticonvulsant medication he had received (diphenylhydantoin, mesantoin, tridione, phenobarbital), the occasional frank grand mal seizures developed only during screen spells. These aspects of the screen spells cannot be accounted for by psychoanalytic theory alone, although the idea of a neurochemical factor in the pathogenesis of personality disorder is not inconsistent with psychoanalytic theory.

In this case, then, both psychologic factors and a focal disturbance in cerebral functioning are necessary to account for the pathologic clinical manifestations. Without either factor, the presenting clinical epileptic syndrome would not have occurred. As a means to test this statement it is obviously not possible experimentally to cancel out one factor to observe the effects of the other factor alone. The supporting evidence for this hypothesis comes from certain relevant clinical observations. The psychomotor seizures stopped after the first six months of psychotherapy and did not recur, although diphenylhydantoin was also discontinued after these six months. A discontinuation of grand mal seizures was associated with the administration of diphenylhydantoin, but screen spells were not blocked by this anticonvulsant. Psychologic factors triggered screen spells and screen spells triggered grand mal seizures. Reducing the effect of psychologic factors through psychotherapy was associated with the absence of all seizures for more than a year after the discontinuation of the psychotherapy during which the patient received no anticonvulsant medication. New external stresses were associated with the recurrence of screen and grand mal seizures during the follow-up period. The patient has now been seizure-free for four years on small doses of diphenylhydantoin. This boy's emotional conflicts have not been canceled out by psychotherapy, but the effectiveness of the emotional factors in stimulating seizures has been reduced. The effect of the cerebral functional disorder which has been shown to be associated with a lowered seizure threshold (Liberson, 1955) presumably persists (as adjudged from a recent electroencephalogram), but its potency has been reduced too, by the diphenylhydantoin (and possibly by the psychotherapy). These points plus the detailed observations of the relationship between the patient's psychologic state and his ictal activity, recounted in the above description of the therapeutic process, attest to the necessity of both psychologic factors and the presence of a paroxysmal cerebral functional disorder (involving corticothalamic and associated pathways) to produce his clinical syndrome.

A search in the medical literature for reports of epileptic reactions associated with looking reveals some highly relevant observations. Bickford et al. (1953) studied the convulsive effects of light stimulation in children. They found twenty-seven children who had convulsive reactions of varying degrees to stimulation by light. Most of the children had convulsive reactions, substantiated by electroencephalograms, to intermittent light. Some had epileptic reactions to steady, nonflickering light. One case, a six-year-old boy, is reported who developed petit mal seizures, accompanied by typical spike-waves in the electroencephalograph, when staring at a window screen, window curtain, finely woven cloth or his father's corduroy jacket! Robertson (1954) has recently reported seven cases of "photogenic epilepsy" in which epileptic attacks were self-precipitated in the patients by movement of the fingers or hand in front of the eyes or by blinking while looking at the sun or strong light. In the case of Ned, his convulsive episodes—"screen spells"—developed when perceiving continuous illumination and there was no rapid interruption of the light by his fingers, hands or eyelids. The similarity of Ned's case to the six-year-old boy reported by Bickford et al. (1953) is striking. The psychoanalytic study of Ned's case provides evidence that psychologic conflicts about looking may be one of the determinants in epileptic susceptibility to visual stimulation. Also, the fact that self-precipitation of such seizures has been commonly observable elsewhere makes more understandable Ned's remarks that he could "hypnotize" himself, for this was the way he saw his role in initiating the seizure state.

Problems for Further Psychophysiologic Research

No extant hypothesis explains satisfactorily the triggering of paroxysmal neural activity and an altered state of consciousness by a self-induced or externally stimulated psychologic conflict or state. In a recent study (Gottschalk, 1955) where paroxysmal slow electroencephalographic activity was correlated with an epileptic subject's tape-recorded verbal associations, it was found that the arousal of separation anxiety facilitated epileptic discharges in this patient's electroencephalogram. Such observations, however, only illustrate that the phenomenon can occur, but they do not explain the mechanism.

A résumé of the observed relationship between Ned's psychologic state, his psychic seizures, and finally his grand mal seizures will be sketched out to indicate some of the gaps in our understanding of this sequence of events. Either a meaningful external situation or a self-initiated series of thoughts aroused in the patient memories of recent and past experiences having to do with dependent, sexual, and aggressive interchanges between key people of the past and recent present. These old perceptions were associated with various feelings—pleasure, displeasure, fear or anxiety (of punishment, of ridicule, of loss of parental support), frustration, and anger. The psychologic compromise between these conflicts was experienced as a compulsion to go to a window screen and look through it. If looking through the screen was not interrupted for 30 seconds, a screen spell invariably started which could, after Ned had been in psychotherapy a while, be modified by maintaining verbal communication with the patient. Presumably, memories and thoughts (cortical activity) and the emotional components (subcortical activity) of these ideas modulated 3 c.p.s. spike and wave activity that in itself was not sufficient to cause a seizure. Under some unknown set of circumstances a psychic seizure, with highly integrated motor activity, could ensue. This seizure was associated with an altered state of consciousness from which the subject could sometimes be aroused. Sometimes—it is not clear how or why—the relatively localized epileptic cerebral discharges (involving predominantly one frontotemporal cortex, the diencephalon, the reticular substance) could spread further and become a diffuse epileptic discharge manifested as a grand mal seizure. As previously indicated, a necessary condition for this sequence of events was a specific anatomical structure and neurochemical basis, without which the behavior associated with the psychologic state would probably have been otherwise.

Some Recent Research, Contributions from Physiologists and Neurologists

There is information which has accumulated elsewhere that fills in some of the gaps of our understanding of the mechanism by which emotions may be associated with epileptic phenomena. Liberson (1955) has recently indicated that emotional stimuli may induce a convulsion through (1) either the creation of a "general excitatory state" with an excessive formation of either acetyl choline (see also Forster, 1945) or insulin, or (2) a preliminary conditioning of certain stimuli which set up epileptogenic states in those areas of the brain which participate in the control and release of emotional processes, such as the rhinencephalon, diencephalon, and mesencephalon. He has collected evidence which shows that rhinencephalic structures, which appear to be involved in the integration of emotional reactions and visceral activity (see also Mac-Lean, 1949, 1952; Papez, 1937; and Yakovlev, 1948), have the lowest threshold to epileptic discharges and that these discharges can be induced by visual and auditory stimuli. Epileptic discharges can be induced experimentally similarly in diencephalic and mesencephalic structures. It is additional data of this sort which is required to account for the general and specific mechanisms of the association of psychologic conflict and epileptic states.

The Epileptic Seizure as a Symbolic Expression of Emotional Conflict

Other authors have seen epileptic seizures as symbolic expressions of repressed desires that are unconscious. The seizure, particularly grand mal seizure, has been described variously as an expression of inhibited rage (Freud, 1928; Bartemeier, 1932), inhibited sexual desire (Greenson, 1944), and frustrated dependency (Heilbrunn, 1950).

The present study found no evidence to support any of these views in so far as the grand mal seizure is concerned. Though Ned's grand mal seizures were observed to occur when he was making premature attempts to establish independence from parental figures, this does not tell us that his grand mal seizures symbolize his conflicts with authority figures or with dependency problems. It simply tells us that such a situation has a temporal relationship, and possibly a causal relationship, with a final event. The testing of any hypothesis one might have about the symbolic function of the experience for the person having the grand mal seizure is virtually precluded by the impossibility of verbal communication with a person having such a seizure. The present study, however, does reveal that condensation and symbolization are demonstrably important processes in certain types of minor epileptic spells where higher levels of cerebral integration are maintained and during which some verbal communication may take place, such as during the patient's "screen spells."

In my opinion, the grand mal seizure probably has no symbolic significance, though it may be precipitated by various kinds of emotional conflicts. My impression is that no symbolic activity is possible at the psychologic level without effective cerebral cortical functioning or, from the psychologic frame of reference, without the intactness of cognitive processes. In grand mal convulsions, integrated functioning of the cerebral cortex does not occur. When cortical functioning is not completely impaired—as in certain types of focal epileptic reactions—symbolic activity may be possible. A grand mal seizure is a kind of mass reflex which is the end product of a potential series of noxious stresses (trauma, electric shock, drugs, metabolic disturbances, emotional problems) to the organism, but it is not specific to any one kind of stress. And the grand mal seizure does not signify the nature of the stress precipitating it. It has no more symbolic function than the circulatory dysfunction of ulcerative colitis or essential hypertension. In less generalized forms of epileptic discharge, however, such as in psychomotor epilepsy and related automatisms or in certain manifestations of petit mal epilepsy and especially in "psychic equivalent seizures," it is likely that epileptic manifestation may symbolize in microcosmic forms some aspects of the subject's old and recent emotional conflicts.

SUMMARY AND CONCLUSIONS

The psychoanalytic study and treatment of a ten-year-old epileptic boy are reviewed. Particular emphasis is laid on the sequence of psychologic conflicts and states associated with one type of seizure that was repeatedly observed in the playroom sessions with him. This type of seizure was an atypical, so-called "psychic equivalent" seizure, with motor components. Interseizure electroencephalograms showed a 3 c.p.s. spike-wave pattern. Also, the psychic equivalent seizures were the prodromal manifestation of infrequent but clear-cut grand mal seizures.

The features and psychologic conflicts of a hysterical character, although manifested both during seizure and interseizure periods, were not found sufficient in themselves to account for the epileptiform manifestations of this patient. The presence of a type of paroxysmal cerebral functional disorder, which has elsewhere been found to be associated with decreased seizure threshold, could not alone account for the epileptic behavior, particularly that manifested during the psychic equivalent seizures. Both complex factors (the hysterical character disorder and the paroxysmal cerebral functional disorder) were considered necessary to produce the clinical syndrome.

The therapeutic problems encountered in this patient illustrate the therapeutic value of psychoanalytic psychotherapy in the management of certain types of epileptic individuals.

The case study is also considered to illustrate the value of psychoanalytic study of epilepsy as an important avenue of furthering our understanding of the interplay of the neural and experiential bases of emotional disorder.

FOLLOW-UP

I had the good fortune to encounter Ned twenty-three years after the termination of his psychotherapy and obtained a color video-tape of the follow-up interview. I learned that the patient had been completely seizure-free for twenty-one years, using no anticonvulsive medication over this period of time, and having no "screen spells," conversion symptoms, or other neurotic symptoms. He had a surprising ability to recall many specific details about what took place during the psychotherapy, especially behavior, feelings, and attitudes expressed or experienced toward the therapist. The patient is happily married, has three children, and is very successful in his vocation.

I had lost personal contact with the patient for over twenty years, but his parents regularly sent me a Christmas card throughout my various moves; when the patient moved to the area where I was living, he personally contacted me. This is how the long-term follow-up interview came about.

11

PSYCHIATRIC IMPLICATIONS OF TEMPORAL LOBE DAMAGE

MARY A. SARVIS, M.D.
(1960)

The case to be presented is one in which organic brain disease could be detected on psychological grounds at a time when the diagnosis had not yet been made by neurological examination. Because the patient was an unusually perceptive boy, the case afforded a striking opportunity to distinguish between organic and psychological factors in the disturbance. Hugh's temporal lobe symptoms, as they were gradually identified in treatment, could be separated from his psychological problems and identified by the patient as the work of "Mr. 'Cephalitis," his name for the organic lesion. The ways in which the patient handled his organic damage and the body-image problems related to it could be distinguished from the symptoms he developed and the defenses he used with respect to his secondary psychological problems.

PRESENTING SYMPTOMS

The parents of a six-year-old boy asked for a consultation, saying "Ever since Hugh was nine months old he had what people call emotional disturbances . . . They call them temper tantrums but they aren't." These eruptions, Hugh's "mads," consisted of frequent, unpredictable, apparently unmotivated aggressive outbursts of murderous intensity in which the boy attacked anyone near him, striking, biting, scratching, kicking, and screaming. His father was the only family member strong enough to restrain him. Until recently, if he had been ignored in an attack, Hugh had followed family members around the house, striking them.

The explosive outbursts were the parents' chief concern; the mother feared Hugh was psychotic. However, the patient also had many other difficulties. He was bound up in extensive compulsive rituals, particularly around eating and bedtime. It took two or three hours to put him to bed because of his anxiety and his rituals; any interference with the rituals produced marked panic and aggressive outbursts. He had a totem toy tiger which had to be with him, especially in bed. He usually refused to eat with the family and restricted his diet almost entirely to popcorn and mush. His food rituals and inhibitions embarrassed him so much that he avoided social events. He could not play with other children because of his unstable behavior and his own self-consciousness. He felt that children regarded him as crazy. He was frequently absent from school because of recurrent illnesses. When he was able to attend school, he showed the strain by increased explosiveness at home.

The patient had frequent low-grade fevers, often on a respiratory basis: during these bouts his symptoms increased markedly. His gait was clumsy and his motor coordination poor; Thomas shoes (which he refused to wear) had been prescribed, and he wore glasses for a mild visual disturbance. On the basis of skin tests, he was said to have mild allergies. Neurological examinations had been negative. The medical reports indicated that all these physical findings were minimal and that no prescriptions would have been given if the parents had not been so desperate to have something done. The common medical impression was that the boy was spoiled and the mother was overprotective. The mother's extreme anxiety level, with its coercive impact, her demands for absolute medical authority, and her scattered, anxious matching of one doctor's opinion against another's reinforced this impression.

DEVELOPMENTAL HISTORY

Infancy

The patient was the third of four adopted children. They had all come from different families and had been adopted a few days after their birth. None of the other children presented any unusual difficulties. Hugh's early infancy was sufficiently socialized and advanced to earn him the family nicknames "Mr. Jaberwocky" and "Mr. Precocious." In the mother's words, "He drank from the cup early. Solids were taken at six weeks. He had an especially lusty fondness for meats. Until nine months he would clutch his spoon and play with food, mess his hands in it and talk and laugh." His sleep was undisturbed and his developmental skills were normal to superior.

Acute Illness

When Hugh was nine months old, his parents went out for three hours, leaving the children with a housekeeper. They returned to find the baby screaming, unable to recognize them and refusing to let anyone touch him. Shortly thereafter, he developed severe, recurrent diarrhea which lasted until he was three. No etiological agent was found, despite exhaustive medical work-ups. The only positive physical finding was moderate leukocytosis of unknown origin. For this, the patient was maintained on sulfa compounds for two or three years.

His behavior changed abruptly with this illness. The mother said, "After nine months, he clenched his mouth tight to avoid the spoon and hit it and us. He wasted away and looked emaciated. . . He would stare at the nipple for awhile, then cry and push it away or accept it greedily for a few moments, then scream and hit it away again. We discovered that he would drink more if we did not hold him and would hold the bottle through the sides of the crib at arm's length. . . He refused to touch the bottle with his hands, and his former habit of fondling the nipple and bottle changed to striking it away. . . He would hold his hands over his genitals and kick violently and scream whenever diapered. We tried leaving off the diapers, but any sight or odor of B.M. caused a tantrum again." The other children in the family had learned to use the toilet by copying, but the mother said of Hugh that "any suggestion that he use the toilet threw him into screams; so we did not pursue it."

His sleeping changed from normal to "light sleep. . . He screamed and fretted till exhausted then took a short nap and woke crying again day and night until almost two years. He began to improve then. At nine months he began head banging. . . He cried and thrashed around in a jerking motion in his crib so much that the sides had to be padded because his head became bruised. He stayed on his back. At fifteen months, he insisted on having lights and vacuum cleaner on to sleep. We moved his crib against the wall so he could turn the wall switch on—we would hear it click on and off all during the night. He insisted on staring into bright lights; day and night the lights had to be kept on or he would become frantic. By eighteen months, he would turn the vacuum cleaner on with the palm of his hand—he never used his fingers. He had violent tantrums unless the lights were on and the vacuum cleaner running loudly. . . If we entered his room, he would awaken screaming. He jerked in his sleep.

"At nine months, he stopped developing, refused to touch anything with his hands until almost two years. He made almost no effort to turn over, crawl or walk. He walked suddenly and clumsily at fifteen months without much previous attempt at sitting or pulling himself up." During this period of acute illness he would "hold his head and cry, walk into objects and get hurt. . . He would not pick up anything or play with toys. . . Between nine months and two years, Hugh would strike anyone who leaned across him or put their arms around him. He could not be loved in our arms or cuddled in any way. He made a special point of hitting anyone who wore glasses and knocked them off and broke them. Until about five, he had a violent spell if his babyhood was mentioned, tore up his own baby pictures, said, 'I hated being a baby.' He covered his ears and wouldn't listen.

"At eighteen months, Hugh discovered music and became obsessed with listening to records. It worried us that he would listen only to Tschaikovsky and that he refused nursery rhymes, yet it encouraged us to realize that he could recognize certain records. At three, he insisted upon taking music lessons."

During the period of acute illness, the patient reacted with indifference to personal events around him. A new-born (adopted) sister arrived when he was thirteen months old, but "he seemed too ill to notice." He acted as if he were unaware of a two-week separation from his mother at fifteen months. An eccentric housekeeper, who had been in the home since Hugh's birth, was fired when he was twenty-one months old, and he did seem to react favorably to that and to the family's move to the country when he was two; he slept uninterruptedly for the first time and shortly began to move his hands again. However, he continued to be unmoved by deaths of close relatives and friends, regardless of how much these upset the family or how close he had been to the person involved.

Hugh's improvement began at about two. At about three, his

diarrhea abruptly ceased and his behavior rapidly began to shift from a psychotic to a more clearly neurotic pattern. The mother said that he "started voiding outside. . . At three and a half, he conformed to sitting on the toilet or standing there, never wet his pants. Until about three and a half, he would only have a B.M. outside the house. By four years, he stopped complaining about the odor of his B.M.'s and became very proud of his feces. He enjoyed flushing the toilet, expressed admiration over the size of his B.M. He annoyed our other children by demanding to flush *their* toilets. He bullied his little sister by insisting, 'I'm the boss of the toilets.' "

When Hugh was four and a half to five and a half, things improved generally in the family, even though the mother was ill for a year in hospital or at home, and had two major operations (on kidneys and back). The patient continued to improve physically and emotionally. The parents assumed that Hugh's difficulties were completely psychogenic, blaming themselves and a housekeeper. This housekeeper (Hugh called her "the Cooker," "the Spanker") was said to be eccentric and was suspected of aggressive behavior toward the children and sexual abuse of the patient. Between four and a half and five and a half, the patient attended a therapeutically oriented nursery school, where the theory of the housekeeper as prime villain of the piece was developed and the parents' view of the psychogenic nature of the difficulty was consolidated. During this period between four and a half and five and a half, Hugh still hid his genitals in bed and bath, became extremely upset if anyone saw them, and had the aggressive outbursts, compulsive rituals, phobias, and inhibitions already mentioned. He feared having his mother leave him, crying, "What if Cooker beats me?" He screamed at nursery school. He tore up his baby books until he was about five, when he gradually "became very affectionate again, permitted physical comforting and loving . . and began talking about his infancy."

INITIAL EVALUATION AND PROCEDURES

Hugh himself, at the time of the evaluation, was a shy, clinging, meticulous boy whose opening remark to me concerned "the Old Witch" (presumably the housekeeper). He was untalkative but responsive to the playroom situation and to me. He was markedly compulsive and showed particular concern with testing his control over spatial boundaries; for instance, when blocking in a colored area, he painted perpendicularly up to a boundary line rather than parallel to it. The content of his play in the three evaluation sessions was violent: snakes and monsters attacked the people of a family. This play was repetitive and rose to a crescendo: "The snakes won the war!" He became progressively more spontaneous in his play and less shy with me.

Diagnostic Impression

This case at first seemed rather puzzling, partly because the parents' information was presented so unquestioningly within a psychogenic framework, which had been supported by the nursery school teachers. I knew, however, that the personnel of this nursery school were given to rather facile psychogenic assumptions, and it seemed likely that there might be retrospective distortion in the parents' presentation. There seemed to be no doubt that, superficially, the wicked housekeeper was the witch to whom the boy referred in the evaluation interviews. On the other hand, the parents were good observers and attentive to their children; there were older, highly articulate, and confiding children in the family; it did not seem likely that the housekeeper could have abused the children very seriously or very long. I felt that "the Cooker" became the personification of the attacking female as a displacement from the mother. The history told of a period of rather striking autistic symptoms, yet Hugh—though he communicated in an oblique and symbolic way and was rather remote in personal relationships—did not impress one as an autistic child. Nor did the quality of family relationships, either currently or in the developmental story, suggest this.

There were two principal factors which directed one's attention to organic brain disease, presumably originating in the acute illness at nine months.

1. The extreme intensity of the mother's anxiety is hard to convey: she was in a state of continual panic and the quality of this panic reminded one of Goldstein's description of the catastrophic anxiety in patients with organic brain disease who experience their mental processes as strange and unpredictable, as not making sense, and who

no longer feel completely responsible for them—not even unconsciously. In a similar way, this patient's mother reacted to her son's disease (despite her conscious, verbal assumption of psychogenesis and responsibility) as if it had this same quality of incongruity, unpredictability, and natural catastrophe.

2. There were, of course, neurotic characterological interactions in the family. However, I could see no evidence that the patterning of family neurotic interactions had any significant causal relationship to the boy's disturbance.

Therefore, an electroencephalogram was recommended. This disclosed extensive focal and degenerative lesions in the right temporal lobe.

Initial Hypotheses and Maneuvers

My working assumption at this point was that the aggressive outbursts were triggered by stimuli from the organically damaged area of the brain. I assumed that the remainder of the boy's symptoms represented his efforts to bind the severe anxiety associated with his organic brain disease, largely by compulsive symptoms, partially by phobias and inhibitions. I did not anticipate that other symptoms, like his "mads," might also be a direct result of stimuli from damaged brain areas.

I felt that the medical aspects of the situation should be brought under control and separated from the psychological management. If Hugh could be stabilized on anticonvulsive drugs, I hoped it would lower the intensity of his "actual" anxiety[1] (that associated with the brain damage) and make his compulsive defenses less crucial to him psychologically. It was also hoped that this approach would reduce the level of the mother's anxiety, help her to stay with one doctor, and give her confidence in beginning to learn to differentiate her son's "mads" from his psychological problems. It was agreed that medical stabilization would be begun before the boy returned to me for psychotherapy.

Hugh was put on Dilantin, which moderated his aggressive behavior but produced intellectual dulling and retardation. A change

---

1 Namely, anxiety associated with physiological excitation, like Freud's concept of "actual neurosis," rather than anxiety associated with psychological conflict.

to Hibicon diminished these side effects.[2] However, six months after the initial contact, Hugh developed a fever, and his aggressive-assaultive outbursts increased violently. The mother once more became catastrophically anxious and again began frantically to seek auxiliary medical advice. A family friend suggested phenobarbital, the boy reacted to it with further excitement, the parents persuaded their doctor that there might be fresh encephalopathy, and the patient was put in a hospital for a pneumoencephalogram. Here he remained for four weeks with a low-grade fever before the neurological work-up could be completed. Hugh was a difficult patient to handle and, despite the known organic lesion, was often treated by the medical and nursing staff like a spoiled or naughty boy. The patient himself, alert, anxious, and curious, listened to discussions on rounds, spied on conversations in the nursing station, became thoroughly conversant with his diagnosis and the opinions concerning his current medical status and behavior. No new encephalopathy was found.

He was reluctant to return to see me; as he admitted several months later, he thought I had put him in the hospital and that I could read his mind. Ten months after the initial contact, when he was seven, he agreed to come to psychotherapy once a month.

Meanwhile, I had seen the parents several times. Both were people who functioned well and did not suffer from gross neurotic symptoms. The mother had a hysterical character structure, with notable suppression and repression of hostility; the father was a moderately passive-aggressive, somewhat inhibited man. Psychological testing (Minnesota Multiphasic Personality Inventory) was within statistically normal limits for both, with considerable evidence of symptom suppression (i.e., high K scores).

It seemed crucial in the management of the family situation to reduce their confusion between organic and psychological symptoms, their guilt and their anxious pressure for objective authority. I agreed to see them regularly once a month and at any other time they wished. They always came in together. In our discussions, I strongly supported the validity of their own observations and urged them to act accordingly. For instance, the mother felt that there was a clear relationship between low fever and exacerbations in Hugh's

2 The patient was stabilized eventually on Milontin.

aggressive behavior. This relationship had always been minimized by doctors because the mother appeared so overprotective. I encouraged the parents to trust their own judgment in this and other aspects of Hugh's management. Because the mother felt that Hugh was able to attend school only at great emotional cost, collapsing as soon as he got home, I asked the school to put him on home instruction, where he remained for a little over a year. Later in treatment, the parents talked with me at times about transient difficulties with the other children, asked my advice about infants they thought of adopting, etc., but the focus of the counseling with the parents was essentially that described above. I also suggested attitudes and maneuvers designed to diminish the intensity of the mother-child relationship and to strengthen the realistic, positive relationship between the father and the boy. The mother concurred in this. No attempt was made to focus on the parents' problems with themselves or each other.[3]

COURSE IN TREATMENT

When Hugh, now seven years old, came into treatment, the initial stage was primarily concerned with the working through of his paranoid transference fantasies via repetitive monster play. All the aggressive animals and robots in the playroom and all the decrepit, mutilated animals were monsters who attacked a child or a whole family and destroyed them. In the third session (third month of treatment), the leader of the monsters became a "crabby lady." Hugh devoted much time to details of the war but always, in an excited, explosive climax, had the people totally destroyed. He was friendly, tentative, and taciturn with me. With his mother he was domineering, clinging, demanding, and angry. However, the family reported progressive stabilization of behavior at home: the clawing, scratching, and fighting had given way in part to verbal assaultiveness. In the third therapy session, Hugh asked me about my notes (which had to be made during the sessions for reasons of expediency). He also referred briefly to the bad lady as a nurse in the hospital.

[3] I do not wish to minimize the fact that the parents' psychological problems influenced the meaning of the patient's illness to them and also their handling of it. The mother's fear of hostility is an obvious case in point. In working with the parents, however, my efforts were directed largely at *counteracting* these attitudes rather than *interpreting* them.

In the fifth month of treatment, he agreed to come in every other week. The monster fantasy theme took on a markedly stereotyped quality with more and more burlesque of a television-type show. The lady villain was sometimes made humorous and the monsters were sometimes defeated. In general, he began to accept himself as a patient, to refer to previous events in the playroom, and to tell me of things that happened at home. I felt there was more modulation in his playroom behavior.

Then during the seventh to ninth month of treatment, Hugh's play shifted markedly to compulsive number play, with great emphasis on boxing in all the numbers and drawings. He became more tense, withdrawn, and uncommunicative. He acted very angry with his mother, hit her, and then spent most of the hour standing at the window to make sure she did not leave the building. I began to discuss his fear that he would be deserted because of his aggressive behavior and the meaning which his hospital experience had had for him. As usual throughout the first phase of treatment, Hugh would not answer such remarks, sometimes turning away or looking angry and stubborn. However, when my comments were appropriate, he would often gradually relax and become involved in play. He continued to be tense, hyperactive, and anxious in the playroom; he refused to come to see me once a week, and he complained of being no good at anything that he tried to do.

His parents reported that he had seen a movie about the cruel Roman emperor, Caligula, had said, "Caligula must have had 'cephalitis like me." He had begun very repetitive, intensive Caligula play at home and induced his parents to read to him at length about this period of Roman history.

I have mentioned his refusal to communicate with me directly. Typically, he would bring up a problem by telling his mother to ask me about something. Cues to his body image and some of his organically determined symptoms had already appeared, though I did not recognize their specificity at the time. Before treatment began, Hugh had complained that at night he feared a tiger jumping out at him in a "bad thought . . a movie in my head." (You will recall the way he fought fire with fire by way of his toy, the totemistic tiger.) He had also described his body as full of little rooms; his illness was always peeking around the corners of the rooms, but he could never catch it. Early in treatment, he asked his parents about his tinnitus and told them to ask me. He talked to his mother about the bad smells he used to smell.

Now in the ninth month of treatment, he told his mother to ask me about my notes. When I took this up with him, he admitted he felt his treatment was not a secret, that I discussed him with other doctors. He also complained to the secretaries of the clinic that I intended to force him back into school. In the next session, he seemed tense and angry. I talked about his feeling that I could read his mind and his paranoid misinterpretations; he admitted his anger at having people tell me about him and went on to discuss his fear in the hospital and his anger about having 'cephalitis. He said he was like Caligula but referred later to "the bad Caligula dream" (see below, "color dreams").[4] He admitted that he had believed I could read his mind and said he tried to think only of Bugs Bunny and not of his worries when he came to see me. Heretofore, he had been unshakable in refusing to listen "officially" to interpretations. By contrast, in this session, he was attentive to my speculations about the meaning of the hospital experience and his relations with me. Two or three times, during pauses, he asked: "Are you thinking?" and let me bring something up. Now after seven months, he agreed to come in once a week. His manner became markedly more relaxed and friendly; his behavior at home and in the waiting room improved dramatically.

In the tenth month, the persecutory play themes shifted to a war between children and adults with the mother as the most frequent malefactor. The essence of this repetitive play was the concept of mothers being deceitful to children—telling them something was for the children's benefit when the real aim was cruelty. Hugh said that the adults "want to make the children horrible people like they are." This play culminated in an almost literal tale of his illness as he saw it: two women put a man on the table, cut his head open, inserted a hydrogen bomb, and sewed him up again, while the bomb ticked. The ensuing explosion killed all the men; all the women escaped unharmed.

Hugh then was willing to tell me, with elaborate diagrams of the

4 The Caligula play waned in the tenth month and ceased with the naming of a Chihuahua pup by that name!

floor plan, about his experiences in the hospital and his confusion about whether he had 'cephalitis or was just bad. His discussion of details of his emotional experiences always was preceded and pointed up by the location of these events on his diagram. He needed to locate himself in space and derive the memory of what happened from this spatial orientation. Shortly thereafter, at his request, I told him about the etiology and course of his illness and how it caused the "mads."

In the next session, he began to discuss his paranoid transference by playing with the doll who previously had been the "crabby lady" who led the monsters, saying, "She is a member of the Bag family who looks something like you." To my question, "The bad lady?" he replied, "Sometimes." He then burlesqued Mrs. Snob-bag and Mrs. Crab-bag, who had just tortured the male members of their families, conversing in a false, mannered, social chit-chat which was a parody of his mother. The next hour he gave me a flower which he said was called either "Heaven in the Mist" or "Devil in the Bush" and asked me which I was. At this time, when his ambivalence and his paranoid fantasies had been expressed, I inquired how long he thought he would have to come. He replied, "Oh, a year, at least!"

During the fifteenth to twenty-fifth months of treatment, his play shifted to problems concerned with his body image and his organic lesion (interpolated with compulsive or smearing activities). His relationship with me was stably positive; he treated me like a benevolent protector (against his phobias), a chum, or a well-liked but a slightly stupid pupil (e.g., in the chess sequence).

Hugh came in with a chess set and insisted that we play. He told me his rules of how each piece was allowed to move but did not disclose the point of the game. After a couple of sessions, I realized that in the game (as described by the patient) the knight seemed to be the only piece that could capture the queen. I said as much and he responded enthusiastically, "Yeah, the knight's called the Queen Killer!" The parents, who did not know what had transpired, told me that until now Hugh had become so upset when his queen was captured in chess that the family had refrained from taking it; now he said it was all right to capture her, the pawn would win her back. The problem was discussed with the patient in terms of its oedipal meaning. The chess ceased in an atmosphere of satiation.

Hugh had also disclosed, through spatial metaphor, his envy of women, saying that the king could only move one space at a time but the queen could move anywhere! The indirect nature of this entire communication was typical.

Early in treatment, certain paintings had suggested the patient's loss of spatial differentiation between his body and the outside world, the merging of figure and ground, and the remote, inhuman feelings connected with it. In white paint on white paper, he drew three paintings: "A Ghostly Gas Station," "Swings in a Snowstorm," and the bubbles which showed on the surface of the water after a swimmer had dived in and disappeared—then the swimmer's track or wake through the water. No figures appeared. These paintings were done in May, 1954, when the patient was seven years old. Hugh's first conventional child's drawing appeared a year and a half later, in October, and his first representational figures—a witch and her cat—at Halloween of that year.

A set of Bender Gestalt figures were presented to the patient in the seventh month of treatment. Hugh's Bender did not give any evidence of his organic brain disease. It did reflect his superior intellectual level and, in its compulsive organization, his concern with enclosing and binding space.

Around the fifteenth month, space binding became the most prominent feature of treatment. The patient diagrammed action drawings of cars and busses with emphasis on danger in space and time; he did a series of elaborate ant-warren diagrams with much accurate detail; he diagrammed a jail, a gas chamber, an electric chair. He spent much time and took elaborate care in boxing in score sheets, constructing boxes for his number work, etc. When he returned to school at the age of eight and a half years, his compulsive activity increased, particularly number play and boxed, compulsive diagrams and drawings. His relationship with me continued to be friendly and he allowed me to explain a pending intravenous pyelogram (after first covering his ears and saying, "No shots!"). Also, for the first time in treatment, he volunteered to tell me about the results of a medical procedure.

About four months followed in which oedipal and castration fears alternated with striking magical, destructive-restitutive play. Hugh drew a "dangerous house"; then he said that since he had made it, he could make it safe and did so, fixing up all the dangerous features. After an earthquake, he drew a skyscraper falling over, then emphasized the body-image meaning by making a sixty-two-story skyscraper (with the stories all counted), showed the top twenty stories falling and called it "Hugh and Co." In this period (after a year and a half of treatment), he came to a session with clear intent to communicate something, drew a witchlike diagram and spent the whole hour removing and interchanging arms, legs, and hat. He gave it a clear personal reference by drawing a box in the brain and describing it as the controlling mechanism. He showed how its connections were wrong when the figure was mutilated; when the figure was put back together correctly, he changed the connection in the brain box to suit. This kind of play was repetitive and persistent. His probable castration fears in the hospital were discussed with him and he elaborated various fearful events in the hospital. Following this period in therapy, he became more direct in his relations to me and less fearful about the clinic. Whereas he had previously insisted that I call for him in the waiting room and escort him back to his mother, and had gone into a panic when he had smeared his clothes or skin lest people laugh at him, he now could get dirty, allowed himself to be called on the public address system, and formally took leave of me at the door to the playroom. It was the next month, the eighteenth, that he drew the witch and her cat—his first "human" forms.

In the next four months of treatment. the patient's body image was explicitly elaborated and it became possible to differentiate symptoms and fantasies which were a result of excitation from damaged brain areas from his other symptoms and problems. I must emphasize again, however, that the parents had reported some body-image concepts (body made up of little rooms) and some symptoms (tinnitus and bad smells) before treatment began; the fact that Hugh would not discuss them explicitly until late in the second year of treatment did not result from repression of a deep nature but from feelings of embarrassment, shame, mistrust, fear of consequences, etc. It seems likely that the body-image concepts and the meaning of the organic symptoms were preconscious, but that the devouring witch fantasies and the paranoid transference had to be worked through before the patient could or would discuss the meaning of the organic disease.

In the organic category, the eating problem was the first symptom to be brought up. The parents and the pediatrician had become increasingly concerned about Hugh's poor diet and loss of weight and had discussed the problem with me. Hugh came in one day looking troubled and tense, seemed anxious to talk about something but unable to do so. Next he brought in a note: "1. I lost 3 pounds. 2. i can't eat good. 3. I only eat mush or popcorn. 4. Lately i can't hardly eat at all." He still could not bring himself to discuss the problem directly. He then requested an extra appointment because of something he had forgotten to show me and brought in a diagram of a "machine" comprising power circuits. I suggested that this had some connection with his fears of food, how food goes through the body (assuming it was related to his protracted diarrhea), etc. Hugh denied this. However, he admitted to fantasies of people in his blood and, when I asked him to paint a diagram of how his brain, heart, and stomach were connected, he readily began to do so.

The body-image drawing was done in three sections on three sheets of newsprint paper in two sessions, a week apart. Though he did not compare the sections, the body outlines were well matched, suggesting a definite spatial concept on the boy's part. The body was outlined in faint pink, while the organs and the "people who live in the blood" were bright red or undiluted black. Hugh drew, on the heart, two stick figures: "The Red King in charge of blood and the Black King in charge of cephalitis." Each King had stick-figure guards around him. Hugh drew a window they could look out of in the head (where the control mechanism was) and had it similarly guarded. "Blood veins" ran from the heart to the head and to the extremities; the soldiers of the Black and Red Kings traveled up and down these. The red and black forces were evenly matched. He omitted the penis; when I commented on this, he said, "Oh yes, the cannon," drew it and described how the guards mounted steps to fire it.

Excited play followed in which a soldier dreamed of a hand with fifty fingers so he could fire more guns at once. Then Hugh did a series of drawings with an erotized theme, in which parts of a boy and girl were interchanged. For the first time, women were defeated;

they ended in a fight and killed each other while the boy escaped unharmed: "He wasn't interested in them anyhow."

A few sessions later, Hugh told of Mr. 'Cephalitis, who lived in one mansion while Hugh lived in another. The mansions, of course, were identically furnished and decorated. He talked first of getting robbers or criminals in jail but having them break out and repeat their crimes, then he said that Mr. 'Cephalitis did the same. He, Hugh, would subdue Mr. 'Cephalitis and make him sign a paper to be good, but Mr. 'Cephalitis would immediately break his word and do it again. Hugh discussed the rooms in his own body where Mr. 'Cephalitis lived: in the arm (big room) and fingers with hall (blood veins) going up to the head. In connection with his trouble in controlling Mr. 'Cephalitis, he said poignantly: "A body has a million rooms."

The eating problem was still troublesome and the family (in response to the pediatrician's urging) was putting pressure on Hugh to overcome it. Presumably in response to this, he returned to play of aggressive women in a number of play sessions. Thinking of the "cannon" he had omitted from his body image, I again discussed his feeling that I had sent him to the hospital, his castration fear, and his fears of women as the aggressor. He talked about his fears of the two housekeepers in the past: one in the home during his mother's illness (when he was four and a half to five and a half), who set no limits, the other (the original witch, "the Cooker"), during his infancy. He called the latter "the Spanker" and said: "I must have thought my mother was the Spanker and she never spanks. I got scared of her." Earlier, he had said, "I didn't know who was the Cooker and who was my mother, so I just hit everybody."

He admitted his paranoid fantasies about his mother (as usual, in spatial terms) in connection with his drug therapy. He told how huge the pills seemed at first and admitted the thought: "What's mother trying to do—fill my mouth to the back and choke me? . . Not really . . . But I thought the pills would swell in my stomach." "And choke your stomach?" "Yeah. . . Now the pills seem small."

Hugh became willing at this point to discuss further the symptoms which—as gradually became clear—were related to excitation from damaged brain areas. You will recall that he had brought up his eating problems, denying fears and fantasies, saying he just didn't like the taste. I had proceeded nonetheless on a psychogenic hypothesis, and requested that he be given a Rorschach, asking particularly about fantasies in this area. The Rorschach interpretation suggested that Hugh did have opposing concepts of "bad-oral aggression" vs. "head-intellectual functioning-control." I told Hugh about this dichotomy; he denied its etiological importance. However, he was willing to discuss his abnormal perceptions. He told me of his nightly bad dreams which were like movies and usually in color. The themes of these bad color dreams all concerned being chased by bad guys, murders, frightening situations, torture dreams, in which some or all of his family were involved. Earlier, he had dreamed of being abandoned himself or lost or given away. Despite the dramatic content, it occurred to me that these dreams had a stereotyped quality reminiscent of organic deliria. Hugh told me, on inquiry, that they all occurred in the early morning and their occurrence in color distinguished them, in his mind, from his other dreams. I wondered if they could originate in excitation from brain-damaged areas and suggested a two-hour delay in the evening dose of Milontin (till bedtime). The dreams promptly ceased and have not recurred.

This called forcibly to my attention the possibility that other symptoms might be related to stimuli from the damaged brain area and I recalled Ostow's article (1955) and Penfield's work (1954) on perceptual disturbances associated with temporal lobe damage. The patient's reaction to my discovery that his bad color dreams seemed to be caused by Mr. 'Cephalitis confirmed his inclusion of them into his damaged body image. He said, "Of course," it was the 'cephalitis causing them—he knew that all the time—if I had wanted to know, why hadn't I asked him?

I asked his mother to keep a diary about his symptoms. Here she described the *déjà vu* phenomena mentioned by Penfield. "Hugh says, 'Sometimes things happen in the day and I think I dreamed them before. Like a man will come to the door and I think it has happened before in my dream. The man will come in the same face and nose and clothes that was in my dream before. But that happens to everybody, doesn't it? . . I know a dream is really a dream because in real life I cannot see my face. If I can see my face then I know it is a dream.'"

On the day he brought in this record, Hugh asked me what further comments I had to make about his food problems. I said I didn't know, except somehow eating seemed to be connected with 'cephalitis. He replied: "Of course it is, by the tongue." I asked: "How does it get to the tongue?" "Well, 'cephalitis is a disease. . . It climbs [to the tongue] by the blood veins." I questioned him further, "You mean tastes are made funny by the 'cephalitis like those sounds[5] you used to hear?" He replied: "Yes . . . They're too strong." He discussed the exacerbation of tastes and how, if the smells are strong, he could not bear to taste the food at all. I suggested that he try holding his nose to see if he could eat more things; this was moderately successful.

The patient talked about certain other symptoms as if they occupied the same place with respect to his body image as the above. He included his hoarse voice which embarrassed him greatly, his clumsiness and incoordination of gait, and his genitourinary difficulties (e.g., his repeated infections and occasional dribbling). The "bladder room" featured prominently in his early discussions of his body image.[6] Periodically Hugh shyly asked me for my thoughts or suggestions on the management of these symptoms.

During the summer in which Hugh was nine years old, the family planned a trip to Europe. In view of the specific relation of some symptoms in the perceptual realm to stimulation from damaged brain areas, I suggested that they consult Penfield, in Montreal, about possible extirpation of focal areas. This obviously traumatizing plan was thoroughly discussed with the patient and, despite an initial phobic reaction, he accepted it calmly. The period before the trip (the last two months of his second year of treatment) was devoted to discussions of this anticipated trauma and to management of Hugh's panic about the shots and other procedures preparatory to the trip. He had a fairly severe regressive, coercive reaction to the shots, but skillful handling by the pediatrician enabled him to get through them.

During the European sojourn, unforeseen difficulties once more

[5] The tinnitus reported by the parents before treatment began.

[6] The patient had been subject to repeated genitourinary infections. All studies, including intravenous pyelograms, were negative and did not disclose any peripheral defect to account for the predisposition.

ensued. Hugh was referred by Penfield to Sir Russell Brain in London, but before he could be worked up neurosurgically, he again developed a refractory genitourinary infection and was hospitalized for several weeks in a children's hospital. The eventual neurosurgical decision was that the brain damage was too extensive for operative intervention. In general, the boy's medical experiences in England were very supportive, in contrast to his previous hospital experience. When his behavior was difficult, a surgeon commented to the mother, "These temporal lobe lesions make it terribly difficult for a little chap, don't they." However, again one surgeon and one nurse told the family that the patient was simply spoiled and they must ignore his complaints. The parents responded with their typical overcompliance to authority and ignored Hugh's complaints of earache until an infection was florid and rupture of the eardrum imminent. During this period, Hugh's aggressive behavior increased.

When Hugh returned to treatment, he did not show direct or indirect resentment of me because of his difficult medical experiences this time. He said, "Well, you told me about it . . and why . . and you couldn't know I'd get bladder trouble." He was readily willing to discuss his hospital experiences in detail. In striking contrast to his previous account of hospitalization, where he had to describe his emotional reactions in relation to the floor plan, he now could focus directly on the interpersonal transactions and his emotional reactions. During the next four months, he continued in a realistic, friendly relationship with me, engaging in nonsymbolic play and using therapy for supportive and ego-oriented purposes. The question of termination was brought up with him at the end of this time because it seemed advisable (for expedient reasons) that further dynamically oriented therapy be deferred. Hugh agreed to a termination date two and a half months in the future.

He promptly began playing with a box of modular blocks which came in five sizes, each about an inch larger than the last. He had never played with these blocks before. At this time in his daily life, Hugh showed little of the incoordination, clumsiness, or perceptual uncertainty which had been characteristic when he was first seen. He had learned to roller skate, to ride a bicycle, and to do reasonably well in all sports save those, like baseball, in which his perceptual difficulties made him uncertain.

However, in his play with the blocks he showed striking retro-gression to much earlier spatial and perceptual confusion. Since he played with nothing else for the remaining months of treatment, it seemed clear that this was a psychologically meaningful change. In every session, he built two-story houses. He showed marked pseudo stupidity in matching the blocks for size, making no effort to use a measuring block or even to look at the blocks carefully. He built by a process of approximation and patching, which at first seemed merely to be far below his current functional and maturational level. After a few times, however, I realized that each two-story edifice, however patched and approximated, was solid except that each one was completed with a definite gap or chink in the second story—very poorly patched, if at all. It then seemed clear that the block play was a recapitulation of Hugh's feelings about his body and his organic damage. I said, "They've all got a hole in the head." He agreed enthusiastically.

In the remaining sessions, he built progressively better and more skillfully erected houses in a clear, magical attempt to create a less damaged body image. He began to select blocks accurately by size, then to use a sample block and lay out enough materials in advance to carry out his plans. Some tendency to improvisation or patching continued until, in the last session, he built a carefully planned, complexly designed, very well-proportioned, perfect building. He was just ten years old when treatment ended.

PROGRESS IN TREATMENT

During the course of treatment, the patient had made remarkable social advances. His aggressive outbursts and his compulsive rituals were strikingly diminished, as was his tormenting demandingness on his family. Hugh himself knew when he needed to increase his drug dosage and could distinguish the symptoms originating from his brain damage from other problems. He still had some eating diffi-culties, fears of shots and medical procedures, and periods of tense, irritable behavior. However, in school, he was performing excel-lently at grade level and had been elected president of his class. His improvement in motor skills has been described. His social relations were good and he was no longer suspicious, withdrawn, or felt that he was crazy.

Dynamically, I believe one can say that Hugh worked out much of the anxiety associated with his brain damage. His basic identification with the female aggressor was only partially modified. This identification represented Hugh's "solution" of the paranoid attitude toward his mother which had resulted from the acute stage of the organic illness. Thus it was ego-syntonic and not as accessible to psychotherapy as his other difficulties. I felt that (1) a continued abatement of the aggressive outbursts and improved social adjustment as a result of medication and psychotherapy might make his identification with the female aggressor less necessary; (2) the consequently improved realistic relationship with his father might enable Hugh later to view the feminine identification as more ego-alien and to work it through with the aid, if necessary, of further formal therapy.

FOLLOW-UP

The parents were retested and Hugh was seen again eight months after termination of treatment. The parents, according to their MMPIs, were relatively unchanged. Not so with Hugh: he presented himself as a strikingly more self-confident and masculine boy who had lost much of the shy, uncertain, indefinably handicapped and somewhat feminine bearing which had characterized him before. He summarized his impression of treatment when I commented that he had "forgotten" some of the dynamic transactions: "Yes . . . but I remember the important problems." To Hugh, these were problems concerning Mr. 'Cephalitis, whom he now demoted to the familiar nickname "Sephy." His previous anger against his father had been repressed; he looked at me in astonishment when I reminded him that he had often written his father notes, saying he hated him; he told me, "I'm a woman hater now." Improved masculine identification had clearly taken place. When I said it looked as if Mr. 'Cephalitis was locked up in jail for good, Hugh smiled broadly and agreed with assurance.

He did another portrait of his body image which showed traces of his previous drawing but also reflected his marked clinical improvement and mastery over aggressive impulses. The Red King in charge of Blood had become the Queen; the Black King in charge of 'Cephalitis had become the Good King, the ruler, and now was blue. The Queen's guards were still red and traces of the connection with the blood remained (e.g., their hospital was in the heart). The King's evil soldiers had become Government Agents (presumably a reflection of ego and superego control over aggression). The control box was gone from the head and the blood veins no longer existed (you will recall that they previously served as "roads" for the conveyance of aggressive impulses and abnormal perceptions). Now, the feet and legs were made repositories for a factory and storehouses containing all kinds of Thanksgiving foods (this was humor, related to the date of the interview). The patient was clearly speaking metaphorically: at first he labeled the kidneys as "filters," then he said, "No, that's what they really are; this is a game; they have to be something different," and made them storehouses for old clothes. Much humor appeared in the drawing. I asked Hugh (recalling the chess sequence) where the knight was. He replied (referring, I believe, to treatment), "Oh, this isn't such olden times!" He had come in with a minor complaint about his hoarse voice (an encephalopathic symptom); probably because of this, he located a dungeon on one side of his neck. This was the only feature of the new body-image drawing done in the original black. Hugh incarcerated Sephy and his guards in it and stated that Sephy was locked up for good there.[7]

His social improvement had continued. His relation with me was friendly, assured, and realistic. His perception of encephalopathic symptoms was unchanged; his memory of psychological attitudes and problems had undergone marked distortion and repression. In contrast to his early fears about confidentiality and his paranoid attitudes, he now was entirely unconcerned to hear that I wanted to write a story about him and Mr. 'Cephalitis to tell to other doctors. I explained the use of a pseudonym; he asked what his would be and,

[7] Further development of a more realistic body image was seen two years after treatment. Hugh made a very aesthetic ceramic paperweight which showed his accurate perception of his organic lesion and his ability to sublimate through creative productivity. He made a semiabstract model of a brain, using coils of clay which were smoothly interwoven and represented the convolutions of the brain. However, precisely in the right temporal area was a distorted, twisted patch of thin, spidery coils. Ends of these coils protruded; the organization and unity shown in the rest of the model were conspicuously lacking in this area. The coils themselves were "deformed" by twisting and unevenness. He had modeled his organic lesion.

when I told him, laughed heartily and said, "That's nothing like my name."

DISCUSSION

The patient's difficulties can be classified under: (1) the organic factors: the perceptual abnormalities and the aggressive outbursts; (2) the boy's efforts to organize these organic symptoms and his view of his disease (a) in terms of body image and (b) in his fantasies about Mr. 'Cephalitis and how to control him; (3) the psychodynamic problems. This third category includes the distortions of psychosexual development, the fixations and the defensive maneuvers which relate (a) to the nature and timing of the organic onslaught and (b) to the characteristic interpersonal transactions in his family.

The Organic Factors

Let us consider first the part Mr. 'Cephalitis played in the picture—the symptoms caused by stimuli originating in the damaged brain area which comprised widespread degenerative and irritative lesions of the right temporal lobe. Penfield and Jaspar (1954) and Ostow (1955) describe the temporal lobe as a receiving station for olfactory and taste stimuli. Sensations of vertigo and disturbances of equilibrium may be produced by stimulation of the lateral aspects of the temporal lobe (Ostow, p. 388). "Perceptual illusions, dreamlike hallucinations, and attempts to repeat the stereotyped automatic behavior were seen. The perceptual illusions included impairment of judgment about the size of a visual object, its distance from the patient, the loudness of noise, the pitch of a voice, or the speed of an event. There was also the well-known *déjà vu*, the illusional impression of familiarity. The hallucinatory sequences might be memories, recent or remote, or dreamlike productions, or actual reproductions of dreams with which the patient was familiar" (Ostow, p. 389). Penfield and Jaspar refer to alimentary seizures, autonomic seizures, etc.: "The attacks from which this patient suffered were obviously in a part of the brain related to the alimentary tract and producing at different times borborygmi, nausea, bad taste, salivation, and sensations referred to stomach, throat, and mouth. Each series of attacks was associated with diarrhea" (Penfield and Jaspar, p. 430).

How do these considerations apply in the case of our patient? In differentiating psychological problems from symptoms directly related to the damaged brain area, my bias was psychogenic: I did not anticipate that temporal lobe damage triggered symptoms other than the aggressive outbursts. Two differentiating criteria seem to apply: (1) Certain symptoms which were described in the literature as occurring with temporal lobe lesions occurred in the patient and, in two of these (the aggressive outbursts and the color dreams), abatement of the symptoms seemed to occur with pharmacological management. (2) The patient's affective-defensive attitude toward certain symptoms seemed to differentiate them from other problems even before the patient became aware of this difference or was willing to tell me which symptoms he felt were related to Mr. 'Cephalitis.

The patient's eating disturbance is a typical example. You will recall that I had proceeded on the assumption that his difficulties were psychogenic, i.e., related to the onset of his illness in the oral stage, the painful diarrhea, and his fantasies of being devoured or torn apart by food and by those who fed him. In actuality, when the issue of hyperreactivity of the perceptual apparatus was raised, Hugh replied that he knew the problem was organic. He said, "Of course . . . 'Cephalitis is a disease. It climbs down the blood veins to the tongue."

Note that this datum was integrated by the patient into his encephalitic body image and taken for granted, not reacted to like a psychological conflict. Schilder (1935) states that organic lesions are perceived by the person as being peripheral rather than central to the ego. "Organic disease and organic change have less to do with the personality than functional disease. A functional disease is connected with the innermost problems of the individual—with the centre of his Ego" (Schilder, p. 156). You have noted that both Hugh and his mother responded to the boy's disease as if it were an external catastrophe which had overwhelmed them.

The symptoms which satisfy the above criteria for organicity include the aggressive outbursts, the bad smells, and the eating disturbance, the tinnitus, the *déjà-vu* experiences, and the color dreams. These can almost certainly be considered as direct results of stimuli from damaged areas of the temporal lobe. Also, it seems likely that certain spatial and visual distortions fall into this category.

Perceptual difficulties in temporal lobe lesions may include impairment of judgment about the size or distance of a visual object, the speed of an event, etc. The patient's specific fear of baseball, persisting after he had mastered other motor skills involving coordination, suggests an origin in such disordered perception. His disturbed perception of the size of his pills may be a neat example of the fusion between his paranoid feeling that his mother was responsible and the spatial distortions relating to the temporal lobe damage.

The patient acted as if his hoarse voice and his clumsy gait were also directly connected with his organic lesion (e.g., he reacted to them with embarrassment and shame rather than repression or distortion). Hugh also included his periodic genitourinary disturbances in this category, but, since retrograde pyelography has not been done, a peripheral cause for these difficulties has not been completely ruled out. The diarrhea which accompanied Hugh's acute illness may be an example of the alimentary seizures referred to by Penfield; at least no peripheral cause was ever discovered.

Hugh's view of all these symptoms is uniform and fits in with Schilder's concept (that they are peripheral in the ego): he reacts to them with marked embarrassment and shame but very little guilt. He is clever in disguising these symptoms. He is afraid of being sold or abandoned because of his aggression, but he regards all these difficulties as enemy aliens rather than problems incorporated into his own psychic economy and condemned by his superego.

Body Image

Loss of Boundaries: Schilder (1935) and Bender (1952) have made extensive studies of the spatial organization of the world (e.g., sidewalk drawings of children, Bender Gestalt test) as projections of body image. Hugh, in his rendering both of his own explicit body image and in his other productions, showed his lack of a firm boundary between his body and the outside world. You remember that, in his early pictures, he did three in white paint on white paper which seemed to reflect this lack of differentiation. Later, in his body-image painting, the interior of his body (showing his conflict with Mr. 'Cephalitis) was painted in bright red and black, but the outline of the figure was done in pale pink. He behaved as if the aggressive outbursts and perceptual distortions had made him literally uncertain of his own spatial boundaries.

Hugh tried to combat this loss of boundaries by preoccupation with binding and enclosing space. During treatment, one of the most prominent features of his graphic productions was repetitive and emphasized boxing in of drawing, numbers, etc. He did drawings in which the danger was that of going too far in space-time. Diagrams of a catacomb type were numerous. His performance on the Bender Gestalt represented a successful effort to conceal his organically determined loss of boundaries by his compulsive and meticulous rendition of the figures (space binding). This boxing in of space did not ebb and flow with other compulsive activities; although certainly an effort to bind anxiety compulsively, it seemed also to be a specific effort to delineate the boundaries of the patient's own body and to contain Mr. 'Cephalitis within that boundary. He typically used spatial metaphor to describe his problems with Mr. 'Cephalitis. He spoke of the body as a series of rooms with a control box in the head representing his disease. He said Mr. 'Cephalitis lived in a mansion with fifty rooms. Efforts to control his aggression were described as putting Mr. 'Cephalitis into jail. In the last phase of treatment, when he was trying to reconstruct a less damaged body image, he did so by repetitively building two-story houses out of blocks. Similarly, he used spatial referrents in describing his own experiences. In his first traumatic hospitalization, for instance, he located his emotional experiences and reactions by reference to a floor plan of his ward. As he improved clinically, Hugh also was less threatened by the loss of spatial boundaries; in his second hospitalization, no floor plan was used to locate or mediate his emotional reactions. His second body-image drawing, likewise, showed his markedly lessened anxiety about his problems of spatial boundaries; now both events inside the body and the outline of the body drawing were equally vivid and definite.

The Autistic Phase

In the light of current discussions of infantile autism, it is particularly interesting to note that such classical autistic symptoms could occur at the most acute stage of Hugh's illness and abate, with-

out formal treatment, as his diarrhea diminished. Physiological variables are highlighted as etiological agents in his autistic reaction.

Hugh did not show the inborn "thin protective barrier against
stimuli" described by Bergman and Escalona (1949). His first nine
months of development were not only normal but relatively lusty
and outgoing. He did suffer a sudden and massive illness at nine
months. This illness caused hyperreactivity of the perceptual apparatus, which, when it occurs at this critical developmental stage, is
a powerful stimulus for autism. His illness, in addition, caused severe
recurrent diarrhea, which lasted until he was about three years old.
This diarrhea constituted a "maximum developmental insult," that
is, it interfered with the developmental modes and zones most highly
cathected at that stage. Also, it constituted a proprioceptive insult.
Mahler (1952) noted that an autistic child she observed was markedly reactive to proprioceptive stimuli, i.e., visceral pain. This was
in sharp contrast to the child's lack of response to exteroceptive pain,
i.e., a burn on the mouth.

Mahler and Gosliner (1955) describe the critical stage for autistic
reactions as that in which the infant is gradually differentiating
himself from the mother and establishing the mother as an external
object. They feel that this developmental stage is typically "still a
very precarious one at twelve to thirty months of age" (p. 195). From
Hugh's case, it seems that differentiation of the mother as a hostile
external object may occur even earlier than twelve months if some
inner or outer source of pain (e.g., diarrhea, an overstimulating
mother) forcibly disrupts the infant's symbiotic gratifications.

Hugh reacted to the double assault on him at nine months with
the predictable developmental response: since his mother was the
primary object, he developed a paranoid reaction to her. The theoretical implications of this primary rejection of the mother will not
be elaborated here, since they are discussed elsewhere (Sarvis and
Garcia, 1960). However, it should be noted that the stimulation of
the paranoid reaction in this boy was physiological and not related
to family psychodynamics. In fact, the family psychodynamics were
so strongly organized against a chronic autistic reaction, that Hugh,
as soon as his diarrhea abated, began to recover from his autism
without any formal psychotherapeutic intervention.

It seems probable that infantile autism is a two-stage process.

Any combination of etiological variables, at the vulnerable developmental stage, may cause a child to reject his mother in a primary autistic reaction. One of these etiological variables may, of course, be the pathology of the mother, but others are clearly physiological, constitutional, etc. Whatever the causes, the child has rejected the mother because, at that age, she is the primary object. Now, the mother has to struggle with her own temptation to counterreject or counterwithdraw from the child. If this counterrejection is marked, it predisposes to the consolidation of the autistic reaction into chronic autistic disease. If the counterrejection is absent, as in the case of Hugh's family, the child's recovery from an autistic reaction is greatly supported.

At times, however, it seems that constitutional variables or physiological assaults may be so overwhelming to the child's ego that no attitude on the part of the mother or the therapist suffices to help the child master an autistic reaction.

12

BEHAVIOR DISORDER AND EGO DEVELOPMENT IN A BRAIN-INJURED CHILD

SHELDON R. RAPPAPORT, Ph.D.
(1961)

In surveying the literature dealing with the disorders of thought processes[1] and behavior found in the brain-injured child and adult, three views are encountered. Each of these views recognizes the presence of behavioral and cognitive disturbances on the one hand and of damaged neural tissue on the other. They differ in what they regard as the genesis of the behavioral disturbance, and consequently in what they recommend for handling such patients.

The oldest and still most prevalent view attributes the observed thought disorder and behavioral deviations to irrevocably damaged neural structures (Hunt and Cofer, 1944; Klebanoff, Singer, Wilensky, 1954). Either impairment in the higher inhibitory cortical centers, or brain-stem lesions are held responsible for hyperactivity, impulsiveness, and hostile or destructive outbursts so commonly found in the brain-injured child (Blau, 1936; Kahn and Cohen, 1934; Strauss and Lehtinen, 1947; Timme, 1952); and their anxiety is also considered to be determined by the organic lesion (Bender, 1949).[2]

The second view in general leaves a hiatus between the organic and the psychological factors, the implication being that the former are irreparable and can only be controlled by means of drugs and/or by delimitation of the environment to make it nonfrustrating. As for the psychological factors, this view advises guidance of the parents

1 This paper is fondly dedicated to the late Dr. David Rapaport. He gave generously of his all-too-limited time so that through his helpful suggestions and editing this paper could take its present form.
2 [See also Birch, 1964; Wender, 1971.]

and treating the "accompanying neurotic problems" of the child (Bender, 1949; Bradley, 1955; Weil, 1958).

According to the third view, the total picture presented is the result of the *interaction* of functional and organic factors (Betlheim and Hartmann, 1924). Indeed, in restating Schilder's position, Rapaport (1951, pp. 660, 288f.) has suggested that organic damage and psychological disturbance may use the same mechanisms, though differing in intensity and extent. The mechanisms referred to are the ego functions. Whether symptoms are characteristic of brain damage, of psychological disturbance, or of both present simultaneously, they still involve the ego functions.

While Mahler (1952), Weil (1953), and others have greatly furthered our knowledge about ego dysfunction in the emotionally disturbed child, the study of the nature of ego functions in the brain-damaged child has been neglected. Perhaps that is primarily because historically the brain has been regarded as a highly vulnerable organ, irreparable when damaged. However, today we know that the brain is a much more resilient organ than it was previously thought to be. We also know that the cerebrum is—by and large—not composed of loci of specific intellectual functions (Hebb, 1949; Landis, 1949), and that the function of a damaged area can be taken over, to a large extent, by other areas. Contrary to previous belief, the minor cerebral hemisphere is also capable of accommodating training for a particular skill when the dominant hemisphere has been extirpated (Nielson, 1946), and children can still learn to speak after the speech areas of the dominant hemisphere are destroyed (Penfield and Roberts, 1959). Therefore it is worth while to study the brain-damaged child centering attention on his ego functions and avoiding the assumption that damage to neural tissue plays the paramount role in his behavior and thought disturbances.

The facts just cited do not mean that damaged neural tissue is of no importance at all. But they do mean that we have yet to learn exactly what role damaged neural tissue does play in the disabilities of brain-damaged children. In fact, there is still considerable disagreement as to what role damaged neural tissue plays in behavioral disturbance in general. Some writers, such as Bender (1947), believe that there is neuropathology underlying all behavioral and emotional disturbance. Investigators have also found abnormal EEG patterns both in children and adults who showed behavioral disturbance but no clinically demonstrable brain damage (Kennard, 1959; Silverman, 1944). The question remains whether or not there is, indeed, a neuropathological matrix, which at times is only manifested sub-clinically, underlying all behavioral disturbance, or whether, as suggested by Morrell's work with monkeys (Morrell and Jasper, 1956; Morrell, Roberts, Jasper, 1956), abnormal EEG patterns can be consequences of a psychological process. In the face of the complexity of such problems, it does not seem warranted to regard the impulsive and driven behavior of the brain-damaged child as solely the result of the damage to neural tissue. To approach the brain-damaged child from the standpoint of ego functioning permits us to study the interaction of neurologic and psychologic factors and provides the opportunity for treating him more efficaciously, as a whole person. As Hartmann (1952, p. 18) has stated, it is particularly the study of ego functions that might facilitate the meeting between the psychoanalytic and the neurophysiologic approaches.

The thesis of this paper is that behavioral disturbance, such as found in the case to be presented, (1) is not due solely to damaged brain tissue per se and therefore is not necessarily irreversible; (2) but is due to a considerable degree to the disturbance which that damage causes in the epigenesis of the ego; (3) the deviant ego maturation fostering a disturbed parent-child relationship that in turn inhibits proper ego development; and (4) the disturbance both in ego development and in the parent-child relationship can be alleviated by psychotherapy and adjunctive therapies.

CASE PRESENTATION

Kenny came from middle-class, second-generation American parents. His father was an assertive but jolly hale-fellow-well-met. His mother spoke in a high, whining, soft voice, which was in keeping with her general demeanor of sweetness and light. Both parents had rather strict, orthodox Jewish backgrounds. The father's family had struggled very hard, so that from an early age he had to make his way in the world by his own wits and aggressiveness. Working while in school he managed to receive a high-school education. After returning from service during World War II, he worked very hard to build his own business and succeeded in providing his family with the usual comforts and conveniences. The mother came from a family that was financially somewhat superior to her husband's. The family was able to go to the seashore for summer vacations and to finance her education at a teacher's college. While teaching, she continued her education and earned a master's degree. She described herself as having been a quiet, shy child who envied her older brother's outgoing nature and many friends. When her brother died, after she finished college, she was very depressed. She described her mother as having been a ravishing beauty whom everyone admired and respected and whom she adored. Her mother had opposed her marriage, feeling that her prospective husband was beneath her. In turn, the husband resented his mother-in-law, feeling that she was forever turning his wife against him. He also felt that his wife owed allegiance first to him and not to her mother. When his wife wanted him to do things for her recently widowed mother and he voiced his resentment, she would coldly pull away from him. She, in turn, resented his mother, a widow, though she, living at a great distance, visited only rarely. Although she never told her husband, she felt that her mother-in-law was a selfish woman; she would not help out when she came to visit and expected to be waited on. According to her report, the mother-in-law would lounge around all day only to put on a great show of industriousness and cooperation when her son came home from work.

Kenny's two-and-a-half-year-older brother was born with diabetes, and although the parents were distressed about this, they soon took it in their stride. Their relationships with him were good, and he made a good adjustment until Kenny's difficulties began to demand too much of their attention. Even then he showed only transitory emotional upsets, which were alleviated by counseling the parents on their handling of him.

Kenny's delivery (twelve hours of labor) was normal and spontaneous. He barely cried at birth and only whimpered when pinched. Because of an Rh incompatibility, he was given multiple transfusions of Rh negative blood. He slept a great deal and his activity level was low, but he did accept the bottle and sucked without falling asleep while feeding. Kernicterus and Rh negative erythroblastosis fetalis were diagnosed.

His mother began to take care of Kenny when he was brought home from the hospital at five weeks of age. Because he slept a great deal and was not responsive, he received little attention from his mother except at feeding time, when he was held and cuddled. At nine months of age he first began to smile in recognition of his mother and could still not support his head to any real degree. He showed no coordination of arm and hand movements until fourteen months of age, and no righting reflex until sixteen months of age. As Kenny's motor activity increased, it proved obviously athetotic.

Starting at five months of age, repeated EEG's were made. At first they were reported to be highly abnormal, with the basic frequency very slow, two to three per second, and the amplitude very high, reaching 300 microvolts. There were numerous plateau type waves and an occasional spike formation. Although the abnormality was described as quite diffuse, there were also apparently zones of hyperirritability in the right motor, occipital, and temporal regions. By seventeen months of age, the electroencephalographic tracings were considered to be within the upper limits of normal, both in rhythm and amplitude, and there were no abnormal wave forms indicative of cortical hyperirritability. After that, the physician in charge felt that no further EEG's were necessary.

Because Kenny did not respond consistently to the usual auditory stimuli in his environment, his hearing was repeatedly examined starting at five months of age. It was thought that he had a bilateral hearing impairment associated with the erythroblastosis and kernicterus, but just how extensive the hearing loss was could not be established at the time.

I first saw Kenny when he was eighteen months of age. Because his EEG's and gross neurologic tests by then had shown improvement, Kenny was brought to me in order to determine his intellectual status. He had just learned to sit alone without support, but as yet made no attempt to pull himself to a standing position. Unlike most youngsters of that age, he sat quietly on his mother's lap for almost an hour and a half. When he became restless, he was put on the floor, where he crawled around for a while. Soon tiring of that, he lay quietly. He showed a less than normal amount of interest in his surroundings. His mother reported that at home he also was quite passive and unresponsive. He smiled only upon tactile contact and caressing from his mother. She related that Kenny made sounds occasionally, but he made none during his two-hour visit with me.

On the Cattell Infant Scale (Cattell, 1947), Kenny obtained an M.A. of 9.8 months, and an I.Q. of 54. He succeeded on all items at the seven-month level and failed all items at the twelve- and thirteen-month levels. He was sufficiently interested in reaching for and examining articles presented to him (such as a shoestring, a bell) to be credited with most items at the eight-month level, and to be credited with such items as recovering a toy hidden under a handkerchief, at the ten-month level. He imitated my poking my finger into the hole of a peg board, at the ten-month level, and also imitated my placing a cube in a cup, at the eleven-month level. However, he had not been taught such simple responses as pat-a-cake or waving bye-bye, at the nine-month level. Kenny also showed a strong grasp and an overhand thumb and forefinger prehension, at the eleven-month level. However, he did not have the coordination to bang two objects together or to rattle a spoon in a cup, at the ten-month level.

On the Vineland Social Maturity Scale (Doll, 1947), Kenny received an S.Q. of 61. At the 0-to-1-year level, he was penalized because he could not stand alone or walk and still drank only from a bottle. At the one-year level, he was credited only with spontaneously starting to pull off his socks and with being able to be in the company of other children without creating antagonism. He still was fed completely by his mother. She held him while feeding him liquids in a bottle and baby foods with a spoon. She had never tried to get him to hold a utensil in his hand, or to eat junior foods or table foods, and she had never allowed him to sit alone in the high chair and eat the baby foods with his fingers. Kenny also had not been introduced to pencils, crayons, picture books, or educational toys for infants.

After seeing Kenny that first time, I had a conference with the mother in order to explain the test findings. I pointed out, for example, that his responses on the Cattell suggested that Kenny had enough interest and attention to learn simple acts, such as pat-a-cake; that he had sufficient muscle strength and prehension to hold a spoon or cup; and that he needed her stimulation in order to learn and to become more self-sufficient. I advised her to stimulate Kenny with activities that would be within his scope and would challenge him without undue frustration. My purpose was to provide Kenny with the pleasure of simple accomplishments, which in turn could serve as motivation for trying more difficult tasks. His accomplishments, I hoped, would also evoke in his mother the desire to give him more attention and to teach him more, which in turn would promote his development.

When I again saw Kenny and his mother, a year and a half later, she had been quite faithful in giving him more stimulation. After teaching him to use a cup, she had weaned him from the bottle (at twenty months); she had encouraged him to feed himself and to use a spoon, and to assist with the dressing process—e.g., taking off his own socks and trousers at bedtime—and she had taught him to play simple games, such as pat-a-cake. She had also started him in physiotherapy at a clinic for cerebral palsied children, at twenty-six months of age. The program was directed at "aiding him with head control, with balance, reciprocation, standing balance, and walking." He resisted the training and was never described as more than "fairly cooperative." Kenny had also had an audiometric test, which showed a 20 to 40 decibel loss at 200 cycles, a 55 decibel loss at 500 cycles, and an 85 decibel loss at 1000 cycles. He had been examined, too, at the cerebral palsy clinic in preparation for speech therapy. The findings were: "He drools. Chewing, sucking, and swallowing reflexes are not normal. Phonation is fairly good. Breathing is mildly irregular. The tongue is depressed at the radix and there is tension in the geniohyoid and mylohyoid muscles. He does not close his lips adequately but there is no particular athetoid involvement and this movement is possible. He should be approached primarily as a severely hard-of-hearing child with athetoid involvement." As a result of these findings, at three years and four months of age, Kenny was started on speech therapy designed for deaf children.

During the visit with me when he was three years of age, Kenny was sociable and showed interest in his surroundings. He was not shy and soon after entering the examining room he sought attention and affection from me. He enjoyed manipulating the various materials in the room, and he especially liked scribbling on paper with a pencil, a feat his mother had taught him. However, most of his behavior was without purpose and was not aimed at accomplishing a goal. For example, he handled the various toys in the room but did not play with them or try to make them do something. He usually would not respond to auditory instruction, and even though he watched what I was doing, he generally did not imitate my actions. Only when he was asked to perform a familiar task, one in which he had already achieved success many times over, did he immediately set out to do it. Those were also the only times he showed any sustained attention. At all other times he was hyperdistractible and pulled away from the task as soon as I asked him to perform it, as though it posed a threat to him. Because it would have reflected his inaccessibility rather than his intelligence, I gave him no intelligence test at that time (Rappaport, 1951, 1953). However, he did show an S.Q. of 51, as opposed to the previous S.Q. of 61. The drop was due to his having made no gain in communication or in locomotion, and what credit he received for the skills that his mother taught him was not sufficient to offset that.

My next contact with Kenny was five years later, at the age of eight. Many important events occurred during that period. Soon after he became three, the cerebral palsy clinic to which he went for physical and speech therapy started a school, and Kenny attended it for full-day sessions, five days a week. His program there was essentially the same as it had been at the cerebral palsy clinic: speech and physical therapies. Up until that time no attempt had been made to toilet train him. The school initiated toilet training and after several months succeeded in making him not soil while at school. He then retained his feces while at school and continued to soil at home. Along with being forced suddenly into bowel control when he entered the school, he was also separated from his mother for the first time. His crying and screaming when his mother left him were vocal verifications of his separation anxiety. The crying and screaming subsided only after he had been going to school for over two months. Kenny hated the school and even today shows his dislike of it by sticking out his tongue each time he passes the building. Despite the fact that this was a very disturbed period of his life, Kenny did learn to walk. He walked without support at three years and ten months of age, with an athetotic gait which is still present.

As I was to learn later (see footnote 4 below), the mother felt inadequate because she had not gotten Kenny to control his bowels at home as he had learned to do at school, and so she started an all-out campaign to *make* him achieve bowel control at home (at this time

Kenny was just about four years old). Even though she kept him on the toilet for periods as long as half an hour, he would do nothing. Instead he would defecate while alone at night and would smear his feces all over his crib and the adjacent wall. This was his "gift" to his mother each morning. At about the same time Kenny began to refuse to go to bed at night. Each time he would be put down, he would get up and go downstairs where his parents were. The father often gave him beatings to stop this. When this did not avail, the parents in their exasperation took to locking him in his room. This enraged him. He screamed, kicked, and beat on the door. As a result he got more severe beatings. Most nights he went to sleep only when overcome by complete exhaustion. The parents were then at their wit's end, and the father restrained Kenny by means of a jacket in his bed. Despite the jacket, Kenny could throw himself backward and bang his head against the headboard. He did this with such vehemence that the parents feared he would "kill himself." They therefore put a football helmet on him at night. The battle of the bed continued for a whole year. Then, although the parents do not know why, Kenny suddenly stopped fighting about going to bed; and the football helmet, the restraining jacket, and the locked door became things of the past. The smearing, however, continued for another six months, a total of a year and a half. It stopped when Kenny, at the age of five and a half, acquiesced to defecate in the toilet, both at home and at times even at school. Nocturnal bladder control was not established until Kenny was over eight years of age.[3]

Between four and five and a half years of age, Kenny's over-all behavior became increasingly disturbed. By five and a half, he flouted his mother's authority in most everyday situations, as though to compensate for his submitting to her in toilet training. He was willful and negativistic when asked to do something. He was also very demanding of his mother, and would have a temper tantrum if not given his way. Even when out in public with her, he would dart off in all directions at once, grabbing this, demanding that.

At six years of age, the school which he had attended closed and Kenny started going to a school for the deaf. This was his first experi-

---

[3] This came about when he began to emulate his father a great deal. The father showed his dislike of Kenny's bed wetting and expressed the hope that Kenny would be a big boy and stop the wetting.

ence in a formally structured classroom situation. He would not mind the teacher, and he disturbed the class by kicking and shoving other children and by running up and down the aisles. The more he was punished—whether by the beatings of his father, by being yelled at, locked in his room, or sent to the principal's office—the more hyperactivity and diffuse hostility he showed. Kenny had always been hyperdistractible, but his hyperdistractibility increased markedly in any situation that made demands on him, such as school did, making him even less manageable there. His mother had such great difficulties with him that she dreaded his being at home, so that each time the telephone rang she was afraid the school was calling to tell her to take Kenny home again. All her difficulties with Kenny brought her into a state of near-panic. She told her husband often that she was afraid she was going to have a nervous breakdown. Her only way of managing Kenny was to cajole or appease him at every turn. This was the state of affairs when I next saw Kenny. He was then almost eight years of age.

It should be mentioned here that when Kenny entered the school for the deaf he also changed speech therapists. During the thirty-two months spent with the first speech therapist, he uttered only occasional sounds which had any kind of inflection. With the second speech therapist, in eight months' time (after which apparently she gave up) he learned some basic pantomime, intended as an intermediary to speech. He also began uttering sounds that did have inflection and sounded like, as McGinnis, Kleffner, and Goldstein (1956) so aptly put it, "scribble speech." He managed to pronounce some words fairly clearly, such as *ar* for *arm,* and even an occasional word distinctly, such as *home.* But in both cases he could not retain the achievement for any length of time. At school he also received instruction in reading, by the method of associating pictures with the word symbol. Kenny was able to learn the meaning of single words, but only in individual instruction, not in a group. The group proved too distracting, and also too stimulating to aggression.

On psychological retest Kenny obtained an S.Q. of 64. This score would have been higher if he had not been penalized partly for his athetosis, which did not permit him to ride a bike and do many other things boys his age do, but primarily for his refusal to conform with such expectations as dressing himself and exercising caution. Under fear of punishment from the father, Kenny showed that he could dress, and in general could take care of himself. In everyday living, however, he would refuse to do so and would flout his mother's authority.

On a nonverbal test of intelligence (Arthur, 1947), Kenny achieved an I.Q. of 60, not significantly different from his previous one. During the testing he showed a fear of challenge, withdrawing from the task as soon as he met with difficulty. He also showed marked hyperdistractibility. For example, during the visual test of attention span, the edge of my gold cuff link was exposed. Although it made no glare and was unobtrusive, it was sufficient to distract him from the task to which he was attending at that moment quite well. But his attention could be regained fairly readily. Kenny also had a disturbance in the structuring of his percepts. For example, on the Healy Picture Completion Test II (a series of ten pictures showing a boy's day at school, from his getting dressed in the morning to his return home at evening), in which a square portion of each picture is cut out, and the subject is to pick from a wide variety of squares the appropriate square to fit each picture, Kenny was unable to select the appropriate square eight out of the ten times. But, when I covered everything except the elements immediately relevant to a particular cutout, Kenny did perceive what was going on in that picture and then was able to choose the appropriate missing square. By covering up everything else I helped him to perceive the essential details and relegate all other details to the background, thus structuring a percept without being lost in a mass of minutiae.

The psychological test findings as well as Kenny's fear of challenge, his hyperdistractibility, his disinhibition, and his "scribble speech" pointed to his suffering from a severe aphasia—which, in turn, was inextricably interrelated with his behavioral disturbance. It seemed clear that to help Kenny it would be necessary to overcome the aphasia, aid him in developing control over his impulses, and assist his parents in their relationships with him.

In a discussion with the parents, we agreed that I would see them once a week to help them cope with the home situations, I would see Kenny twice a week for psychotherapy, and Kenny would get speech therapy again.

The first step was to help the mother overcome her morbid fear of

Kenny, which prevented her from relating with him effectively and often immobilized her in her dealings with him. At first she was completely unable to admit her anger and resentment over Kenny's behavior. In her sweetness-and-light voice, and without one word of anger toward him, she would tell me about his kicking and hitting her in his temper tantrums, and would complain of being afraid to be with him and of not knowing how to cope with him. I pointed out to her repeatedly that his behavior was extremely hard to bear and that anyone would be angry about it. She gradually became able to tell me about how angry she was with Kenny. Even then it was still difficult to get her to describe exactly what Kenny did and how she handled any specific situation. It took four months before she could allow herself to describe in detail an entire "crisis" with Kenny. The more she became able to admit her anger toward Kenny and to take a look at her reactions to him, the less she had to appease him, and she started to manage him effectively.[4] In the process of helping

[4] The changes in the mother resulted without delving into the unconscious conflicts which, as it was revealed later, played a role in her relationship with Kenny. This is what happened:

Fourteen months after therapy with Kenny began, the maternal grandmother took care of Kenny and his brother while the parents went away for a week end. Kenny objected to his mother's leaving and gave his grandmother a bit of a hard time. The grandmother, who had a coronary condition, suffered a slight heart attack that week end. A couple of weeks later, she died of a coronary attack. The week after Kenny's mother got up from sitting in mourning, she suddenly became fed up with the children's bickering between themselves and ran out of the house on a cold, rainy morning, clad only in a raincoat pulled around her nightgown. That evening her husband found her, sitting in a deserted railroad station. As a result of that incident, I saw the mother a number of times over the next two and a half months. During this time she brought out memories of many instances in her childhood and adolescence in which she felt that she was left out and unwanted, whereas her brother was the center of attraction. She felt that she was always wrong. Even after she married, her mother disapproved of her choice of a husband; and when she had children, even they did not bring her praise and a sense of pride. Similarly, she mentioned the fact that the school had been able to toilet train Kenny when she had not been able to do so. She also felt bad that she had not been able to handle Kenny and had to tell me her mistakes so that I could tell her what to do. In general, the material she brought out, among other things, suggested unresolved hostility to her mother and brother, which, attended by guilt, caused her feelings of inadequacy. In turn, she projected her feelings about her bad, defective self onto Kenny. It is probable that this was one of the direct unconscious factors in her inability to tolerate her angry feelings toward him. But she became able to tolerate such feelings toward Kenny and to examine her own reactions to him without the uncovering of these unconscious factors. Even after she had brought out feelings of hostility and guilt in her sessions with me, she never connected this with her relation to Kenny. The cathartic relief afforded by these interviews apparently reinstated her established defenses and she did not want to probe any further into her unconscious.

her to reach this point, we worked out plans for handling the major situations that caused stress in everyday living. Limits were established and when Kenny would not conform to those limits, he was "bounced" (Redl and Wineman, 1951, p. 39) from the situation. In so doing he was not, however, restrained, locked in, or excluded for very long. By gesture it was indicated to him that he was acting like a baby and when he could act like a big boy again, he could rejoin the group.

As the father became aware of Kenny's aphasia and the frustrations which it imposed on the boy, he tolerated Kenny's negativism and aggression without feeling that such behavior was a personal threat to him both as a man and a father. He began to develop projects in which the boy could find gratification in building simple things while sharing his father's company. Kenny enjoyed these times with his father and eagerly looked forward to them.

As the months went by, the "bouncing" became less and less necessary and the gestures of "big boy" or "baby" were sufficient to aid Kenny in controlling his impulses. Kenny now spent more time with his father. He began "shaving" with him in the morning and imitated in many ways the father's activities and mannerisms.

Kenny's "identification" with his father brought another interesting change. To lead up to that change, from three years of age on, Kenny showed preoccupations with various objects. First, as he learned to scribble, he became overattached to pencils. Wherever he was, whenever he saw one, he would seize it and begin scribbling with it. When Kenny was taught at school how to brush his teeth, his fascination shifted from pencils to toothbrushes. Each time the family visited someone's house, Kenny would dash into the bathroom to use the toothbrushes there. Later the fascination shifted to keys. He would sneak into his parents' bedroom and make off with any or all of his father's keys. Some mornings his father would be furious because Kenny had made him late for work by running off with the ignition key. Along with his attraction to keys, he was enchanted by cars. Walking down a street, he had to touch each new car he saw. Whenever he saw a toy model of a car, he nagged his parents for it. When he became frustrated and angry, he would break whichever object fascinated him at that particular time. As Kenny identified increasingly with his father, his preoccupation with taking keys diminished. Instead, he was satisfied to have his own set of keys, "like Daddy's." He also came to tolerate seeing model cars without insisting that they be purchased for him, and he could walk past a new car on the street without touching it and merely gestured that it was new.

In my discussions with the parents, we also worked on Kenny's hyperdistractibility and his difficulty in foregoing immediate gratification of his wishes. The approaches I suggested to the parents were the same as I used in the therapy sessions. The hyperdistractibility was handled by helping him not to deviate from his intended goal. For example, he would indicate that he had to urinate and be on his way to the bathroom, only to be distracted by something and never get there. At such a time, he would be shown, through gesture, that first he should go to the bathroom and then he could pursue the other activity. After this type of external structuring went on for a number of months, Kenny himself proudly would gesture the sequence of activities to those around him, without being distracted. Still later, he was able to pursue a goal to completion even without gesturing.

Designating the sequence of activities also helped him to delay gratifying his wishes. For example, he was told that big boys do not just take; first they ask for what they want. That led into helping him accept the concept that part of growing up is knowing we just cannot have everything we want. It also led into helping him accept the fact that he had to earn many of the things he wanted, either by first showing big-boy responsibility, or by earning money in little jobs around the house.

Along with Kenny's other improvements, he also began showing an interest in learning to communicate. Within a year's time he learned and retained a good fund of gestures and even a few actual words.[5] His ability to write words increased noticeably. As his interest grew and as success came, he was able to concentrate on schoolwork quite well. He no longer showed hyperdistractibility and hyperactivity while in class.

Now let us turn to Kenny's behavior during his therapy sessions.

[5] Not being familiar with aphasic children, the speech therapist remained convinced during all the time she worked with Kenny that he was severely deaf. It was proven later that this was not the case. Aphasia, not hearing loss, was the primary cause of his not being able to speak. Had she been trained to work with aphasic children, Kenny's over-all progress would most likely have been substantially accelerated.

Therapy started when he was eight years and four months of age. For the first six months, I saw him twice a week, and for the next year and a half, once a week. In the beginning Kenny's behavior during these sessions was primarily destructive. His interest was confined to toy cars and trucks, which he would run back and forth vigorously, only to smash them suddenly underfoot. Without any sign of remorse or a glance at me, Kenny would indicate that the car or truck was broken, and he would throw it out. When given a new car he would be very pleased with its newness and shininess and would want to share his pleasure with me. When the car was no longer shiny he would polish it with his saliva and his sleeve, or put Scotch tape over its surface in order to pretend that it was new and shiny again. Then he would bring it to me to be admired. In short order he would nevertheless suddenly smash it. In his ambivalence toward the car, his using it as an object for his hostility always won out. When he was not being destructive, he showed a great deal of pleasure in being able to control the movements of the cars. He would back them up, make them turn sharply, make them speed around obstacles, and so on. All the while he would keep his eyes down on the level of the car so as to make his fantasy of driving the car more realistic.

That period of his play was also characterized by his wanting to take home with him whatever caught his fancy. When I would indicate it was time for us to stop, Kenny would seize an object and dash out with it. He might take a pad of paper, a paper clip, a railroad timetable, a car, or just about anything. During that same period of time he would crunch hard candy voraciously during his sessions.

I made no attempt initially to help Kenny curb either his acquisitive or destructive wishes, because I thought that he was enacting with me his wish for the giving, good parent who would not retaliate and whom he could incorporate. After several months he began looking at me with a sheepish smile when he smashed a car, and I communicated to Kenny through gestures that I knew how much he liked the new cars and was sorry he smashed them. A bit later I communicated that I would not let him smash the cars because he would feel bad afterwards and would have no shiny car until I had a chance to get a new one. Gradually Kenny began to inhibit his destructiveness and finally merely signaled his intention to destroy so that I could intervene. He would smile happily then. His signaling his intention to destroy and my intervention became a game that was repeated many, many times. Through this game Kenny did gain mastery over his destructive impulses, which seemed to have been a defense against his fear of being "smashed and broken" by his father. This type of play recalls Freud's statement (1920) about the ego gaining mastery through turning a passive situation in which one is overwhelmed into a situation of action and preparedness.

After such games had gone on for a while, Kenny turned to the miniature life dolls. He would pull off their arms and legs, indicating to me that I should cry in order to show that I was sorry. My crying would at first send him into gales of laughter. Later he would ask me to fix the dolls. He also began discovering minute defects in the cars. For example, a speck of plastic had run over on the wheelbase of one car, and this made it "broken." He would want me to "fix" it for him. When I indicated that Kenny wished that the cars or dolls were broken instead of himself, he vigorously denied it. As it happened, during that time Kenny had an accident with his bicycle. (He had learned to ride a bicycle which had training wheels.) He lost control of it, smashed into a wall, and broke his collarbone. When I first saw him after the accident, he indicated through gestures that the bone was broken and that the doctor, a very good man, had fixed it for him. I indicated that he did not like to have the broken bone and was glad to have it fixed. He agreed heartily. In the following weeks I then had the opportunity to point out to him that *he* did not like to feel broken, as he showed in his anger at not being able to ride a bicycle without training wheels, at not being able to build models as his brother did, at not being able to talk, and at having to wear a hearing aid (which many times he had refused to wear when he came into session). Because he did not want to feel that he was broken, he would rather the car or doll be broken. Although Kenny made no overt response to such interpretations, his play entered a new phase.

Kenny brought in a book from school. In the book he showed me a story about a child whose father was reading the newspaper and fell asleep. The child sneaked up on the father and said, "Boo!" This startled the father and he shook his finger at the child, saying, "You naughty boy!" In playing out the story Kenny at first wanted me to be the father. As I shook my finger at him, he would laugh. Later he reversed the roles. In this play Kenny used the role of the boy to assimilate the anxiety (Peller, 1954; Waelder, 1932) associated with his earlier hostility for which he had received more than ample punishment at the hand of his father. In the play, it was a relief to find that even though father was angry at him, nothing terrible resulted; i.e., he was not castrated. In playing the role of the father, Kenny employed, apparently for the first time, the defense of identification with the aggressor (A. Freud, 1936): Kenny did the admonishing instead of being the bad boy who got hurt by his father. That role also provided him with the gratification of not being defective, of being able to hear. In the months that followed, Kenny brought in many stories which gave him an opportunity to deny his feeling of being hurt or damaged, and which allowed him to identify with the aggressor.[6] His mother also reported that at home he would admonish her by calling her a baby when he had done something wrong, as though anticipating her admonition.

During those months I asked the mother to come and participate in the play also.[7] My purpose in doing so was to help her develop a better relationship with Kenny by understanding what he was struggling with at that particular time (his ways of handling his fears about his earlier beatings and his dread of being defective) so that she could help him with similar behavior at home. I also hoped that her participating in the play would aid in the fusion and neutralization of his aggressive energy, making it available for ego use (A. Freud, 1949, p. 41f.; Kris, 1950, p. 35). The opportunity for bringing the mother into the play occurred naturally. When Kenny began playing out the "naughty boy" story, he was so delighted that he wanted his mother to see him playing it and invited her in. At first she was tense and uneasy about participating, but as she understood his play as a means of working out his fears, she entered into it readily. Kenny, in turn, showed genuine affection toward his mother for participating

6 Another reason for that type of play seemed to be that it furnished him with still another opportunity to deny his defectiveness through being able to read. Each time he brought in a new story, he would read it to me in his "scribble speech," pointing to each word. Later on, when he stopped bringing in that type of story, he delighted in showing me how well he did his homework. When he finished the homework, he would gesture how smart he was.

7 For a discussion of the mother's entering into the therapeutic situation, see Schwarz (1950).

in the play, and his affection also carried over into the home. That seemed to contribute to his needing less and less external prohibition in order to maintain control over his impulses. He then also lost interest in the candy which was available to him in the office and showed less interest in taking things home with him on leaving.

Kenny's controls developed to the point where he was able to go to an amusement park without being overwhelmed and without dashing madly into all the enticing concessions. Instead, when he was interested in a concession, he would excitedly ask permission to go.

During that same period of time, Kenny also began showing reaction formations to his hostility. He showed pity for those who were sick or injured. Whereas previously he delighted in his mother's being ill, in his brother's being hurt, or in his brother's getting injections of insulin, Kenny no longer laughed gleefully in such situations but showed compassion. Similarly, if he stained his underpants, he was disgusted. He also began smelling his clothing, rejecting any that did not smell clean. In addition, he started taking some interest in keeping his belongings in a fairly orderly fashion.

After having worked with me for a year and a half, Kenny was able to spend the summer at an overnight camp for cerebral palsied children. While there he gained a few new motor skills, got along well with the other boys, and became quite popular. When he returned home, he showed only token hostility to his mother for having been separated from her. This was followed by a show of more than usual affection.

When Kenny returned from camp, he entered a stage of trying to show his prowess. Whereas previously he had displayed only vestigial indications of phallic aggressiveness—in his preoccupation with pencils, toothbrushes, keys, and cars, and in his coming out of his room and intruding on his parents instead of going to sleep at night —he now was intent on being big and strong, of flexing his muscles and performing feats of strength. He also began to show pride in his intellectual accomplishments at school. In both cases he wanted particularly to impress his mother with his feats and gain her praise through them. He also liked hugging her and noted that she had a bosom and men did not.

Therapy with Kenny and counseling his parents were terminated after twenty-five months in preparation for Kenny's going to the Aphasic Unit of the Central Institute for the Deaf, in St. Louis, in order to receive speech therapy. Even though I no longer see him for therapy, I have seen him on occasion as a "friend," and his parents have kept me posted on his progress.

I do not mean to give the impression that Kenny's growth was continuous or that it was a positively accelerated curve without peaks and valleys. It was not. During the two-year course of his development described above, he showed many discouraging, but temporary, setbacks. For about six months after he stopped therapy, he occasionally started to aim a hostile outburst at his mother but did not follow through. These abortive outbursts appeared to be triggered by situations in which he felt inadequate; i.e., he felt others were demonstrating their prowess or showing their adequacy, whereas he could not do likewise. Helping him to understand that he too could become proficient in many skills, if he only practiced them enough, aided in aborting the outbursts. For the past six months Kenny's controls have been as good as would be expected of a child of his age.

Kenny's sense of adequacy has been greatly enhanced and his controls stabilized by his learning to speak while at the Central Institute. Though he had a working vocabulary of less than six words at ten and a half years of age—after a total of six years of speech therapy—with the help of Central Institute's special methods (McGinnis, Kleffner, Goldstein, 1956), he learned in only five months' time to speak and to write seventy-five words and to put them together into sentences! This was accomplished without the use of a hearing aid, and without his having to learn gestures as an intermediary step to speech. As Kenny became able to say words at will, he showed a great eagerness to learn more words. Even though in the year he has been taught by Central Institute's methods he still does not have full command of speech, being able to talk has given him an obvious sense of accomplishment and pride, the equal of which he never showed when he learned to make gestures. Being able to speak has fostered in Kenny a greater sense of identity. This in turn has enabled him to internalize parental wishes more completely, so that he shows, for example, a sense of pride when he is cooperative and well mannered.

DISCUSSION

During his first three years of life, Kenny did not walk or talk; he did not comprehend adequately; he did not show normal interest in or perception of his environment; and he was unusually passive and phlegmatic. These are signs that his ego apparatuses of motility, language, perception, and intention (Hartmann, 1939) had not matured in accord with the normal timetable. Unlike the average child, he therefore was not born with the intact ego apparatuses which serve as the primary guarantees of the organism's adaptation to its environment (Hartmann, 1939, 1952; Erikson, 1937, 1940).[8] The lack of intactness of these primary ego apparatuses in turn fostered a lack of responsiveness on the part of his mother, thus interfering with his first stage, the mutuality phase (Erikson, 1950, 1953) of ego development. Had Kenny been born a normally alert and responsive child, he would have stimulated in his mother the natural desire to interact with him more, thereby aiding his further ego development. If Kenny had been a normal baby, he would have been the wished-for extension of the mother, which would have further enhanced the likelihood of her providing him with the necessary stimulus nutriment (Rapaport, 1958a) for further ego growth. However, as is evident from her becoming able to manage Kenny effectively as she could admit her anger toward him, without resolving the unconscious roots of that anger (see footnote 4 above), the mother's unconscious conflicts played only a small, secondary role in her difficulties with him. Unlike the mothers described by Rank (1949; Rank and Mac-Naughton, 1950), Kenny's mother *was capable* of a giving relationship with her child, but the instrumentation of that capacity was obstructed by Kenny's not having the necessary ego intactness to stimulate it. Hence Kenny's ego development was impeded primarily by his not being equipped at birth with the primary givens that insure adaptation and only secondarily by his mother's unconscious reaction to his defectiveness. But both together contributed to his not developing a sense of being "all right," the basis for developing a sense of identity (Erikson, 1950).

[8] For a discussion of Hartmann's and Erikson's concepts of the primary and secondary apparatuses of ego autonomy, see Rapaport (1956, 1958a, 1958b).

During his early years, one congenitally inadequate ego apparatus, the apparatus of motility, in particular would seem to have
played the major role in impeding his development. Unlike other
toddlers, Kenny did not experience the pure pleasure of functioning
and of being able to master new functions. He did not experience
the stature of "one who can walk"—as Erikson (1950) puts it—nor
could he get parental confirmation of being such a one. This certainly interfered with the natural development of an early sense of
self-esteem and the development of identity. The inadequacy of his
motor apparatus was also a road block to an important avenue of
developing other ego functions. At any given early age Kenny did not
have the normal motor development required for exploring the environment and for differentiating between himself and the external
world; nor did he have the fine coordination with which to get added
information about the environment so as to test reality better and to
widen his scope of interests and pleasures. Hence his inadequate
motor apparatus interfered with his developing the ego functions of
mastery, integration, reality testing, and control of impulses (Mittelmann, 1954, 1957).

It is interesting that the first time he mastered an object, when
he learned to scribble with a pencil, he became preoccupied with it.
It is as though he had to keep repeating the new-found gratifications
of motor mastery and maternal praise. Because of his faulty motor
and perceptual apparatuses, it seems as though Kenny had not
learned to distinguish clearly between himself and his mother, and
in hoarding the object and repeatedly deriving pleasure through it
he was attempting to introject the good mother into himself. His
seizing and hoarding the cherished objects only to break them and
throw them away whenever frustrated would seem to reflect Kenny's
ambivalence toward his mother (Hartmann, Kris, Loewenstein,
1946): breaking them representing projection of the bad mother.
Later on, even at eight to nine years of age, he apparently did not
yet have an adequately differentiated self-image, because whenever
he could not have what he wanted or could not succeed in accomplishing what he was striving to do, he would hit or kick his mother.

His newly developing sense of ego identity was further interfered
with just when he began to find increased gratification through his
mother's teaching him motor skills: he was suddenly separated from

her, he feared losing her love when he would not consent to be toilet trained, and he feared castration and abandonment (Mittelmann, 1954) when beaten and restrained because he would not consent to go to bed. Thus, at a time when he was really just starting the process of achieving a sense of identity, he suffered all these traumatic restrictions on his budding self-expressions. The behavioral disturbance which followed would seem more likely due to Kenny's attempt to preserve his embryonic ego identity than to any organic drivenness. As Erikson (1950, p. 212) has stated, just as an animal defends itself with astounding strength when attacked, so will a child when deprived of all the forms of expression which allow him to develop and to integrate the next step in his ego identity, for "in the social jungle of human existence there is no feeling of being alive without a sense of ego identity." Hence, by means of his disturbed behavior he was trying to ward off being swamped by external demands so that he could survive as a psychic entity. When his mother tried to force him to be toilet trained, his *refusal* to be toilet trained was carried over to his *refusal* to go to bed and to his *refusal* to comply with the teacher's (a mother substitute) requests—all being manifestations of the same retaliatory wish toward his mother for the threat which she posed (Fraiberg, 1950). His fighting at bedtime and his banging his head even when restrained were also attempts to ward off the same threat, the head banging probably also being a substitute for attacking his father (Mittelmann, 1954, 1957). When Kenny was able to give up refusing to go to bed and refusing to defecate in the toilet, he did. But in doing so he became increasingly hostile, negativistic, and demanding, which continued until he achieved a better sense of identity and a more adequate ego organization during therapy.

To summarize Kenny's problem, he was born with damaged ego apparatuses, without the intact function of which it is difficult to develop a sense of ego identity. In addition to the failure to develop a feeling of self-esteem at the usual time of life, when he did begin to find some gratification in achievement and in showing some beginning signs of phallic aggressiveness, he was so traumatized that he developed a fear of abandonment and castration. That served to reinforce and solidify his feeling of defectiveness. The behavioral disturbance which he developed as a means of protecting his budding identity was nonadaptive and only further impeded development.

In the initial stage of therapy, both through the changes brought about in the mother herself and through his relationship with me, Kenny was helped to work through his ambivalence toward his mother. His anal-sadistic wishes, as evidenced in his destroying cars and throwing them away and in his negativism toward his mother, waned. His oral-sadistic demandingness of his mother and his having to get everything he wanted also diminished. In time he was better able to see his mother as an individual and not as an omnipotent extension of himself. He began to obey her more and show affection toward her. Apparently he began to fuse his hostile and libidinal impulses, thereby binding and partially neutralizing his hostile impulses, so as to be able to form a libidinal attachment to her.

During that same period of time, the father was no longer punitive and spent considerable time with Kenny, teaching him various motor skills which were masculine in nature. Kenny delighted in these new achievements. He then began imitating his father, forming a motor identification (Mittelmann, 1954, p. 156f.) with him. As he did so, he no longer had to *be* the father, by incorporating partial objects which represented the father. Instead he was able to be *like* the father; viz., his not having to steal his father's keys, but being able to have keys like his father's.

Kenny also began working out in play, during the initial stage of therapy, his castration fear by turning the passive role into an active one. The nature of his destructiveness indicated that in the face of the trauma his beginning phallic aggressive wishes had regressed to an anal-sadistic level, but it was still primarily the castration fear he was dealing with. Hence, in his play *Kenny* did the smashing, at the same time showing his wish to be the father in his agile maneuvering of the cars. He attempted to work through the same fear in his pulling off the extremities of the dolls and wanting me to fix them; that is, make them not castrated, but whole.

Soon after therapy began, his mother, his father, and I, all related to him so as to supply his faulty ego apparatuses with the external structure they needed in order to develop. Whereas he did not have the ability for anticipation and delay, we supplied it for him by designating the sequence of activities. As he internalized that, he became less distractible and he was able to delay seeking gratification. Moreover, for the first time in his life, what was expected of him by his parents was communicated to him consistently and in a way which he comprehended.

As Kenny worked out his ambivalence to his mother and developed a healthier libidinal attachment to her, as he identified with his father, as he worked through his castration fear, and as he developed the means for anticipation and delay, as well as a clear and consistent idea of parental expectation, his ego controls grew steadily stronger. Hyperactivity and hyperdistractibility diminished, and he had sufficient neutralized energy available for concentrating in school and learning his work well.

In his next developmental step, Kenny employed the defense of identification with the aggressor, which paved the way for his internalizing parental demands and developing his superego (A. Freud, 1949, p. 124f.). With that he was able to control his impulses even under seductive circumstances, such as an amusement park. He then also manifested reaction formation against his anal-sadistic impulses: compassion, disgust with dirt, and neatness—substantial ego and superego achievements.

After these reaction formations were established Kenny displayed strong and widespread phallic aggressive wishes. It seems as though his libidinal development progressed only after his ego development had reached the stage at which it should have been normally when the libido reaches its phallic stage. We may speculate that he would have entered fully into the phallic stage if he had not suffered the traumata just as the phallic impulses were emerging, but in view of all the help his ego needed in order to develop, that seems doubtful.[9]

Even though Kenny's ego controls developed greatly during the two years of therapy, they were not truly stabilized until he overcame his aphasia. This is understandable in that overcoming it greatly enhanced his self-esteem and also contributed substantially to the consolidation of his ego. It is indeed doubtful whether Kenny would

[9] In Kenny, as in many other brain-damaged children, libidinal development seemed to be arrested along with ego development and to progress along with it. Although Kenny did show vestiges of phallic aggressiveness, the phallic impulses were not really evident until his ego was quite developed. This is in contrast to the psychogenically ego-disturbed child who appears to have a fragmented or disturbed ego development but whose libido shows evidence of all stages of psychosexual development. Even though the libidinal development is not integrated, it is there, in apparent contrast to many of the brain-damaged children I have seen. This apparent contrast presents an interesting problem for further research.

have had so severe a behavioral disturbance if he had been helped
to overcome his aphasia around four years of age. On the other hand,
if he had received only speech therapy appropriate for deaf children
—even though he did show a high-frequency hearing loss—and therefore had not overcome his aphasia, in all likelihood he would not
have achieved the ego intactness he now shows.

CONCLUSION

The damage to Kenny's brain tissue in itself did not cause an
irrevocable enslavement to his hostile impulses and ultimately did
not prevent his gaining autonomy from them. Control of his impulses was commensurate with his ego development, which was
brought about by psychoanalytically oriented psychotherapy in conjunction with the McGinnis method of speech therapy for aphasia
and techniques designed to structure his innately faulty primary ego
apparatuses.

Whether or not most brain-damaged children, or even most
aphasic children, would respond to similar handling could be determined only by further research. However, in a number of children
having congenital brain damage, which Kenny exemplifies, approaching their rehabilitation from the standpoint of ego psychology has
been fruitful.

Perhaps the time is nearing when those who have been concerned
with the brain-damaged child will enlarge their scope sufficiently to
view him from the framework of ego development. For example, the
symptoms which Myklebust (1954) recognizes as associated with the
aphasic child's *lack of organismic integrity* could be considerably
amplified and clarified if examined in terms of the concepts developed by Hartmann, Kris, Erikson, and Rapaport. Similarly, in
their new book, Strauss and Kephart (1954) emphasize the importance not only of considering all the possible effects of brain injury
on the total organism but also of considering the effect of the injury
"upon the development which is in process and the effect upon the
organism which will eventually result from the deviation of this
development" (p. 1). They trace the brain-damaged child's disturbances to dysfunctions of such basic processes as perception, language,
and concept formation. What they are discussing is the epigenesis of

the nervous system and its effect on the organism's later activities. Perhaps it is not a giant step from the epigenesis of the nervous system to Erikson's concepts of the epigenesis of the ego (1937, 1939, 1940, 1950), so that the damaged cognitive processes which they discuss could be viewed as the ego's primary apparatuses of autonomy. To combine their work, together with that of Hebb (1949), Piaget (1924, 1927a, 1927b, 1936, 1937), Richter (1941), Gottschalk (1956), and others, into the conceptual matrix of ego psychology would not only enhance our knowledge of the cognitive and behavioral distortions of the brain-damaged child, but would also further our knowledge of cognitive and behavioral structures in general.

Summary

Kenny's congenital brain damage manifested itself in athetosis, aphasia, and faulty ego apparatuses in general. His faulty ego apparatuses, which resulted from the congenital brain damage, and environmental punishment and restriction, interacted to cause a hostile and impulsive behavioral disturbance. Hence, it was necessary to help him structure those faulty ego apparatuses and work through his emotional conflicts arising from the aforementioned traumata in order for him to develop adequate ego function and a sense of identity. That was achieved through the aid of psychotherapy and counseling the parents, conjoined with the McGinnis method of speech therapy for aphasia and techniques designed to provide external structure to his faulty primary ego apparatuses. In so doing, his hostile and impulsive behavioral disturbance was overcome.

BIBLIOGRAPHY

C.P. = *Collected Papers*

P.S.C. = *The Psychoanalytic Study of the Child*, Volumes 1–25, New York: International Universities Press, 1945–1970; Volumes 26–30, New Haven: Yale University Press, 1971–1975.

S.E. = *The Standard Edition of the Complete Psychological Works of Sigmund Freud*, 24 Volumes. London: Hogarth Press, 1953–1974.

W. = *The Writings of Anna Freud*, 7 Volumes. New York: International Universities Press, 1968–1974.

ARTHUR, G. (1947), A Point Scale of Performance Tests, Revised Form 2. New York: Psychological Corporation.

BARTEMEIER, L. H. (1932), Some Observations on Convulsive Disorders in Children. *Amer. J. Orthopsychiat.*, 2:260–267.

BEACH, F. (1948), *Hormones and Behavior.* New York: Hoeber.

BECK, H. L. (1959), Counselling Parents of Retarded Children. *Children*, 6:225–230.

BELL, A. I. (1961), Some Observations on the Role of the Scrotal Sac and Testicles. *J. Amer. Psa. Assn.*, 9:261–286.

——— (1964), Bowel Training Difficulties in Boys. *J. Amer. Acad. Child Psychiat.*, 3:577–590.

——— (1965), The Significance of Scrotal Sac and Testicles for the Prepuberty Male. *Psa. Quart.*, 34:182–206.

BENDER, L. (1947), Childhood Schizophrenia. *Amer. J. Orthopsychiat.*, 17:40–56.

——— (1949), Psychological Problems of Children with Organic Brain Disease. *Amer. J. Orthopsychiat.*, 19:404–415.

——— (1952), *Child Psychiatric Techniques.* Springfield, Ill.: Thomas.

BENEDEK, T. (1950), Climacterium. *Psa. Quart.*, 19:1–27.

——— (1959), Parenthood as a Developmental Phase. *J. Amer. Psa. Assn.*, 7:389–417.

BERGMAN, P., & ESCALONA, S. K. (1949), Unusual Sensitivities in Very Young Children. *P.S.C.*, 3/4:333–352.

BERGMANN, T. (1945), Observation of Children's Reactions to Motor Restraint. *Nerv. Child*, 4:318–328.

——— & FREUD, A. (1965), *Children in the Hospital.* New York: Int. Univ. Press.

BETLHEIM, S., & HARTMANN, H. (1924), On Parapraxes in the Korsakow Psychosis. In: *Organization and Pathology of Thought*, ed. D. Rapaport. New York: Columbia Univ. Press, 1951, pp. 288–307.

BIBRING, G. L. (1959), Some Considerations of the Psychological Processes in Pregnancy. *P.S.C.*, 14:113–121.

303

BIBRING, G. L. ET AL. (1961), A Study of the Psychological Processes in Pregnancy and of the Earliest Mother-Child Relationships. *P.S.C.*, 16:9–72.

BICKFORD, R. G., DALY, D., & KEITH, H. M. (1953), Convulsive Effects of Light Stimulation in Children. *Amer. J. Dis. Child.* 86:170–183.

BIRCH, H., ed. (1964), *Brain Damage in Children.* Baltimore: Williams & Wilkins.

BLAU, A. (1936), Mental Changes Following Head Trauma in Children. *Arch. Neurol. Psychiat.*, 35:723–769.

BLOS, P. (1960), Comments on the Psychological Consequences of Cryptorchism. *P.S.C.*, 15:395–429.

BOWLBY, J., ROBERTSON, JAMES, & ROSENBLUTH, D. (1952), A Two-Year-Old Goes to Hospital. *P.S.C.*, 7:82–94.

BRADLEY, C. (1955), Organic Factors in the Psychopathology of Childhood. In: *Psychopathology of Childhood*, ed. P. H. Hoch & J. Zubin. New York: Grune & Stratton, pp. 82–104.

BURLINGHAM, D. (1951), Precursors of Some Psychoanalytic Ideas about Children in the Sixteenth and Seventeenth Centuries. *P.S.C.*, 6:244–254.

——— & FREUD, A. (1942), *Young Children in Wartime.* London: Allen & Unwin.

CALEF, V. (1959), Report of Panel: Psychological Consequences of Physical Illness in Childhood. *J. Amer. Psa. Assn.*, 7:155–162.

CATTELL, P. (1947), *The Measurement of Intelligence of Infants and Young Children.* New York: Psychological Corporation.

COLEMAN, L. L. (1950), The Psychologic Implications of Tonsillectomy. *N.Y. State J. Med.*, 50(1):1225–1228.

COMFORT, A. (1960), Darwin and Freud. *Lancet*, 2:107–110.

CONNELL, L. F. (1953), Tonsils: In or Out? *Parents Mag.*, 28:40–44.

DEUTSCH, H. (1942), Some Psychoanalytic Observations on Surgery. *Psychosom. Med.*, 4:105–115.

——— (1945), *The Psychology of Women*, Vol. 2. New York: Grune & Stratton.

DI GEORGE, A., & WARKANY, J. (1959), The Endocrine System. In: *Textbook of Pediatrics*, ed. W. E. Nelson. Philadelphia: Saunders, 7th ed., pp. 1150–1204.

DOLL, E. A. (1947), *Vineland Social Maturity Scale.* Philadelphia: Educational Test Bureau.

DUBO, S. (1950), Psychiatric Study of Children with Pulmonary Tuberculosis. *Amer. J. Orthopsychiat.*, 20:520–528.

EDELSTON, A. (1943), Separation Anxiety in Young Children. *Genet. Psychol. Monogr.*, 28:3–95.

EISSLER, K. R. (1955), *The Psychiatrist and the Dying Patient.* New York: Int. Univ. Press.

ENGEL, G. L. (1961), Is Grief a Disease? *Psychosom. Med.*, 23:18–22.

ERICKSON, F. H. (1958), Play Interviews for Four-Year-Old Hospitalized Children. *Child Develpm. Monogr.*, Vol. 23, No. 3.

ERIKSON, E. H. (1937), Configuration in Play. *Psa. Quart.*, 6:139–214.

——— (1939), Observations on Sioux Education. *J. Psychol.*, 7:101–156.

——— (1940), Problems of Infancy and Early Childhood. In: *Outline of Abnormal Psychology*, ed. G. Murphy & A. Bachrach. New York: Modern Library, 1954, pp. 714–730.

——— (1950), *Childhood and Society.* New York: Norton.

——— (1953) Growth and Crisis of the "Healthy Personality." In: *Personality in Nature, Society, and Culture*, ed. C. Kluckhohn & H. A. Murray. New York: Knopf, pp. 185–225.

——— (1956), The Problem of Ego Identity. *J. Amer. Psa. Assn.*, 4:56–121.

ESCALONA, S. K. (1949), The Psychological Situation of Mother and Child upon Return from the Hospital. In: Senn (1949), pp. 30–51.

FAUST, O. A. ET AL. (1952), *Reducing Emotional Trauma in Hospitalized Children* [A Report by Departments of Pediatrics and Anesthesiology]. Albany, N.Y.: Albany Medical College.

FENICHEL, O. (1936), The Symbolic Equation: Girl = Phallus. *C.P.*, 2:3–18. New York: Norton, 1954.

FINEMAN, A. D. (1959), Preliminary Observations on Ego Development in Children with Congenital Defects of the Genitourinary System. *Amer. J. Orthopsychiat.*, 29:110–120.

FORD, C. S., & BEACH, F. A. (1952), *Patterns of Sexual Behavior.* New York: Harper.

FORRER, G. R. (1959), The Mother of a Defective Child. *Psa. Quart.*, 28:59–63.

FORSTER, F. M. (1945), Action of Acetylcholine on Motor Cortex. *Arch. Neurol. Psychiat.*, 54:391–394.

FRAIBERG, S. (1950), On Sleep Disturbances of Early Childhood. *P.S.C.*, 5:285–309.

———— (1960), Homosexual Conflicts. In: *Adolescents*, ed. S. Lorand & H. I. Schneer. New York: Hoeber, pp. 78–112.

FREUD, A. (1936), *The Ego and the Mechanisms of Defense.* New York: Int. Univ. Press, 1946.

———— (1949), Aggression in Relation to Emotional Development. *P.S.C.*, 3/4:37–48.

———— (1952), The Role of Bodily Illness in the Mental Life of Children. *P.S.C.*, 7:69–81.

———— (1952a), The Mutual Influences in the Development of Ego and Id. *P.S.C.*, 7:42–50.

———— (1953), Film Review: A Two-Year-Old Goes to Hospital. *W.*, 4:280–292.

———— (1954), In: Problems of Infantile Neurosis. *P.S.C.*, 9:16–71.

———— (1961), Answering Pediatricians' Questions. *W.*, 5:379–406.

———— (1975), Remarks on Receiving the C. Anderson Aldrich Award. *Pediatrics*, 56:332–334.

———— & BURLINGHAM, D. (1943), *War and Children.* New York: Int. Univ. Press.

FREUD, S. (1900), The Interpretation of Dreams. *S.E.*, 4 & 5.

———— (1905), Three Essays on the Theory of Sexuality. *S.E.*, 7:125–243.

———— (1911), Formulations on the Two Principles of Mental Functioning. *S.E.*, 12:213–226.

———— (1912), Contributions to the Psychology of Love. *C.P.*, 4:192–202.

———— (1914), On Narcissism. *S.E.*, 14:67–102.

———— (1915), The Unconscious. *S.E.*, 14:159–215.

———— (1917), Mourning and Melancholia. *S.E.*, 14:237–260.

———— (1920), Beyond the Pleasure Principle. *S.E.*, 18:7–64.

———— (1923), The Ego and the Id. *S.E.*, 19:3–66.

———— (1923a), The Infantile Genital Organization of the Libido. *C.P.*, 2:244–249.

———— (1926), Inhibitions, Symptoms and Anxiety. *S.E.*, 20:77–175.

———— (1928), Dostoevsky and Parricide. *S.E.*, 21:175–196.

FRIES, M. E. (1946), The Child's Ego Development and the Training of Adults in His Environment. *P.S.C.*, 2:85–112.

GOTTSCHALK, L. A. (1953), Effects of Intensive Psychotherapy on Epileptic Children. *Arch. Neurol. Psychiat.*, 70:361–384.

———— (1955), Psychologic Conflict and Paroxysmal EEG Patterns. *Arch. Neurol. Psychiat.*, 73:656–662.

———— (1956), The Relationship of Psychologic State and Epileptic Activity. *P.S.C.*, 11:352–380.

GREENACRE, P. (1944), Infant Reactions to Restraint. *Trauma, Growth, and Personality*. New York: Norton, 1952, pp. 83–105.

———— (1947), Vision, Headache and the Halo. *Psa. Quart.*, 16:177–194.

———— (1952), Some Factors Producing Different Types of Pregenital and Genital Organization. In: *Trauma, Growth, and Personality*. New York: Norton, pp. 293–302.

———— (1953), Certain Relationships between Fetishism and Faulty Development of the Body Image. *P.S.C.*, 8:79–98.

———— (1954). In: Problems of Infantile Neurosis. *P.S.C.*, 9:16–71.

———— (1955), Further Considerations Regarding Fetishism. *P.S.C.*, 10:187–194.

———— (1956), Re-evaluation of the Process of Working Through. *Int. J. Psa.*, 37:439–444.

GREENSON, R. R. (1944), On Genuine Epilepsy. *Psa. Quart.*, 13:139–159.

HAMPSON, J., & MONEY, J. (1955), Idiopathic Sexual Precocity in the Male. *Psychosom. Med.*, 17:1–35.

HARTMANN, H. (1939), *Ego Psychology and the Problem of Adaptation.* New York: Int. Univ. Press, 1958.

———— (1950), Comments on the Psychoanalytic Theory of the Ego. *P.S.C.*, 5:74–96.

———— (1952), The Mutual Influences in the Development of Ego and Id. *P.S.C.*, 7:9–30.

———— KRIS, E., & LOEWENSTEIN, R. M. (1946), Comments on the Formation of Psychic Structure. *P.S.C.*, 2:11–38.

HEBB, D. O. (1949), *The Organization of Behavior*. New York: Wiley.

HEILBRUNN, G. (1950), Psychodynamic Aspects of Epilepsy. *Psa. Quart.*, 19:145–157.

HENDRIK, I. (1949), Discussion. In: Senn (1949), p. 119.

HOFFER, W. (1950), Oral Aggressiveness and Ego Development. *Int. J. Psa.*, 31:156–160.

HUBBLE, D. (1963), The Psyche and the Endocrine System. *Lancet*, 2:209–214.

HUNT, J. McV., & COFER, C. N. (1944), Psychological Deficit. In: *Personality and the Behavior Disorders*. New York: Ronald Press, 2:971–1032.

HUSCHKA, M., & OGDEN, O. S. (1938), The Conduct of a Pediatric Prophylaxis Clinic. *J. Pediat.*, 12:794–800.

JACKSON, E. B. (1942), Treatment of the Young Child in the Hospital. *Amer. J. Orthopsychiat.*, 12:56–63.

JACKSON, K. (1951), Psychologic Preparation as Method of Reducing Emotional Trauma of Anesthesia in Children. *Anesthesiology*, 12:293–300.

———— ET AL. (1952), Problem of Emotional Trauma in the Hospital Treatment of Children. *J. Amer. Med. Assn.*, 149:1536–1538.

———— ———— (1953), Behavior Changes Indicating Emotional Trauma in Tonsillectomized Children. *Pediatrics*, 12:23–28.

JACOBSON, E. (1954), The Self and the Object World. *P.S.C.*, 9:75–127.

JANIS, I. L. (1958a), *Psychological Stress*. New York: Wiley.

———— (1958b), Emotional Inoculation. In: *Psychoanalysis and the Social Sciences*, 5:119–154. New York: Int. Univ. Press.

JESSNER, L., BLOM, G. E., & WALDFOGEL, S. (1952), Emotional Implications of Tonsillectomy and Adenoidectomy on Children. *P.S.C.*, 7:126–169.

———— & KAPLAN, S. (1949), Reactions of Children to Tonsillectomy and Adenoidectomy. In: Senn (1949), pp. 97–118.

JOLLY, H. (1955), *Sexual Precocity*. Oxford: Blackwell.

KAHN, E., & COHEN, L. C. (1934), Organic Drivenness. *New Eng. J. Med.*, 210:748–756.

KAPLAN, S. (1952), Discussion of "A Child's Reaction to Adenoidectomy." In: *Case Histories in Psychosomatic Medicine*, ed. H. W. Miles, S. Cobb, & H. C. Shands. New York: Norton, pp. 178–188.

KAVKA, J. (1962), Ego Synthesis of a Life-Threatening Illness in Childhood. *P.S.C.*, 17:344–362.

KENNARD, M. A. (1959), The Characteristics of Thought Disturbances as Related to Electroencephalographic Findings in Children and Adolescents. *Amer. J. Psychiat.*, 115:911–912.

KLEBANOFF, S. G., SINGER, J. L., & WILENSKY, H. (1954), Psychological Consequences of Brain Lesions and Ablations. *Psychol. Bull.*, 51:1–41.

KRIS, E. (1950), Notes on the Development and on Some Current Problems of Psychoanalytic Child Psychology. *P.S.C.*, 5:24–46.

—— (1955), Personal communication.

LANDIS, C. (1949), Psychologic Changes Following Topectomy. In: *Selective Partial Ablation of the Frontal Cortex*, ed. F. A. Mettler. New York: Hoeber, pp. 306–312.

LEUBA, J. (1950), 'Women Who Fall.' *Int. J. Psa.*, 31:6–7.

LEVY, D. M. (1928), Finger Sucking and Accessory Movements in Early Infancy. *Amer. J. Psychiat.*, 7:881–918.

—— (1944), On the Problem of Movement Restraint, Tics, Stereotyped Movements, Hyperactivity. *Amer. J. Orthopsychiat.*, 14:644–671.

—— (1945), Psychic Trauma of Operations in Children. *Amer. J. Dis. Child.*, 69:7–25.

LEWIN, B. D. (1933), The Body as Phallus. *Psa. Quart.*, 2:24–47.

LIBERSON, W. T. (1955), Emotional and Psychological Factors in Epilepsy. *Amer. J. Psychiat.*, 112:91–106.

LINDEMANN, E. (1941), Observations on Psychiatric Sequelae to Surgical Procedures in Women. *Amer. J. Psychiat.*, 98:132–139.

—— (1944), Symptomatology and Management of Acute Grief. *Amer. J. Psychiat.*, 101:141–149.

LUSSIER, A. (1960), The Analysis of a Boy with a Congenital Deformity. *P.S.C.*, 15:430–453.

McGINNIS, M., KLEFFNER, F. R., & GOLDSTEIN, R. (1956), Teaching Aphasic Children. *Volta Rev.*, 58.

MacKEITH, R. (1953), Children in Hospital. *Lancet*, 265:843–845.

MacLEAN, P. D. (1949), Psychosomatic Disease and the "Visceral Brain." *Psychosom. Med.*, 11:338–353.

—— (1952), Some Psychiatric Implications of Physiological Studies on Fronto-temporal Portion of Limbic System. *EEG Clin. Neurophysiol.*, 4:407–418.

MAHLER, M. S. (1952), On Child Psychosis and Schizophrenia. *P.S.C.*, 7:286–305.

—— & GOSLINER, B. J. (1955), On Symbiotic Child Psychosis. *P.S.C.*, 10: 195–212.

—— LUKE, J. A., & DALTROFF, W. (1945), Clinical and Follow-up Study of the Tic Syndrome in Children. *Amer. J. Orthopsychiat.*, 15:631–647.

MEERS, D. R. (1966), A Diagnostic Profile of Psychopathology in a Latency Child. *P.S.C.*, 21:483–526.

MENNINGER, K. A. (1934), Polysurgery and Polysurgical Addiction. *Psa. Quart.*, 3:173–199.

MICHAELS, J. J. (1943), Psychiatric Implications of Surgery. *Family*, 23:363–369.

MILLER, M. L. (1951), The Traumatic Effect of Surgical Operations in Childhood on the Integrative Functions of the Ego. *Psa. Quart.*, 20:77–92.

MITTELMANN, B. (1954), Motility in Infants, Children, and Adults. *P.S.C.*, 9:142–177.

MITTELMANN, B. (1957), Motility in the Therapy of Children and Adults. *P.S.C.*, 12:284–319.

MONEY, J., HAMPSON, J., & HAMPSON, J., (1955a), Hermaphroditism. *Bull. Johns Hopkins Hosp.*, 97:284-300.

—— —— —— (1955b), Sexual Incongruities and Psychopathology. *Bull. Johns Hopkins Hosp.*, 98:43–57.

MOORE, W. T. (1975), The Impact of Surgery on Boys. *P.S.C.*, 30:529–548.

MORRELL, F., & JASPER, H. H. (1956), Electrographic Studies of the Formation of Temporary Connections in the Brain. *EEG Clin. Neurophysiol.*, 8:201–216.

—— ROBERTS, L., & JASPER, H. H. (1956), Effect of Focal Epileptogenic Lesions and Their Ablation upon Conditioned Electrical Responses of the Brain in the Monkey. *EEG Clin. Neurophysiol.*, 8:217–236.

MYKLEBUST, H. R. (1954), *Auditory Disorders in Children*. New York: Grune & Stratton.

NIELSEN, J. M. (1946), *A Textbook of Clinical Neurology*. New York: Hoeber.

NOVACK, E. (1944), The Constitutional Type of Female Precocious Puberty. *Amer. J. Obst. & Gyn.*, 47:20–42.

OREMLAND, E. K., & OREMLAND, J. D., eds. (1973), *The Effects of Hospitalization on Children*. Springfield, Ill.: Thomas.

OSTOW, M. (1955), A Psychoanalytic Contribution to the Study of Brain Function, Part 2. *Psa. Quart.*, 24:383–423.

PAPEZ, J. W. (1937), A Proposed Mechanism of Emotion. *Arch. Neurol. Psychiat.*, 38:725–743.

PASCHKIS, K., RAKOFF, A., & CANTAROW, A. (1958), *Clinical Endocrinology*. London: Cassell.

PEARSON, G. H. J. (1941), Effect of Operative Procedures on the Emotional Life of the Child. *Amer. J. Dis. Child.*, 62:716–729.

PELLER, L. E. (1954), Libidinal Phases, Ego Development, and Play. *P.S.C.*, 9:178–198.

PENFIELD, W., & JASPER, H. (1954), *Epilepsy and the Functional Anatomy of the Human Brain*. Boston: Little, Brown.

—— & ROBERTS, L. (1959), *Speech and Brain Mechanisms*. Princeton: Princeton Univ. Press.

PETO, A. (1959), Body Image and Archaic Thinking. *Int. J. Psa.*, 40:223–231.

PIAGET, J. (1924), *Judgment and Reasoning in the Child*. New York: Harcourt, Brace, 1928.

—— (1927a), *The Child's Conception of the World*. New York: Harcourt, Brace, 1929.

—— (1927b), *The Child's Conception of Physical Causality*. New York: Harcourt, Brace, 1930.

—— (1936), *The Origins of Intelligence in Children*. New York: Int. Univ. Press, 1952.

—— (1937), *The Construction of Reality in the Child*. New York: Basic Books, 1954.

PICKERILL, C. M., & PICKERILL, H. P. (1954), Elimination of Hospital Cross-Infection in Children. *Lancet*, 266:425–428.

PILLSBURY, R. M. (1951), Children Can Be Helped to Face Surgery. *Child*, 15:122–124.

PLANK, E. N. (1971), *Working with Children in Hospitals*. Cleveland: Case Western Reserve Univ. Press, 2nd. ed.

—— & HORWOOD, C. (1961), Leg Amputation in a Four-Year-Old. *P.S.C.*, 16:405–422.

PROVENCE, S. (1961), Personal communication.

PRUGH, D. G., ET AL. (1952), A Study of Emotional Reactions of Children and Families to Hospitalization and Illness. *Amer. J. Orthopsychiat.*, 23:70–106, 1953.

RANK, B. (1949), Adaptations of the Psychoanalytic Technique for the Treatment of Young Children with Atypical Development. *Amer. J. Orthopsychiat.*, 19:130–139.
——— & MACNAUGHTON, D. (1950), A Clinical Contribution to Early Ego Development. *P.S.C.*, 5:53–65.
RAPAPORT, D., tr. & ed. (1951), *Organization and Pathology of Thought.* New York: Columbia Univ. Press.
——— (1956), Present-Day Ego Psychology. In: Rapaport (1967), pp. 594–623.
——— (1958a), The Theory of Ego Autonomy. In: Rapaport (1967), pp. 722–744.
——— (1958b), A Historic Survey of Psychoanalytic Ego Psychology. In: Rapaport (1967), pp. 745–758.
——— (1967), *The Collected Papers of David Rapaport*, ed. M. M. Gill. New York: Basic Books.
RAPPAPORT, S. R. (1951), The Role of Behavioral Accessibility in Intellectual Function of Psychotics. *J. Clin. Psychol.*, 7:335–340.
——— (1953), Intellectual Deficit in Organics and Schizophrenics. *J. Consult. Psychol.*, 17:389–395.
——— (1961), Behavior Disorder and Ego Development in a Brain-Injured Child. *P.S.C.*, 16:423–450.
REDL, F., & WINEMAN, D. (1951), *Children Who Hate.* Glencoe, Ill.: Free Press.
——— ——— (1952), *Controls From Within.* Glencoe, Ill.: Free Press.
REICH, A. (1954), Early Identifications as Archaic Elements in the Superego. *J. Amer. Psa. Assn.*, 2:218–238.
RICHTER, C. P. (1941), Biology of Drives. *Psychosom. Med.*, 3:105–110.
ROBERTSON, E. G. (1954), Photogenic Epilepsy. *Brain*, 77:232–251.
ROBERTSON, JAMES (1953), Film: *A Two-Year-Old Goes to Hospital.* London: Tavistock Clinic; New York: New York University Library.
——— (1953a), A Two-Year-Old Goes to the Hospital. *Nursing Times*, 49(1):388–393.
——— (1953b), Some Responses of Young Children to Loss of Maternal Care. *Nursing Times*, 49:382–386.
——— (1958), *Young Children in Hospital.* New York: Basic Books.
ROBERTSON, JOYCE (1956), A Mother's Observations on the Tonsillectomy of Her Four-Year-Old Daughter. *P.S.C.*, 11:410–433.
RUBIN, E. (1951), An Experiment in the Prediction of Children's Reactions to Stress by Means of Psychological Test Measures. Ph.D. Thesis, Boston University Graduate School.
SARVIS, M. A. (1960), Psychiatric Implications of Temporal Lobe Damage. *P.S.C.*, 15:454–481.
——— & GARCIA, B. (1960), Etiological Variables in Autism. *Psychiatry*, 24:307–317, 1961.
SCHILDER, P. (1935), *The Image and Appearance of the Human Body.* New York: Int. Univ. Press., 1950.
SCHWARZ, H. (1950), The Mother in the Consulting Room. *P.S.C.*, 5:343–357.
SENN, M. J. E. (1945), Emotional Aspects of Convalescence. *Child*, 10:24–38.
——— ed. (1949), *Problems of Infancy and Childhood: Transactions of the Third Conference.* New York: Josiah Macy, Jr. Foundation.
——— & SOLNIT, A. J. (1968), *Problems in Child Behavior and Development.* Philadelphia: Lea & Febiger.
SILVERMAN, D. (1944), The Electroencephalograph of Criminals. *Arch. Neurol. Psychiat.*, 52:38–42.
SOCARIDES, C. (1960), The Development of a Fetishistic Perversion. *J. Amer. Psa. Assn.*, 8:281–311.

SOLNIT, A. J. (1950), Hospitalization. *Amer. J. Dis. Child.*, 99:155–163.

———— & GREEN, M. (1959), Psychologic Considerations in the Management of Deaths on Pediatric Hospital Services. *Pediatrics*, 24:528–539.

———— & PROVENCE, S. A., eds. (1963), *Modern Perspectives in Child Development.* New York: Int. Univ. Press, see esp. Parts III & IV.

———— & STARK, M. (1959), Pediatric Management of School Learning Problems of Underachievement. *New Eng. J. Med.*, 261:988–993.

———— ———— (1961), Mourning and the Birth of a Defective Child. *P.S.C.*, 16:523–537.

SPENCE, J. C. (1946), *The Purpose of the Family.* London: Epworth Press.

———— (1947), Care of Children in Hospital. *Brit. Med. J.*, 1:125–130.

SPITZ, R. A. (1954). In: Problems of Infantile Neurosis. *P.S.C.*, 9:16–71.

STRAUSS, A. A., & KEPHART, N. C. (1954), *Psychopathology and Education of the Brain-Injured Child*, Vol. 2. New York: Grune & Stratton.

———— & LEHTINEN, L. E. (1947), *Psychopathology and Education of the Brain-Injured Child.* New York: Grune & Stratton.

SYMONDS, E. M. (1960), Precocious Sexual Development. *Report of the Adelaide Children's Hospital*, 3.

THOMAS, R. ET AL. (1963), The Search for a Sexual Identity in a Case of Constitutional Sexual Precocity. *P.S.C.*, 18:636–662.

TIMME, A. R. (1952), What Has Neurology to Offer Child Guidance? *Neurology*, 2:435–440.

WAELDER, R. (1932), The Psychoanalytic Theory of Play. *Psa. Quart.*, 2:208–224.

WEIL, A. P. (1953), Certain Severe Disturbances of Ego Development in Childhood. *P.S.C.*, 8:271–287.

———— (1958), Seminar held at the Institute of Philadelphia Association for Psychoanalysis.

WENDER, P. H. (1971), *Brain Dysfunction in Children.* New York: Wiley-Interscience.

WERNER, H. (1940), *Comparative Psychology of Mental Development.* New York: Int. Univ. Press, 1957.

WILKINS, L. (1948), Abnormalities and Variations of Sexual Development During Childhood and Adolescence. *Advances in Pediatrics*, 3:159–217.

———— (1957), *The Diagnosis and Treatment of Endocrine Disorders in Childhood and Adolescence.* Springfield: Thomas, 2nd ed.

WILLIAMS, D. (1953), A Study of Thalamic and Cortical Rhythms in Petit Mal. *Brain*, 76:50–69.

———— & PARSONS-SMITH, G. (1949), The Spontaneous Electrical Activity of the Human Thalamus. *Brain*, 72:450–482.

———— ———— (1951), Thalamic Activity in Stupor. *Brain*, 74:377–398.

WILSON, S. H. K. (1940), *Neurology*, Vol. 2. Baltimore: William Wood.

WINNICOTT, D. W. (1953), Transitional Objects and Transitional Phenomena. *Int. J. Psa.*, 34:89–97.

———— (1961), The Effect of Psychotic Parents on Emotional Development of the Child. *Brit. J. Psychiat. Soc. Work*, 6.

YAKOVLEV, R. I. (1948), Motility, Behavior, and the Brain. *J. Nerv. Ment. Dis.*, 107:313–335.

INDEX

Abreaction, 21–22
Accident proneness, 41–46, 104, 107–09, 122–24, 130, 133–34
  prior to surgery, 64, 77
Activity
  compensatory, 209
  in mastery of handicap, 200–18
  see also Passive into active
Actual neurosis, 254
Adaptation
  of brain-damaged child, 295–301
  role of fantasy in, 208–09
Adolescence, Adolescents, 160, 182, 206–07
  of handicapped boy, 217
  with life-threatening illness, 161–78
  reckless in matters of health, 11
  schizophrenic, reaction to surgery, 55
  see also Puberty
Aggression
  in brain-damaged child, 248–73, 283–301
  and confusion, 108–10
  defense against, 149
  defused, 177–78
  and headache, 108, 117
  increase prior to surgery, 63–64, 77
  to mother, 111; *see also sub* Ambivalence
  and motor restraint, 4–5
  and seizures, 223–45
  following surgery, 71, 90
  turned against self, 50, 122; *see also* Accident proneness, Self-injury
  urinary and anal, 165
  see also Rage
Aggressive child, reactions to surgery, 50–53
Alimentary seizure, 270, 272
Ambivalence
  and body image, 122
  to mother, 78, 215, 296–99

  of parent, 17–18
Anesthesia, 154, 158
  conceived as: oral attack, 76; primal scene, 155; punishment, 25–26; sexual union, 150
  meanings of, 25–27, 30
  reactions to, 7, 66–67
  reconstruction of impact, 169–77
  and sleep disturbances, 77
Anxiety
  about abnormality, 144–46
  actual, 254–55
  anal, 151–52, 168
  anticipatory, 7, 77
  catastrophic, 253–54
  focus of, 30–31
  homosexual, 203
  and hospital atmosphere, 17
  hypochondriacal, 43
  lack of, 57
  of mother: 82, 95; impact on physician, 157
  narcissistic, 152
  oral, 151–52
  and pain, 7–9
  phallic, 168–69, 175–76
  phase-specific, 118, 133
  of physician, 82, 192
  and preparation for surgery, 19–22
  real and neurotic, 79–80
  verbalization, 57
  see also Castration anxiety, Fear, Mutilation fear, Separation anxiety, *and sub* Body image
Anxiety attacks, 236
Anxiety states following surgery, 40–47
Aphasia, 286–89, 294, 300–01
Arthur, G., 286
Atypical child, 105
  reactions to surgery, 54–55

311